California's Ozone-Reduction Strategy for Light-Duty Vehicles

Direct Costs, Direct Emission Effects, and Market Responses

Lloyd S. Dixon

Steven Garber

RAND

The Institute for Civil Justice

This research is supported by The Institute for Civil Justice.

ISBN: 0-8330-2392-6

© Copyright 1996 RAND

RAND is a nonprofit institution that helps improve public policy through research and analysis. RAND's publications do not necessarily reflect the opinions or policies of its research sponsors.

Published 1996 by RAND
1700 Main Street, P.O. Box 2138, Santa Monica, CA 90407-2138
RAND URL: http://www.rand.org/
To order RAND documents or to obtain additional information, contact Distribution
Services: Telephone: (310) 451-7002;
Fax: (310) 451-6915; Internet: order@rand.org

California's Ozone-Reduction Strategy for Light-Duty Vehicles

Direct Costs, Direct Emission Effects and Market Responses

Lloyd S. Dixon

Steven Garber

RAND

The Institute for Civil Justice

The mission of the Institute for Civil Justice is to help make the civil justice system more efficient and more equitable by supplying policymakers and the public with the results of objective, empirically based, analytic research. The ICJ facilitates change in the civil justice system by analyzing trends and outcomes, identifying and evaluating policy options, and bringing together representatives of different interests to debate alternative solutions to policy problems. The Institute builds on a long tradition of RAND research characterized by an interdisciplinary, empirical approach to public policy issues and rigorous standards of quality, objectivity, and independence.

ICJ research is supported by pooled grants from corporations, trade and professional associations, and individuals; by government grants and contracts; and by private foundations. The Institute disseminates its work widely to the legal, business, and research communities, and to the general public. In accordance with RAND policy, all Institute research products are subject to peer review before publication. ICJ publications do not necessarily reflect the opinions or policies of the research sponsors or of the ICJ Board of Overseers.

PREFACE

California has adopted an aggressive plan to bring the state into compliance with national ambient air quality standards. California's strategy includes strict emission standards on mobile and stationary sources and on area sources such as solvents, paints, and consumer products.

The cost and efficacy of California's plan have generated substantial debate. Studies by different interest groups and by government agencies have produced widely ranging estimates of the cost and emission reductions produced by various components of the plan, and there is little commonly accepted empirical information on which to base policy decisions.

Because of the importance of this policy issue for all Californians, the Institute for Civil Justice undertook an evaluation of a key component of California's plan--the strategy for reducing emissions from light-duty vehicles. The project is funded by a grant from the California Manufacturers' Association and by the Institute's general research funds.

In light of the diverse audiences interested in this subject matter, we present our findings in three different forms. This report details our methods and findings. A non-technical summary is contained in *California's Ozone-Reduction Strategy for Light-Duty Vehicles: An Economic Assessment*, MR-695/1-ICJ. Finally, some of our findings on the zero-emission vehicle mandate are presented in *Making ZEV Policy Despite Uncertainty: An Annotated Briefing for the California Air Resources Board*, DRU-1266-2-ICJ.

For information about the Institute for Civil Justice, contact

Dr. Deborah Hensler, Director
Institute for Civil Justice
RAND
1700 Main Street, P.O. Box 2138
Santa Monica, CA 90407-2138
TEL: (310) 393-0411 x7803
Internet: Deborah_Hensler@rand.org

A profile of the ICJ, abstracts of its publications, and ordering information can be found on RAND's home page on the World Wide Web at http://www.rand.org/centers/icj/.

CONTENTS

APPENDIX

FIGURES

TABLES

ACKNOWLEDGMENTS

During the course of this project, many people provided us with information, pointed us to the most recent available information, explained key concepts, suggested others we should talk to, or reviewed an initial draft. We thank them all for their time. Below, we list, alphabetically by organization, several who deserve special mention.

Steven Douglas, Gerald Esper, and Richard Klimisch, American Automobile Manufacturers Association; Jeff Jetter, American Honda; Steven Albu, Thomas Cackette, Edie Chang, Paul Hughs, Karen Irwin, Terry McGuire, Rod Summerfield, and John Urkov, California Air Resources Board; Steven Gould and Larry Sherwood, California Bureau of Automotive Repair; Bill Van Amburg and Paul Hellicker, CALSTART; Michael Berabe and Reginald Modlin, Chrysler; Alan Eisenberg, Patricia Little, and David Millerick, Ford; James Ehlmann and Harry Foster, General Motors; Veronica Kun, Natural Resources Defense Council; James Lyons, Sierra Research; Charles Walz, Texaco; Rowland Hwang, Union of Concerned Scientists; Timothy Lipman and Daniel Sperling, Institute of Transportation Studies, University of California at Davis; and Michael Wang, Western States Petroleum Association;

We also thank the members of the advisory board for this project: Winston Harrington, Resources for the Future; Robert Sawyer, University of California at Berkeley; Daniel Sperling; Ruben Mettler, Chairman Emeritus, TRW; and Michael Traynor, Cooley, Godward, Castro, Huddleson, & Tatum. Their input helped ensure a balanced and comprehensive report.

Three formal technical reviewers provided valuable comments on the first draft: Kenneth Girardini and Steven Popper, RAND; and Winston Harrington. We appreciate the care, speed, and insight with which they completed their reviews.

Many people at RAND also made important contributions to the project. Mary Vaiana provided tireless, expert advice for making our ideas clearer and more accessible. John Adams designed and wrote the computer programs that approximated the statistical distribution of electric vehicle operating costs, and Lewis Evans provided very useful comments on interim drafts. Jerry Aroesty, Milton Kamins, and Robert Lempert were valuable sources of information, and Susan McGlamery in RAND's library tracked down many information sources. Patricia Williams did a superb job correcting and formatting the document; Pat Bedrosian quickly edited and formatted the document for publication; John Anderson provided research assistance; Geoffrey Sommer alerted us to newly available materials and commented on the first draft; and Kevin McCarthy provided advice and encouragement in developing the initial project proposal. Finally, we thank Deborah Hensler for her guidance, patience and unflagging support.

GLOSSARY

Term	Definition
AC	Alternating Current
ADP	Alternate Durability Program
AFV	Alternatively Fueled Vehicle
ATC	Average Total Costs
AVC	Average Variable Cost curve
AVR	Accelerated Vehicle Retirement
BAR	State of California Bureau of Automotive Repair
BER	Benefit-Effectiveness Ratio
Big 7	Automobile manufacturers subject to the ZEV mandate in 1998: Chrysler, Ford, General Motors, Honda, Mazda, Nissan, and Toyota
Biogenic Emissions	Emissions from biological sources
BTAP	California Battery Technical Advisory Panel
CA93 Vehicle	California 1993 vehicle. Internal combustion engine vehicle meeting California 1993 exhaust standards
California LDV Strategy	California's strategy for reducing emissions of ozone precursors from light-duty vehicles
California Strategy	California's strategy for reducing emissions of ozone precursors
CAPUC	California Public Utilities Commission
CARB	California Air Resources Board
Carrying Capacity	The maximum emissions the regional atmosphere can absorb without producing a violation of federal ozone standards
CEC	California Energy Commission
Clean Air Act	Federal legislation passed in 1970 and amended in 1977 and 1990 that regulates air quality
CO	Carbon monoxide
CP2G	California Phase 2 reformulated gasoline
Consumers' Surplus	A measure of the total value consumers place on a good minus what they must pay for it

DC	Direct Current
Demand Elasticity	The ratio of the percent change in quantity demanded to the percent change in price
Direct Costs	Social costs that count in evaluating narrow cost effectiveness
Direct Emission Effects	Change in emissions of ozone precursors that count in evaluating narrow cost effectiveness
Economic Efficiency	Using resources as they are most highly valued by society as a whole
EDF	Environmental Defense Fund
EEE Regulations	Enhanced Evaporative Emissions Regulations
EGR	Exhaust Gas Recirculation
EMFAC (EMFAC7F)	A computer model used by CARB (among others) to estimate on-road motor vehicle emissions
Emissions Inventory	An estimate of the amount of pollutants emitted from mobile, stationary, and area sources (often expressed in tons per day)
Exhaust Emissions	Emissions produced during combustion and emitted in vehicle exhaust
EV	Electric Vehicle
Evaporative Emissions	Emissions resulting from fuel evaporation from a vehicle when it is operating or resting
FTP	Federal Test Procedure. The driving cycle used in laboratory testing of vehicles and intended to simulate in-use driving conditions
GM	General Motors
HC	Hydrocarbons
I&M	Inspection and maintenance program
ICE	Internal combustion engine
ICEV	Internal combustion engine vehicle
IM240	The equipment used to test tailpipe emissions in some inspection and maintenance programs. Requires a dynamometer that can operate at various speeds and loads
In-Use Compliance Program	A CARB program that allows the recall of LDVs for emission related defects during the certification period

LDV	Light Duty Vehicle. All passenger vehicles and trucks with gross vehicle weight rating of 6,000 pounds or less
LEV	Low Emission Vehicle. A vehicle that is certified to emit no more than 0.075 g/mi NMOG, 0.2 g/mi NOx, and 3.4 g/mi CO at 50,000 miles
Marginal Cost	The additional cost of producing another unit of a good
Marketing Emissions	Emissions that occur during delivery and storage of gasoline at gas stations and refueling of vehicles
Mobile Sources	Sources of air pollution that can move around (e.g., automobiles, motorcycles, trucks, off-road vehicles, boats, airplanes)
MOBILE (MOBILE5a)	A computer model, used by U.S. EPA (among others) to estimate on-road motor vehicle emission factors
NAAQS	National Ambient Air Quality Standards
Narrow Cost-Effectiveness Analysis	An analysis that estimates costs per unit of benefit but is too limited to provide a complete guide for policy decisions
Narrow Cost-Effectiveness Ratio	The ratio of direct costs to direct emission effects (generally measured in dollars per ton)
NCER	Narrow cost-effectiveness ratio
NERA	National Economic Research Associates
NMOG	Non-Methane Organic Gases. ROG other than methane (a gas with low reactivity in the atmosphere)
NOx	Oxides of nitrogen--NO and NO_2. These gases are ozone precursors
OBD II	On-Board Diagnostics II
ORVR	On-Board Refueling Vapor Recovery
Ozone Precursors	Gases (ROG and NOx) that combine in the presence of sunlight to form ozone
PIVCO	Personal Independent Vehicle Company
PM	Particulate Matter
Producers' Surplus	The difference between what suppliers sell goods for and the minimum amount for which they would be willing to produce and sell them

Reactivity	Propensity of gases to chemically react with other gases in the atmosphere
Remote Sensing Devices	Devices not on-board the vehicle that measure vehicle tailpipe emissions by passing infrared beams through the vehicle exhaust
Resource Allocation	How productive resources are used
RF-A	Reformulated Fuel A (the industry average gasoline in 1989)
RFG	Reformulated Gasoline
ROG	Reactive Organic Gases. ROG consists of methane, many other hydrocarbons (compounds consisting solely of hydrogen and carbon) and oxygenated compounds such as aldehydes, alcohols, ethers, and ketones
RRIS	Random Roadside Inspection Survey
RVP	Reid Vapor Pressure. A measure of the surface pressure required to keep a liquid from vaporizing at a temperature of $100°$ F
SC II	Smog Check II. California's enhanced inspection and maintenance program
SCAB	South Coast Air Basin. Bounded by the Pacific Ocean to the west, the San Gabriel, San Bernardino, and San Jacinto Mountains to the north and east, and the southern border of Orange County to the south
SCAQMD	South Coast Air Quality Management District. The SCAQMD has jurisdiction over all of Orange County and the non-desert portions of Los Angeles, Riverside, and San Bernardino Counties
SIP	California State Implementation Plan
Smog Check	California's inspection and maintenance program
Stage II Vapor Recovery Nozzles	Nozzles on gasoline pumps designed to limit ROG emissions during refueling
Stationary Sources	Sources of air pollution that have a fixed location
Social Costs of Pollution	All costs imposed on society by pollution, including costs of damage to health, vegetation, and ecosystems and reductions in visibility
Sunk Costs	Costs that have already been incurred and cannot be recovered

Supply Elasticity	The ratio of the percent change in the quantity of a good supplied to the percent change in price
TCM	Transportation Control Measures
THC	Total hydrocarbons
Tier 1 Vehicle	Vehicles that are certified to emit no more than 0.25 g/mi NMOG, 0.4 g/mi NOx, and 3.4 g/mi CO at 50,000 miles. (Same exhaust standard as a California 1993 vehicle)
TLEV	Transitional Low Emission Vehicle. A vehicle that is certified to emit no more than 0.125 g/mi NMOG, 0.4 g/mi NOx, and 3.4 g/mi CO at 50,000 miles
ULEV	Ultra Low-Emission Vehicle. A vehicle that is certified to emit no more than 0.040 g/mi NMOG, 0.2 g/mi NOx, and 1.7 g/mi CO at 50,000 miles
UNOCAL Program	UNOCAL's accelerated vehicle retirement program
U.S. EPA	United States Environmental Protection Agency
UST	Underground Storage Tank
VERS	Vehicle Emission Reduction Studies
VMT	Vehicle miles traveled
WTA	Willing to accept. The minimum amount of money a car owner would be willing to accept to give up his or her vehicle for scrap
Willingness to Pay	The maximum amount an individual would pay for the right to a good or some other thing of value
Zero Mile Emission Rate	The rate at which vehicle emits when it has zero miles on the odometer
ZEV	Zero Emission Vehicle. Vehicles that directly emit zero grams of any air pollutant into the atmosphere. Indirect emissions, such as power plant emissions, are not included

1. INTRODUCTION

1.1 THE POLICY PROBLEM

In several parts of California, ozone concentrations in the air exceed federal and state standards on many days of the year. The South Coast Air Basin, which includes all of Orange County and the non-desert portions of Los Angeles, Riverside, and San Bernardino Counties, violates these standards more often than any other area in the nation. Ozone levels in the air basins containing the cities of Sacramento, San Diego, and Ventura, and in the San Joaquin Valley and the Southeast (Mojave) Desert, also violate the standards on many days.

The federal Clean Air Act Amendments of 1990 require California--like other states that have not achieved compliance with federal standards--to adopt a comprehensive strategy for bringing all areas of the state into compliance. The South Coast has the furthest to go, and its deadline for compliance is 2010. All other areas of the state are required to achieve compliance between 1999 and 2007 depending on the current levels of pollution (CARB, 1994d, Volume 1, p. I-6).

The responsibility for demonstrating to the United States Environmental Protection Agency (U.S. EPA) that California has a comprehensive ozone-reduction strategy lies with the California Air Resources Board (CARB), a part of the California Environmental Protection Agency. The strategy contains elements that must be adopted at various levels of government. Some elements, such as regulations for airplane emissions, must be adopted by the federal government. Others, such as regulations for passenger vehicles and light-duty trucks, are adopted at the state level. Still others, such as regulations for stationary sources and on vehicle travel (e.g., car-pooling plans), are adopted by local air districts, such as the South Coast Air Quality Management District.

The most recent additions to the California strategy are summarized in the State Implementation Plan for Ozone or SIP (CARB, 1994d). The SIP describes plans to bring each area that does not currently meet the federal ozone standards (non-attainment areas) into compliance. Many of the statewide, and even federal, elements of the SIP are driven by what seems needed in the South Coast, because achieving compliance there is the greatest challenge.

The following estimates suggest the magnitude of the challenge. Ozone is formed when reactive organic gases (ROG) and nitrogen oxides (NOx)--so-called ozone precursors--react chemically in the presence of sunlight.[1] Table 1.1-1 compares recent CARB estimates of ROG and NOx emissions in the South Coast Air Basin in tons per day--what is called the emission inventory--and estimates of the maximum levels of ozone precursors that can be emitted without violating the ozone standard--the carrying capacity of the basin.

Table 1.1-1

1990 Emissions of Ozone Precursors and Carrying Capacity in South Coast Air Basin (tons per day)

	ROG[a]	NOx
1990 Inventory	1,517	1,351
Mobile	851	1,116
Stationary	666	235
Carrying Capacity	323	553
Reduction Needed		
Tons per day	1,194	798
Percent	-79	-59

[a]Biogenic emissions are excluded.
SOURCE: CARB, 1994c Volume I, p. I-17.

As can be seen from the table, compliance in the South Coast is believed to require dramatic reductions of emissions from both mobile and stationary sources. Attaining the ozone standards in the South

[1]ROG is composed primarily of hydrocarbons, which are released into the atmosphere when petroleum-based fuels evaporate or are burned incompletely. NOx is produced during combustion when nitrogen and oxygen combine at high temperatures. Besides hydrocarbons, ROG is composed of many different gases, and different studies discussed below focus on different subsets such as hydrocarbons (HC) or non-methane organic gases (NMOG). Distinctions among ROG, HC, and NMOG appear to be of minor significance for our purposes--e.g., they are swamped by other sources of uncertainty such as those we describe--and in this report we simply use the term ROG to refer to any of them.

Coast is estimated to require ROG emissions to fall by 79 percent and NOx emissions by 59 percent from their 1990 levels. Such reductions must occur even while increases in population, driving and industrial activity are working in the opposite direction.

To achieve emission reductions of such magnitude, ozone-reduction policies must be aggressive. Various parts of the California strategy have generated considerable debate. Much of the debate is driven by efforts of various parties to protect their interests. Nonetheless, underlying the debate are high stakes for Californians and for non-Californians as well. Reducing ozone levels would confer major health and other benefits on the state and might aid the state economy--for example, by making California a more desirable place to work and to visit. At the same time, reducing ozone levels will have substantial negative effects on Californians and on the state economy.

1.2 PURPOSE AND SCOPE OF THIS STUDY

California's ozone-reduction strategy includes strict emissions standards for new vehicles, enhanced smog check, regulation of stationary sources, and regulation of some consumer products. Studies by different interest groups and by government agencies have produced widely ranging estimates of the cost and emission reductions produced by various elements of the strategy, and there is little commonly accepted empirical information on which to base policy decisions.

The purpose of this report is to provide an empirical foundation for decisionmaking. We analyze the cost and effectiveness of California's strategy for reducing emissions from light-duty vehicles (passenger cars and light-duty trucks), focusing--as does the SIP--on the South Coast. We report ranges of estimates across different light-duty vehicle (LDV) studies; characterize the areas of, and reasons, for agreement and disagreement; evaluate the technical adequacy and credibility of individual studies; and identify issues that have not yet been addressed.

We focus on LDVs in the South Coast basin for several reasons. First, the goal of attainment in the South Coast basin drives many of the policies adopted for the entire state. Second, as Table 1.2-1

shows, mobile-source reduction targets for the South Coast are
proportionally largest for light- and medium-duty vehicles. Third, 1990
ROG emissions from LDVs are estimated to be higher than the ROG targets
for 2010 from all mobile and stationary sources combined (Table 1.2-1).
Finally, in terms of total tons, the reduction goals for light-duty
vehicles are much more extensive: 503 tons per day of ROG and 280 tons
per day of NOx, 42 percent and 35 percent of the targets for total
emission reductions from all sources.

Table 1.2-1

Emission Reduction Targets by 2010 for the South Coast Air Basin

Source	1990 Inventory (tons per day)		2010 Emissions (tons per day)		Percent Reduction	
	ROG	NOx	ROG	NOx	ROG	NOx
Stationary	666	235	207	100	-69	-57
Mobile	851	1,116	116	453	-86	-59
On-Road	694	744	108	303	-84	-59
Light-duty	582	391	79	111	-86	-72
Medium-duty	75	124	15	60	-80	-51
Heavy-duty	37	229	14	132	-62	-42
Off-Road	114	368	75	203	-34	-45
Other[b]	43	5	12	7	-72	+40
Unallocated			-79[a]	-60[a]		

[a]These reductions remain to be allocated to the components of mobile
source emissions. Once they are allocated, some of the percent
reductions for mobile sources in the last two columns will be larger.
[b]Includes motorcycles and off-road recreational vehicles.
SOURCE: CARB, 1994d, Volume II, p. I-27.

We examine the key components of California's strategy for reducing
emissions of ozone precursors from LDVs, or *the California LDV strategy*
for short. The strategy--as we define it--includes policy actions the
SIP adopted in 1994 and other ozone-reduction policies aimed at LDVs
that are not yet fully implemented.[2] We analyze separately the

_____

[2]By "not yet fully implemented," we mean that the policy action's
costs and benefits could still be changed by varying the policy. In
contrast, emissions standards for new vehicles for model years up
through 1995 have been fully implemented.

following policy actions, each of which we refer to as an *element* of the California LDV strategy:[3]

- new standards for tailpipe emissions,
- new standards for evaporative fuel emissions,
- requirements for on-board recovery of vapors during refueling,
- new standards for on-board monitoring of emission systems,
- changes in California's Smog Check program,
- a program to purchase and retire older vehicles,
- changes in gasoline formulation, and
- the zero-emission vehicle (ZEV) mandate.[4]

The analysis puts particular emphasis on the ZEV mandate, the most controversial aspect of the strategy. We emphasize the ZEV mandate because it is currently under review, poses particularly difficult analytic challenges, and the economic and environmental stakes are very high. However, we believe that the ZEV mandate cannot be usefully analyzed in isolation from the other elements of the strategy. Our analysis of the ZEV mandate relies crucially on the analyses of the other elements of the California strategy.

1.3 MAJOR UNCERTAINTIES

Major uncertainties plague the search for policies that will achieve California's air quality goals most economically. Some of these uncertainties are fundamental to economic issues--for example, costs of achieving emission reductions in various ways, emission reductions that will result from various policies, performance of machines and people, reactions of markets, and means other than those proposed available to reduce ozone. We use various analytic means of dealing with such uncertainties.[5]

---

[3]In this report, we do not analyze the transportation control measures that have been proposed by several air pollution control districts.

[4]We analyze the ZEV mandate in place as of January 1996. CARB is currently reviewing the mandate. Significant modifications appear likely, but no final decisions have yet been made.

[5]Other sets of uncertainties that are fundamentally economic involve the relative costs of achieving the same level of ozone by varying the targets for total ROG and NOx reduction or changing the allocation of any total reduction targets across categories of emissions

Other major uncertainties do not involve economics, but are crucial to wise policymaking. These include uncertainties about factors underlying the emission reduction targets in the SIP, including: the links between emission levels and ozone levels, the current level of emissions, and the proportionate emission reductions needed to meet air quality goals. (See Appendix 1.A for further discussion.) We do not analyze non-economic uncertainties; however, it is important to keep them in mind when evaluating policies designed to achieve emission-reduction targets based on such estimates.

1.4 ORGANIZATION OF THE REPORT

Our discussion is organized as follows.

- In Section 2, we provide an overview of our analytic approach.
- Section 3 summarizes estimates of current internal combustion engine emissions.
- Section 4 reviews the history of LDV regulations and discusses the effectiveness of past regulations.
- Section 5 describes elements of California's strategy to further reduce LDV emissions.
- Section 6 analyzes what we call the direct costs and benefits of the hardware-based elements of the strategy. These include new tailpipe emission standards, new evaporative emission standards, requirements for on-board recovery of refueling vapors, and on-board emission system monitoring requirements.
- In Section 7, we analyze costs and benefits of the hardware-based elements of the strategy that involve market responses to the regulations.
- Section 8 analyzes the direct costs and benefits of the non-hardware based elements of the strategy: a new inspection and maintenance program, an accelerated vehicle retirement program, and changes in gasoline formulation.

---

sources (light-duty vehicles, stationary sources, etc.). We cannot analyze these uncertainties in this report because they require an analytic scope much broader than LDVs.

- Section 9 considers market responses to the non-hardware based elements.

- In Section 10, we analyze direct costs and benefits of the zero-emission vehicle mandate.

- Section 11 analyzes market responses to the ZEV mandate.

- In Section 12, we bring together our findings, interpret them and discuss policy implications.

2. ANALYTIC APPROACH

2.1 OVERVIEW

We took the following basic approach to analyzing California's ozone-reduction strategy.

- We developed an economic framework for identifying costs and benefits that should be considered in evaluating any component of California's LDV strategy;

- We reviewed and critiqued the most informative or influential existing studies of various elements of California's LDV strategy and interviewed stakeholders to locate and interpret information;

- We applied standard economic principles to interpret data and estimate effects;

- We characterized ranges of reasonable disagreement about key estimates;

- We developed models to predict the costs, emission reductions, cost effectiveness, and market effects of various components of the strategy;

- We identified issues that have not been addressed and analyzed them qualitatively;

- We also identified issues that may be important to the policy decision at hand but about which we have essentially no information.

In this section, we discuss our analytic approach in more detail. We begin by defining the policy problems and explaining the basic economics of air pollution. We review basic concepts, principles, and techniques of cost-benefit analysis. We then provide an overview of our analytic approach, including how we define policies and alternatives, our sources of information, pitfalls of cost-effectiveness analysis as typically applied to the policy issues at hand, how we analyze market effects of policies, our means of dealing with economic uncertainties, and how we deal with interdependencies among policies. We conclude by proposing how policymakers might best use the limited information available to them to make economical policy choices.

2.2 DEFINING THE POLICY PROBLEM

As is standard in economic analysis of public policy, we conceptualize the fundamental economic policy goal of California's ozone reduction strategy as economic efficiency, which means providing members of society *in the aggregate* with their best possible opportunities for well being.[6]

When setting out to analyze the economic efficiency consequences of California ozone-abatement polices, we immediately encounter two fundamental issues that suggest different versions of the policy problem. The first is whose costs and benefits should be considered? The second is the leeway available to policymakers in pursuing economic efficiency. We discuss each issue briefly.

We consider two alternative definitions of "members of society": Californians and all U.S. residents. We consider the first because the policies we analyze are the province of California policymakers, who appear to be most concerned about Californians. We consider effects on Americans as a whole because other environmental policymakers--e.g., federal legislators and officials at the U.S. EPA--have this broader constituency, and because California policy is driven to a large degree by federal air-quality policies.

The second fundamental issue is whether--for analytic purposes-- ozone levels in California should be considered as a constraint that policymakers must satisfy or a choice that policymakers can make. We provide analyses relevant to both possibilities because the answer differs according to which policymakers we have in mind.

Under present law, California policymakers are required to achieve compliance with the national ambient air quality standards (NAAQS)

---

[6]The goal of economic efficiency does not concern itself with how economic welfare is distributed among members of society. We do, however, develop and present estimates concerning how the costs and benefits of various elements of California's new ozone-reduction strategy can be expected to be distributed among various groups inside and outside the state.

developed by the U.S. EPA in implementing the federal Clean Air Act. Thus, California policymakers are viewed as making ozone policy choices under the constraint that compliance must be achieved.

The NAAQS, being a creation of federal policy, can also be changed by federal policy. To federal policymakers--at least in the Congress-- ozone levels are not a constraint, they are a choice for which the social costs and benefits of relaxing or tightening air-quality standards are fundamental considerations. In fact, the economic wisdom of federal environmental regulations are issues of considerable concern in Washington.

Combining each of the two definitions of "members of society" with each of the two views of the leeway available to a particular policymaker leads to four versions of the policy problem. These are summarized in Table 2.2-1. The four policy problems are described in the four cells of the table. Each version results from combining a choice of whose costs and benefits count (row headings) with one of two levels of flexibility available to policymakers (column headings). For example, in one version of the policy problem, we assume that California policymakers (e.g., CARB) must accept the NAAQS as a constraint, but within that constraint seek economically efficient policies. If these policymakers' concerns are limited to the well-being of Californians, they would seek policies to attain the NAAQS in a way that minimizes the costs to Californians of doing so, adjusted for any additional benefits to Californians. The U.S. Congress, on the other hand, has the power to change the NAAQS and is assumed to be concerned about the well-being of all U.S. residents. Accordingly, the version of the policy problem they face (bottom right cell) is to choose the standards for California so that whenever emissions are abated, the costs to U.S. residents of doing so are no greater than the benefits to U.S. residents.

Our analyses provide information relevant to all four versions of the policy problem.

Table 2.2-1

Four Policy Problems

Constituency	Degree of Latitude in Pursuing Economic Efficiency	
	Ozone Standard Given (e.g., CARB)	Ozone Standards Can Be Chosen (e.g., U.S. Congress);
California residents	NAAQS attainment in California at minimum cost--net of subsidiary benefits-- to Californians	Reduce emissions in California only when extra costs to Californians are less than extra (ozone-reduction and other) benefits to Californians
All U.S. residents	NAAQS attainment in California at minimum cost--net of subsidiary benefits-- to all U.S. residents	Reduce emissions in California only when extra costs to U.S. residents are less than extra (ozone-reduction and other) benefits to U.S. residents

2.3 THE MICROECONOMIC POLICY PROBLEM

We now review some basic economic perspectives used in our analysis of California's LDV strategy. We describe why totally free markets are likely to produce too much air pollution for economic efficiency, provide some quantitative feel for the size of the problem at the level of the individual LDV, and suggest how we might provide incentives for efficient behavior and identify efficient policy initiatives.

2.3.1 Why Would Totally Free Markets Produce Too Much Pollution?

Actions that pollute the air use a valuable social resource: clean air. In a totally free market--i.e., a setting very different from our current one, in which there is *no* government action to influence *any* of the actions that cause air pollution--individuals and companies would be allowed to use this resource without having to bear the social costs of doing so. Economists generally agree that allowing people to use resources without paying the cost encourages overuse or waste of resources--in this case too much use of clean air or, equivalently, too much air pollution. To put this in the context of emissions from LDVs: the behavior of several groups jointly determines emission levels.

Drivers, auto companies, oil companies and others make decisions affecting air quality; the resulting pollution involves costs to all members of society.

As Table 2.3-1 highlights, none of these types of decisionmakers can be counted on to treat air quality as a primary factor in making decisions. Drivers generally don't think of emissions as a performance factor affecting their willingness to pay for different vehicles, vehicle maintenance, or different fuels, and they don't generally worry much about air pollution when they consider driving extra miles. Individual drivers may care a lot about the environment and take action to protect it (e.g., ride a bicycle), but we can't count on drivers in the aggregate voluntarily to use up clean air only when it is socially worthwhile.

Automobile and oil companies may be willing to take some actions to protect the environment voluntarily--perhaps out of public spiritedness or because of benefits to company reputations--but we can't count on companies voluntarily to use up clean air only when it is socially worthwhile.[7] Companies would pay more attention to air quality if their customers (i.e., drivers) were to provide them with significant incentives to do so. But because most drivers will not voluntarily pay much more for cleaner vehicles, automobile companies would often lower their profits by incurring extra costs to improve emission performance. Similarly, oil companies cannot be expected voluntarily to bear large costs of producing cleaner fuels if drivers are unwilling to pay substantially more for them.

A totally free market, then, would not the give key actors who determine the quality of our air the right incentives to factor air quality into their decisions. This is because most of the social benefits of the necessary sacrifices would be enjoyed by others, and we can't expect individuals or companies voluntarily to make major sacrifices for the benefit of others.

---

[7]For example, companies that are motivated to take costly, voluntary actions to protect the environment would leave themselves vulnerable to competition from less environmentally active companies.

Table 2.3-1

Decisions of Drivers, Auto and Oil Companies Affecting Air Quality and the Primary Concerns That Affect Those Decisions

Decision-makers	Primary goals	Decisions that affect air quality	Primary factors considered
Drivers	Own economic well being, convenience	What vehicle to own	Price and performance of vehicle
		How to maintain it	Costs of maintenance and effects on performance
		What fuel to use	Price per mile of driving, performance with different fuels
		How much to drive	Costs per mile (gas, maintenance) and benefits of mobility
Motor vehicle companies	Company profits	Design features and manufacturing processes affecting emission levels, durability	Company costs of designing and producing cleaner vehicles
			Competitive advantages of cleaner vehicles
Oil companies	Company profits	Fuel formulas	Company costs of developing and producing cleaner fuels
			Competitive advantages of cleaner fuels
		Fuel distribution methods	Costs and competitive advantages of cleaner distribution methods

2.3.2 What Would Happen If Polluters Were Forced to Bear the Costs They Impose on Others?

If those who create pollution were forced to pay the social costs of the amounts they pollute, they would choose to reduce their pollution whenever it cost them less to do so than the resulting savings in pollution payments. To gauge how behavior would respond to such efficient incentives, we used existing estimates of annual pollution costs from vehicles with different emission rates (grams of ROG and NOx emissions per mile of driving) and existing estimates of costs per ton of emissions. (Appendix 2.A provides the details.)

Existing estimates imply that:

- Drivers of vehicles with average emissions levels[8] in the South Coast generate pollution costs on the order of $250 to $700 per year if they drive 12,000 miles; in Sacramento, the cost is about $340 a year; in other air basins, the amount is considerably lower, roughly $50 to $150.

- Drivers of vehicles with higher emissions[9] in the South Coast generate pollution costs in the range of $1,000 to $3,000 per year. In other basins, the corresponding figures are about $1,225 in Sacramento, and much lower--roughly $125 to $300-- elsewhere.

- Drivers of vehicles with extremely high emissions[10] generate pollution costs in the South Coast on the order of $4,000 to $15,000 per year; in Sacramento the cost is approximately $6,000; in the other areas, it would be about $600 to $1,100.

What changes in behavior would result if drivers were charged taxes equal to the costs of pollution they generate? These are the kinds of changes that policymakers should strive to achieve, because these are the ones that would promote economic efficiency.

With corrected incentives, drivers of vehicles with average emissions would have noticeable, but not overwhelming, incentives to reduce emissions. For example, driving 8,000 miles per year rather than 12,000 would reduce a driver's annual emissions taxes by roughly $100 or less. The responses of drivers of vehicles with high emissions, who would face taxes roughly three to four times higher, depend on their

---

[8]For the purposes of discussion here, an average vehicle is one that emits at the average rate for the vehicle fleet in 1992. (ROG = 3.76 gm/mi and NOx = 1.26 gm/mi, as shown in Table 3.3-1.)

[9]To represent vehicles with high emissions rates, we took the average measured emissions of 74 vehicles scrapped as part of the 1990 UNOCAL vehicle-retirement program. These emissions rates are the average tailpipe emissions test--ROG = 16.6 gm/mi and NOx = 2.4 gm/mi (Hsu and Sperling, 1994, Table 2).

[10]To represent a very high emissions rate, we used the single highest rate measured among the 74 vehicles in the UNOCAL program (ROG = 85.4 gm/mi and NOx = 9.0 gm/mi). As discussed in Appendix B, even these rates are likely to understate emissions rates for the dirtiest vehicles on the road.

costs of reducing emissions in various ways, but they are likely to take more action than drivers of vehicles with average emissions. We expect that drivers of vehicles with extremely high emissions in the South Coast and Sacramento, faced with thousands of dollars per year in taxes, would see *any* sensible means of reducing emissions as preferable to persisting with, and paying for, their current emission rate.[11]

If drivers had substantial incentives to reduce emissions, this would create profit-based incentives for vehicle manufacturers and oil companies to help them do so. In the case of manufacturers, the prospect of high emission taxes would make consumers willing to pay considerably more for new vehicles whose emissions levels don't increase with vehicle age or can easily be fixed when they do. In the case of oil companies, consumers would be willing to pay considerably more for fuels that produce fewer emissions. For example, suppose a company could supply fuels that reduce emissions by 25 percent. Given the kinds of emission taxes discussed above, a driver of an average car in the South Coast Basin would be willing to pay 10 to 40 cents more per gallon (i.e., the tax savings per mile from reducing emissions 25 percent). If companies could produce emission reductions for their customers at costs below what consumers are willing to pay for the emission reductions, then it would be profitable to do so. Companies failing to respond to such incentives would lose out in competition to those that do respond.

2.3.3 What Does the Economic Perspective Tell Us About Policy Options?

For a variety of reasons, including the uncertainty about damage costs per ton of emissions and the current infeasibility of measuring emissions from individual vehicles, we cannot precisely allocate the costs of pollution to individual polluters and wait for their behavior to adjust.[12] It may be possible to design tax schemes--approximating

---

[11]For example, such taxes would be more than enough to cover the cost of leasing a new vehicle for a year.

[12]Many economists are very favorably disposed to policies that correct incentives and then rely on (corrected) market forces to determine appropriate resource use. This approach to policy--which many would describe as "flexible and market-based"--is favored in many cases because it relies on responses of people who have the relevant information and personal stakes in making efficient choices. Compared

efficient taxes--based on indicators of emission rates such as annual emission test results and odometer readings that would lead to worthwhile changes in individual and corporate behavior. It is unclear, though, how well feasible schemes could correct incentives and how much they would cost. In any event, such approaches are not part of the California strategy. The strategy is to regulate the behavior of drivers, auto and oil companies directly.

Nevertheless, thinking in terms of what efficient incentives would involve can be helpful.

- First, it provides a sense of the magnitude of the policy problem. The benefits to society of reducing pollution are significant, and the size of the costs being imposed on other Californians, especially by vehicles with unusually high emission rates, are very large. These costs suggest very substantial amounts of economic waste--using valuable air resources to very little benefit.

- Second, focusing attention on the behavior of different groups of decisionmakers can help identify potential gaps in proposed policies.

- Third, it suggests what types of policies may be most promising. It is clear, for example, that the dirtiest vehicles are a part of the problem.

What else might we learn by thinking about efficient incentives? For example, if we required people to pay the costs of their air pollution, would we find them voluntarily testing vehicle emission levels and repairing problems promptly? scrapping vehicles with emission problems more costly to repair than the vehicle is worth? driving fewer miles and carpooling more often? Would they willingly pay enough extra to cover the costs of: cleaner fuels? vehicles with more durable emission-control systems? electric vehicles?

Cost-benefit analysis is designed to answer questions like these.

---

with direct regulatory ("command and control") approaches, flexible, market-based approaches may have much less difficulty in getting people to do things that are contrary to their own interests.

2.4 SOCIAL COSTS AND BENEFITS AND COST-BENEFIT ANALYSIS[13]

When considering policy options that appear to promote a social goal, policymakers must analyze the options to determine which are sufficiently promising to be implemented. Evaluation involves identifying and estimating the benefits (socially desirable outcomes) and costs (socially undesirable outcomes) of the policies and comparing the benefits with the costs.

Microeconomics provides a widely accepted conceptual foundation for understanding the nature of social costs and benefits and hence the efficiency consequences of public policies. The branch of microeconomics called cost-benefit analysis applies these concepts to quantifying costs and benefits, comparing them and making judgments about whether specific policy measures promote efficiency--that is, have benefits in excess of costs--and, if so, by how much.[14]

Let's consider the nature of the social costs and benefits of proposed policies to reduce ozone levels in California.

2.4.1 Social Costs

The social costs of a policy include *all* of the effects that are undesirable to any members of society that have not yet been incurred.[15] These costs are relevant to economic evaluation whether or not they are intended or foreseen consequences of the policy that caused them. It is

---

[13]Some especially useful texts on cost-benefit analysis are Just, Hueth and Schmitz (1982), and Sugden and Williams (1978).

[14]The principles of microeconomics provide a powerful conceptual framework for evaluation, most notably by allowing identification of the components of social costs and benefits. In the present context, we cannot perform a complete cost-benefit analysis because many of the relevant factors cannot be quantified. Many factors that can't be quantified appear to be important nonetheless. Making policy wisely requires understanding what factors are relevant, understanding what is known about those factors, and keeping in mind the potential importance of factors that have not been or cannot be quantified.

[15]Costs that have already been incurred--so-called *sunk* costs--can no longer be avoided and are, then, no longer relevant to evaluating options still available to policymakers. For example, a policymaker can decide whether to *continue* a policy that has been instituted, but that person can no longer decide whether to institute the policy in the first place.

helpful to think about economic costs as involving either *resource costs* or *direct reductions in well-being.*

Resource costs. These costs include the social value of the resources used up because of the policy. For example, all elements of the California LDV strategy involve use of resources by public agencies to administer and enforce regulations. Different elements of the strategy involve different types of other resource costs. Many elements require technology advancements and the use of scientific and engineering resources. In the case of regulations that will cause manufacturers to upgrade the hardware for internal combustion engine vehicles, much of the resource costs are the costs incurred (but not necessarily borne) by vehicle manufacturers to design, manufacture, and install additional hardware. In the case of a smog-check program, much of the resource costs include the time and effort of vehicle owners and mechanics in getting vehicles inspected and repaired and the costs of the test equipment and parts used for repairs.

Direct reductions in well-being. Some undesirable effects of policies are more naturally thought of as directly reducing the well-being of members of society. Examples include any inconvenience or aggravation involved in smog check or mandatory car-pooling programs (beyond time cost, per se), reductions in employment opportunities for individuals, and reductions in well-being that might result from reduced vehicle performance caused by additional emissions controls.

2.4.2 Social Benefits

A policy's social benefits are the effects that are desirable to any members of society. Benefits include any savings in resource use or any direct ways that members of society are made better off.

The policies analyzed in this report are implemented primarily for the purpose of reducing ozone concentrations in non-attainment areas in California. But these policies may have other desirable effects of considerable social consequence, and *all* socially desirable effects of these policies are relevant in an economic evaluation of them.

The benefits of ozone reduction are improvements in human health (decreases in coughing spells, asthma, etc.), reduced ozone damage to plants and animals, etc. But there are several potential, socially beneficial side effects of policies designed to reduce ozone.[16] For example,

- NOx is a precursor of particulate matter (PM) suspended in the air as well as of ozone, and PM is believed to have very serious health effects. Therefore, reductions in detrimental health effects from PM that result from policies to reduce ozone are also benefits of those policies.

- Motor vehicles emit pollutants other than ozone precursors that are believed to have undesirable environmental impacts, for example, carbon monoxide. Ozone-reduction policies that reduce emissions of such pollutants confer social benefits due to these reductions.

- Regulations that spur technology development may lead to advances in science and engineering that would benefit members of society in ways other than ozone reduction.

- Ozone reduction policies might enhance employment opportunities.[17]

2.4.3 Valuing Costs and Benefits

Identifying costs and benefits is one thing, putting dollar values on them is quite another.

Valuing resource costs. Valuing resource costs is relatively easy because resources are often traded in markets and their market prices often provide a reasonably accurate reflection of their social value.[18]

Valuing changes in well-being. Valuing costs or benefits that involve direct changes in well-being is often much more difficult. There are at least two reasons for this: (1) effects of a policy on

---

[16]We emphasize that all benefits of ozone-reduction policies are relevant to evaluation--whether or not they are intentional consequences of the policy--and that such side benefits might be of considerable consequence. However, we do not analyze such benefits.

[17]This would be especially beneficial, economically, if it involved reallocation of people to activities in which they are more productive.

[18]When this is not the case, quantification of resource costs often involves adjustment of market prices to reflect factors that make market prices of resources deviate from their social values.

factors such as health, visibility, employment, and convenience are relatively difficult to estimate, and (2) it is difficult to put a dollar value on many of these factors.

Economists attempt to value such factors using the fundamental principle that the social value of a change that makes individuals better off is the total value placed on that change by the individuals receiving the benefits. To operationalize such values, economists think in terms of the maximum amount the beneficiary would be willing to pay to receive the benefit.

Consider, for example, reduced incidence or severity of asthma episodes resulting from an ozone-reduction policy action. To estimate such a benefit, analysts would attempt to estimate several quantities and combine the estimates to produce an estimated dollar value for the asthma-mitigation benefits. These quantities are the:

- reduction in emissions of ozone precursors resulting from the policy action;
- reduction in ozone levels resulting from the emission reductions;
- reduction in incidence and severity of asthma attacks resulting from the reduction in ozone levels;
- the amounts the individuals who suffer less from asthma episodes would be willing to pay for these health benefits.

Note that the first three factors--which involve engineering, behavioral, atmospheric chemistry, and epidemiological issues--can be very difficult to estimate, and that they have nothing to do with valuation in dollar terms. As we shall see, cost-effectiveness analysis attempts to avoid the difficulties of expressing benefits in dollar terms, but must still cope--somehow--with difficulties in estimating and combining benefits expressed in non-monetary terms.

Valuing costs and benefits that accrue at different times. The costs and benefits of some ozone-reduction policies accrue over years, and sometimes decades. Generally, it is assumed that costs incurred further into the future, other things equal, involve lower social costs than those same costs if they were to occur sooner, and that benefits occurring further into the future, other things equal, are of less social value than those same benefits if they were to occur sooner.[19]

The standard approach to adjusting values of benefits and costs to a common time basis is to discount them to present values (i.e., express future benefits and costs in terms of the equivalent values if costs or benefits were experienced today).[20]

Comparison of costs and benefits in the same time units is especially important when the time profiles of costs and benefits differ substantially. The dissimilarity in time profiles of costs and benefits varies considerably across elements of the California strategy. For example:

- The administrative costs of vehicle-retirement programs tend to occur at the time a vehicle is scrapped, but emission reductions would accrue over the future months or years that a scrapped vehicle would have remained on the road if it were not for the program.

- Most of the costs of improving emission controls for new vehicles are incurred by the time that the new vehicles are built, but the air-quality benefits can last over the lifetime of the vehicle.

2.4.4 Estimates of the Benefits of Ozone Reduction

To get a sense of the value of reducing emissions of ozone precursors, we examined several estimates of the dollar value of the social cost per ton of emissions. These estimates are based on different approaches and range widely. We have not analyzed these studies in detail and do not view them as definitive. (See Appendix 2.B

---

[19]The discussion here assumes that all dollar values--no matter when they accrue--are expressed in constant dollars (i.e., do not reflect any price inflation). Unless indicated otherwise, all dollar values in this report should be interpreted as being expressed using current price levels.

[20]Discounting to present value is more controversial--among non-economists--in the context of environmental benefits than in the context of many non-environmental benefits or costs generally, but there is a solid conceptual basis for doing so. For discussions of discounting environmental benefits, see Cropper and Portney (1990), Cropper, Ayedede, and Portney (1991), and Kopp (1994).

for a discussion of the sources of the estimates, the approaches used to develop them, and their values.) We interpret these estimates to indicate that the benefits of reducing emissions in the South Coast Air Basin are likely to exceed $5,000 per ton of ROG or NOx emissions, perhaps by a substantial amount, but are probably less than $25,000; these benefits may be almost as high in Sacramento as in the South Coast; and in San Diego, Ventura, and San Francisco benefits per ton are much lower, possibly less than $1,000. These estimates suggest that there may be significant benefits to reducing emissions, depending on how costly it is to do so.

2.4.5 Incremental Costs and Benefits of Emission Reduction

As discussed in Appendix 2.B, it is generally expected that each additional ton of emissions causes more health and other damage than the previous ton did. In the jargon used by economists, the marginal or incremental damage of emissions increases with the level of emissions. The *benefits* of reducing emissions are *avoiding the damage* that the avoided emissions would have caused. Since the incremental damage of emissions increases as emissions increase, the incremental benefits of reducing emissions decreases as we reduce emissions more and more.

As almost everyone agrees, California policymakers find themselves considering more and more costly ways to reduce each additional ton of emissions. There don't seem to be many low-cost ways to reduce emissions that haven't already been implemented. The marginal or incremental costs of reducing emissions increase as we reduce emissions more and more.

That incremental benefits decline and incremental costs rise suggests:

- Policymakers who must meet the NAAQS are likely to find that policies that have yet to be adopted involve higher and higher costs per ton of emission reduction to get smaller and smaller benefits per ton. In short, to achieve attainment, they need to implement less and less economically desirable policies. In addition, policies implemented statewide because they are

required for attainment in the South Coast may have very low
benefits relative to costs in other parts of the state.

- Policymakers who are free to change the NAAQS should keep in
  mind that, at some point, the benefits of even the most
  efficient emission reductions in California yet to be
  implemented may fall below the costs of achieving them. If so,
  it would be economically efficient to relax the NAAQS.

2.4.6 Distribution of Costs and Benefits

The costs and benefits of different elements of the California
strategy are suffered or enjoyed by different California residents.
Non-residents are also affected by the California policies. Strictly
speaking--given a definition of "members of society" or constituency of
concern to a policymaker--the distribution of costs and benefits among
those people is irrelevant to economic efficiency, which counts costs
and benefits in the aggregate.

However, the distribution of costs and benefits across various
groups is of considerable interest in the present context for at least
two reasons:

- Different policymakers focus on different constituencies (e.g.,
  California and U.S. policymakers on Californians and Americans,
  respectively) and therefore want to know which benefits and
  costs accrue to their constituents and which don't.
- Many policymakers are very concerned about distributional
  impacts of their policies even *within* their own constituencies
  (e.g., between consumers and producers, rich and poor,
  residents of different regions within California or the U.S.).

Fortunately, estimation of aggregate costs and benefits--for
purposes of cost-benefit analysis--is often most effectively
accomplished by estimating costs and benefits as they accrue to
different groups. We provide such information--distinguishing consumers
and producers of various types of vehicles, and Californians from non-
Californians--as a by-product of our analyses of market responses to
various elements of the strategy.

2.4.7 Cost-Effectiveness Analysis

Often, quantifying a policy's benefits in dollar terms is so difficult or controversial that attempting to do so would be counterproductive. Cost-effectiveness analysis is a response to this difficulty. In cost-effectiveness analysis, benefits (e.g., asthma episodes avoided) or some surrogate for them (e.g., reduction in ozone levels, tons of emissions reduced) are expressed in whatever units they can be accurately measured, and an attempt is made to compare policies in terms of costs per unit of benefit.

This form of evaluation can be very revealing--under the right conditions. Consider two situations in which a cost-effectiveness analysis could be especially helpful to policymakers.

First, suppose two policies under consideration are projected to have identical benefits. In such a case, cost-effectiveness analysis would require estimating the costs of the two policies, and the policy with the lower costs would be deemed to be preferable--more "cost effective."

Second, suppose two policies aimed at the same kinds of benefits were projected to have the identical costs. In this case, a cost-effectiveness analysis would focus on estimating the benefits (but not quantifying them in dollar terms), and the policy with the larger benefits would be deemed to be more cost effective.

The basic ideas of these examples are, respectively, that it is always better to get the same benefits for lower cost or to get larger benefits for the same cost. Unfortunately, things are not nearly so simple when it comes to the policies under study here. We discuss the limitations of cost-effectiveness analysis as applied to the California LDV strategy in Section 2.5.3.

2.5 MAJOR COMPONENTS OF OUR ANALYSIS

We now describe the major components of our analysis: how we define policy alternatives, our sources of information, the limitations of cost-effectiveness analysis as typically applied, our approach to market-mediated effects, and how we deal with economic uncertainties and interdependencies among policies.

2.5.1 Definition of Policies and Alternatives

The policies we analyze are the following "elements" of the California strategy:

- new standards for tailpipe emissions,
- new standards evaporative fuel emissions,
- requirements for on-board recovery of vapors during refueling,
- new standards for the on-board monitoring of the emission system,
- changes in California's Smog Check program,
- a program to purchase and retire older vehicles,
- changes in gasoline formulation, and
- the zero-emission vehicle mandate.

We analyze each element as it exists under the current regulations.[21]

A given policy option can be analyzed only in comparison to an explicit alternative, and the alternative chosen can have important effects on the conclusions one might draw about the policy. To consider the effects of each policy element, we attempt to compare the outcomes of the entire California LDV strategy to the outcomes resulting from the strategy without that one element.

Figure 2.5-1 helps make this point. We seek to compare the costs and benefits of the entire California LDV strategy, with the costs and benefits of the strategy minus one element. In effect, we are looking at the costs and benefits of adding the element to the remaining N-1 elements of the California strategy.

_____

[21]For example, when we analyze reformulated gasoline (RFG) we assume--as the current regulations allow--that new vehicles can be certified using RFG, and when we analyze the ZEV mandate, we assume--as the current regulations allow--that the calculation of fleet averages for NMOG include electric vehicles. While we do develop information relevant to consideration of some modifications of elements, we do not systematically explore such modifications.

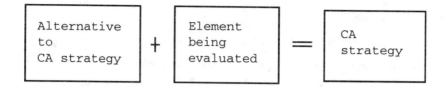

Fig. 2.5-1—Comparing Policy Alternatives

There are other ways to choose policies to be evaluated--for
example, we could add policy elements one at a time, or add or delete
sets of elements. We have chosen the method described above because it
seems highly relevant to the current decision task of California
policymakers. The strategy has been adopted, and California is
obligated under federal law to reduce emissions at least at the rate
expected under the strategy.

2.5.2 Information Sources

For each element of the California strategy, we review and
critique--in terms of conceptual foundations, comprehensiveness, and
reliability--empirical and conceptual analyses bearing on the costs and
emission reductions that can be expected. We used information from
three basic sources:

Scholarly, trade, and popular publications. As detailed in
citations and collected in the reference list, we consulted numerous
books and journal articles from several research fields as well as
articles in the trade and popular presses. Such publications were
identified through electronic searches of various bibliographic
databases, references in other documents, and leads supplied by people
we interviewed.

Unpublished reports. We also rely on numerous unpublished reports
from government agencies, consulting firms and research organizations.
Most of these were identified in (and, in many cases, obtained through)
in-person or telephone interviews with personnel from CARB,

environmental groups, and industry groups (see below).[22] In addition, several very useful unpublished reports were located from the discussion paper catalog of Resources for the Future, a research organization in Washington, DC.

Interviews. We also obtained information from in-person or telephone interviews. We interviewed researchers, consultants, and staff at state regulatory agencies. We also interviewed policy and technical staff of the various stakeholders in the process: automobile companies, environmental groups, the electric power industry, and electric vehicle industry interests. In general, we rely on such information when there were no written accounts. Of particular import are details of key analyses that do not appear in the reports summarizing the analyses.[23]

2.5.3 Limitations of the Narrow Cost-Effectiveness Approach[24]

Most of the studies we have reviewed for this project--and virtually all of the ones that attempt to evaluate elements of the California strategy--summarize their results in cost-effectiveness terms.

Usually the analysis involves four basic steps:

---

[22]Because we anticipated that much of the most relevant material would be unpublished, and unpublished materials are very difficult to locate, we made it a point in each of our in-person interviews to ask what the interview subjects would encourage us to consider. People tended to recommend materials that supported their views, but because we interviewed very knowledgeable people representing very diverse sets of positions, we are hopeful that we have located and considered the most relevant and important unpublished materials for our purposes. In addition, an earlier draft of this report was circulated to dozens of analytically oriented personnel from a comparably diverse set of organizations, and this enabled us to locate and consider some unpublished reports that we had initially failed to identify.

[23]In particular, as detailed below, we obtained such information from CARB staff, personnel at the three U.S. motor vehicle manufacturers, and Sierra Research.

[24]See Lareau (1994) for another critique of cost-effectiveness analyses of policies to reduce emissions of ozone precursors. While we think he makes several excellent points, Lareau appears to be more sanguine than we are about the prospects for reliably expressing policy choices solely in cost-effectiveness terms.

- Estimating the costs per vehicle of a policy action during some time period (often from the present to the year 2010);
- Estimating the emission reductions (often from the present to the year 2010) of ozone precursors per vehicle affected by the policy;[25]
- Multiplying each of the per-vehicle figures by the number of vehicles projected to be affected by the policy (to obtain projections of total dollar costs and tons of emission reductions);
- Computing a cost-effectiveness ratio by dividing the total dollar costs by the tons of emission reductions (expressed in dollars per ton).

Note that the *higher* this ratio, the *less* attractive a policy appears to be because it appears to take more dollars per unit of benefit.

Direct costs and direct emission reductions defined. Different studies purporting to estimate cost effectiveness for California ozone-reduction policies take account of different costs and emission reductions. The nature of these costs and emission reductions differs substantially from one policy element to the next, and, to a lesser but still considerable extent, from one study of a particular element to the next. We use the terms *direct* costs and *direct* emission reductions to refer to the costs and emission effects that we take the NCER for a particular element to incorporate. Generally speaking, we define direct costs and direct emission reductions for a particular element to correspond to what most, or all of the studies of that element that we reviewed, appear to take into account in analyzing cost effectiveness.[26]

---

[25]Often this is done using an elaborate computer model such as the latest version of U.S. EPA's MOBILE or CARB's EMFAC.

[26]Usually, the cost-effectiveness studies we reviewed ignore behavioral responses to policies at the level of individual drivers or vehicle owners and they almost always ignore market responses; we define direct costs and emission benefits accordingly. An exception is cost-effectiveness studies of inspection and maintenance programs, many of which purport to take account of behavioral issues such as evasion and fraud, and hence we define direct costs and emission benefits to include such behavioral responses in the case of I&M programs.

We begin each analysis of direct costs and emission reductions (in Sections 6, 8 and 10) by explaining what direct costs and emission benefits mean in that context.

Information on direct costs and emission reductions can be very useful for making policy decisions, but it is important to recognize the limitations of these kinds of calculations as a guide to policy. To remind the reader of these limitations we refer to *narrow* cost-effectiveness analyses or *narrow* cost-effectiveness ratios (NCERs).

Why do NCERs by themselves provide an inadequate foundation for policy decisionmaking? The reasons are several.

A ton is not a ton is not a ton. Tons of emission reductions of ozone precursors is a surrogate for actual benefits of health improvements, etc. Although such a surrogate may be the best possible given current knowledge, it is worth remembering that it is very crude. Sometimes reductions in ROG will reduce ozone, and sometimes they won't. Sometimes reductions in NOx will reduce ozone, and sometimes they won't. The benefit measure often used--tons of emission reduction of ROG plus tons of emission reduction of NOx--assumes not only that there are benefits to reducing each precursor, but also that at the margin these benefits are the same--i.e., that the social value of reducing a ton of NOx is the same as the social value of reducing a ton of ROG <u>and</u> that the benefit provided by reducing each additional unit of emissions is the same as the benefit provided by reducing the first unit.[27] In some studies, researchers express the benefit measure in terms of tons of only one of the precursors to avoid making the former assumption, but this assumes that the benefits of reducing the other precursor are zero. Further difficulties pertain to the fact that the benefits of ozone reduction differ over space (e.g., they are considerably higher in the South Coast than in most other areas in California), and time of year (due to differences in sunlight and other atmospheric factors).

---

[27]For discussions of the difficulties of allocating benefits of ozone reduction between ROG and NOx for cost-benefit or cost-effectiveness purposes, see Small and Kazimi (1995, pp. 15-16) and McConnell and Harrington (1992, pp. 22-27).

Ozone levels before and after the year 2010 matter. Much of the analysis of cost-effectiveness focuses on the year 2010, the target date for South Coast compliance with federal standards for air quality. Although this date is extremely important for legal reasons, from an economic perspective, it is artificial. It is hardly a foregone conclusion that by 2010 ozone will cease to be policy concern in South Coast. Thus, decisionmakers are well advised, as they do at least sometimes, to look beyond the year 2010.

Benefits include more than ozone reduction. As noted above, policies that reduce emissions of ROG and NOx may involve important social benefits other than ozone reduction, such as reductions of other pollutants. Such benefits are relevant to policy evaluation.

Direct costs include more than is generally quantified. Most of the cost-effectiveness studies we review take a limited view of costs. They generally focus on direct resource costs to the exclusion of what we have called direct decreases in well-being. The latter can be very important in evaluating some policies, for example transportation control measures and enhanced inspection and maintenance. Other costs can result if policies divert scientific and engineering effort towards relatively unproductive activities or worsen employment opportunities for Californians.

We can't implement just the policies with low NCERs. Often people attempt to defeat a policy proposal by claiming--or even demonstrating-- that the proposed policy has a much higher NCER than past policies or other policies being proposed or implemented. Even if NCERs did not suffer from the other kinds of limitations discussed elsewhere, such claims or demonstrations really don't tell us very much. For example, they don't tell policymakers who must meet the NAAQS how else to get the tons of reduction necessary to comply with federal law. Moreover, the narrow cost-effectiveness (or even economic efficiency) of a policy that has already been implemented is irrelevant to any policymaker unless we can extend or fortify the past policy in some way and get more emissions reductions with cost-effectiveness (or efficiency) similar to what we have gotten in the past. As discussed above, we should expect that our current opportunities to get additional emission reductions are not as attractive as the ones we have implemented in the past. In addition, there is no good reason to expect that all of the remaining options worth adopting have similar levels of cost-effectiveness or efficiency.

Costs to Californians are of particular concern. Many of the analyses we reviewed estimate the additional costs of producing LDVs, while not analyzing who will bear these costs. Some people assume that vehicle-production costs should be irrelevant to California policymakers because, for example, these costs will be absorbed by vehicle manufacturers, who are assumed not to be Californians. Both premises are wrong. Sometimes analysts or commentators suggest that all of these costs will be borne by Californians because all costs to manufacturers will be passed on in higher vehicle prices. This is also wrong. In estimating costs and benefits, we pay particular attention to the issue of how costs are shared between Californians and others, which requires analysis of the extent to which additional costs of vehicle manufacture will lead to price increases.

Indirect effects are mediated through market adjustments. The way that analysts and commentators typically treat the issue of who bears the additional costs of producing vehicles is symptomatic of a larger phenomenon: Most analysts don't consider how markets will adjust to the policies they are evaluating, or do so naively, or fail to consider implications of these adjustments. For example, if a policy leads to higher prices for new vehicles, we should expect that the price increases will reduce new vehicle sales and delay retirement of older vehicles, which on average produce higher emissions. Thus policy-induced changes in prices have implications for how policies affect emissions.

Despite such limitations, we believe that NCERs can be very helpful in making policy choices--if used with care and judgment. How we think this might best be done is explained in Section 2.6, which concludes this section.

2.5.4 Analyses of Market-Mediated Effects of Policies

Many of the policies under consideration are likely to change the prices of new and used vehicles in California, the well-being of

consumers and the profits of vehicle manufacturers and their dealers.
Such market responses have important implications for the economic
efficiency of the policies, but are typically ignored in narrow cost-
effectiveness calculations.

We go beyond the narrow cost-effectiveness frameworks used in most
studies to consider how markets will respond to implementation of many
of the policy elements and what the implications are for costs and
benefits of the policies. In addition, we develop information about the
distribution of costs and non-emission benefits among various groups
inside and outside California.[28] In all cases we offer the analyses as
providing information that can and should be used along with NCERs in
arriving at a policy decision.

We analyze market responses using standard economic models and
reasoning. When we have sufficient information to calibrate models
numerically, we simulate ranges of effects of some policy elements on
new internal combustion engine vehicle or electric vehicle markets. In
some instances--for example, the effects of scrappage programs on used
LDV markets--we use a supply and demand framework to develop qualitative
implications that are helpful in critiquing studies of narrow cost
effectiveness and identifying pitfalls in policy design and
implementation.

2.5.5 Dealing with Economic Uncertainties

The elements of the California strategy have very diverse economic
effects. There is very considerable uncertainty about: costs of
achieving emission reductions in various ways, emission reductions that
will result from various policies, performance of machines and people,
reactions of markets, and means of reducing ozone that are not part of
the California LDV strategy. Generally, it would be very helpful to
policymakers to have a sense of the numerical range in which the

---

[28]Depending on the policy element under discussion, we estimate
effects separately for groups such as: buyers of new ICEVs in
California, buyers of new EVs in California, owners of used vehicles in
California, buyers of used vehicles in California, sellers (vehicle
manufacturers and their dealers combined) of new ICEVs in California,
and, in the case of the ZEV mandate, vehicle manufacturers and dealers
that are and are not subject to the mandate before 2002.

relevant quantities are likely to fall. In some cases, available information does not support such quantification. In other cases, it does.

Various means of dealing with uncertainties. We deal with uncertainties as best we can with the information we have. In some contexts we merely point out the existence of an uncertainty that seems important and describe its apparent sources. In some contexts we describe the degree of uncertainty verbally. In many contexts we attempt to reduce uncertainty by developing new information or integrating old information in informative ways. In many cases we attempt to quantify the degree of uncertainty. Sometimes we display quantitatively the range of disagreement about various costs and benefits; often we are able to illuminate the sources of the disagreement.

Lower and upper bounds. When it seems feasible to do so, we use principles of microeconomics and cost-benefit analyses and available empirical information to develop ranges of estimates. The details of how we do this differ from case to case, but the general interpretation of one of our ranges is typically the same. Specifically, it is the narrowest range we are able to develop within which we are very confident the true value lies. Thus we refer to the end points of these ranges as lower and upper bounds. It is implausible to us that the true value lies outside such a range; however, it is not necessarily the case that all values within the range are plausible to us. We would prefer, of course, to have ranges within which all values are plausible and outside which no values are plausible, but available information does not allow such precision.

Some of the values we bound are quantities that have been estimated by others, for example, the cost of additional hardware required to meet stricter certification standards for exhaust emissions or the production cost of an electric vehicle. In these cases, our bounds are usually estimated values from other studies: our lower-bound estimate is an estimate that we believe is very likely too low, and our upper-bound estimate is an estimate that we believe is very likely too high. In

each of these cases, we discuss our reasons for choosing the lower and
upper bounds in question.

In other cases we estimate bounds on quantities not estimated in
other studies (e.g., the effect of the ZEV mandate on the prices of new
internal combustion engine vehicles), starting with ranges of estimates
for underlying parameters taken directly or adjusted from other studies.
Although we have no firm basis for emphasizing or choosing particular
values within such ranges, we explain our methods in sufficient detail
to allow readers to develop economic implications using parameter values
they think are particularly plausible.

2.5.6 Accounting for Interdependencies Among Policies

The effect of adding a particular element of the strategy with the
others in place depends on the effectiveness of the other policies.[29]
This is particularly true on the benefits (emission reduction) side. For
example, the effectiveness of a vehicle-scrappage program depends on the
emission levels of scrapped vehicles, which depends (in part) on the
effectiveness of the smog-check program.

Such interdependencies reflect the fact that various elements of
the strategy are aimed at controlling the same emissions. The number of
such interdependencies or interactions that might be important is quite
large. We consider many, but not nearly all, of them.

Given our strategy of analyzing an element with the others in
place, accounting for interdependencies involves assuming the
effectiveness of some policies while analyzing another. The difficulty
comes in when the effectiveness of policies is highly uncertain. In
several instances we accommodate such uncertainty by analyzing the
effectiveness of one element under various assumptions about the
effectiveness of other elements that appear to be particularly relevant
in that context. Such an analytic strategy is often called "sensitivity
analysis."

---

[29]See, for example, Lareau (1994) for a discussion of this issue in
the context of ozone-reduction policies.

2.6 HOW SHOULD NARROW COST-EFFECTIVENESS INFORMATION BE USED?

We have explained why economical choice of ozone-reduction policies cannot be reliably reduced to mechanical use of narrow cost-effectiveness ratios. Despite this, we devote substantial attention to studies that calculate NCERs and in some cases we present our own ranges of estimates. In this section we explain why we do this and how narrow cost-effectiveness information might best be used.

2.6.1 Why Pay So Much Attention to NCERs?

We pay attention to NCERs for three reasons:

(1) The idea of cost-effectiveness and studies purporting to estimate cost-effectiveness are very influential with policymakers;

(2) Most of the quantitative information useful for our purposes is imbedded in such studies; and

(3) If interpreted with care, cost-effectiveness calculations can be very helpful in making policy decisions.

Reasons to use NCERs do not provide guidance on *how* to use them. As background for considering how NCERs might best be used, we first step back and look at the dilemma facing policymakers who must make decisions.

2.6.2 The Decision Problems Facing Policymakers

Policymakers should always be on the lookout for polices that are more attractive than the ones they are presently considering for implementation. In keeping with the focus of this report on evaluation of elements of the existing California LDV strategy, we do not dwell on this crucial issue.

Different goals call for different decision rules. As discussed in Section 2.2, some policymakers (e.g., the U.S. Congress) have the power to change ozone standards, and in principle are free to pursue economic efficiency. Other policymakers (e.g., California regulators) are bound by law to achieve air-quality goals set by others. In this discussion we allow--relying on existing estimates of dollar benefits and costs of emission reductions--for the possibility that attainment of current air-quality standards in the South Coast will require some actions with social costs higher than their social benefits.[30] For ease of exposition, we also leave it implicit that policymakers interpret costs and benefits to mean costs and benefits to their own constituents.

Cost and benefit information is useful to both types of policymakers, but policymakers with different goals have different (general) decision rules (Table 2.2-1):

- Policymakers pursuing economic efficiency would want to implement a policy if and only if all of the social benefits taken together exceed all of the social costs taken together.

- Policymakers bound to achieve target levels of emission reductions would seek to achieve these targets at the smallest excess of all of the social costs taken together over all of the social benefits taken together.

What do policymakers know about costs and benefits? When a decision must be made, some of the costs and benefits have been quantified, some much more precisely or convincingly than others. Other costs and benefits have not been quantified at all. Costs and benefits that have been quantified seem to get disproportionate emphasis in the policy process, but those that have not been quantified are not necessarily less important.

NCERs contain much useful information, but it is important to understand what information they do and do not contain. We develop information that should be helpful to policymakers on this score. More specifically, we review and critique many studies that express their findings in terms of NCERs, sorting out the basic conceptual issues, highlighting implicit assumptions, exploring the sensitivity of estimates to alternative assumptions, and analyzing sources of discrepancy between conflicting estimates.[31] Equally important, if not

---

[30]This possibility is suggested by some of the information we review below. However, there is considerable uncertainty about various fundamental factors, and new information might establish that current ozone standards are not more stringent than economic efficiency requires. For example, we may learn that emissions cause much more damage than is currently believed or we may discover new ways to reduce emissions at much lower costs.

[31]Such as differences in underlying concepts, assumptions, and sources of information.

more so, we point out potentially important costs and benefits that are not accounted for in the NCERs no matter how well these ratios are developed.

Concerning the factors that are not incorporated--which we refer to as "uncounted" costs and benefits--it is important to consider them as well as available information allows. We provide new information on such factors, primarily on those related to market-mediated effects.

Policymakers inevitably, however, make decisions not knowing nearly as much as they (and we) would like. We attempt to help them by identifying (and periodically reemphasizing) uncounted costs and benefits. Among factors that have been quantified to some extent, we help the reader understand the nature and sources of what appear to be the key economic uncertainties. When possible, we do this by developing ranges (as described above) of NCERs and other relevant factors and exploring what one would have to believe about underlying issues (e.g., how effective some other element of the strategy is, how much it will really cost to produce electric vehicles) to focus on particular parts of these ranges.

2.6.3 How Do We Propose That NCERs Be Used?

Thus, the policy choices cannot be reduced to simple formulas: there is much too much uncertainty for that. But choices must be made. We offer the following general guidance, to which we return in Section 12.

Follow the steps:

Step 1: Use your beliefs about factors underlying the NCERs (based on information about the reliability of the data and methods used) to determine the narrowest range that you find plausible.

Step 2: Make a list of the potentially important costs and benefits that are not accounted for in the NCERs you have, consider what you know about them, and form as precise a judgment as you can about the relative magnitudes of uncounted costs and uncounted benefits.

Step 3: Consult Table 2.6-1, perhaps modified to your liking, which provides some rough rules of thumb for the South Coast.

Table 2.6-1

Illustrative Rules of Thumb for Using Narrow Cost-Effectiveness Ratios (NCERs) to Choose Ozone-Reduction Policies for the South Coast

If you think the NCER is about:	And you must find more tons of reductions, then:	And you are free to pursue economic efficiency, then:
$5,000/ton or less	Implement the policy unless uncounted costs appear to far outweigh uncounted benefits	Implement the policy unless uncounted costs appear to far outweigh uncounted benefits
$10,000/ton	Implement the policy unless uncounted costs appear to far outweigh uncounted benefits and alternative ways to reduce tons look even less promising	Implement the policy as long as uncounted costs appear not to much outweigh uncounted benefits
$25,000/ton	Don't implement the policy unless uncounted benefits appear to outweigh uncounted costs or alternative ways to reduce tons look even less promising	Don't implement the policy unless uncounted benefits appear to far outweigh uncounted costs
$50,000/ton or more	Don't implement the policy unless uncounted benefits appear to far outweigh uncounted costs and alternative ways to reduce tons look even less promising	Don't implement the policy unless uncounted benefits appear to outweigh uncounted costs by tens of thousands of dollars per ton

The numbers in Table 2.6-1 are based on current estimates of the benefits of emission reductions in the South Coast. As reported in Section 2.4.4, we do not view these estimates as definitions and urge policymakers to adjust the numbers in Table 2.6-1 as they see fit.

Consider first policymakers pursuing economic efficiency. Estimates for the South Coast (discussed in Section 2.4.4 and detailed in Appendix 2.B) suggest that benefits of ROG and NOx emission reductions are probably more than $5,000 per ton but below $25,000.[32] NCERs of roughly $10,000 per ton, then, would be taken to mean that a policy is efficient as long as uncounted costs appear not to be much larger than uncounted benefits. NCERs of considerably less than $10,000 per ton--say, $5,000--require a less encouraging judgment about uncounted costs relative to benefits, and NCERs of considerably more than $10,000 per ton--say, $25,000--require an encouraging judgment about uncounted benefits relative to costs, the more so the higher is the NCER.

Rules proposed for policymakers who must find more tons of emission reductions (e.g., as required within the SIP process) are based on adjusting the rules for the policymakers free to pursue efficiency.[33] Two major considerations guide the adjustments: a) attainment of air-quality goals in the South Coast currently appears to require adopting measures whose costs exceed their benefits, and b) in such cases, it is especially important to consider alternative ways to get the same tons of reduction. Thus, the rules proposed for policymakers who must meet emission reduction targets involve less stringent requirements for optimism about uncounted benefits relative to costs for any given NCER level, but explicitly remind the policymaker to consider alternatives when leaning towards implementing policies that appear to be inefficient.

The inevitable imprecision of such rules, while regrettable, at least serves to remind the reader that:

- Even though we'd like to know a lot more before making a decision, decisions must be made.
- Economical decisionmaking cannot be reduced to precise rules in the context of the policies we are analyzing.
- NCERs contain useful information.
- NCERs often ignore important costs and benefits that are no less relevant because they are uncounted in the calculation.

---

[32]Recall that the relevant figures appear to be almost as high in Sacramento, but much lower in San Diego, Ventura, and San Francisco.

[33]Note that for very large or very small NCERs the decision rules tend to converge.

- We may know a lot or very little about costs and benefits that are uncounted in the NCERs.

- Policymakers obligated to meet emission-reduction targets (e.g., California policymakers in obeying federal law) must be bolder than policymakers free to pursue economic efficiency.

- Even policymakers obligated to meet emission-reduction targets should try to find the most economical ways to do so.

We offer these rules in the belief that decisions made systematically considering all of the relevant issues--even if that requires considerable judgment about factors that are uncounted, unquantified, unquantifiable, or even effectively imponderable--will tend to turn out better than decisions based on mechanical processing of numbers that fail to account for many relevant factors.

3. INTERNAL COMBUSTION ENGINE VEHICLE EMISSIONS

In this section, we discuss estimates of internal combustion engine vehicle (ICEV) emissions in California. We first describe the sources of these emissions and discuss the factors that influence emissions from these sources. We then summarize estimates of average ICEV emissions and how they are distributed across vehicles.

To preview our findings:

(1) There is a substantial uncertainty about the amount of real world emissions from light-duty vehicles. This uncertainty is due both to which vehicles are tested and to how they are tested.

(2) Current emission estimates may understate actual emissions.

(3) Lifetime average vehicle emissions per mile are substantially higher than vehicle certification standards because certification tests do not accurately represent real world driving conditions and because emissions per mile increase with age.

(4) A small proportion of vehicles account for a relatively large percent of total emissions, although disagreement remains on the extent of the concentration.

3.1 SOURCES OF EMISSIONS

There are main three sources of internal combustion engine vehicle emissions: exhaust emissions, evaporative emissions, and marketing emissions.[34]

Exhaust emissions. ROG, NOx, and CO are produced during the combustion process and emitted in vehicle exhaust.

Evaporative emissions. Evaporating fuel generates ROG emissions both while the car is running and when it is resting. There are three basic types of evaporative emissions that are generally thought to occur in the following decreasing order of importance (Calvert et al., 1993,

---

[34]Crankcase or blowby emissions are another source of emissions. These have been almost completely eliminated by positive crankcase ventilation valves, and we ignore them here. Positive crankcase ventilation valves have been required in California since 1965 (CARB, 1995e, p. 34).

p.38). *Diurnal emissions* are associated with diurnal breathing of the fuel tank as the ambient air temperature rises and falls. *Hot soak emissions* occur when the fuel system is exposed to high under-hood temperatures after the vehicle is turned off. They mainly occur in the 30 minutes after the car is turned off. *Running losses* occur as fuel in the fuel tank is heated up during vehicle operation.

Marketing emissions. Fuel spillage and the escape of fuel vapor into the atmosphere during refueling also cause ROG emissions. Included in this category are emissions due to the delivery of gasoline to gas stations, storage of gasoline at the gas station, and vehicle refueling.

3.2 DETERMINANTS OF EMISSIONS

The emissions generated from each of these sources depend on a large number of factors that involve technology, human behavior, and driving conditions. A description of some of the key factors follows.

Technology. The engine design and emission control devices installed on the vehicle affect tailpipe and evaporative emissions, and as we will see below, may affect refueling emissions. Critical to vehicle emissions are both how these technologies perform when the car is new and how their performance degrades over time.

The characteristics of fuel also influence emissions. Fuel with lower Reid Vapor Pressures (RVP)[35] produce less evaporative emissions, and tailpipe emissions vary in a complicated way with fuel composition.[36]

The technology used in gasoline distribution affects emissions. Vapor recovery nozzles at gasoline stations may reduce ROG emissions during refueling, and regulations on gasoline underground storage tanks affect emissions while gasoline is stored.

The technology used in vehicle inspection and maintenance (I&M) programs may also affect vehicle emissions. The technology affects the extent to which high emitting vehicles are identified and can help in

---

[35]Reid Vapor Pressure is a measure of the surface pressure required to keep a liquid from vaporizing at a temperature of 100°F (CARB, 1990a, p. 4).

[36]See Calvert et al. (1993).

diagnosing malfunctions and verifying whether the vehicle has been
repaired.

Human behavior. Emissions are integrally linked to many dimensions
of driver behavior. The number of miles driven and the number of
vehicle starts affect emissions. The relation between miles driven and
emissions is obvious. Given the number of miles driven, the more
starts, the more emissions, because substantial emissions are generated
until the car warms up.

Driving style also affects emissions. Aggressive drivers, those
who accelerate frequently and drive rapidly, generate more emissions
than other drivers. The fraction of time air conditioning is used also
affects emissions. Drivers who run the air conditioning more frequently
generate more emissions than drivers who operate air conditioning less
often.

Vehicle maintenance can have an important effect on emissions. The
emission systems of poorly maintained vehicles may deteriorate more
rapidly than those of properly maintained ones.

Human behavior also determines the effectiveness of automobile
warranty and recall programs. Even if a malfunctioning component of the
emission control system is under warranty, a driver may choose not to
take the car in for repair if vehicle performance is not affected.
Recall programs are effective only to the extent that drivers bring
their vehicles in for repair.

Human behavior is a central component of vehicle inspection and
maintenance programs. Drivers who try to skirt the program and smog-
check mechanics who try to bypass the requirements may seriously
compromise its effectiveness.

Driving conditions. Regional driving conditions and ambient
temperature affect emissions--the higher the temperature the more
evaporative and marketing emissions. So does average travel speed:
Stop and go traffic on congested freeways or surface streets will
increase emissions per mile.

3.3 IN-USE EMISSIONS

Vehicle emissions vary importantly with model year, model, and mileage. Emissions also vary substantially even over vehicles of a given model year, model, and mileage.

Figure 3.3-1 qualitatively depicts average ROG emission in grams per mile for vehicles of particular model and model year as mileage increases. The vertical bars on the plot illustrate the dispersion of individual vehicles around the average. One might expect the dispersion around the average to increase as vehicles age.

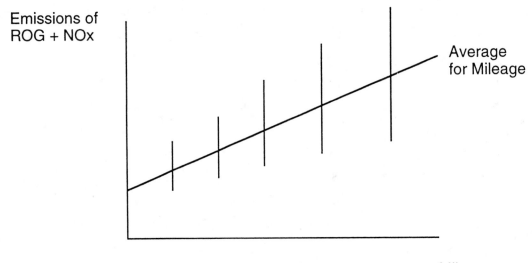

Fig. 3.3-1—Average Emissions and Spreads for Vehicle of a Given Model and Model Year

Figure 3.3-2 qualitatively illustrates the emission distribution of vehicles that are new (zero miles) and at 100,000 miles. Even though the means of the two distributions are different, the two distributions may overlap--there may be some new vehicles that emit more than the cleanest vehicles with 100,000 miles. As we discuss below, there is strong evidence that a small fraction of vehicles are responsible for a relatively large share of overall emissions. Thus, there is reason to believe that the right tails of the distributions in Figure 3.3-2 taper off slowly.

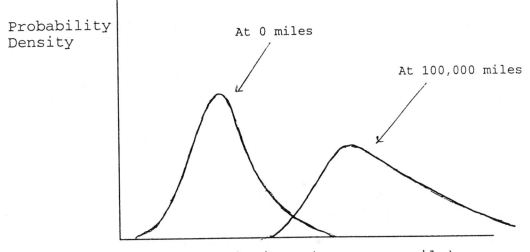

Fig. 3.3-2—Distribution of Vehicle Emissions for Given Model and Model Year When New and at 100,000 Miles

There is considerable uncertainty over actual vehicle emissions because vehicle emissions are not measured directly but predicted by models that may be only partly accurate. Estimates of mobile source emissions in California are primarily made using CARB's EMFAC and U.S. EPA's MOBILE models. These models predict fleet emissions based on data on in-use vehicle emissions, surveys of vehicle miles traveled and starts, average driving speeds, and fleet composition. The models have been continually revised as new data have become available; however, a great deal of uncertainty remains about how well these models capture real-world emissions.

There are three main reasons for the uncertainty in the models' accuracy. First, the test procedure used to measure in-use vehicle tailpipe emissions does not correspond well to real-world driving conditions. The Federal Test Procedure (FTP) used both by U.S. EPA and CARB was developed before test equipment could simulate rapid accelerations and under-represents the frequency and severity of rapid accelerations (Ross et al., 1995, p. 22). In 1992 CARB developed a test cycle that it thought more accurately represented driving behavior in the South Coast Air Basin. This so-called Unified Cycle was developed by using chase vehicles to measure the speed and acceleration of randomly selected vehicles on the road. Exhaust emissions on the Unified Cycle are approximately 100 percent higher for ROG and CO and 60 percent higher for NOx than on the FTP (CARB, 1994c, p. 8). The FTP also does not test vehicle emissions with the air conditioning on. Preliminary data suggest that air conditioning increases NOx emissions roughly 75 percent (German, 1995). Thus using the FTP to estimate emissions in areas such as the South Coast where air conditioning is widely used will significantly understate emissions.

Second, it is difficult to measure real-world evaporative emissions. They are commonly estimated based on emissions during a test protocol. In the past, these test protocols have not adequately represented areas such as Southern California that experience very high air temperature during certain parts of the year (Calvert et al., 1993, p. 38). In recent years, CARB has been revising its models to better represent evaporative emissions. (CARB, 1990a, p. 14)

Third, the vehicles on which in-use emission estimates are based may not be representative of the fleet as a whole. CARB bases its vehicle emission factors on in-use surveillance programs that are done roughly once a year. The vehicles in these tests may not be representative of the in-use fleet for several reasons:

- **Small sample size.** Emissions of between 200 and 300 vehicles are measured in each surveillance program.[37] This is a very

---

[37]In the most recent surveillance program (Light-Duty Surveillance Program 12 completed in 1994), 232 vehicles were tested (CARB, 1994c, p. 1).

small number of observations with which to estimate the emissions of hundreds of different engine and car types. The small sample sizes also make it difficult to accurately measure the emissions of the small percent of vehicles that account for a large percentage of emissions.

- **Low response rate.** CARB recruits vehicles from the fleet on a voluntary basis. The participation rates for these efforts are very low.[38] Higher emitting vehicles may be underrepresented because it seems likely that owners with the most poorly maintained vehicles or with vehicles whose emission control equipment has been tampered with will not participate.[39]

- **Oldest vehicles are not tested.** Vehicles more than 10 years old are typically not tested. This excludes many vehicles from testing: roughly 60 percent of vehicles of a given model year are still on the road 10 years later (Sierra, 1994a, p. 52). There is thus reduced information on which to project the emissions of the vehicles with the highest mileage and probably the highest emissions.

Several different types of studies have recently suggested that CARB's model underestimates mobile source emissions. Measurement of ambient concentrations of ROG, CO, and NOx in automobile tunnels in Los Angeles indicated that emissions of ROG and CO were 3.8 and 2.7 times higher than predicted by California's EMFAC model, version 7C--a past version of the model. These ratios may even understate the true differences because cold engines are probably underrepresented in tunnel studies, and a disproportionate share of vehicle emissions occur when the engine is cold.[40] Data from remote sensing devices also suggest

---

[38]The response rate in Light-Duty Surveillance Program 12 was between 7 and 16 percent, depending on how it is calculated (CARB, 1994c, pp. 1-2). Aroesty et al. (1994, p. 108) report that response rates in previous programs were typically around 5 percent.

[39]In a study that compared readings from on-road remote sensing devices with those on the FTP, Klausmeier et al. (1995, pp. 3-53) found remote sensing readings for carbon monoxide were substantially higher for vehicles that were not brought in for FTP testing.

[40]Tunnel studies are usually done on main arteries, and most cars are warmed up by the time they get to the tunnels. Albu, Kao, and

that ROG emissions may be understated relative to NOx. (Small and Kazimi, 1995, p. 11).

As a result of this evidence, emission estimates have increased in successive versions of EMFAC. The recently released revision of EMFAC, version 7G, increases 1990 light-duty vehicle ROG emissions in the South Coast by 31 percent, CO emissions by 91 percent, and NOx emissions by 66 percent over the version 7F (CARB, 1995f, p. I-24).[41] The latest emission estimates are still fundamentally based on the FTP without air conditioning, and thus likely continue to understate real world emissions.

Table 3.3-1 presents several estimates of lifetime average vehicle and fleet emissions in grams per mile. Two observations about the numbers in this table are noteworthy. First, the various estimates differ significantly. Small and Kazimi's ROG estimate is over two times larger than CARB's. Estimates of ROG exhaust, NOx, and CO emissions from a vehicle certified to 1993 California standards by Hwang et al. using a preliminary version of EMFAC version 7G are 20 to 25 percent higher than CARB's using EMFAC version 7F. Second, the in-use emissions are substantially larger than the certification standards. Estimates by Hwang et al. are roughly twice the certification standard for a 1993 California vehicle, and Ross's estimates for a 1993 vehicle meeting federal standards are over 3 and 5 times the certification standards for ROG exhaust and CO emissions, respectively. In-use emissions are substantially larger than certification standards because certification tests do not replicate real world driving conditions and because emission control systems deteriorate over time.

Estimates of the evaporative emissions on a grams-per-mile basis are scarce, but those available suggest that evaporative emissions account for a substantial portion of overall ROG emissions. Estimates in Table 3.3-1 vary from 0.5 to 0.72 grams per mile and approximately 30 to 65 percent of overall ROG emissions.

Cackette (1992, p. 31) claim that 70 percent of trip emissions occur during the cold start period.

[41]These changes appear to be in part due to an increase in VMT, but the effect of this increase appears to be small.

Table 3.3-1

Estimates of Internal Combustion Engine ROG and NOx Emissions
(gm/mile)

| | ROG | | | | |
	Exhaust	Evap.	Exhaust + Evap.	NOx	CO
Calif. fleet average CARB estimate for 1993 fleet[a]	1.0	0.5	1.5	1.2	13.6
Small and Kazimi estimate for 1992 fleet[b]			3.76	1.26	13.0
1993 California Vehicle					
New car standard[c]	0.25			0.4	3.4
CARB estimate[d]	0.38			0.63	5.6
Sierra estimate[e]	0.42	0.72	1.14	0.67	6.2
Hwang estimate[f]	0.52			0.74	7.0
1993 Federal Vehicle					
New car standard[g]	0.41			1.0	3.4
Ross estimate[h]	1.3	0.5	1.8	1.48	18.9

[a]Refueling and storage emissions included (CARB, 1994b, pp. E-3, E-4). CARB estimates use EMFAC7F.

[b]Small and Kazimi (1995), p. 13.

[c]At 50,000 miles. Standards for evaporative emissions are specified as emissions allowed during a test procedure, not as grams per mile.

[d]CARB (1994a), p. 46. CARB uses EMFAC7F to estimate emissions during vehicle lifetime. Translated to gm/mile assuming 100,000 mile vehicle life.

[e]Sierra (1995c). Number based on emissions reductions of zero-emission vehicle relative to a California 1993 vehicle. Assumes basic I&M and 130,000 vehicle life. Based on EMFAC7F. Evaporative emissions probably do include refueling emissions, but may not include storage emissions.

[f]Hwang et al. (1994), p. 42. Estimates based on Preview EMFAC7G. Evaporative emissions estimates from Hwang are not presented here because they include effects of evaporative emission controls regulations that will be phased in between 1995 and 1998.

[g]Small and Kazimi (1995), p. 13.

[h]Upstream emissions (gasoline refining emissions) excluded. Ross et al. (1995), p. 5.

Estimates of refueling emissions we were able to locate were low on a grams-per-mile basis, mainly because, as we will discuss in Section 4, the control technology on gasoline distribution emissions is thought to be quite effective. CARB puts gasoline distribution emissions at 0.06

gm/mile for an ultra low emission vehicle (ULEV) in 2000 (CARB, 1994b, p. E-4). These may be close to present day marketing emissions because the control technology is not expected to become much more effective over the next five years.

3.3.1 The Distribution of Emissions Across Vehicles

One of the most significant findings in recent years is that a small proportion of vehicles in use account for a relatively large percent of total emissions. Although analysts generally agree on this point, debate remains about how uneven the distribution is. During interviews conducted for this project, CARB staff estimated that 10 percent of vehicles account for approximately one-third of total emissions, and Sierra staff estimated that 25 percent of the vehicles account for 50 percent of emissions.[42] Studies using data based on remote sensing devices commonly conclude that 5 to 10 percent of vehicles account for upwards of one-half of total emissions (Aroesty et al., 1994, p. 5).

The truth is likely somewhere in between the CARB and remote sensing estimates. As we discussed above, CARB's in-use emission tests may miss the highest emitters. In contrast, remote sensing may overstate the concentration because it measures emissions only at one point in time, and the emissions of an individual vehicle vary substantially over time. In fact, if multiple readings are taken for an individual car, one finds that a small percent of the readings account for a high percent of emissions. Remote sensing is usually done under conditions where vehicle speed and acceleration are at least partially controlled, but this may only partially correct the bias.[43]

High emitting vehicles are found among both older and new vehicles, although older, high mileage vehicles are far more likely to be high

---

[42]Sierra Research, Inc., is a well established consulting firm that specializes in mobile source emissions policy.

[43]Studies that report remote sensing measurements usually rerank the data when reporting the distribution of emissions for individual pollutants across vehicles. Because pollutants are not perfectly correlated across vehicles (particularly ROG and NOx), such a presentation likely overstates the concentration of *combined* emissions (ROG plus NOx plus CO) across vehicles.

emitters (Aroesty et al., 1994, p. 5). Vehicles drop out of the fleet over time and older vehicles are driven less than new vehicles. Thus, even though high emitters may be most common among the oldest vehicles, the proportion of total fleet emissions produced by relatively new vehicles, say 4 to 8 years old, is greater than that produced by older vehicles, say over 12 years old (see Calvert et al., 1995, Figure 2).

4. LIGHT-DUTY VEHICLE REGULATORY HISTORY

California has attempted to reduce vehicle emissions since the mid-1960s, and emissions have fallen over time. Comparison of 1993 fleet emissions with pre-control emissions suggests that ROG, NOx, and CO have dropped between roughly 70 and 85 percent on a grams per mile basis (see Table 4.0-1). Of course, vehicle miles traveled have increased dramatically over the same period, so the actual reduction in mobile source emissions is much lower.

Table 4.0-1

Improvement in Average Fleet Emissions

	gm/mi		Percent Change
	1992 Fleet Average[a]	Pre Control[b]	
ROG	3.76	17	-78
NOx	1.26	4	-68
CO	13.0	85	-84
ROG+NOx	5.02	21	-76

[a]Small and Kazimi (1995), p. 13.

[b]Based on figures from Sierra (1994a, p. 16) and Calvert et al. (1995, p. 1).

In this section we examine the regulatory system in California as of 1993. We evaluate how the various components of the regulatory system affect the emission-related behavior of the central players in the process--car companies, oil companies, drivers, and smog-check mechanics. We rate the effectiveness of the system's components in reducing emissions. This will allow us to understand how thoroughly various sources of vehicle emissions have been addressed and provide background for interpreting the new elements of California's light-duty vehicle ozone reduction strategy.

To preview our findings:

(1) Exhaust and evaporative emission certification has been effective in inducing automobile companies to build vehicles that are cleaner when new, but has done only a moderate job of reducing emissions

due to the deterioration of emission control equipment over the life of the vehicle.

(2) Warranty and recall programs have also been moderately successful in reducing emissions due to equipment deterioration, but do not address emissions due to tampering or improper maintenance.

(3) California's Smog Check program appears to have done a poor job of reducing emissions due to component aging, tampering, and improper maintenance. The reasons are many, but fraud by smog-check technicians, vehicle emission variability that makes it possible to pass emission tests if repeated often enough, and low repair-cost ceilings in past programs are likely among the most important.

(4) Refueling regulations appear to have been quite successful in reducing evaporative ROG emissions.

4.1 REGULATING EMISSIONS MEANS CHANGING HUMAN BEHAVIOR

To be effective, California's emission control programs must affect the behavior of several different sets of people. Table 4.1-1 presents the principal components of California's regulatory program and denotes which actors have to take action for the policy to work.

Table 4.1-1

Components of California's Regulatory Policy on Emissions and Actors Who Must Respond for Components to Work

Regulatory Components	Automobile Manufacturers	Oil Companies	Drivers	Smog-Check Technicians
Certification	x			
Warranty	x		x	
Recall	x		x	
Inspection & Maintenance (I&M)			x	x
Gasoline formulation	x	x		
Refueling	x	x	x	

- **Certification** regulations require car manufacturers to verify that their vehicles meet certain emissions standards and works to the extent that manufacturers design and build clean vehicles.

- Emission-related **warranty** and **recall** programs attempt to induce auto makers to build durable emission control equipment, but for these programs to work, drivers must bring their vehicles in for repair.

- Vehicle **inspection and maintenance** (I&M) programs depend on a complex set of interactions between drivers and smog-check technicians.

- Regulations that require lower-emitting **gasoline formulations** require gasoline manufacturers to reformulate their product and car manufacturers to design vehicles and emission control systems that work well with it.

- **Refueling regulations** designed to reduce emissions during vehicle refueling depend not only on hardware installed by either car companies or oil companies (the gasoline nozzle in the case of oil companies), but on whether this hardware is properly used by drivers.

In the sections that follow, we describe and evaluate each component of California's regulatory program.[44]

4.2 CERTIFICATION

Before an automobile manufacturer can sell a car model in California, it must certify that the model meets various emission standards. Standards are specified for tailpipe emissions of ROG, NOx, and CO in grams per mile and for the evaporative emissions generated during specified test protocols. From 1966 through 1992, manufacturers were required to demonstrate that their vehicles met these standards at 50,000 miles, and starting in 1993, they were also required to demonstrate that vehicles meet the standards at 100,000 miles for ROG and CO.[45] Tests of exhaust emissions are done on vehicle dynamometers

---

[44]Transportation control measures are a component of California's emission control strategy that we do not address in this report. Transportation control measures attempt to reduce emissions by reducing vehicle miles traveled.

[45]A 100,000 mile NOx certification the TLEVs, LEVs, and ULEVs will be gradually introduced starting in the second half of the 1990s.

using the FTP. Aging of the vehicle may be simulated on automobile test tracks or by using laboratory engine dynamometers.

Table 4.2-1 presents exhaust certification standards for three different periods. The certification standards have dropped dramatically over time: The 1993 standards are 80 to 90 percent below the 1971 standards.

Table 4.2-1

California Emission Certification Standards
(gm/mi)[a]

	1971	1983-1992	1993
50,000 miles			
ROG[b]	2.2	0.39	0.25
NOx	4.0	0.4	0.4
CO	23.0	7.0	3.4
100,000 miles			
ROG[b]			0.31
NOx			--
CO			4.2

[a]Bureau of National Affairs (1992).
[b]ROG is hydrocarbons for 1991 and non-methane hydrocarbons for other years.

Vehicles have been required to pass evaporative emission tests since 1970 (Calvert et al., 1993), and the test procedure has become more stringent over time. As of 1993, vehicles were allowed to emit no more than 2 grams of hydrocarbons during a test that simulated one day of diurnal emissions where fuel temperatures range between 60°F and 84°F and hot soak emissions over one hour when the ambient air temperature is between 68°F and 86°F (CARB, 1990a, p. 3).

CARB's certification standards apply to vehicle-fuel combinations. Thus, manufacturers use the fuel that the vehicle is designed to run on in certification tests. Until now, however, the fuel used in the certification of gasoline vehicles has not been the same fuel consumers actually use. U.S. EPA regulations specify that gasoline-powered vehicles be certified on indolene, which is cleaner than the fuel commercially available. As we will see in later sections, manufacturers will probably start certifying gasoline-powered vehicles on the new gasoline formulation soon required in California (Phase 2 gasoline).

Emissions from vehicles that run on different kinds of fuels are composed of different combinations of ROG and NOx species, and these different species vary in their ozone-forming potential. Some species are highly reactive in the atmosphere, others are less so. To evaluate vehicle emissions on an equal basis, CARB has developed a set of Reactivity Adjustment Factors based on a fuel's reactivity relative to conventional gasoline (the industry average gasoline in 1989, called Reformulated Fuel A, or RF-A). Manufacturers then adjust emissions by these factors when certifying vehicles.

We now consider the strengths and weaknesses of the certification program for controlling emissions.

4.2.1 Strengths

Manufacturers cannot circumvent certification requirements because they cannot sell vehicles in California that have not been certified. Certification standards have required manufacturers to develop and produce technology to reduce exhaust and evaporative emissions when the vehicle is new. Requirements that the components be certified at 50,000 and 100,000 miles have also required them to pay attention to the durability of emission control equipment.

4.2.2 Weaknesses

Several features of the current certification process may compromise its effectiveness in reducing emissions.

(1) Certification is determined using tests that do not accurately reflect real world operating conditions.

- Certification of exhaust emissions is done using the FTP, which misses important real-world driving conditions. As discussed in Section 3, evidence suggests that real-world drivers accelerate more often and more rapidly than is represented in the FTP.[46] Certification tests are also done with the air

---

[46]Ross et al. (1995, p. 2) estimate that so-called high-power ROG emission is about 10 percent of the 1993 federal exhaust certification standard for ROG and 125 percent of the certification standard for CO.

conditioner off. Because so-called hard accelerations and air conditioning are not included in the test, auto makers have little incentive to control emissions during these driving conditions.

- The evaporative emission tests are also not representative of the real world, particularly in areas like Los Angeles that have many hot days. The current certification tests use emissions over a one day diurnal, but CARB studies (1990a, pp. 6-7) have shown that approximately 20 percent of vehicles are not driven on a given day and that two-thirds of these have been sitting for two or more days.[47]

- Vehicles running on the fuel actually used by consumers generate more emissions than vehicles running on the fuel used in certification (indolene). Lippincott, Segal, and Wang (1993, p. 3) found that ROG emissions were 23 percent higher and NOx emissions were 19 percent higher when the average gasoline sold in 1989 (Reformulated Fuel A or RF-A) was used rather than indolene.[48]

(2) In-use deterioration may be very different from that simulated in the lab or on test tracks. Aging in the certification process is done over short periods of time and under relatively controlled conditions. For example, catalytic converters are aged by heating in ovens, but therefore are not exposed to fuel and oil contamination that can occur in actual use.

(3) As Aroesty et al. point out (1994, p. 15), 40 percent of the California fleet has more than 100,000 miles on it, meaning that many

---

[47]Studies have also shown that the one-hour test used to simulate a 24 hour diurnal may substantially understate emissions. Evaporative emissions are several times higher when diurnal tests are done over 24 hours with temperatures that range from 72°F to 96°F than in the one-hour test currently required for certification where fuel temperature range from 60°F to 84°F (CARB, 1990a, pp. 6-7). The difference is not only proportionately large but also very large in absolute value--for example 8.6 versus 25.5 grams for a 1983 Toyota Tercel (CARB, 1990a, pp. 6-7).

[48]These results were for prototype low-emission vehicles (TLEVs, LEVs, and ULEVs) developed by domestic and foreign vehicles. The results may be different for vehicles currently on the road.

vehicles are driven beyond the mileage for which components were designed.

4.2.3 Performance

In Table 4.2-2 we rate the effectiveness of each component of California's past LDV emission control strategy as high, moderate, or low in reducing each source of emissions. Components are *highly effective* if they appear to have eliminated a substantial portion of the emissions from a given source. Components are *moderately effective* if they appear to produce significant emission reductions, but the reductions are not large relative to the uncontrolled emissions from the given source. Effectiveness is rated *low* if the reductions appear small compared to the overall emissions from the particular source.

There may still be substantial emission reductions possible from a particular source even if a component's effectiveness is rated high. Similarly, the quantity of emission reductions from a source may be substantial even though moderate relative to the uncontrolled emissions from the source. A dash is entered in a cell when the component does not address the particular source of emissions.

There can be little doubt that certification requirements have reduced both exhaust and evaporative emissions from new vehicles at low mileage. We thus rate the effectiveness of the program on new car tailpipe and exhaust emissions as high. Even for new car emissions, however, there is room for improvement. The certification tests for both exhaust and evaporative emissions can be modified to more accurately reflect in-use operating conditions.

The effect of certification requirements on emissions due to component aging is less clear: many vehicles are driven beyond the certification mileage and vehicles are not aged under real world conditions. We rate the effect of certification requirements on emissions due to component aging as moderate. Note that tampering and poor maintenance are not addressed by the certification program.

Table 4.2-2

**Effectiveness of Emission Control Strategy on Source of
Emissions When Applicable**

| | New Vehicles | Emission System Deterioration | | | Fuel Marketing |
		Tampering	Poor Maintenance	Aging	
Certification	High	--	--	Moderate	--
Warranty	--	--	--	Moderate?	--
Recall	--	--	--	Moderate	--
I&M	--	Low	Low	Low	--
Gasoline formulation	?	?	?	?	?
Refueling regulations	--	--	--	--	High

4.3 WARRANTY

CARB requires automobile manufacturers to offer a 3 year or 50,000 mile bumper-to-bumper warranty on emission control equipment for 1990 model year and later vehicles. During this period, if a car fails a smog-check inspection, the manufacturer is required to make all necessary repairs and adjustments. In addition, CARB requires manufacturers to offer a 7 year or 70,000 mile warranty on high cost emission control components. These are components that cost more than $300 in 1990 dollars to repair or replace, including both parts and labor (California Health and Safety Code, Title 13, Article 6). Under CARB's Emission Warranty Information Reporting Program, manufacturers must notify CARB once one percent of any emission control part in a particular engine family and model year has been replaced under warranty and then provide quarterly reports on the subsequent number of parts replaced (California Health and Safety Code, Title 13, Article 2.4).

4.3.1 Strengths

CARB's warranty requirements give automobile manufacturers an important financial incentive to produce durable emission control equipment. It also reduces the cost to drivers of fixing malfunctioning emission control equipment and makes them more likely to get their vehicles repaired.[49]

4.3.2 Weaknesses

CARB's warranty provisions have several weaknesses.

- There is no guarantee that malfunctioning emission control devices will be identified. For example, without a properly functioning I&M program, there may be little chance that some malfunctions will be identified.

- Even if a malfunction is identified, the driver may have little incentive to take the car in for repair. Again, the effectiveness of the warranty program may depend in part on the effectiveness of the I&M program.

- Most vehicles in California are driven for more than 7 years or 70,000 miles. Manufacturers may have not much incentive to design parts that last longer than the warranty period.[50]

- The effectiveness of the program in reducing emissions depends in part on whether repairs reduce emissions. This may not be the case if the mechanic does not know how to properly repair the car or if replacement parts quickly malfunction.

- Warranties require that the car be properly maintained.[51] Vehicles that are not properly maintained may not be fixed.

4.3.3 Performance

According to CARB staff, there have been a substantial number of warranty repairs since the program started in 1990.[52] CARB staff have

---

[49]Time and inconvenience costs to the driver remain.

[50]Manufacturers may still be concerned about how long-term reliability affects the perceived quality of their products.

[51]What this actually implies is fuzzy. Presumably car owners would be required to complete the recommended maintenance, but car warranties only say they *may* deny coverage if the vehicle is not properly maintained.

[52]Staff estimated that, for the 10 manufacturers with the largest vehicle sales in California, over 1 percent of 400 to 500 different components are being replaced in 1990 model year cars.

also observed that the number of warranty repairs has fallen significantly in recent model years.[53]

According to CARB staff, there are three main reasons that drivers bring vehicles in for emission-related warranty repairs. (1) The emissions system malfunction makes vehicles more difficult to drive, (2) the malfunction (e.g., loose substrate material in the catalyst) causes rattles, and (3) the engine malfunction light goes on. CARB staff do not think there were many warranty claims due to inspection and maintenance failures, but this could indicate that the inspection and maintenance program is ineffective, not that malfunction rates are low.

It is not clear whether the warranty program is having a significant impact on emission system durability. We do not know if the costs of warranty repairs--either in dollars or in damaged product image--are substantial. And, we do not know if the recent decline in warranty repairs is due to the warranty program or to other components of the California strategy such as the recall program. In addition, the warranty program presumably has little effect on emissions after the warranty period. Thus in Table 4.2-2, we rate the effectiveness of the program on emissions from component aging as moderate, but append a question mark to denote that the effectiveness might well be low. Note that the program does not address emissions due to tampering and poor maintenance.

4.4 RECALL

CARB has two programs for requiring manufacturers to recall entire engine families for emissions system failures. The first is tied to the warranty monitoring program discussed above. Once more than 2 to 4 percent, depending on model year, of an emission system component has been replaced under warranty, CARB can require the manufacturer to replace the part on all vehicles with that engine family (California Health and Safety Code, Title 13, Article 2.4, Section 2143).[54] CARB's

---

[53]CARB staff could not be specific on how much it has fallen, but when probed for orders of magnitude, they thought 25 percent might be a reasonable guess.

[54]The warranty failure rate thresholds are 4 percent in 1990 and 1991 model years, 3 percent in 1992 and 1993, and 2 percent in 1994 on.

decision to recall such vehicles depends on both the type of malfunction and the projected impact on emissions.

The second program is the CARB In-Use Compliance Testing Program. CARB has authority to recall engine families if their FTP emissions exceed certification standards during the certification period (0 to 100,000 miles). Thus, vehicles can be recalled for up to 50,000 miles prior to the 1993 model year and up to 100,000 miles for 1993 model year and later vehicles.

Between 30 and 45 engine families are usually tested each year under the In-Use Compliance Testing Program (CARB, 1995a). Once an engine family has been selected, CARB uses DMV registration data to solicit owners of the targeted vehicle to participate in the program. Participation is voluntary. Manufacturers are responsible only for vehicles that are properly maintained, so to avoid manufacturer challenges, CARB carefully screens the recruited vehicles.

To be included in the test, vehicles must have

- Been driven at least 30,000 and not more than 50,000 miles,
- Completed the 30,000-mile required service by 30,500 miles,
- Not been in a crash,
- Done no extended towing of heavy trailers.

The proportion of vehicles that survive these screens is small. For example, in a December 1994 test, 2,500 drivers were solicited by mail, 168 responded and of those 33 vehicles were considered acceptable. CARB ultimately tests 10 to 14 vehicles in each engine family with the manufacturer present (CARB, personal communication). CARB can require a recall if the average emissions of the vehicles tested is higher than the certification standard. Whether a failing vehicle is actually recalled depends on the amount by which emissions exceed the certification standards. For example, vehicles that exceed the standard by less than 15 percent are usually not recalled. To increase the number of drivers who take their vehicles in for emission-related

CARB has the authority to apply the 4 percent threshold to all post 1990 model years (California Health and Safety Code, Title 13, Article 2.4, Section 2143).

recalls, recall repairs must be done before the car can pass the inspection and maintenance program (BAR, 1995, p. 67).

4.4.1 Strengths

Recalls are costly to manufacturers both because of the costs of replacement parts and labor and because of possible negative effects on the firm's reputation. The recall program thus provides strong incentives for manufacturers to build durable emissions control equipment. As with warranty repairs, recalls also reduce the cost to drivers of repairing an emissions system defect and makes them more likely to get their vehicles repaired.

4.4.2 Weaknesses

CARB's recall program has several weaknesses.

- Recalls can only be done during the certification period, but many vehicles are driven greater distances.
- The certification period has recently increased to 100,000 miles, but the very stringent recruiting requirements may make it difficult for CARB to find vehicles that have had all the required maintenance at the appropriate intervals (30,000, 60,000, and 90,000 miles). Thus CARB may find it difficult to expand its surveillance program to higher mileage vehicles.
- The recall program does not address emissions due to tampering, poor maintenance, or vehicle accidents.
- Because the sample is small, it may include few high emitters, and manufacturers may be able to successfully challenge these vehicles as poorly maintained.
- If the inspection and maintenance program does not enforce requirements that recalled vehicles be fixed, drivers may have little incentive to bring a vehicle in for repair.

4.4.3 Performance

As shown in Table 4.4-1, the number of recalls triggered by the in-use compliance testing program peaked at 12 in 1988 and 1989 and then fell to between 4 and 7 per year in the most recent years for which data are available. The percent of engine families tested that have been recalled has also generally dropped since the program began. In the early years of the program, upwards of 80 percent of the engine families tested were recalled. The percentages were 15 and 11 percent in 1993 and 1994.

Table 4.4-1

Engine Families Tested and Recalled in CARB's In-Use Compliance Testing Program

Year	Recalls	Engine Families Tested	Percent Recalled
1983	1	5	20
1984	5	6	83
1985	4	5	80
1986	3	5	60
1987	11	25	44
1988	12	32	38
1989	12	32	38
1990	9	32	28
1991	2	30	7
1992	4	17	23
1993	7	46	15
1994	5	45	11

Source: CARB (1995a), Attachment 2.

Overall there were 32 engine families and 150,850 vehicles recalled in 1994 (CARB, 1995a, Attachment 3). Five of these were triggered by the in-use compliance program, but we do not know how the remaining 27 break down into voluntary recalls by the manufacturers and recalls triggered by the warranty monitoring program.

We have not been able to collect information on recall compliance rates for vehicle owners. However, anecdotal information from major auto makers suggests that recall costs have been substantial. We also have not seen information estimating the emissions reductions due to recalls.

The number of recalls suggests that automobile manufacturers have to take this program seriously. The drop in the percentage of engine families that fail in-use compliance tests also suggests that auto makers have improved the durability of their emission control equipment over time. This is a significant benefit of the program even if the emission reductions from the recalls themselves are not great.

As shown in Table 4.2-2, we rate the program as having a moderate impact on emissions due to component aging. We do not assign a higher rating because (1) the recall program does not apply to the oldest, highest mileage vehicles, (2) CARB may have difficulty extending its program to vehicles that have close to 100,000 miles, and (3) due to the small sample sizes used in the tests, manufacturers may be able to challenge the high-emitting vehicles that raise the average emission of the tested vehicles over the average. As shown in Table 4.2-2, the recall program does not address emissions due to tampering, poor maintenance, or other potential causes of high emissions such as accidents.

4.5 INSPECTION AND MAINTENANCE

California has had a wide-ranging inspection and maintenance program since 1984. The Smog-Check Program requires every vehicle to pass an emission inspection every two years.[55] The inspections consist of

- a visual inspection to determine whether the required emission control equipment has been tampered with or obviously damaged in some way;

- a functional test to determine whether particular vehicle components important to emissions control are operating properly;[56]

- a tailpipe emission test.

Inspections and repairs can be done in any of the approximately 8,400 privately owned test and repair stations that have been licensed by the state.

The tailpipe emissions test measures exhaust concentration of ROG and CO when the vehicle is idling at high and low revolutions per

---

[55]For a brief history of California's I&M programs, see Sommerville (1993), pp. 32-36.

[56]For example, the smog check inspector must check engine timing and also check that the EGR (exhaust gas recirculation) valve behaves as expected in different engine operating states.

minute. Vehicles fail the test when the measured concentrations exceed cut points that have been established for different vehicle model years. According to CARB staff involved in setting cut points, cut points are selected to ensure that

- a sizable proportion of excess emissions are identified. (Excess emissions are vehicle FTP emissions in excess of the certification standard.)

- a very high percentage of vehicles that fail the smog check would also fail an FTP certification test. (The target false failure rate is less than 1 percent.)

- not more than one-third of vehicles fail. (Failure rates greater than one-third are thought to be politically unacceptable.)

There is not a precise mapping between the smog-check cut points and FTP emissions, but vehicles failing the smog-check inspection will likely emit many multiples of their certification standards on the FTP.[57]

Drivers' repair costs are capped. Between and 1990 and 1994, the ceiling ranged between $50 and $350 depending on model year.[58] On January 1, 1995, the ceiling increased to $450 for all vehicles. A driver can receive a waiver for repairs that would put the total repair bill over the ceiling.[59]

The program is run by the Bureau of Automotive Repair (BAR) in California's Department of Consumer Affairs. BAR currently runs several surveillance and monitoring programs to induce smog-check stations to perform tests properly.

---

[57]For example, in an evaluation of different test equipment, Radian uses cut points on the IM240 test of 0.97 gm/mi for HC, 1.99 gm/mi for NOx, and 23.30 gm/mi for CO for 1981 and later vehicles (Klausmeier et al., 1995). These are 2.5, 5.0, and 6.8 times FTP certification levels.

[58]The costs ceilings were $50 for 1971 and earlier model years, $90 for 1972-74 model years, $125 for 1975-79 model years, $175 for 1980-89 model years, and $300 for 1990 and later model years. The ceiling does not apply to repairs of tampered equipment.

[59]No ceiling applied to repairs related to tampering.

4.5.1 Strengths

The current Smog Check has several strengths. First, unlike the previously discussed components of the strategy, it covers vehicles that have been poorly maintained or tampered with. Second, it covers vehicles over their entire life. Third, the high cut points focus the program on only the highest emitters, which may result in the lowest cost per ton of emissions reduced. The high cut points can still apparently capture a high percentage of fleet excess emissions. Radian (Klausmeier et al., 1995, pp. 2-19) found that CARB's cut points caused 32 percent of a sample of 1981 and newer vehicles to fail but captured 85 to 95 percent of excess emissions.

4.5.2 Weaknesses

The current Smog Check has several weaknesses.

- **Inadequate tests.** There is no NOx or evaporative emission test. Smog-check programs rely on visual and functional tests for these pollutants.[60] Nor does Smog Check test emissions when the vehicle is cold. This is an important omission because by some estimates up to 70 percent of trip emissions occur when the vehicle is cold (Albu, Kao, and Cackette, 1992, p. 31), and many emissions control components are designed specifically to control cold start emissions. There is also evidence that high emitting vehicles may exhibit substantial emission variability. Simply repeating the test may result in a pass after a few trials.

- **Low cost ceilings for waivers.** Prior to 1995, the cost waiver was very low for many vehicles. Many emission-related malfunctions could not be fixed within the cost limits.

- **Technician fraud.** It is very easy for mechanics to falsify tests. At one extreme they can simply "clean pipe" the car, which means testing the exhaust of a clean car in place of the subject car. Mechanics can also make adjustments to enable the car to pass the test and then undo the adjustments afterward,

---

[60]NOx emissions are not highly correlated with the ROG and CO emissions that are tested in the current program.

or simply state that visual and functional test were satisfied when they were not. The ability of drivers to shop around until they find a technician that passes their car puts pressure on mechanics to falsify tests.

- **Predictable tests.** Drivers can select the time and place of the test and thus may make temporary adjustments to increase the chance that their vehicles can pass the test.

- **Inability of technicians to fix vehicles.** Even if high emitting vehicles are properly identified, emissions will not improve if auto repair technicians cannot fix the vehicles or if the repairs deteriorate rapidly.

4.5.3 Performance

The effectiveness of California's smog-check program is hotly debated. Some argue that the program makes little difference (Glazer et al., 1995). Others argue that the program is significantly reducing emissions but falls far short of its potential. We briefly review the data available on the program's performance.

Random Roadside Inspection Surveys (RRISs) have been conducted annually by BAR and CARB since 1983 (Aroesty et al., 1994, p. 59). Each year thousands of vehicles are pulled over with the assistance of the California Highway Patrol and a complete inspection and maintenance test is done. Participation is voluntary, but participation rates appear to be high.[61] The RRISs consistently find that the failure rate for vehicles that recently received a smog-check certificate are no lower than those due for inspection shortly. In the 1988 survey, 39 percent of those vehicles due for a smog check in the next 90 days failed the roadside test compared with 42 percent of the vehicles that had a smog check in the previous 90 days. In 1991, 32 percent of the pre smog-check vehicles failed compared with 37 percent of the post smog-check vehicles (Glazer et al., 1995, p. 86).

---

[61]Apparently, no response rate statistics were kept, but Aroesty et al. (1994, p. 66) found that, anecdotally, the response rates are over 90 percent.

These RRIS data suggest that Smog Check is having little effect on emissions. But this conclusion may be unwarranted for two reasons. First, these studies evaluated only whether or not vehicles passed the roadside inspection program; they did not measure actual changes in emissions. Even though vehicles continue to fail a smog-check test in the 90 days after they received a smog-check certificate, their emissions might still be lower than their pre-smog check levels. Second, even if individual smog checks had no impact on emissions, the program may cause both pre- and post-test levels to be lower. For example, drivers may take better care of their cars and more readily approve emission-related repairs when a smog-check program is in place than without one. The decline in both the pre- and post-failure rates in the RRIS between 1988 and 1991 may be evidence of this.

Evidence on tampering rates over time also suggests that the program is having some effect. Random roadside studies of pre-1980 cars in California found tampering rates of 48 percent in 1987, 45 percent in 1989, 41 percent in 1991, and 38 percent in 1992 (cited in Glazer et al., 1995, p. 88). However, caveats must be given about the significance of this trend. The vehicles tested were growing older over time, and it may be that only the better maintained ones survive.

California's I&M Review Committee, a panel of experts appointed by the legislature, directed an extensive review of the smog-check program in 1992 (Sommerville, 1993). Using a sample of 1,100 vehicles that failed CARB-conducted smog checks and then were sent out to randomly selected commercial smog-check shops, the Review Committee estimated that in 1992 the smog-check program reduced the emissions of vehicles subject to the program by approximately 18 percent for ROG, 15 percent for CO and 7 percent for NOx (Sommerville, 1993, p. 2).

Several key analytical issues make it difficult to know how much weight to give these estimates.

First, CARB employees and student volunteers, not the actual owners, took the vehicles to commercial smog-check stations. They may not have put the same pressure on smog-check technicians to control repair costs as owners would. After an initial fail, actual vehicle owners may shop around for a station that will pass them with no or only minimal repairs.[62]

Second, there is not enough information in the report to evaluate what assumptions the I&M Review Committee made about the deterioration rate of repaired vehicles or how benefits of previous smog-checks are calculated. Conversations with Sierra and CARB suggest that repaired vehicles deteriorate at the same rate as the fleet as a whole, but we could not determine if this is the assumption used in the I&M Review Committee Report or review the data, if any, on which this belief is based.[63] The benefits of Smog-Check are not just the emission reductions in the last required smog-check for a vehicle, but the cumulative emission reductions by all previous smog-checks. The 1,100 car study allowed the Review Committee to estimate the effectiveness of one round of smog checks, but did not provide information on how much lower emission levels were because of previous smog-checks. The Committee relied on CARB's CALIMFAC model for this, but little information is provided with which to evaluate the appropriateness of these adjustments.

Finally, the Review Committee did not tackle the very difficult issue of what the effects of Smog Check are on the background levels of vehicle maintenance and emission-control system repair.

Some of the analytical issues we have discussed would tend to make the emission reductions calculated by the Review Committee overly optimistic, others would make them overly pessimistic. We believe that driver behavior is critical in the system, and suspect that the use of CARB employees and students as surrogate owners may cause the Review Committees estimates of effectiveness to be too high.

---

[62]The number of false passes appears to be higher in the real world than in the 1,100 car study. The RRIS suggest that 40 percent of cars should fail a smog-check test, but only 20 percent do. We thus might expect half of the 1,100 vehicles to receive passes--but only 24 percent do. The I&M Review Committee adjusts for this, however, by using the 1,100 car study to calculate emission reductions only for the vehicles that actually fail their smog-check tests in the real world.

[63]The I&M Review Committee planned to follow the emission behavior of the repaired vehicles in their study over time, but we do not know the status of these reports.

Even though there is substantial uncertainty about the effectiveness of the current I&M program, it seems clear that the program is falling far short of its potential for reducing emissions due to component aging, poor maintenance, and tampering. Fraud by smog-check technicians who falsely pass vehicles either on an initial test or after repairs were attempted appears to be a significant problem. Sierra (1994a) estimates that test results are falsified for 15 to 20 percent of vehicles, although we have not been able to evaluate the basis for this estimate. BAR staff believe that 15 percent of smog-check stations falsify tests on *every* car and that these stations test 27 percent of all cars.[64]

Whether due to fraud or incompetence, the percent of vehicles that fail smog checks in roadside surveys is much higher than the percent that fail in smog-check stations. In an analysis of the 1993 RRIS, Aroesty et al. (1994, p. 60) found that the failures rates were 20, 20, 24, and 41 percent for the visual inspection, functional inspection, emission test, and overall test, respectively. The corresponding initial failure rates during 1993 in smog-check stations were 3, 5, 14, and 17 percent.[65] Similarly, California's I&M Review Committee found that 26 percent of the vehicles in their 1,100 vehicle study were improperly passed by commercial smog-check stations (Sommerville, 1993, p. 49). And, for the reasons discussed above, this may understate the actual percentage in practice.

It also appears that smog-check technicians have difficulty fixing vehicles. Using the 1,100 vehicle database, Glazer et al. (1995, p. 88) found that overall ROG emissions actually increased after repairs for the

---

[64]Interview with Larry Sherwood, BAR. Note that all cars may not have failed a properly done test.

[65]BAR staff suggested that part of this discrepancy may be due to improper measuring of the number of vehicles failing their first I&M test. For example, smog-check technicians may improperly code a follow-up test after repairs are done as an initial test. This would decrease the failure rate in BAR's data on initial tests. Analysis that links vehicle identification number to test data is needed to resolve this issue.

50 percent of vehicles with the lowest ROG emissions prior to repair. The same was true for CO emissions.[66]

Because there is some evidence that Smog Check is having little impact on emissions and other evidence that the program is falling well short of its potential, we rate its effect on emissions due to tampering, poor maintenance, and aging as low in Table 4.2-2.

4.6 GASOLINE FORMULATION

Since January 1, 1992, all gasoline sold in California must meet Phase 1 reformulated gasoline standards (Phase 1 RFG). The Phase 1 standards require

- that the Reid Vapor Pressure (RVP) not exceed 7.8 pounds per square inch (9.0 psi had previously been common),
- a minimum amount of detergents and deposit control additives, and
- no more than 0.05 grams of lead per gallon (which was the standard for unleaded fuel in 1991) be purposely added (CARB, 1990b).

Lower RVP lowers evaporative ROG emissions, and the detergents and deposit control additives keep engine parts cleaner which reduces exhaust emissions of both ROG and NOx (CARB, 1990b, p. 87). Reducing the lead in gasoline reduces atmospheric lead. Lead does not affect ozone levels, but is highly toxic to humans.

4.6.1 Strengths

The fundamental strength of reformulated gasoline is that it can quickly affect the emissions of all vehicles in operation.

4.6.2 Weaknesses

Reformulated gasoline may have little or no overall effect on the emission of vehicles produced after reformulated gas is introduced because RFG may change the design of these vehicles. If manufacturers certify vehicles on the new fuel, presumably they will, over time, re-engineer their emission control systems so that the vehicles continue to

---

[66]This is not quite as bad as it sounds because the cleanest 50 percent of cars accounted for only approximately 15 percent of ROG emissions in the sample. The same was true for CO.

meet the certification requirements by similar margins. If the fuel used in certification does not change, however, the reformulated fuel may reduce emissions even in new vehicles.[67]

There are also ways that the effects of reformulated gas could be compromised even for vehicles not certified on it. If RFG adversely affects vehicle performance, drivers may compensate by using fuel additives. These additives may increase emissions. Drivers may also try to compensate by tuning vehicles in ways that increase emissions.

4.6.3 Performance

CARB estimates that the cost of the Phase 1 standards is low--on the order of 2 or 3 cents per gallon (CARB, 1990b, pp. 133, 142).[68] We have not evaluated the effectiveness of the Phase 1 standards. This is in part because it will only be marketed for four years before it is replaced by Phase 2 RFG. Most of our analysis of emission reductions focuses on Phase 2 RFG.

Phase 1 RFG may affect all sources of emissions. Vehicles have continued to be certified on indolene since Phase 1 gasoline was introduced, so there may be some effect on new vehicle emissions. The deposit control additives may reduce emissions due to component aging. Vehicle emissions when the vehicle has been tampered with or poorly maintained may also be lower with reformulated gasoline than without. For example, if the activated charcoal canister used to control evaporative emissions is removed, evaporative emissions will presumably be less when the fuel RVP is lower. Using similar reasoning, reformulated gasoline may also reduce marketing emissions. Because the magnitude of these effects is unknown for Phase 1 RFG, we enter question marks for each source of emissions in Table 4.2-2.

-----

[67]It may be that even vehicles certified on the new fuel generate some emission reductions. A vehicle certified on reformulated gas may emit no less under the operating conditions captured by the certification test, but it may emit less under so-call "off-cycle" conditions.

[68]Costs of the reformulated gas also include the reduction in vehicle performance it might cause, or in the extreme, any engine or fuel system damage. CARB did not evaluate such costs.

4.7 REFUELING REGULATIONS

California requires most gasoline stations to equip gasoline nozzles with vapor recovery systems. These systems return the gasoline vapor displaced from the fuel tank during refueling to the large gasoline storage tanks of the service station. These so-called Stage II vapor recovery systems have been in widespread use in the metropolitan areas of California since 1980.[69] It is estimated that 95 percent of total gasoline sales in California are currently through Stage II nozzles (CARB, 1995b, p. 2).

4.7.1 Strengths

The primary strength of Stage II vapor recovery systems is that they address an important source of emissions associated with the operation of all ICEVs.

4.7.2 Weaknesses

The controls on refueling emissions have two major weaknesses. First, enforcement programs are needed to ensure that gasoline stations install and properly maintain the Stage II nozzles. There are thousands of gasoline stations in the state, and it may be difficult and expensive to effectively enforce the regulations. Second, consumers may use the nozzles in ways that compromise their effectiveness. In actual use, consumers may not insert the nozzle in the gasoline tank neck so that there a snug fit between the nozzle and the neck, or consumers may cause fuel spills when they try to "top-off" their tank in spite of warnings not to.

---

[69]Vapor recovery control applied during bulk fuel drops into the gasoline station's storage tank is referred to a Stage I vapor recovery and during the refueling of vehicles as Stage II vapor recovery (CARB, 1995b, p. 2).

4.7.3 Performance

CARB estimates that the in-use efficiency of Stage II vapor recovery systems ranges from 86 to 92 percent *in areas with annual enforcement programs* (CARB, 1995b, p. 2). We have not investigated what percent of areas have annual enforcement programs. We also have not evaluated the CARB studies on which estimates are based to see if they accurately capture real-world consumer behavior. It appears to be widely accepted, however, that the Stage II nozzles work well. From the information available, we rate their performance as high in Table 4.2-2.

5. CALIFORNIA'S LIGHT-DUTY VEHICLE STRATEGY

California, in conjunction with U.S. EPA, has adopted a very aggressive strategy to further reduce emissions of ozone precursors from light-duty vehicles. This strategy attempts to plug many of the holes in the existing light-duty strategy identified in Section 4. In this section we briefly describe each of the elements of the California strategy. The costs, emission reductions, and cost-effectiveness of each element will be investigated in Sections 6 through 11.

5.1 EXHAUST EMISSION STANDARDS

Starting in 1994, each manufacturer must meet increasingly stringent certification requirements for exhaust emissions. Fleet-average non-methane organic gas (NMOG) emissions from all passenger cars and light-duty trucks with loaded vehicle weight of less than 3,750 pounds must fall from 0.250 grams per mile in 1993 (the certification standard for a California 1993 vehicle) to 0.062 in 2003 (see Table 5.1-1).[70] This is a four-fold decrease in exhaust ROG emissions--which account for perhaps one-half of total ROG light-duty vehicle emissions (exhaust and evaporative). Slightly higher fleet average requirements have been established for light-duty trucks with loaded vehicle weight between 3,751 and 5,750 pounds.[71]

Manufacturers may meet these standards by combining vehicles that have been certified to different emissions standards. Table 5.1-2 shows the 50,000 and 100,000 mile certification standards for the five different emission standards available: California 1993 vehicles (CA93), transitional low-emission vehicles (TLEVs), low-emission vehicles (LEVs), ultra low-emission vehicles (ULEVs), and zero-emission vehicles (ZEVs). These vehicles can be produced in any mix so long as the average of the 50,000 mile certification levels is less than or

---

[70]Because this requirement is so commonly known as the "NMOG Standard," we use the term NMOG rather than ROG when referring to it.

[71]Loaded vehicle weight is the average of gross vehicle weight and curb weight.

equal to the NMOG standard, and, as will be seen below, a minimum percent of zero-emission vehicles are produced.

Table 5.1-1

**Fleet Average NMOG Requirements for
Light-Duty Vehicles
(grams per mile)[a]**

Year	Fleet Average NMOG
1994	0.250
1995	0.231
1996	0.225
1997	0.202
1998	0.157
1999	0.113
2000	0.073
2001	0.070
2002	0.068
2003 and beyond	0.062

[a]All passenger cars and light-duty trucks with loaded vehicle weight less than 3,750 pounds.
SOURCE: CARB (1994a), p. 3.

U.S. EPA is currently redefining the Federal Test Procedure used in certification tests to be more representative of real world driving. In particular, more rapid accelerations will be included in the FTP. If adopted, such a revision would in effect further tighten certification requirements on exhaust emissions. CARB is also currently implementing its Alternate Durability Program (ADP) to make the component aging requirements in the certification process more reflective of real-world conditions. This may in effect increase the durability needed for certification.

The NMOG standard applies both in California and in many northeastern states that have adopted the California program.[72] Judging by vehicle registrations by state in 1994, vehicle sales in these states

---

[72]States are able to choose between the federal mobile source control program and California's. In the northeast, Connecticut, Delaware, the District of Columbia, Maine, Maryland, Massachusetts, New Hampshire, New Jersey, New York, Pennsylvania, Rhode Island, Vermont, and Virginia have chosen California's program.

are approximately 2.5 times as large as those in California (*Automotive News*, 1995, p. 40).

Table 5.1-2

**Certification Standards for Vehicles That Can Be Used
to Meet NMOG Standard for LDVs
(grams per mile)**

Certification Standard	NMOG	NOx	CO
At 50,000 miles			
CA93	0.250	0.4	3.4
TLEV	0.125	0.4	3.4
LEV	0.075	0.2	3.4
ULEV	0.040	0.2	1.7
ZEV	0	0	0
At 100,000 miles			
CA93	0.310	--	4.2
TLEV	0.156	0.6	4.2
LEV	0.090	0.3	4.2
ULEV	0.055	0.3	2.1
ZEV	0	0	0

NOTE: Passenger cars and light-duty trucks with loaded vehicle weight less than 3,751 pounds.
SOURCE: CARB (1994a), p. 2 and Bureau of National Affairs (1992), p. 127.

Table 5.1-3 shows the emission sources targeted by the new components of the California ozone-reduction strategy for light-duty vehicles. To see how the new components build on the components implemented as of 1993, the table also duplicates our evaluation of the effectiveness of the preexisting components from Section 4.

The new exhaust emission standards and the new FTP protocol further tighten exhaust certification standards that have already been very effective in reducing exhaust emission in new vehicles. The Alternate Durability Program focuses on an area where California has not been as effective in reducing emissions: emissions due to component deterioration.

Table 5.1-3

Emission Sources Targeted by New Regulations

	Where Program Applies	Implementation Date	New Vehicle Emissions	Deterioration Emissions			Marketing Emissions
				Tampering	Poor maintenance	Aging	
A. Effectiveness of current program							
Certification			High	--	--	Moderate	--
Warranty			--	--	--	Moderate?	--
Recall			--	--	--	Moderate	--
I&M			--	Low	Low	Low	--
Gasoline formulation			?	?	?	?	?
Refueling regulations			--	--	--	--	High
B. Emissions targeted by new program							
NMOG standard	CA and NE	1994-2003	x			x	
Enhanced evap. requirements	U.S.	1995-1998	x				x
ORVR	U.S.	1998-2003					x
OBD II	U.S.	1994-1996		x	x	x	
Smog Check II	CA	1996		x	x	x	
AVR	CA	1996			x	x	
CP2G	CA	1996		x	x	x	x
ZEVs	CA,MA,NY	1998	x	x	x	x	x

5.2 ENHANCED EVAPORATIVE EMISSION STANDARDS

As discussed in Section 4.2, manufacturers must certify that their vehicles emit more no more than 2 grams of reactive organic gases during a specified test procedure. New tests that are more representative of real world conditions in California will be phased in between 1995 and 1998.

Instead of measuring hot soak emissions for one hour after a driving event when the ambient temperature is between 68°F and 86°F, hot soak emissions will be measured over one hour at an ambient temperature of 105°F. The old test procedure attempted to simulate a one-day diurnal by heating the fuel in the gas tank from 60°F to 84°F over one hour and measuring the emissions during that hour. The new test will heat and cool the whole vehicle from 65°F to 105°F and measure emissions over three full days. Manufacturers are required to certify that their vehicles do not emit more than 2 grams during these more stringent tests at both 50,000 and 100,000 miles (CARB, 1990a, pp. 2-5).

The old procedure did not measure running losses. The new procedure requires running losses to be less than or equal to 0.05 grams per mile when the ambient temperature is 105°F (CARB, 1990a, p. 5).

U.S. EPA has also set new evaporative emissions standards for the nation as a whole. These requirements are apparently quite similar to the CARB requirements, although we have not done a thorough comparison.

5.3 ON-BOARD REFUELING VAPOR RECOVERY REQUIREMENTS

CARB is in the process of adopting U.S. EPA's on-board refueling vapor recovery (ORVR) requirements with some slight modifications (CARB, 1995b, p. 2). ORVR systems capture the fuel tank vapors displaced during refueling in a canister on-board the vehicle. The regulations require that the vehicle emit no more than 0.20 grams per gallon during a detailed test procedure. At 27.5 miles per gallon (the corporate average fleet mileage requirement), this amounts to 0.007 grams per mile. Vehicles must achieve this standard whether or not they are fueled with vapor recovery nozzles. Once ORVR systems are in widespread use throughout the vehicle fleet, U.S. EPA can drop requirements for Stage 2 nozzles in non-attainment areas (CARB, 1995b, p. 1).

ORVR requirements are phased in between 1998 and 2000 for passenger cars and between 2001 and 2003 for light-duty trucks (CARB, 1995b, p. 6).

5.4 ENHANCED EMISSION SYSTEM MONITORING REQUIREMENTS

To reduce emissions due to component aging, tampering, and poor maintenance, CARB substantially strengthened requirements for on-board emission component monitoring systems in 1989 (CARB, 1989a). These requirements build on an initial set of requirements adopted in 1985 and are referred to as OBD II (OBD standing for on-board diagnostics).[73] OBD II requires an on-board system to determine whether all emission-related components and systems are working properly, and to illuminate a dashboard light (the "Check-Engine" light) when they are not.

When it detects a failure, OBD II requires that an on-board computer store the nature of the failure and the vehicle operating conditions at the time of failure. It is hoped that such information will facilitate diagnosis and repair. OBD II requires standardized fault codes and a standardized connector located below the instrument panel that would allow access to the on-board computer (CARB, 1989a, p. 9).

CARB requires manufacturers to phase in OBD II between 1994 and 1996 (CARB, 1989a, p. 17). U.S. EPA has adopted on-board diagnostic regulations very similar to CARB's.

5.5 SMOG-CHECK II

In 1996, California will implement an enhanced vehicle inspection and maintenance program known as Smog Check II (SC II). SC II will be required in the urbanized portions of Sacramento, Fresno, and Kern counties, southern Ventura County, the South Coast Air Basin, and western San Diego County (BAR, 1995, p. D-1).[74] Approximately 10.4

---

[73]We have not examined the effectiveness of OBD I. It appears, however, that the requirements for OBD I are very weak compared to OBD II.

[74]These are the areas that have been classified as serious, severe, or extreme nonattainment areas for ozone or moderate or serious nonattainment areas for CO (BAR, 1995, p. 2).

million of the 17.4 million vehicles in the state will be subject to SC
II. The remaining vehicles will be subject to the existing program
(BAR, personal communication, 1995).[75]

SC II will differ from the current program in seven fundamental
ways: (1) a proportion of the fleet must be tested in stations that test
but do not repair vehicles (*test-only* stations); (2) high-emitting
vehicles that have been identified on the road by remote sensing devices
will be required to be inspected within 30 days; (3) some vehicles will
be required to be tested annually rather than every second year; (4)
waiver requirements will be stricter; (5) emission tests will be done
using more sophisticated equipment; (6) transmission of test results to
a central database will occur in real time; and (7) smog-check
technician licensing requirements will be tightened. We discuss each of
these in turn.[76]

Test-Only Stations. Initially, California will require inspections
in test-only stations for 15 percent of the vehicles due for inspection
each year (BAR, 1995, p. 9). This amounts to about 750,000 vehicles a
year. Vehicles required to go to test-only stations include

- A 2 percent random sample of vehicles due for inspection
  (approximately 100,000 vehicles per year).
- Vehicles in commercial fleets that travel more than 50,000
  miles a year.
- High-emitters or tampered-with vehicles that have been
  identified in previous inspections.
- High emitters identified in test-and-repair stations.
- Likely high emitters identified by remote sensing with the help
  of a high emitter profile (200,000 vehicles per year).

The percent of vehicles required to go to test-only stations may be
increased if BAR determines that SC II is not producing the emission
reductions required in the SIP or meeting the emissions reductions

_____

[75]The existing biennial program will cover about 6.4 million
vehicles, and about 0.6 million vehicles will require testing only in
the event of a change of ownership.

[76]See BAR (1995) for a more detailed description.

standards required by U.S. EPA (BAR, 1995, p. 9). According to BAR staff, there will be 50 to 75 test-only stations.

Remote Sensing. Remote sensing equipment, in combination with a profile of vehicles likely to have high emissions, will be used to detect high emitters on the road. BAR currently plans to identify 250,000 vehicles per year and require them to obtain an inspection within 30 days and obtain repairs, if required, within another 30 days. Fines for failure to obtain an inspection and failure to obtain necessary repairs will each be $500. (BAR, 1995, pp. 5, 12).

Increased Test Frequency. Annual inspections will be required for 2 to 5 years for vehicles that have been identified as high-emitters. Also, vehicles identified as high emitters by remote sensing devices will have to come in for inspection before their regular biennial inspection.

Stricter Waiver Requirements. There will be no cost waiver for high-emitting vehicles. The cost waiver increased to $450 for all vehicles in January 1995 (see Section 4.5), and waivers cannot be issued for two consecutive inspections.

More Sophisticated Tests. The idle tests of the current program will be replaced by a loaded mode test that will measure NOx emissions. Also, the evaporative emissions system will be tested using a gas-cap pressure test.

Electronic Transmission of Test Results. Transmission of test results to a centralized database will occur in real time. This will help with station surveillance. Also, both overt and covert audits will be increased.

Technician Licensing. Requirements for licensing as a smog-check technician will be tightened. Technicians must be certified by the Institute for Automotive Service Excellence and have more work experience before they can be licensed (BAR, 1995, pp. 58-61).

The California legislature authorized BAR to subsidize the repair costs of low-income drivers with high-emitting vehicles. BAR is authorized to pay 80 percent of the repair bill up to $450. The legislature also authorized BAR to scrap vehicles identified as high polluters by SC II. BAR can offer market value up to $800 for the vehicles. A fund was set up for these programs, but according to BAR, as of July 1, 1995, the funding was inadequate to initiate either program (BAR, 1995, p. 32).

The relation between the SC II and the accelerated vehicle retirement (AVR) program discussed below is not clear. BAR includes "system-wide use of AVR" as one of the strategies it will use if the program fails to meet the emission reductions in the SIP.

5.6 ACCELERATED VEHICLE RETIREMENT PROGRAM

Beginning in 1999, up to 75,000 older, high-emitting vehicles a year will be purchased and retired in the South Coast Air Basin. A smaller number of vehicles will be retired between 1996 and 1998 (CARB, 1994d, Volume 2, p. B-2). The program was instituted by SB 501, which was signed into law on October 14, 1995. Currently, there is no detailed plan for how the AVR program will work, or, as just mentioned, how it will be linked to SC II. Yet to be determined are how older or high-emitting vehicles will be defined, how these particular types of vehicles will be recruited, or how offers to buy vehicles will be determined. As shown in Table 5.1-3, accelerated vehicle retirement attempts to reduce emissions from older vehicles on the road due to component aging and poor maintenance. To avoid encouraging tampering, most proposals disqualify vehicles that have been tampered with.

5.7 GASOLINE FORMULATION REQUIREMENTS

On June 1, 1996, all gasoline sold in California must meet CARB's Phase 2 reformulated gasoline standards. California Phase 2 gasoline (CP2G) must meet a detailed set of specifications, the most important of which for emission reductions are vapor pressure and sulfur content. Lower vapor pressure means less evaporative emissions, and lower sulfur content increases catalyst efficiency (Calvert et al., 1993, p. 42). Reid Vapor Pressure will not be allowed to exceed 7.0 psi (down from 7.8 for Phase 1 RFG) and sulfur content will be reduced 80 percent from pre-control levels.

Reformulated gasoline targets emissions of vehicles that are currently on the road (see Table 5.1-3). The main effect on vehicles produced after CP2G is introduced may be to reduce emission control costs rather than emission levels. We return to this complex issue in Section 8.

5.8 ZERO-EMISSION VEHICLE MANDATE

Starting in 1998 automobile manufacturers must produce and deliver for sale zero-emission vehicles (CARB, 1995b, pp. 3-13).[77] A zero-emission vehicle (ZEV) is defined as a vehicle which produces zero emissions of specified pollutants under any and all possible operating modes and conditions (CARB, 1995c, pp. 2-8).[78] Large manufacturers are required to initially produce and offer for sale a number of ZEVs equal to 2 percent of their annual sales of passenger cars and light-duty trucks. The percentage rises to 5 percent in 2001 and 10 percent in 2003. Large volume manufacturers are defined as manufacturers selling 35,000 or more light- and medium-duty vehicles per year in California between 1989 and 1993 (CARB, 1990c, p. I-14). Intermediate volume manufacturers (those with average sales between 3,000 and 35,000 vehicles between 1989 and 1993) are not required to offer ZEVs for sale until 2003, but their mandated quantity starts at 10 percent. Small volume manufacturers (those with volumes less than 3,000) are not subject to the ZEV mandate (CARB, 1990c, p. I-14). Manufacturers must pay a $5,000 fine on each unit of their mandated quantities not met by the production of ZEVs or the purchase of ZEV credits (see below).

Table 5.8-1 presents the projected number of ZEVs that must be offered for sale by seven large manufacturers (the Big 7), starting in 1998, to cover their mandated quantities. The quantities are based on current sales volumes in California. Massachusetts and New York have adopted the California ZEV mandate and their participation approximately doubles the required number of ZEVs that must be offered for sale.

To provide some flexibility, the mandate allows for sales of ZEV credits. Manufacturers can use credits bought from other manufacturers who sell ZEVs (whether traditional ICEV manufacturers or not) to offset

---

[77]CARB is currently reviewing the mandate described here. Significant modifications appear likely, but no final decisions have yet been made.

[78]Indirect emissions produced in generating electricity are not considered.

obligations under the mandate. Performance requirements for vehicles that generate ZEV credits are still vague. Currently, the only requirements are that the vehicles have four wheels and be registered for on-road use in California. Presumably the rules will have to be more completely specified before a credit market develops.

As shown in Table 5.1-3, zero-emission vehicles address all sources of internal combustion vehicle emissions.

Table 5.8-1

Number of Zero-Emission Vehicles Required To Be Produced for Sale by Manufacturer
(vehicles per year)

Manufacturer	1998-2000[a] (2 percent)	2001-2002[b] (5 percent)	2003 on[b] (10 percent)
General Motors	6,600	16,500	33,000
Ford	6,400	16,000	32,000
Toyota	3,900	9,750	19,500
Chrysler	2,700	6,750	13,500
Honda	2,500	6,250	12,500
Nissan	1,800	4,500	9,000
Mazda	900	2,250	4,500
Total	24,800	62,000	124,000

[a]*Automotive News* as cited in Moomaw et al. (1994), p. 5-2.
[b]Derived from column 1 by multiplying by ratio of the mandate percentages.

6. DIRECT COSTS AND BENEFITS OF HARDWARE-BASED ICEV ELEMENTS

OVERVIEW AND PREVIEW OF FINDINGS

In this section, we consider the direct costs and emission reductions of the proposed ICEV hardware regulations and the implications for narrow cost effectiveness. However, these views of costs and emission reductions fail to tell the whole story because they ignore *market-mediated effects*--that is, how markets will respond to the costs of upgrading ICEV hardware. Considering these responses enables us to understand, for example, who bears the direct costs and to consider how market effects will alter the composition of the vehicle fleet, with possibly substantial effects on emissions in the short term. We discuss the market-mediated effects of the hardware-based regulations in Section 7.

By *direct costs*, we mean the extra resources needed to design, produce, and install the hardware to meet the regulatory requirement. These costs include research and development, plant and equipment, parts, and assembly costs. These costs are the focus of the studies we review.

By *direct emission* reductions we mean the decreases in tons of ROG and NOx emissions that would result if the only effects of the policy on emissions were to upgrade emission-control systems on the vehicles that otherwise would be sold in California. *Narrow cost-effectiveness* is the ratio of direct costs to direct emission reductions.

These are the concepts that have been emphasized by previous studies.

To preview the findings of this section:

(1) The hardware-based elements of the California LDV strategy will increase production costs of the vehicles sold in California. Reasonable bounds for incremental costs relative to a 1993 California vehicle are $200 and $1,000 per vehicle.

(2) There is great deal of uncertainty about how much these regulations will reduce light-duty vehicle emissions. Estimated emission reductions vary up to a factor of three depending on which

emission model is used and what is assumed about the other elements of the LDV strategy such as I&M. Underlying all the estimates is the substantial uncertainty discussed in Section 3 about how well emission estimates correspond to real world emissions. Using our current knowledge, we cannot construct upper and lower bounds for emission reductions from the studies reviewed.

(3) Relative to other hardware measures, projected narrow cost effectiveness ratios for EEE are low and do not vary a great deal across the studies reviewed ($400 to $2,500 per ton of ROG plus NOx).

(4) There appears to be general agreement that ORVR requirements are redundant.

(5) There is wide variation in the studies reviewed on NCERs of TLEVs relative to 1993 California vehicles and LEVs relative to TLEVs. Estimates of these NCERs range from $1,100 to $40,000 per ton of ROG plus NOx. The NCERs for ULEVs relative to LEVs are higher and there is less variation across the studies reviewed ($22,000 to $48,000). Because of the uncertainty over emission reductions, however, we do not view these as ranges into which NCERs will almost certainly fall.

(6) The choice between CARB's and U.S. EPA's emission models affects absolute levels of estimated NCERs. This choice may or may not affect comparison of narrow cost-effectiveness ratios across different policies. If, for example, the emission reductions for different model years and mileages are all off by a common multiple, relative rankings would not change. If, on the other hand, projections vary a great deal in accuracy across vehicle ages, policy comparisons could be distorted. Such might be the case in comparing AVR and the NMOG standard--which requires information on the emissions of both existing and future vehicles.

6.1 DIRECT COSTS OF ICEV HARDWARE REGULATIONS

We first examine the direct costs of the proposed regulations. In keeping with our approach as described in Section 2, we seek to evaluate the costs and emission reductions of adding each of the hardware-based elements of California's LDV strategy, assuming that all the other elements are in place. Thus, for example, we assume that vehicles run on Phase 2 gasoline and are subject to Smog Check II. The baseline used for reference is a vehicle meeting all California requirements for the 1993 model year (CA93 vehicle). The direct costs examined in this section are the costs of adding the hardware required to meet the new regulatory standards to a CA93 vehicle.

In our discussion, we (1) review direct cost estimates for regulation of exhaust emissions, (2) review direct cost estimates for regulations on evaporative emissions and emission control system monitoring requirements, and (3) consider the total direct costs of all the hardware-based elements of California's ozone-reduction strategy. The principal studies we reviewed for this discussion are CARB (1990a, 1994a and 1994b) and Sierra (1994a).

6.1.1 Direct Costs of Exhaust Regulations

Sierra Research, Inc., and CARB provide detailed cost estimates of the exhaust regulations. These appear to be the only comprehensive analyses publicly available. We base our review and critique of both the CARB and Sierra estimates on published studies as well as on interviews with both staffs. We augment this information with confidential interviews conducted with technical staff at Chrysler, Ford, and General Motors in July 1995.

Sierra Estimates

Sierra (1994a) developed a comprehensive framework for estimating the incremental cost of TLEV, LEV, and ULEV vehicles over the cost of a CA93 vehicle. Sierra estimates incremental manufacturer variable and fixed production costs and dealer margin. Incremental variable costs are costs that vary with the number of vehicles produced. They include component, assembly, shipping, and warranty costs. Fixed costs are independent of the number of vehicles produced and include research and development costs, assembly line equipment and tooling, testing facility costs, manufacturer overhead, and the cost of capital. Dealer margin is the cost to the dealer of financing and selling vehicles.

Table 6.1-1 lists some of the key features and assumptions of the Sierra study.

Table 6.1-1

Overview of Estimates of ICEV Hardware Costs

	CARB (1994a)	Sierra (1994a)
Source of Information	CARB projections of engineering design and personnel requirements. Vendors of emission control componentry for variable costs.	Confidential data supplied by five major manufacturers, vendors of emissions control components, Sierra engineering assumptions (pp. 93, 97).
Cost Categories		
Variable costs	Based on CARB engineering designs and prices from component suppliers. Warranty based on CARB assumptions, basis not specified (p. 34). Changes in assembly costs detailed.	Components of variable costs not detailed. No significant warranty costs assumed (p. 103).
Equipment, tooling, and facilities	Components bought from vendors included in component prices.	Included, but magnitude not reported separately.
R&D	R&D for some components included in supplier prices, other incremental costs listed.	Included, but magnitude not reported separately.
Manufacturer overhead and profit	Manufacturer overhead based on costs of activities assumed (p. 20). Some incremental legal costs assumed. Small increase in administrative costs (p.39). 6% cost of capital (p. 42).	Included but magnitudes not reported separately.
Dealer margin	1.5% increase in vehicle cost to cover dealer financing, 3% dealer sales commission on incremental car cost (p.42).	50% of standard markup, but standard markup not reported (p.98).
Performance offsets	None.	None (p. 103).

Table 6.1-1 (Cont'd.)

Analytic Issues	CARB (1994a)	Sierra (1994a)
Costs discounted?	No.	Costs discounted at 5% annual real rate of interest (p.96).
Experience effects	None assumed although assume initial bugs have been worked out.	Experience reduces variable costs by 5% per year.
Technological innovation	Technological innovation will keep catalyst costs constant even if more precious metal loading required (p. 27).	None.
Amortization period	8 years for most fixed costs; emissions testing equipment amortized over 15 years (p. 40).	3-5 years for equipment, tooling, facilities, and R&D (p. 94).
Recurring costs?	None--one product cycle only.	R&D and equipment, tooling, and facilities fall 50 percent in each successive 5-year product cycle.
Control introduced at beginning of product design cycle	Yes.	Yes (p. 94).
Fuel parameters	Apparently, California Phase 2 fuel (p. 6).	Not specified.
Production volume	100,000 units for 8 years (p.38).	California and nationwide.

Sierra assumed that manufacturers phase in TLEVs, LEVs, and ULEVs, according to the schedule projected by CARB in its 1990 analysis of the proposed NMOG regulation. The fixed costs required for each type of vehicle were allocated between 1993 and 2010 as needed to meet the phase-in schedule, and costs were discounted back to 1993 using a 5 percent real rate of interest.

Sierra assumed that experience with production would reduce variable costs 5 percent per year. Sierra also assumed that the fixed cost required in each successive 5-year product cycle would decline 50 percent. Sierra does not specify what type of fuel it assumed in its costing exercise. Cost estimates will likely be lower if it is assumed that vehicles can be certified on California Phase 2 gasoline rather than on the gasoline currently used in certification (indolene).[79]

Sierra's cost estimates are based on confidential data provided by five major automobile manufacturers in 1993 and on data collected from vendors of emission control components. The framework and data developed by Sierra seem appropriate for evaluating the costs of emission control hardware. The main shortcoming of the Sierra estimates is that they do not provide sufficient information to allow evaluation of the magnitudes reported. Manufacturers' assumptions about the type of emission control system needed and their costs are not reported, nor are the components of variable or fixed costs. This is in part due to the need to maintain confidentiality, but it makes assessment of the findings difficult.

---

[79]Lippincott, Segal, and Wang (1993) compared data from 3 manufacturers on the emissions of 20 prototype TLEVs, LEVs, and ULEVs when using the industry average gasoline in 1989 (reformulated fuel A, or RF-A), the fuel used in certification (indolene), and California Phase 2 gasoline. They found emissions were 23 percent and 19 percent lower for total hydrocarbons (THC) and CO respectively when Phase 2 gasoline was used rather than indolene. NOx emissions were 8 percent higher, but in contrast to the changes for THC and CO, the estimated increase was not statistically significant. The findings suggest that emission control systems need to be less effective and thus may be less costly on vehicles certified on Phase 2 gasoline compared to those certified on indolene.

Sierra estimated the incremental costs when production volumes equal (1) the volumes projected for California and (2) the volumes projected if the NMOG standard applied nationwide. Twelve northeastern states and the District of Columbia have adopted California Low-Emission Vehicle Program, and in our analysis we assume that manufacturers produce enough vehicles to meet the NMOG requirement in both California and the northeastern states. As detailed in Appendix 6.A, vehicle sales in all 14 states are approximately 3.5 times sales in California alone. We use this figure to interpolate between Sierra's California and nationwide estimates to estimate production costs at volumes required in the 14 states.

The manufacturers' estimates of the incremental costs of TLEVs, LEVs, and ULEVs compiled by Sierra are reported in the first panel of rows in Table 6.1-2. Fixed costs have been allocated over the total number of vehicles assumed to meet the NMOG standard through 2010, and the estimates are presented on a cost-per-car basis. The TLEV and LEV numbers reflect a mix of 4-, 6-, and 8-cylinder engines (although Sierra does not detail what mix is assumed). Because CARB estimates that auto manufacturers will be able to satisfy the NMOG standards with no more than 15 percent ULEVs, car makers may only have to produce 4-cylinder ULEVs. Thus, the costs for 4-cylinder and 6-cylinder ULEVs are reported separately.

After reviewing the engineering assumptions behind each manufacturer's estimates, Sierra identified the particular emission control approach that seemed most appropriate from a cost and performance standpoint. According to Sierra (1994a, p. 97) this was generally the "lowest-cost system found for each combination of control measure and vehicle size category (e.g., 4-cylinder car, 6-cylinder car)." As seen in Table 6.1-2, Sierra's "best-case" estimates are roughly 40 to 65 percent below the manufacturer estimates. The main reasons Sierra (1994a, p. 100) cites for the difference are:

- Manufacturers sometimes allocated the costs of more sophisticated engine designs to the emission standard. Sierra did so only when it appeared such modifications were essential for compliance with the emission standard.

- Manufacturer estimates did not project any cost reductions as experience with production increased over time.
- Sierra included only one-half of the dealer markup assumed by manufacturers.

Table 6.1-2

Adjusted Sierra and CARB Estimates of the Incremental Costs of a TLEV, LEV, and ULEV over a 1993 California Vehicle
(dollars per vehicle)

	TLEV	LEV	ULEV 4-cyl	ULEV 6-cyl
Sierra manufacturer (discounted to 1993, 1993 dollars)[a]				
Variable costs	280	657	902	1,260
Fixed costs	210	538	663	927
Dealer margin	48	118	136	190
Total	538	1,312	1,701	2,377
Sierra best-case (discounted to 1993, 1993 dollars)[a]				
Variable costs	150	406	305	688
Fixed costs	112	333	224	506
Dealer margin	26	73	46	104
Total	288	812	575	1,298
CARB (undiscounted, 1994 dollars)[b]				
Variable costs	35	83	167	180
Fixed costs	23	26	31	31
Dealer margin	3	5	9	10
Total	61	114	207	221

[a]Estimates assume production volumes required for 14 states (including California) that have adopted California's Low-Emission Vehicle Program. See Appendix 6.A.
[b]CARB, 1994a, p. 44.

CARB Estimates

In 1994, CARB updated its estimates of TLEV, LEV, and ULEV costs (CARB, 1994a, 1994b). Using its engineering expertise and cost data solicited from emission-control component suppliers, CARB put together an emission control system for each standard and engine size. As shown in Table 6.1-1, the types of costs CARB considered seem as comprehensive as those considered in Sierra's study. If fact, as in the case of warranty costs, CARB included some costs that Sierra (and apparently the manufacturers) did not.

CARB's cost estimates assume that the prototypical manufacturer produces 100,000 TLEVs, LEV, or ULEVs a year over an 8-year product cycle. CARB did not calculate costs for subsequent product cycles, but presumably costs would be less per car than during the first 8-year cycle. Variable costs were estimated separately for 4-, 6-, and 8-cylinder engines, then combined into a single estimate for each standard using the current proportions of engine sizes in the California fleet. CARB did not discount costs back to a base year.[80]

In contrast to the Sierra study, the assumptions behind the CARB estimates are explicit. However, CARB is often not very explicit in its written documents about the basis for these assumptions. For example, there is no explanation of what the warranty costs were based on, and the reader has little basis to judge whether the assumptions for the various components of fixed costs (e.g., research and development or legal costs) are appropriate for the very large firms that produce automobiles.

Interviews with CARB staff suggest that CARB based its estimates on empirical information, informed judgment, or both. For example, CARB staff described how warranty cost estimates were based on data on past warranty costs for emission-related components, and research and development and legal costs were based on CARB's extensive experience with the automobile industry and on many contacts with industry experts.

CARB's analysis focuses on the low-cost producer (CARB, 1994a, p. 19). CARB estimates should therefore be most comparable to the Sierra best-case estimates because the best-case estimate also concentrates on the low-cost system. In contrast, the Sierra manufacturer estimates are likely averages over both high- and low-cost producers.

---

[80]When asked about this issue, CARB staff responded that they included a cost of capital factor in their analysis--total costs were increased by 6 percent. It is unclear to us how this adjustment compares with spreading costs into the future and discounting.

The bottom panel of Table 6.1-2 reports CARB's estimates for TLEV, LEV, and ULEV costs. CARB's estimates are lower than Sierra's best-case estimates by roughly a factor of five and lower than Sierra manufacturer estimates by roughly an order of magnitude. All components of CARB's estimates are substantially below Sierra's.[81]

Judging by our review of the Sierra and CARB documents and interviews with both Sierra and CARB staff, the following appear to be the most important factors explaining the difference between the CARB and Sierra estimates.

- **Cost-structure of producer.** CARB (1994a, p. 19) examines the low-cost producer. The Sierra manufacturer estimate, in contrast, averages estimates of both the high-cost and low-cost producers.

- **Number of components.** CARB (1994a, p. 19) thinks that Sierra and the manufacturers assume more components than needed to meet the standards. Sierra (1994a, p. 102) says CARB assumes too few.

- **Cost of components.** Sierra (1994a, p. 102) claims that the costs of components used by CARB are lower than the uninstalled cost of components.

- **Type of fuel used in certification.** Neither study is explicit about the type of fuel used in certification, but CARB (1994a, p. 6) appears to be using California Phase 2 gasoline while Sierra does not.

- **Incorporation of emission control changes into normal product development cycles.** This is difficult to quantify, but CARB appears to assume that many emission control changes are more readily incorporated into normal product development cycles than Sierra assumed. For example, CARB incorporates no incremental costs for plant tooling modifications (1994a, p. 39).[82]

---

[81]Table 6.1-2 compares cost estimates that are discounted to 1993 (Sierra's) with CARB's undiscounted costs estimated using 1994 prices. Discounting CARB costs would make them even lower.

[82]Incremental costs of plant tooling modifications would be low if manufacturers use pre-assembled exhaust system modules bought from

- **Amortization period.** CARB assumes an 8-year product cycle and Sierra assumes a 5-year cycle. Fixed costs do fall 50 percent in each successive product cycle in Sierra's analysis, but perhaps CARB does not believe that Sierra's costs are falling quickly enough.

- **Discounting.** Sierra discounts its costs to 1993, CARB does not discount and is presumably basing costs on 1994 prices.

- **Overhead costs.** Sierra assumes overhead costs are a standard proportion of variable and other fixed costs. CARB specifies the tasks that need to be done.

Each of these factors except discounting tends to reduce CARB's cost estimates relative to Sierra, and the combined effect of all the factors results in the major differences in Table 6.1-2.

In fact, comparing Sierra's discounted costs to CARB's undiscounted costs actually understates the difference in the two sets of estimates. As we will see in Section 6.2, Sierra presents information on both discounted and undiscounted benefits, and comparison of the two sets of numbers suggests that discounted emission reductions are approximately 30 percent smaller than undiscounted benefits. Costs may be loaded more toward the beginning of the period, so the difference between discounted and undiscounted costs may not be as great, but it may still be substantial. If the difference between discounted and undiscounted costs were 30 percent, the factor of five differences between some of the CARB and Sierra best-case estimates would be closer to a factor of seven when discounting was considered.

Data from the Big 3

In July 1995, we met with the technical and regulatory personnel of Chrysler, Ford, and General Motors to better understand the data that they provided Sierra. As a condition for these discussions, we agreed not to divulge any information they considered confidential. They explained their cost estimates and in some cases updated the numbers they provided Sierra.

---

suppliers. CARB staff reports that this is typically the case (CARB, personal communication).

On the basis of these discussions, we offer the following observations. First, like CARB's cost estimates, the manufacturers' estimates appear to result from serious costing efforts. Their estimates were prepared as part of elaborate production planning processes. We were not able to audit the manufacturer estimates, but they seemed to be based on a careful engineering evaluation of the technology required to meet the standards and the associated costs. Second, the estimates the companies gave us were roughly consistent with Sierra's best-case estimates.[83] This may be partly because we interviewed only three of the five firms that provided data to Sierra. But, it also suggests that manufacturer estimates have come down in the two years since they provided their initial estimates to Sierra. Engineering designs appear to have changed and some of the fixed costs have already been incurred. Third, there was considerable variation in the cost estimates across manufacturers. As a result, the difference between CARB and manufacturer estimates is considerably smaller for some companies than for others.

Because the data provided us by the manufacturers were similar to Sierra's best-case estimates, in the analysis that follows, we take the Sierra best-case estimates to be an updated estimate of average manufacturer costs.

The variation in estimates across the companies may explain the difference between the CARB and Sierra best-case (updated manufacturer) estimate. The data provided us by the auto makers suggest that there indeed are firms that use cost projections similar to CARB's, which projected costs for the low-cost firms.

In evaluating the costs of the exhaust standards, we are concerned with the compliance costs of all firms, not just the low-cost firms, because the cost of all firms are the resource costs due to the regulations.[84] This suggests that the Sierra estimates are in principle

---

[83]Manufacturers gave us undiscounted numbers and these undiscounted numbers were similar to and, if anything, somewhat higher than Sierra's discounted numbers. When discounted to make them comparable to Sierra best-case estimates, they may be lower than the Sierra best-case numbers. However, we do not have the detailed information on time pattern of expenditures needed to make this adjustment.

more relevant at least initially. But how long they will be relevant depends on how quickly the high-cost producers will match the costs of their low-cost competitors. There will certainly be strong competitive pressures to do so, and high-cost producers may be able to quickly reverse engineer the emission systems of their low-cost competitors.

Additional data have recently become available on the costs of low-emission vehicles. First, in August 1995, Honda announced that it had received LEV certification from CARB and U.S. EPA for several of its Civic models (Honda, 1995).[85] Honda's LEV relies on design changes incorporated into the normal product cycle and requires little if any emission-control hardware.[86] The incremental cost of the LEV is expected to be small. A Honda press release said that there would be little added cost to the consumer, and Honda staff interviewed for this project said they would not be surprised if there was no added production cost. This small cost increase compares to Sierra's $812 estimate and CARB's $114 estimate.[87] Some costs are not included in the Honda estimate. The Honda staff interviewed believed that the estimate did not include R&D, vehicle testing programs, and building prototypes. Staff thought, however, that these costs were not large and would likely not bring the overall cost up to even CARB's estimate.

Second, Honda has also announced that it has produced and tested a prototype Accord meeting ULEV standards that it plans to introduce in the 1998 model year (*USA Today*, Jan. 13, 1995).[88] Honda's ULEV also does not appear to be hardware intensive. Honda estimates that the

---

[84]Basing resource costs on the average costs weighted by production volume of producers currently in the market implicitly assumes market shares will not change. We discuss this issue in Section 7.2.4.

[85]Civics have 4-cylinder engines.

[86]The emission control system relies on more accurate electronic control of the air-fuel ratio, a new "tumble port" cylinder head design that allows a more complete mixture of air and fuel, and a catalyst close to the engine (a so-called *close-coupled* catalyst) that warms up quickly (Honda, 1995).

[87]Note that the CARB and Sierra estimates average over 4-, 6-, and 8- cylinder engines. CARB's estimate for a 4-cylinder LEV is $86 (CARB. 1994a, p. 44).

[88]CARB verified that the car met the ULEV standard. CARB memo from Bob Cross, Assistant Chief, to Don Drachand, Chief, Mobile Source Division, December 14, 1994.

incremental cost will be approximately $300 due to the use of an extra
oxygen sensor, more advanced computer chips, and a second catalyst.
This estimate also does not include R&D, testing, and prototypes. Honda
staff also thought the cost may well turn out to be less than $300 if
computer chip costs continue to fall and design improvements are made.
Honda's cost estimate compares to CARB's $207 and Sierra's $575 estimate
for a 4-cylinder ULEV.

Third, auto makers have started to produce some TLEVs. CARB
(1994a, p. 18) found from the certification documentation for eight 1994
production TLEVs that TLEVs cost $35 more than CA93 vehicles. CARB does
not say so explicitly, but because the figure is based on certification
documentation, it probably includes only variable costs and, if so, is
close to CARB's TLEV variable cost estimate (see Table 6.1-2). Other
uncertainties remain about these data. For example, we have not
reviewed what type of financial information manufacturers typically
report on certification documentation--and whether it is cost or sales
price information.

Honda's announcements suggest that there are producers that will be
able to produce TLEVs, LEVs, and ULEVs at costs close to CARB's
estimates. And they can apparently do so without the hardware-intensive
systems assumed necessary by Sierra. However, this does not mean that
the average cost of all low-emission vehicles produced by all
manufacturers will have these low costs. The costs of all manufacturers
may not be as low as Honda's. In addition, the emission control costs
on some types of vehicles may be more than others. Honda's four-
cylinder cars and the TLEVs that have been produced so far may be the
least expensive to adapt to the low-emission standards.

In the analyses of narrow cost-effectiveness below, we use the CARB
estimate to construct lower bounds and the Sierra best-case estimate to
construct upper bounds. CARB estimates are appropriate lower bounds
because they appear to approximate the incremental costs of the low-cost
producers but apparently ignore the existence of higher cost producers.
The Sierra best-case estimates are appropriate upper bounds because they
may well approximate the average costs currently estimated by producers,
but ignore the possibility that the higher cost firms may quickly

reverse engineer the systems of the low-cost producers. The lower bounds most likely understate the true resource cost of the regulations; the upper bounds most likely overstate the resource cost.

6.1.2 Direct Costs of Evaporative Emission Regulations and Emission System Monitoring Requirements

Sierra uses the methodology described above to estimate the direct costs of EEE, ORVR, and OBD II. Because these regulations apply nationwide, we use the Sierra estimates that assume national production volumes. CARB's estimates for the costs of these regulations are not nearly as comprehensive as their cost estimates for TLEVs, LEVs, and ULEVs.

CARB's estimates for EEE controls are based on its own engineering designs. The variable costs include the cost of the hardware required for an enlarged activated charcoal canister, fuel vapor lines, and a fuel cooling system (CARB, 1990a, pp. 17-18). There is no discussion of any incremental assembly and warranty costs, and fixed costs are only briefly addressed. The cost of enhanced testing facilities is estimated to be negligible. There is no discussion of any associated research and development costs, tooling and equipment costs, assembly costs, or warranty costs. There are thus no fixed costs to amortize. Finally, variable costs incurred in the future are not discounted back to a base year.

Because CARB's EEE analysis was done before its ORVR analysis (discussed shortly), it is unlikely that it presupposes ORVR. The same is probably true of Sierra's estimates, although Sierra is not explicit about the cost interactions of the two systems.

CARB (1995a, p. 18) uses U.S. EPA's cost estimate for ORVR with no additional discussion. We have not reviewed U.S. EPA's cost estimate to determine what types of costs are included and what the estimates are based on. ORVR systems will most likely be integrated with the EEE system, but neither CARB nor Sierra explicitly discusses whether its cost estimates presuppose EEE. Given the low magnitudes of the estimates, it seems likely that both CARB and Sierra assumed that ORVR was added onto an existing EEE system.[89]

CARB's cost estimate for OBD II is based on the cost of only the incremental sensors it projects are necessary (CARB, 1989a, p. 16). Again, the variable cost estimate does not appear to include assembly and warranty costs, fixed costs are not discussed, and costs are not discounted back to a base year.

These costs do not include any savings that accrue to either the manufacturer or the vehicle owner. OBD II may make it easier to catch and diagnose manufacturing defects at the assembly plant, possibly reducing manufacturer warranty costs. OBD II may also enable mechanics to diagnose and fix power train problems more quickly. This may save vehicle owners both time and money.

Table 6.1-3 reports the Sierra and CARB cost estimates for EEE, ORVR, and OBD II. As before, CARB's variable cost estimates are significantly below even the Sierra best-case estimates, although this time the differences are factors of 2 or 3 rather than factors of five.[90] The dollar differences between the Sierra best-case and CARB variable cost estimates for EEE and ORVR are not large, particularly considering that CARB apparently does not include some variable costs in its estimates (e.g., additional assembly costs). Variable costs account for a greater proportion of Sierra's total cost estimates for EEE, ORVR, and OBD II (approximately 70 percent) than they did for TLEVs, LEV, and ULEVs (approximately 50 percent). This is likely to be because fixed costs are now amortized over the national production volumes rather than over the California volumes.

---

[89]Neither CARB nor Sierra discusses what costs ORVR might impose on gas stations. For example, gas stations may have to install pressure-vacuum valves on their underground storage tanks to deal with the interaction between Stage 2 vapor recovery nozzles and ORVR systems.

[90]To be strictly comparable, the cost estimates would have to be converted to a common baseline. In this case, adjusting CARB's 1989 cost estimate for OBD II and its 1990 estimate for EEE to 1993 dollars to account for inflation would increase the cost estimates, but discounting future outlays back to 1993 would reduce them.

Table 6.1-3

**Sierra and CARB Estimates of the Cost of Adding EEE, ORVR,
and OBD II to a 1993 California Vehicle
(dollars per vehicle)**

	EEE	ORVR[a]	OBD II
Sierra manufacturer (discounted to 1993, 1993 dollars)[b]			
Variable costs	109	50	204
Fixed costs	33	18	58
Dealer margin	14	7	26
Total	156	75	288
Sierra best-case (discounted to 1993, 1993 dollars)[b]			
Variable costs	32	13	111
Fixed costs	9	5	31
Dealer margin	4	2	14
Total	45	20	157
CARB (undiscounted)[c]			
Variable costs	18[d]	5[e]	45[f]
Fixed costs	?	?	?
Dealer margin	?	?	?
Total	?	?	?

[a]Costs most likely assume preexistence of EEE.
[b]Sierra (1994a), pp. 101, A-10.
[c]Dollars assumed to be in year of report.
[d]CARB (1990a), p. 17.
[e]CARB (1995a), p. 18.
[f]CARB (1989a), p. 16.

The reasons for the big difference between the CARB and Sierra estimates for OBD II are probably analogous to those outlined above for TLEVs, LEVs, and ULEVs. CARB (1989a, p. 16) states that the major reason the manufacturer estimates are higher is that the manufacturers assume that OBD II will require a second computer. CARB argues, however, that vehicles need more sophisticated computers anyway to control electronic transmissions, suspensions, throttles, and other components, and that these systems will be able to support OBD II at no extra cost. CARB also believes that long lead times provided before implementation (6 years) will allow manufacturers to incorporate OBD II functions into ongoing vehicle redesigns at very low costs (1989a, p. 17). This belief might explain why CARB pays little attention to fixed costs. It makes sense that these long lead times would help reduce fixed costs, but that does not mean that they would reduce the fixed costs to zero.[91]

6.1.3 Total Direct Hardware Costs

Table 6.1-4 combines numbers from Tables 6.1-2 and 6.1-3 to present estimates of the total incremental direct costs of a TLEV, LEV, and ULEV that also meet the EEE, ORVR, and OBD II requirements. We use these combined costs in our examination of market mediated effects in Section 7. We imputed missing CARB fixed cost and dealer margin estimates for EEE, ORVR, and OBD II using the ratios between fixed cost and variable cost and between dealer margin and variable costs reported by Sierra for each regulation. We then converted the Sierra and CARB estimates to 1995 dollars, but the CARB numbers remain undiscounted.[92]

The estimated incremental cost of a TLEV sold in California that meets the EEE, ORVR, and OBD II regulations ranges from $175 according to CARB to $532 according to the Sierra best-case estimate. The cost estimate for LEV ranges from $229 to $1,079, 4-cylinder ULEVs from $324 to $831, and 6-cylinder ULEVs from $339 to $1,587. We use the CARB estimates as lower bounds in the analysis below and the Sierra best-case estimates as upper bounds.

---

[91]The Bureau of Labor Statistics (BLS) recently estimated that OBD II added $59.43 on average to the retail price of twenty 1996 model year passenger cars (Bureau of Labor Statistics, 1995). Whether or not this figure includes fixed costs is not specified. If it does not, the BLS estimate is probably close to the CARB estimate for variable costs (once the CARB figure is adjusted to 1996 dollars and dealer margin is netted out from the BLS figure). If it does, it may well be lower than the CARB estimate. We have not been able to review the basis of the BLS estimate, and thus cannot determine whether it provides strong evidence that OBD II costs will turn out closer to CARB's estimates than Sierra's.

[92]We have insufficient information about the time profile of CARB costs to discount them.

Table 6.1-4

Total Incremental Costs of a TLEV, LEV, and ULEV Including EEE, ORVR, and OBD II over a 1993 California Vehicle
(dollars per vehicle)

			ULEV	
	TLEV	LEV	4-cyl	6-cyl
Sierra best-case (discounted to 1993, adjusted for inflation to 1995)				
Variable costs	320	587	482	882
Fixed costs	164	395	281	576
Dealer margin	48	97	69	130
Total	532	1,079	831	1,587
CARB (undiscounted, adjusted for inflation to 1995)				
Variable costs	115	164	250	263
Fixed costs	47	50	55	55
Dealer margin	13	15	19	20
Total	175	229	324	339

Note: CARB estimates do not equal sum from Tables 6.1-2 and 6.1-3 because costs adjusted for inflation to 1995.

6.2 DIRECT EMISSION REDUCTIONS

We now review and critique estimates of the direct emission reductions of ICEV hardware elements. We ignore market-mediated emission effects such as increased fleet emissions due to slower fleet turnover caused by higher new car prices. These effects are discussed in Section 7. The principal studies we reviewed on direct emission reductions are CARB (1990a, 1994a and 1994b) and Sierra (1994a).

The emission reductions generated by adding hardware-based elements to the other elements of California's strategy depend importantly on how well the other elements of the system are functioning. The effects of exhaust and evaporative emission hardware depend on the effectiveness of Smog Check II and OBD II. Scrappage must also be considered because it influences how long the vehicle stays in service (as does the I&M program). In the analyses below, we estimate the effectiveness of the hardware-based elements of California's strategy under different assumptions about the effectiveness of the remainder of the program.

The primary studies on the emission reductions of the hardware-based elements of the California strategy were done by CARB and Sierra. We first review their estimates of the emission reductions due to the exhaust regulations and then turn to evaporative emission regulations. Because the effectiveness of OBD II is so closely intertwined with the effectiveness of Smog Check II, the effectiveness of OBD II is discussed in Section 8 along with the effectiveness of the non-hardware based elements of the California strategy.

6.2.1 Direct Emission Reductions of Exhaust Regulations

CARB uses its EMFAC7F model to estimate emission reductions and Sierra uses both EMFAC7F and U.S. EPA's MOBILE5a. These models predict fleet emissions based on a large number of technical and behavioral assumptions. The top panel of Table 6.2-1 lists some of the assumptions used by CARB and Sierra in model runs predicting TLEV, LEV, and ULEV emission reductions. All these parameters affect the estimates, but the most important are the zero-mile emission rates and emission deterioration rates.[93] We first discuss the zero-mile emission and deterioration rates used in the models, assuming that there is no I&M program, then consider the effect of I&M.

MOBILE5a assumes that zero-mile emission rates for TLEVs, LEVs, and ULEVs are reduced relative to those CA93 vehicles by the ratio of their certification standards to the CA93 certification standard, but that their deterioration rates are the same as those for a CA93 vehicle. EMFAC7F makes the same assumptions for zero-mile emission rates but assumes that the deterioration rates are also proportionately reduced. U.S. EPA argues that the new vehicles will deteriorate just as rapidly as CA93 vehicles, while CARB argues that vehicles must deteriorate more slowly if they are to meet 50,000 and 100,000 mile certification and in-use emission requirements (i.e., companies have strong incentives to meet these requirements).

---

[93]The zero-mile emission rate is the emission rate in grams per mile when the car is new. The emission deterioration rate is the increase in emissions per mile for every 10,000 miles driven.

CARB is correct that CA93 deterioration rates would cause the low emitting vehicles to surpass their certification standards quickly,[94] but whether in-use deterioration rates for low-emission vehicles will be substantially lower remains an open question. CARB staff detail the technologies that could be used to attain lower deterioration rates (Albu, Kao, and Cackette, 1992, pp. 8-28), but the in-use performance of these technologies over time is not yet known.[95] The certification and in-use surveillance programs may not provide adequate incentives for manufacturers to achieve the assumed deterioration rates in on-road use. For example, as discussed in Sections 4.2 and 4.4, certification tests are not done using real-world driving conditions, and vehicle surveillance programs may miss the dirtiest vehicles.

CARB's estimates assume no I&M program and no OBD. Sierra predicts emission reductions under three different I&M scenarios: no-I&M, basic I&M, and enhanced I&M. The basic I&M scenario apparently models a program similar to the California Smog Check program. The enhanced I&M scenario models a program that meets U.S. EPA performance criteria for a smog-check program (Smog Check II was designed to perform up to U.S. EPA requirements). Sierra's analysis thus allows us to look at emissions under two different I&M effectiveness scenarios, but, as we will discuss in Section 8, there is considerable doubt about whether these scenarios accurately represent any real-world I&M programs.

---

[94]The NMOG deterioration rate assumed for a CA93 vehicle in MOBILE5a is 0.03 gm/mi/10,000 miles (Sierra, 1994a, p. 67) so that a ULEV with even negligible zero-mile emission will violate the NMOG standard after 20,000 miles.

[95]One of the key advantages of new emission control systems is that they are adaptive. Thus, they can compensate for component deterioration and wear as the vehicle ages (Albu, Kao, and Cackette, 1992, p. 34).

Table 6.2-1

Overview of Empirical Estimates of ICEV Hardware Emissions Reductions

Assumptions for TLEV, LEV, and ULEV	CARB (1994a, 1994b)	Sierra (1994a, 1994c)
Model used	EMFAC7F	MOBILE5a and EMFAC7F
Temperatures	Not specified	Summer runs based on 69°F-94°F for EMFAC7F (1994c, p.7)
Fuel parameters	Not specified	CARB Phase 1 fuel with RVP of 7.8 (1994c, p. 7)
Discount rate	None	5 percent (1994c, p. 9)
Refueling emissions	Not included (according to Sierra, 1994a, p.12)	Included. 0.07 g/mi (1994c, p. 12)
I&M scenarios	No I&M (1994a, p.43)	Three different scenarios: no, basic, and enhanced I&M
OBD2 included?	No (1994a, p. 43)	No
Deterioration rates	Zero-mile emissions and deterioration rates reduced from Tier 1 rates according to ratio of vehicle standard to Tier 1 standard	In EMFAC7F zero-mile emissions and deterioration rates reduced from Tier 1 rates according to ratio of vehicle standard to Tier 1 standard. In Mobile5a, zero-mile rate proportionally reduced but deterioration rate unchanged (1994c, p. 9)

Table 6.2-1 (Cont'd.)

	CARB (1994a, 1994b)	Sierra (1994a, 1994c)
Assumptions for EEE		
Methods Used	EMFAC7F (1990a, p. 14)	MOBILE5a and EMFAC7F
Ambient temperatures	Separate estimates for daily max of 75°F, 95°F, and 105°F all year round	69°F-94°F in EMFAC7F
Basis of emission reduction calculations	90% reductions in running losses and in hot soak and diurnal emissions (1990a, p.17)	Assumptions in MOBILE5a: 75% reduction in running losses, 50% reduction in hot soak emissions, 40-75% reduction in diurnals depending on duration (1994a, p. 59)
Deterioration rates	Not discussed	Appear to use EPA data on vehicles failing pressure/purge test (1994a, p. 61)
Fuel parameters	9.0 RVP	CARB Phase 1 fuel with RVP of 7.8 (1994c, p. 7)
Assumptions for ORVR		
Basis for emission reduction calculations	Engineering analysis of joint effectiveness of ORVR and Stage 2 nozzles	Assumptions slightly modified from MOBILE5a: 98% of vapor displacement emission reduced, no reduction in spillage (1994a, p. 61)
Stage 2 Vapor Recovery Nozzles	In place and working effectively (1995a, p. 18)	Not in place (1994a, p. 116)
Deterioration rates	Not discussed	Appear to use EPA data on vehicle failing pressure/purge tests (1994a, p. 61)
Interaction with Stage 1 emissions	Evaluated	Not evaluated

CARB's estimates of the lifetime emission reductions of TLEVs, LEVs, and ULEVs are reported in the first column of Table 6.2-2. The reductions are relative to the lifetime emissions of a CA93 vehicle (see first row), and the reductions are not discounted back to a base year. The CA93 vehicle emissions and reductions predicted by CARB are substantially less than the undiscounted reductions predicted by Sierra using the same model (compare columns 1 and 2). This appears to be in large part because CARB assumes a vehicle life of 100,000 miles and Sierra assumes 150,000 miles. On a grams per mile basis the two estimates are comparable.[96] As can be seen by comparing the Sierra estimates in columns 2 and 3, discounting emission reductions at 5 percent annually reduces the emission reductions by about one-third from their undiscounted levels.

Switching from no-I&M to enhanced I&M reduces both the baseline CA93 vehicle emissions and emission reductions from TLEVs, LEVs, and ULEVs from 20 to 25 percent (see columns 3 and 4). It is understandable why the emissions of a CA93 vehicle would be less with enhanced I&M than with no I&M. However it is not obvious why the emission *reductions* should be less. On the one hand, an effective enhanced I&M program means that there are less emissions to reduce; on the other, an effective program would ensure that the hardware-based elements perform better over time and thus reduce emissions more than if there were no I&M program.

As expected, the emission reductions predicted by MOBILE5a are lower than those predicted by EMFAC7F. Comparison of the last two columns of Table 6.2-2 shows that projected CA93 vehicle emissions with enhanced I&M are about twice as high in MOBILE5a and that the emission reductions are about one-half as large.

---

[96]Average vehicle lifetime mileage in California is approximately 130,000 miles, and may be closer to 150,000 miles in the South Coast Air Basin.

Table 6.2-2

Emission Reductions Relative to CA93 Vehicle
(lifetime pounds of ROG+NOx per vehicle)

	CARB Using EMFAC7F	Sierra Using EMFAC7F			Sierra Using MOBILE5
	Undiscounted	Undiscounted	Discounted		Discounted
				Enhanced	Enhanced
	No I&M	No I&M[b]	No I&M[c]	I&M[c]	I&M[d]
CA93 (level)	339[a]	529	364	251	421
Reduction from CA93					
TLEV	40[a]	66	43	31	15
LEV	132[a]	204	137	109	44
ULEV	142[a]	223	149	119	51
EEE	34-113[e]	132	82	37	78
ORVR	0[f]	--	--	--	0

[a]CARB (1994a), p. 46. Evaporative emissions not reported by CARB. Here they are assumed to be 0.5 gm/mi for 100,000 mile vehicle life.

[b]Sierra (1995c).

[c]Sierra (1994c).

[d]Sierra (1994a).

[e]Calculated from CARB (1990a), p. 17.

[f]CARB (1995b), p. 18.

6.2.2 Direct Emission Reductions of Evaporative Emissions Regulations

Enhanced Evaporative Emissions Regulation

Sierra's estimates of the emission reductions due to the enhanced evaporative emissions (EEE) regulations are based on the effectiveness assumptions in MOBILE5a (see Table 6.2-1). There is no discussion of the basis for these estimates in Sierra's report, and we have not examined U.S. EPA documentation of MOBILE. CARB estimates that EEE will cause running, hot soak, and diurnal emissions to fall 90 percent. CARB's estimates are derived by comparing emissions of vehicles with standard evaporative emission control systems during a new test protocol with the maximum evaporative emissions allowed under the protocol.

Table 6.2-2 presents estimated emission reductions of EEE regulations. CARB's 1990 estimates varied from 34 to 113 pounds of ROG over the life of the vehicle, depending on whether the maximum daily

over the life of the vehicle, depending on whether the maximum daily temperature *year round* was 75°F or 105°F. The reduction when maximum daily temperature follows a real-world pattern is probably somewhere in between. Sierra's 1995 estimate, using an updated versions of EMFAC (version 7F), is 132 pounds. In contrast to the results for exhaust emissions, emission reductions calculated by Sierra using MOBILE5a are substantially larger than when using EMFAC.

The ranges found in the studies illustrate uncertainty over the emission reductions of EEE. Our review of the methods on which these estimates are based illustrates some of the reasons for this uncertainty.

- As we discussed in Section 3, there is a great deal of uncertainty over the magnitude of current evaporative emissions.

- Some of the emission reduction projections appear to be based on very small data sets. For example, CARB appears to use only 3 vehicles when estimating how much the emissions generated by standard evaporative emission systems exceed the new requirements.

- How EEE systems will function over time is based on U.S. EPA data on pressure and purge tests of the evaporative emission control system in current vehicles (Sierra, 1994a, p. 59). These data may or may not be relevant for the new systems.

On-Board Refueling Vapor Recovery

Both CARB and Sierra conclude that ORVR systems will produce no reductions in refueling emissions if Stage II vapor recovery systems are in place. CARB concludes this because it estimates that Stage II systems are 86-92 percent effective in districts *that have annual enforcement programs* to ensure that gasoline stations comply with nozzle requirements, and an estimated 95 percent of total California gasoline sales are made through Stage II nozzles (CARB, 1995b, p. 2).[97] This

---

[97]CARB (1995a, p. 11) even warns that without installation of a pressure/vacuum valve on the underground storage tank (UST) vent pipe, emissions from gasoline station underground storage tanks may increase when refueling vehicles with ORVR systems.

still leaves some uncertainty about the effectiveness of Stage II
nozzles: no information is given on what percent of districts have
annual enforcement programs, and consumers may not use Stage II nozzles
properly.

ORVR may have an advantage in terms of reducing emissions over
Stage II nozzles if it requires less compliance monitoring and
enforcement. But, ORVR is not likely to eliminate the need for such
programs. Inspection systems will still be needed to ensure that
underground storage tanks are functioning and properly maintained and
that the pressure/vacuum valves required by ORVR are installed and
properly functioning. ORVR may also be advantageous if a significant
number of consumers improperly use Stage II nozzles and if it is
difficult to misfuel an ORVR system. However, we have seen no analysis
of this issue. Overall, we find it reasonable to conclude that ORVR
will indeed have very little impact on refueling emissions.

6.2.3 Synthesis

The preceding discussion illustrates the complexities involved in
predicting reductions of exhaust and evaporative emissions. The
differences in emission reductions are due to differences in:

- Emission model used. Emission reductions predicted using EMFAC
  are roughly twice as high as in MOBILE for exhaust emissions.
  Evaporative emission reductions using EMFAC are roughly one-
  half those using MOBILE.

- Effectiveness of I&M. Emission reductions are 20 to 25 percent
  lower with enhanced I&M.

- Vehicle life. The longer vehicle life assumed by Sierra
  results in approximately 50 percent greater emission reductions
  than the vehicle life assumed by CARB.

CARB combines two assumptions that tend to increase emission
reductions (EMFAC model and no I&M). Sierra combines longer vehicle
life with different assumptions about I&M and the emission model.

Undermining our confidence in all these estimates is the continuing
uncertainty discussed in Section 3 of what on-road lifetime vehicle
emissions actually are. We concluded our discussion of the direct costs

of the hardware based regulations in Section 6.1 stating that the true resource costs of the regulations were likely contained in the bounds we developed. Judging by the information we have gathered to date, we think it premature to do the same for emission reductions. We have reported the reductions projected in different studies and provided some explanation for why they differ. Whether actual emission reductions will turn out to lie within the emission reductions projected in these studies is far from certain.

Hopefully, the information provided will help the reader to determine which emission reduction estimates seem more plausible. For example, the MOBILE estimates would be more relevant if the reader expected little deterioration improvement for TLEVs, LEVs, and ULEVs relative to CA93 vehicles. The EMFAC model would be more relevant if the reader thinks significant improvements in deterioration rates likely.

6.3 NAPROW COST-EFFECTIVENESS RATIOS

A narrow cost-effectiveness ratio (NCER) is an estimate of the direct cost of an emission control measure per ton of emissions reduced. We calculate NCERs in dollars per ton of ROG plus NOx reduced. Recall from Section 2 that NCERs can provide information about the desirability of pollution control measures, but they exclude some important costs and benefits. In the case of the hardware-based elements of California's strategy considered here, issues not considered that could importantly affect the costs and benefits include

- Effect on fleet turnover. If the hardware-based elements of the ICEV control strategy cause ICEV prices to rise, as analyzed in Section 7, fleet turnover may slow and ICEV emissions may rise.

- Location and time of emission reductions. All ROG and NOx emission reductions, wherever and whenever they occur, are included in the NCERs below. However, some reductions will undoubtedly be in areas where, and at times when, pollution levels are low and thus may be of little value.[98]

- Incidence of costs. The NCERs below are calculated from a national perspective in that all costs, whether they are borne by Californians or not, are included. NCERs for Californians will be lower to the extent that costs are shifted outside California.

- Reductions of emissions other than ROG and NOx. For example some hardware based elements may reduce carbon monoxide or particulate emissions.

The first two issues would tend to make emission control measures less desirable than suggested by their NCERs. The last two would tend to make them more desirable.

Table 6.3-1 presents narrow cost effectiveness ratios for the hardware-based elements of the California strategy using the cost and emission reduction estimates in the CARB and Sierra studies. For the exhaust emission standards, NCERs are calculated both relative to the same baseline--a CA93 (top panel of Table 6.3-1) and incrementally as the standard tightens (bottom panel). The NCER for EEE does not vary a great deal across studies (from $364 to $2,541 per ton of ROG plus NOx). Both CARB and Sierra agree that ORVR makes no sense. There is a great deal of variation in NCERs for the exhaust standards. The proportional differences are particularly large for TLEVs an LEVs, but it narrows somewhat for the incremental NCERs of ULEVs over LEVs (last line of Table 6.3-1).

---

[98]CARB and Sierra both consider all emission reductions in California wherever and whenever they occur. Sierra takes this approach for ozone precursors in California because it thinks that air quality benefits are associated with the control of precursor emissions during the majority of the year in Southern California--the region that accounts for the majority of vehicles sold in California--and because the vast majority of vehicles sold in California are sold in non-attainment areas (Sierra, 1994a, p. 44).

Table 6.3-1

Narrow Cost-Effectiveness of ICEV Hardware Based Regulations
(Dollars per Ton of ROG+NOx)[a]

| | CARB[b] | Sierra Best-Case Costs[c] | | |
| | EMFAC | EMFAC | | MOBILE |
	No I&M	No I&M	Enh. I&M	Enh. I&M
Relative to CA93 Vehicle				
TLEV	3,083	13,992	19,408	40,110
LEV	1,746	12,382	15,563	38,553
ULEV4	2,947	8,062	10,094	23,553
ULEV6	3,147	18,199	22,787	53,169
EEE	364-1,206	1,146	2,541	1,205
ORVR	infinite	infinite	infinite	infinite
CA93 to TLEV	3,083	13,992	19,408	40,110
TLEV to LEV	1,165	11,645	14,034	37,747
LEV to ULEV				
4-cyl (45%)	24,668	--	--	--
6-cyl (47%)	17,591	--	--	--
8-cyl (8%)	28,307	--	--	--
All (100%)	21,635	27,967	33,561	47,944

[a]1995 dollars.
[b]Based on undiscounted costs and emission reductions.
[c]Based on discounted costs and emission reductions.

The most important factor explaining the variation in NCERs is the variation in projected costs. As discussed above, CARB's estimates are lower than Sierra's by a factor of five in most cases. Differences in estimated emission reductions are important as well, varying by up to a factor of three when the various estimates of discounted emission reductions are compared. CARB's NCERs combine low costs and the relatively large emission reductions projected by EMFAC with no I&M; Sierra combines high costs with varying estimates of emission reductions.

As implied by our discussion of emission reductions above, the NCER ranges in Table 6.3-1 are not ranges into which we think it highly likely that the actual NCERs will necessarily fall. We have attempted to review and critique the assumptions that underlie the different estimates. Hopefully, this exercise helps the reader to come to his or her own conclusion about the likely NCERs for the hardware-based elements of California's ozone reduction strategy.

The fundamental uncertainty over emissions and emission reductions raises questions about how far we can go with evaluation of strategy elements on narrow cost-effectiveness grounds. We need not throw up our hands and go home, however. If the emission models are all off by a common factor, relative rankings by NCER will not change. If, on the other hand, projections vary a great deal in accuracy across vehicle segments, policy rankings could be distorted. An example might be comparison of the AVR and NMOG elements of the California strategy which requires information on emissions of vehicles of very different vintages and mileage levels.

7. MARKET-MEDIATED EFFECTS OF ICEV HARDWARE ELEMENTS

OVERVIEW AND PREVIEW OF FINDINGS

The regulatory elements aimed at hardware improvements for new California LDVs will increase the costs of producing them. Well-accepted economic principles then suggest that these elements will--at least to some extent--increase prices and decrease sales of new California LDVs. Understanding such effects on prices and sales is key to understanding how the costs of the regulations will be distributed among various stakeholders such as actual and potential California new vehicle purchasers, California vehicle dealers and their salespeople, and stockholders of automobile manufacturers residing in California and elsewhere.

We should also expect increased prices and decreased sales of new LDVs to reduce the rates at which older vehicles are retired. Thus, regulations that increase the costs of new ICEVs will lead, on average, to an older vehicle fleet. To the extent that older vehicles tend to have higher emission rates (per year) than new vehicles, feedback effects on emissions--mediated through the market--are relevant for estimating the emission benefits of the regulatory elements affecting ICEV hardware.

Should we expect such effects to be trivial or substantial? What determines their size? How might they differ across different segments of the new LDV market? What empirical evidence is available to inform such questions? What are the key uncertainties?

To preview our findings:

(1) Using ranges of variable production cost increases developed in Section 6, we estimate that the hardware-based elements of the California LDV strategy could

- Increase average selling prices of new LDVs in California by $100 to $500,

- Decrease new LDV sales in California by up to 4 percent,

- Cost new car buyers in California somewhere between $150 million and $700 million per year,
- Cost vehicle manufacturers and dealers between $100 million and $800 million per year in profits

(2) Declines in new car sales and resulting delays in the retirement of older vehicles due to the regulations suggest that estimates of direct emission reductions are likely to overstate the actual emission reductions. If price effects are large, the new regulations could increase emissions for roughly three to five years and substantially attenuate direct emission benefits of the regulations for several years more.

7.1 OVERVIEW OF THE ANALYSIS

The market for new LDVs in California is very complex. There are more than a dozen manufacturers offering hundreds of models at far flung geographic locations. There are several distinct market segments. Automobile segments include subcompact, compact, mid-sized, and full-sized sedans (which might be further divided by distinguishing luxury or high-performance models from others), sports cars, etc. Market segments for light-duty trucks might be defined in terms of body style (e.g., pickups, mini-vans) numbers of passengers, payload, etc.

Some market segments are very competitive, with several manufacturers offering vehicles that potential buyers view as quite similar; other market segments are less competitive. The nature of demand also differs across market segments; in some, price is likely to be the paramount consideration of most buyers; in others, buyers may be much more willing to pay more for quality or performance improvements.

These complexities and others dictate that no analysis of the market for ICEVs can be nearly definitive. This does not mean, however, that analysis is futile. Economic models (simplified, abstract representations) of the LDV market or segments of it can--if interpreted with care--be helpful in understanding major factors determining prices and sales levels. At the very least, they are useful for clarifying the logical basis for any claims about market effects and for identifying issues that are likely to be overlooked in the absence of structured reasoning.

We analyze price and quantity determination for new California LDVs using three different, well known, economic models. In each case, prices and sales levels result from the behavior of automobile manufacturers, who attempt to maximize their profits, and of consumers, whose vehicle-purchase behavior depends on the prices of vehicles. The models differ according to how the form of competition or interdependencies among manufacturers is specified:

Competitive model (supply and demand). In this model, each manufacturer is assumed to offer products that are identical in the eyes of consumers and to have a small enough impact on the overall market that each chooses its production level ignoring any potential impact of its sales on the market price of LDVs. This model is of considerable relevance because of the generally competitive nature of the contemporary California LDV market, where, in most market segments, several companies compete for sales with largely similar products and significant price increases by a single company would lead to substantial decreases in its sales.

Imperfectly competitive model with identical products. Here sellers in a particular market segment are assumed to offer identical products but to be relatively few in number and to recognize that their actions will affect market level outcomes. This recognition leads them to take such effects into account in deciding how to act. This model captures important aspects of market segments where there are relatively few products that are viewed by buyers as being quite similar. Because of the complexity of such situations, we explicitly consider a market with only two sellers.

Imperfectly competitive model with differentiated products. Here sellers in a particular market segment are assumed to offer products that are viewed as substantially different by buyers. Under these conditions, different companies can charge different prices for products that are in direct competition with each other. Consideration of this possibility allows us to address how the relative prices of different vehicles might change in response to the ICEV hardware regulations. Again, complexity leads us to use a model with only two sellers.

Each model allows us to

- Consider in general terms what we should expect to happen as a result of increases in the production cost of ICEVs,

- Address how such conclusions are likely to differ according to the number of sellers in a market segment and whether buyers perceive major differences between the products within a particular segment, and

- Consider what determines the sizes of these effects, what ranges are for them as implied by different estimates of increases in ICEV hardware costs, and how these effects may differ across market segments and companies.

More detailed expositions of these models are presented in Appendices 7.A, 7.B and 7.C, respectively. Below we summarize what each model implies for the price and quantity of new California LDVs, given the ICEV hardware regulations. Most of our discussion focuses on the competitive model.

7.2 EFFECTS OF THE NEW REGULATIONS ON EQUILIBRIUM PRICES AND QUANTITIES: COMPETITIVE MODEL

For some of the issues we discuss below, it is useful to consider the competitive--or supply and demand--model as applying to the entire market for all LDVs in California; for other issues, we consider it to represent a particular segment of that market. For convenience, we refer to the former as the *market interpretation* and the latter as the *segment interpretation*. Under the market interpretation, there is only one type of vehicle in the California LDV market--which we think of as the average (or prototypical) vehicle. Quantities are annual sales of all new LDVs in the California market, and prices are those of the average vehicle. Under the segment interpretation, prices and quantities are those of the single vehicle type in that segment (e.g., all sub-compact sedans, all small pickup trucks).

We focus on predicting effects in the short-run, a period of time during which sellers cannot adjust their production capacities. We think of this as a period of at least several years. In a competitive model, the sizes of short-run price increases and sales decreases that would result from the new regulations depend on three factors (or parameters of the model):[99]

- The size of marginal production cost increases, which drive the effects;
- The elasticity of demand, which is a measure of the responsiveness to price increases of the number of vehicles that buyers will buy;
- The elasticity of supply, which is a measure of the responsiveness to price increases of the number of vehicles that sellers will sell.

We compute ranges of estimates of price and quantity effects using data characterizing the California LDV market, various combinations of values for the elasticities, and bounds developed from the cost estimates reviewed in Section 6.1. This helps us to understand some of the social stakes in the disagreement about direct cost estimates that are not reflected in the NCERs in Table 6.3-1.

Marginal cost increases. The marginal cost of a vehicle is the increase in production and selling costs experienced by the manufacturer and dealer when an additional vehicle is produced and sold. In Section 5.1, we reviewed CARB and Sierra estimates of the additional costs of ICEVs to comply with the new regulations that require improvements in ICEV hardware. The cost components used there are fixed costs, variable costs and dealer margins. We use the estimated increases in variable cost per vehicle from Table 6.1-4 to represent the increase in marginal cost due to the regulations.[100]

---

[99]Application of a competitive model would imply that in the long run--a period long enough for companies to change their production capacities, product offerings, dealer networks, and even enter or leave the California market--all cost increases lead (dollar-for-dollar) to price increases. We do not analyze long-run implications of the new ICEV hardware regulations for reasons explained in Appendix 7.A.

[100]Fixed costs are not included because (by definition) they do not increase with increases in production levels. Some of the costs of selling reimbursed through dealer margins are fixed and others are variable. The only apparent reason additional emission control equipment would increase selling costs is the cost of the extra money tied up in dealers' inventories. We have no empirical basis for estimating the size

Considering the entire range of vehicle types (i.e., TLEVs, LEVs, and ULEVs), and--more important--whether CARB or Sierra did the estimation, the range of estimated increases in marginal cost is $115 to $882 per vehicle. Since under the market interpretation the increase in marginal cost represents an average across all vehicles, it seems appropriate to focus on cost estimates for LEVs. Here the range of increase (average variable costs from Table 6.1-4) is $164 to $587 per vehicle. We also perform calculations for two intermediate values: $300 and $450 per vehicle.

Values of elasticity of demand. We use values of the demand elasticity of -1 and -2 to represent the sensitivity of quantities demanded of new LDVs in California.[101]

Values of elasticity of supply. Choice of plausible values for the (short-run) elasticity of supply of LDVs to the California market is based on the following reasoning. The elasticity of supply has logical extreme values of zero[102] to infinity.[103] The actual value depends on how quickly marginal costs increase with increases in production for the California market. In our initial calculations, we use values for the supply elasticity from 1 up to 50. We view values at the lower end of

---

of variable dealer costs, but because we expect that the fixed-cost component is predominant, we don't include any part of dealer margin in our estimates of marginal cost increases. The potential inaccuracy introduced is minor because the estimates of variable cost increases are substantially larger than estimates of dealer margins.

[101]As discussed in Appendix 7.A, the former value is standard in the industry, assuming that the prices of all vehicles increase by the same proportion. We also consider the value of -2 to account for the possibility that costs of California ICEVs (and therefore prices) will increase more than in other states and that this will induce some California residents to purchase vehicles in neighboring states, despite the existing impediments for doing so. Note that vehicles imported from other states will also tend to have higher emissions than California vehicles.

[102]Corresponding to a case where supply to the California market cannot be increased at all--i.e., no matter how large the increase in price in the California market, no more vehicles would be offered for sale in California.

[103]Corresponding to a case where any tiny increase in price would make producers willing to sell as many vehicles as California buyers want.

the range of supply elasticities--below 5, say--as implausible unless plants are operating near full capacity.[104]

Estimates of price and quantity effects. As detailed in Appendix 7.A, cost increases tend to increase market prices and decrease market quantities.[105] In Table 7.2-1 we present various predictions of the increases in the average ICEV price in California and decreases in market-level sales attributable to the new hardware regulations. In the table, the upper and lower panels differ only by the assumed value for the demand elasticity. Price increases--expressed in dollars per vehicle--are on the left side of each panel, and quantity (sales) decreases--expressed in thousands of vehicles per year--are on the right side.

In all calculations we assume an average baseline price (i.e., without the cost increase) of $20,000 per vehicle and baseline annual sales of 1.5 million vehicles.

The formulas used to calculate the price increases and quantity decreases in the table are:

Price increase = (Cost increase) x (Supply Elasticity)/(Supply Elasticity - Demand Elasticity).

Quantity decrease = (-Demand elasticity) x (Price increase/$20,000) x (1.5M vehicles)

Thus, for example, if the elasticity of supply is 5 and the elasticity of demand is -2, the model predicts that 5/7 of any increase in marginal cost will be passed through in price.

----

[104]For example, a supply (to California) elasticity of 5 means that expanding production by 5 percent for the California market--which would require an expansion of production at a plant by 1 percent if 20 percent of the plant's production is shipped to California--increases marginal production costs at the plant level by 1 percent. There seems to be little reason for marginal costs to increase at all with increases in production rates if the plant is operating below capacity.

[105]Following standard economic principles, the analysis predicts that additional costs of producing vehicles only for California do not affect prices of vehicles outside California. This prediction is controversial in the context of the ZEV mandate. See Section 11 for a discussion.

Table 7.2-1

Projected Price Increases and Sales Decreases for ICEVs from New ICEV Hardware Regulations

A. Demand elasticity = -1

Increase in marginal cost:

Supply elasticity:	Price increase ($/vehicle):				Quantity decrease (000 vehicles/yr)*			
	164	300	450	587	164	300	450	587
1	82	150	225	294	6	11	17	22
5	137	250	375	489	10	19	28	37
10	149	273	409	534	11	20	31	40
50	161	294	441	575	12	22	33	43

B. Demand elasticity = -2

Increase in marginal cost:

Supply elasticity:	Price increase ($/vehicle):				Quantity decrease (000 vehicles/yr)*			
	164	300	450	587	164	300	450	587
1	55	100	150	196	8	15	23	29
5	117	214	321	419	18	32	48	63
10	137	250	375	489	21	38	56	73
50	158	288	433	564	24	43	65	85

*Assuming a baseline of 1.5 million vehicles sold per year and a price of $20,000 per vehicle

As an example of these calculations, consider the case of the elasticity of supply of 5 and elasticity of demand of -2. Here, predicted price and quantity effects range from a price increase of $117 per vehicle and a sales decline of 18,000 vehicles per year (using the CARB cost estimate) to $419 per vehicle and 63,000 vehicles (using the Sierra cost estimate). As the table indicates, the predicted price and quantity effects are much more sensitive to the cost estimate than the choice of demand elasticity or choice among supply elasticities of 5 (which seems as low as is plausible) or more. For supply elasticities as low as 5, considerably more than half of the cost increase is passed on in prices. Assuming a larger demand elasticity leads to smaller predicted effects on prices for any cost increase but also larger decreases in sales.

7.2.1 Estimating Annual Dollar Costs and Their Distribution

What do such figures represent in terms of total dollar costs per year? How are these dollar costs distributed between consumers (buyers of new California ICEVs) and producers (vehicle manufacturers and their dealers)?

Figure 7.2-1 provides a graphical representation of how economists calculate these quantities.[106] Note also that the environmental benefits due to the regulations--which are the motivation for incurring costs--are not represented in the diagram. These benefits are discussed above in Section 6.2 and below in Section 7.4.

---

[106]The analysis assumes that consumers are equally satisfied with the performance characteristics of their vehicles (apart from emission rates) with the regulations as they would be without the additional hardware required to comply with the new regulations. (See Bresnahan and Yao (1985) for an analysis of this issue in the context of regulations during the 1972-1981 period.) We do not further consider effects on performance characteristics, but the issue is relevant to a complete analysis of the costs and benefits of the regulations.

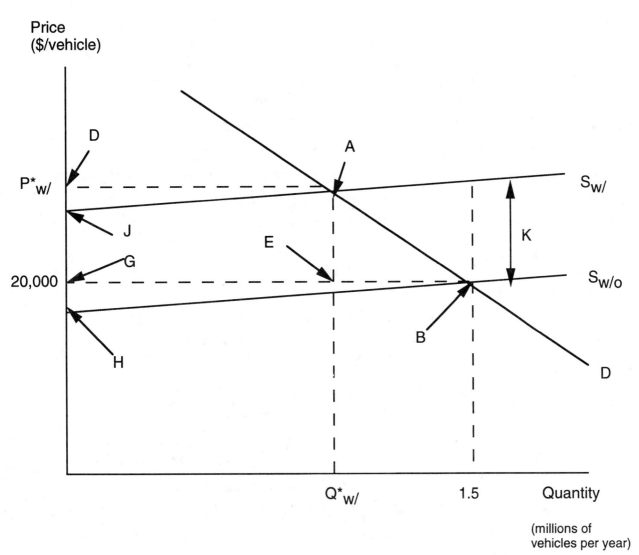

Figure 7.2-1

Consumer and Producer Losses Due to the New ICEV Hardware Regulations Ignoring Benefits of Emission Reduction

Notes:
•Benefits of emission reduction are analyzed in subsections 7.2 and 7.4.4.
• $S_{w/o}$ and $S_{w/}$ are the supply curves without and with the new ICEV hardware regulations
•$P^*_{w/}$ = projected average price of ICEVs in California with new hardware-based regulations.
•$Q^*_{w/}$ = projected annual sales of ICEVs in California with new regulations.

•K is increase in marginal production cost of ICEVs for California due to the new regulations.
•The area of trapezoid DABG is cost to California consumers (loss in consumers' surplus) due to the new regulations
•The annual loss to producers (lost profits)--inside and outside California-- is the additional fixed costs annually due to the new regulations (not shown) plus the change in producers' surplus, which is the area of the triangle DAJ minus the area of the triangle GBH.
•The annual loss to Californians is the loss to California consumers plus the portion of producers' loss borne by stockholders and dealers inside California.

Figure 7.2-1 depicts two competitive equilibria for the California ICEV market. Point B represents the equilibrium without the new ICEV hardware regulations: an average price of $20,000 per vehicle and annual California sales of 1.5 million vehicles. Point A represents the equilibrium with the regulations; the higher price and lower quantity are estimated as described above. K represents the increase in marginal (and average variable) cost of the average California ICEV due to the regulations. Areas in the figure represent millions of dollars per year.

The following quantities are of separate interest as components of the costs of the regulations:

Cost to consumers. The cost of the new regulations to California consumers is represented by the area of the trapezoid DABG. Economists call this the loss of *consumers' surplus* due to the price increase.[107] This loss encompasses losses of two types: (a) the rectangle DAEG (whose area is the increase in price times the number of vehicles purchased with the regulations) is the extra payments consumers make for the vehicles they actually buy; and (b) the area of triangle ABE is (net of the expenditures they avoid) the loss to consumers associated with the vehicles they would have purchased if the price had not increased.[108]

Cost to manufacturers and dealers. This cost is the lost profits of manufacturers and California dealers combined. Lost profits have two components. The first, increases in fixed costs, is not shown in the figure; according to standard economic reasoning, fixed costs are not loaded into prices in the short run because willingness to supply is driven by marginal costs. The second component is the loss of what economists call *producers' surplus*, which is the excess of what producers get for selling over what they would have been willing to accept. In the figure, producers'

_____

[107]Consumers' surplus is the total value buyers place on the vehicles they buy minus how much they actually pay for these vehicles.

[108]Vehicles not purchased are valued according to the amount that consumers would have been willing to pay for them, which is more than the price without the regulations but less than the price with the regulations.

surplus without and with the regulations respectively are the areas of the thin triangles GBH and DAJ.[109]

Cost to Californians. We consider all of the cost to consumers to be costs to Californians on the assumption that virtually all buyers of new vehicles in California reside in the state. Some, but not all, of the losses to producers are borne by Californians even if we assume that all vehicle production takes place outside the state. Some of the stockholders of vehicle manufacturers, wherever they are based, are Californians, and their share of lost profits is a cost to California. Moreover, since the analysis here treats manufacturers and their dealers as unified entities (i.e., "producers" or "sellers"), part of lost producer profits represents losses to California-based dealers. This component of lost profits also represents a cost to California of the new regulations.

7.2.2 Estimates of Annual Dollar Costs and Their Distribution

How large might these dollar figures be? Table 7.2-2 gives a sense of their magnitude.

The top panel of the table details the assumptions used to calculate the figures in the lower two panels.

(1) The change that leads to all of the effects under consideration is the increase in marginal production cost. The calculations in Table 7.2-2 consider the same four values--reproduced in the first row of the table--as in the previous table.

(2) Three other parameters are assumed constant throughout the exercise: (a) the average price of an LDV in California is assumed to be $20,000 without the new regulations; (b) California sales of new LDVs without the regulations are assumed to be 1.5 million vehicles per year; and (c) the elasticity of supply is assumed to be 5.[110]

(3) We consider values for the demand elasticity of -1 (first four columns) and -2 (last four columns).

---

[109]As suggested by the figure, these quantities will be relatively small if the supply curve is relatively flat (i.e., supply is somewhat elastic). In fact, if the supply curve were perfectly flat, there would be no producers' surplus in either situation.

[110]We argued above that this is a lower bound for the supply elasticity, and it is apparent from Table 7.2-1 that price effects are not very sensitive to increases in this elasticity.

Table 7.2-2
Projected Annual Costs to Consumers, Producers and Californians of New ICEV Hardware-Based Regulations
(Ignores Benefits of Emission Reductions)

Assumptions:

Increase in marginal cost ($/vehicle)	164	300	450	587	164	300	450	587
Average vehicle price without new regulations ($ thousands)	20	20	20	20	20	20	20	20
Sales without new regulations (million vehicles/year)	1.5	1.5	1.5	1.5	1.5	1.5	1.5	1.5
Elasticity of demand	-1	-1	-1	-1	-2	-2	-2	-2
Elasticity of supply	5	5	5	5	5	5	5	5

Implied prices and quantities:

Price increase (dollars per vehicle)	137	250	375	489	117	214	321	419
Proportionate price increase	0.0068	0.0125	0.0188	0.0245	0.0059	0.0107	0.0161	0.0210
Sales decrease (thousands of vehicles)	10.3	18.8	28.1	36.7	17.6	32.1	48.2	62.9
Proportionate sales decrease	0.0068	0.0125	0.0188	0.0245	0.0117	0.0214	0.0321	0.0419
Sales with new regulations (million vehicles/year)	1.4898	1.4813	1.4719	1.4633	1.4824	1.4679	1.4518	1.4371

Implied dollar costs ($M/yr):

Cost to California new ICEV buyers	204	373	557	725	175	318	474	616
Additional Fixed Cost--Low (CARB LEV)	75	75	75	75	75	75	75	75
Additional Fixed Cost--High (Sierra LEV)	592	592	592	592	592	592	592	592
Lost Manufacturer and Dealer Profits (CARB fixed costs)	116	150	186	220	145	202	265	321
Lost Manufacturer and Dealer Profits (Sierra fixed costs)	633	667	703	737	662	719	782	838
Cost to Californians (CARB FC and 15% profit share)	222	395	585	758	196	348	514	664
Cost to Californian (Sierra FC and 15% profit share)	299	473	663	835	274	426	592	741

The second panel of the table uses these assumptions to calculate price and quantity effects, along the lines of Table 7.2-1, expressed in alternative ways:

- Calculated price increases range--as they did in Table 7.2-1 for a supply elasticity of 5--from $117 to $489 per vehicle

- Expressed relative to the assumed $20,000 price of a vehicle without the regulations, price increases range from roughly .6 percent to 2.4 percent.

- Calculated sales decreases range from about 10,000 to 63,000 vehicles per year

- Expressed relative to the assumed annual sales of 1.5 million vehicles without the regulations, calculated sales decreases range from about .7 percent to 4.2 percent.

The last panel includes dollar costs per year:

- Projected annual costs of the new regulations to California consumers range from a low of $175 million (using the CARB estimate of increased marginal cost and a demand elasticity of -2) to a high of $725 million (Sierra cost estimate, demand elasticity of -1).

- Additional fixed costs of the regulations (expressed on an annual basis) are approximated by multiplying 1.5 million vehicles per year by estimates of per-LEV fixed costs by CARB ($50) and Sierra ($395)--see Table 6.1-4--to obtain values of $75 million and $592 million per year.[111] The last four rows of the table use these fixed cost estimates as alternatives.

- Annual lost profits of manufacturers and California new-vehicle dealers are calculated as the indicated value for annual fixed

---

[111]Recall, however, from Section 6.1 that CARB assumes that the fixed costs are incurred only once and that they amortize these over eight years. Thus, according to CARB assumptions there would be no additional fixed costs after eight years. Recall also that Sierra assumes that fixed costs recur over the 1994 to 2010 period, but are 50 percent lower each product cycle. Thus the fixed cost figure for Sierra used in Table 7.2-2 may understate annual fixed costs in early years and overstate them in later years.

costs[112] plus the decrease in producers' surplus implied by the changes in marginal cost, price and quantity in the relevant column. Calculated lost profits range from $116 million per year to $838 million per year.

- Finally, the cost to Californians is calculated as losses to consumers plus 15 percent of lost profits. The 15 percent figure is considered illustrative.[113] It represents a rough guess of the fraction of profits from the California new-LDV market that accrues to California residents as stockholders of vehicle manufacturers and to California residents who own new-vehicle dealerships in California. Calculated as described, annual costs to Californians of the new hardware-based regulations range from a low of $222 million to a high of $835 million.

7.2.3 Reinterpreting in Terms of Market Segments

The qualitative conclusions above can be reinterpreted if we think of the analysis as being applied to a segment of the California new ICEV market--for example, subcompacts, pickup trucks, and large sedans. In addition, this "segment interpretation" provides a basis for addressing issues that cannot arise in the market interpretation context. In

---

[112]We include in these calculations all of the fixed costs incurred because of the new regulations. These include the costs of designing the new hardware, building plants to manufacture and install the hardware, and manufacturing and installing equipment to manufacture the hardware. Clearly, some of these fixed costs have already been incurred (by the winter of 1996) and cannot be recovered (i.e., some resources have already been absorbed or used up because of the new regulations); as discussed in Section 2.4.1, these costs are now "sunk." It is important to recognize, then, that policy can no longer save these costs and, therefore, that in a cost-benefit analysis aimed at reconsidering these regulations, these costs are now irrelevant. (They were highly relevant in the past, *before* they were incurred.) We do not eliminate sunk costs from our calculations because we have no basis for estimating their magnitude. The estimates in Table 7.2-2 are reported in sufficient detail to allow readers to make whatever adjustments they think appropriate.

[113]There is sufficient information in the table to recalculate the total cost to Californians using other fractions.

particular, it allows us to consider how price and quantity effects might vary across market segments.[114]

Briefly, reinterpreting the results discussed above in terms of market segments allow us to conclude that, other things equal, the increase in price of a particular type of ICEV will be larger:

- The larger the production cost increase for this type of vehicle to comply with regulations;
- The less responsive to price buyers are in this market segment;
- The more responsive quantities supplied are to price in this market segment.

Numerical calculations analogous to those reported in Tables 7.2-1 and 7.2-2 could also be performed to apply at the market-segment level. For example, with estimates of marginal cost increases and supply and demand elasticities specific to a particular segment, we could predict the price and sales effects and estimate losses to buyers in particular segments. We do not pursue those extensions, but note for those who might that particular attention should be paid to the choice of values for demand elasticities. We used demand elasticity values of -1 and -2 to apply to the California new-LDV market as a whole. For market segments, one would expect the appropriate demand elasticity to be considerably higher (in absolute value terms), the more so the more vehicles in other market segments are viewed by consumers as similar to those in the segment under consideration. For example, new mini-vans have closer substitutes--various other types of new LDVs--than do new LDVs as a whole.

7.2.4 Different Compliance Costs Across Companies: The Competitive Case

To this point, we have assumed that all producers incur the same per-vehicle increase in marginal production cost to comply with the new regulations. However, as we discussed in Section 6.1, there was variation across the three American manufacturers in the estimates of these cost increases that they reported to us. Should we expect price

---

[114]This question cannot be addressed at the level of the entire market because in the model used here there is only one type of vehicle and one price.

increases to be driven by the cost increases of the lowest-cost compliers? The highest-cost ones? Some amount in between?

Supply and demand analysis can be used to examine these questions, albeit with considerable complication. Briefly, the answer is: "It depends on conditions that can be analyzed." We provide an overview of some analyses we've done and what these suggest about the conditions that determine the outcome.

Suppose several producers experience identical cost increases that are the lowest in the industry, and other companies experience higher cost increases. In a supply and demand framework, the size of the lowest cost increases will determine the increase in price if the lowest-cost compliers have enough capacity to supply the entire market at a marginal cost lower than the marginal costs of any higher-cost producers. In this case, which is implausible in the real-world context under discussion, the higher-cost compliers would be driven from the market even in the short run. Alternatively, suppose that the lowest-cost compliers cannot serve the entire market because their capacities are limited. Then the price prevailing in the market will be determined by the cost increases of the highest-cost compliers that can survive in the market given their costs. If all producers are able to survive, then the cost increases of the highest-cost compliers will drive the increase in price for the market as a whole.

In sum, we conclude that:

- Ignoring differences in compliance costs--as we did in Tables 7.2-1 and 7.2-2--may tend to overestimate or underestimate price increases due to the new regulations,

- If differences in compliance costs across companies are substantial, the figures in Tables 7.2-1 and 7.2-2 will tend to underestimate actual price increases if high-cost companies survive in the short-run,

- Companies that are able to comply with regulations at lower costs will tend to expand their sales and profits relative to their higher cost competitors.

We emphasize that these predictions result from competitive models that--by definition--assume that firms take price as given when they make their production decisions. This, in turn, leads to the prediction that low-cost firms will tend to price at their own cost levels and high-cost firms will be driven from the market if low-cost firms have enough production capacity to serve the whole market (given the level of demand).

7.3 IMPLICATIONS OF NON-COMPETITIVE MODELS

Thus far, we have ignored some possibilities that may be important in the real world, particularly in market segments with relatively weak competition. Here are two examples.

(1) If competitive forces don't drive prices down to costs, as they would tend not to in market segments--such as sports cars--with relatively few sellers, then low-cost compliers may take advantage of the fact that their rivals have experienced higher cost increases and increase price more than is driven by their own cost increases. Such strategic possibilities are outside the scope of competitive analysis, but are at the heart of non-competitive models such as the two models we consider presently.

(2) Low-cost producers don't drive high cost producers out of business even if they have the production capacity to serve the entire market segment because some consumers prefer the products of high-cost producers enough to pay prices high enough to cover their higher costs. This kind of possibility is captured in models with "product differentiation," one of which is discussed in closing this section. In fact, the possibility of major differences across firms in compliance costs is one of the key reasons we think it important to consider non-competitive models.

We considered two non-competitive models. In the first, (the Cournot duopoly model),[115] the only two sellers in a market segment are assumed to offer identical products but to recognize that their actions will affect market level outcomes. Because their products are

---

[115]The development here borrows liberally from Tirole (1988, pp. 218-220). The analysis involves applications of the fields of mathematics and economics called "game theory."

identical, their prices must be the same if both are to survive in the market. The model and some results are presented in Appendix 7.B.

In this model, the price increase due to the ICEV hardware regulations is determined not by one or the other of the cost increases, but by the average of them. Sales in the market decline in reaction to the increase in price. In addition, the profits of both firms decline because of the regulations unless one firm's cost increase is considerably larger than the cost increase of the other.

These results are consistent with predictions derived in the competitive analysis above, namely that increased costs due to regulations will tend to

- Increase selling prices of new LDVs in California;
- Decrease new LDV sales in California;
- Decrease benefits to California consumers;
- Decrease profits of vehicle manufacturers and dealers.

We also considered a model with differentiated products in which two sellers in a market segment are assumed to offer products that are substantially different in the eyes of buyers. Some buyers prefer the product of the first firm, and some prefer the product of the second firm. Thus, unlike the situations with the previous models, both sellers can survive in the market even if one charges a higher price. This model provides some basic insights about how strategic behavior in less competitive segments of the California LDV market where products are not very similar--e.g., sports cars--would modify conclusions drawn from the competitive analysis. For example, this model allows us to address conditions under which cost increases due to the new hardware regulations might lead to price increases of different sizes for different products

The model and some results are presented in Appendix 7.C. The model predicts that:

- If both firms have the same cost of compliance, then the two firms raise their prices by the same amount;
- If compliance costs are not identical, the firm with the higher compliance cost will raise price more than its rival;

- The firm with the larger cost of compliance (which we have concluded will raise price more) will lose sales relative to its rival.

Thus this model is also consistent with the conclusions derived from the competitive and Cournot analyses that cost increases due to regulations will

- increase selling prices of new LDVs in California, and
- decrease benefits to California consumers.

Moreover, it is also consistent with the results of the previous analyses that firms that have lower costs of compliance will tend to expand their sales and profits relative to higher-cost compliers.

7.4 MARKET-MEDIATED EFFECTS ON EMISSIONS

How will the market effects we have just discussed affect the emission reductions resulting from the new hardware regulations?

To recap the market effects:

We have shown that several different models of the California new ICEV market point in the direction that increases in production costs required to comply with the new regulations will result in increased prices for new ICEVs in California. The magnitude of the price effect cannot be estimated precisely, and a leading cause of uncertainty is the wide range of estimates of the effects of the regulations on the marginal costs of the hardware.

We also concluded--based on the standard economic reasoning that consumers will buy less of a commodity the higher is its price--that increases in prices of new ICEVs in California will decrease sales of new ICEVs in California.

Finally, we conclude that increases in prices of new ICEVs should increase the demand for used vehicles, thereby increasing their value and reducing the rate at which older vehicles are retired.

This chain of economic reasoning implies that the new regulations will tend to cause the vehicle fleet in California to be older on average (due to fewer new vehicle sales coupled with slower retirement of older vehicles) than it would otherwise be. To the extent that older vehicles have higher emission rates per year than newer vehicles, this market-mediated effect on the composition of the vehicle fleet implies that the actual emission benefits of the new regulations will tend to be less than suggested by estimates of direct emission benefits which ignore effects of changes in fleet composition.

Should we expect such indirect effects on emissions to be substantial or trivial? Should we expect them to be short-lived or long-lived? There is some evidence to bring to bear on these questions.

Gruenspecht (1982a,b) examined empirically the possibility that emission regulations would lead to more emissions (at least temporarily) because of the effects of increased prices on fleet composition. As summarized in Gruenspecht (1982a),[116] Gruenspecht studied the effects of the 1981 tightening of federal emission regulations, which he estimated to increase costs per vehicle by $475 ($350 for hardware modifications and $125 as the present value of the fuel-economy penalty of the extra hardware over the first four years of a vehicle's life). He then estimated that the regulations would increase emissions of ROG for the first five years (1981 to 1986), increase CO emissions in 1982 to 1984, but reduce NOx emissions in all years.[117]

But what about the indirect emission effects of the new California ICEV hardware regulations? Sierra (1994a, pp. 130-133) summarizes an analysis considering a "Hypothetical LEV Standard" involving 40 percent LEVs in 1997, 80 percent LEVs in 1998, and 100 percent LEVs in 1999, which it assumed to increase the price of new vehicles by $850 from a baseline of $14,000. To estimate the effects of this price increase on fleet composition, Sierra assumes that the price elasticity of demand for new vehicles is -1 and that for each new vehicle not sold because of a price increase, .7 of an older vehicle is not retired.[118] It then modifies the registration distribution in MOBILE5a accordingly.

---

[116]See also, Crandall, Gruenspecht, Keeler and Lave (1986, pp. 96-97, App. D).

[117]Econometric estimates of equations for new car sales and used car scrappage rates were used to estimate the effects of the 1981 regulations on fleet composition and then U.S. EPA's MOBILE 2 model was modified to reflect these estimates of changes in fleet composition.

[118]Sierra relies on Charles River Associates for these estimates. It reports that CRA based the -1 figure on a review of "a variety of

The results of this exercise are summarized in Table 6-9 of Sierra (1994a, p. 133). Reminiscent of Gruenspecht's results, Sierra estimates that the fleet-turnover effects of the hypothetical LEV regulation would more than outweigh the direct emission benefits in 2000; i.e., that emissions would increase in 2000 because of the regulation.[119] For the years 2005, 2010, 2015, and 2020, Sierra estimates that the hypothetical LEV regulation would (through combined direct and fleet-turnover effects) lower emissions, but that the fleet-turnover effect eliminates 62 percent, 30 percent, 17 percent, and 15 percent of the direct emission benefits in the four years, respectively.[120]

We have not tried to replicate these analyses or performed any similar analyses of our own. We merely offer the following observations on an issue that seems potentially important:

- Conceptually, the fleet turnover argument is economically sound;

- The basic approach used by Gruenspecht and Sierra seems sensible (i.e., estimate price increases, estimate sensitivity of new vehicle sales and scrappage rates to price changes for new vehicles, modify the registration distribution in a model like MOBILE or EMFAC);

- The demand elasticity of -1 and the .7 figure (number of vehicles not scrapped when one less new vehicle is purchased) used by Sierra (1994a) seem plausible, although we argued above that the appropriate price elasticity might be higher (we also considered -2) because when considering the effects of California regulations we should not expect prices outside California to rise along with California prices. Table 7.2-2

---

economic studies" and the .7 figure on Berkovic (1983). (Sierra, 1994a, p. 131).

[119]In particular, Sierra estimates that exhaust VOC emissions would average .95g/mi without the hypothetical LEV regulation, that the standard approach to estimating (direct) emissions benefits would lead to an estimate of .943 g/mi, but that if fleet turnover effects were considered emissions would be .961 g/mi in 2000.

[120]DRI/McGraw-Hill and Charles River Associates (1994, pp. 42-44) report the results of an analysis of fleet turnover on emissions, but give so little explanation of how it was done that we do not comment further on their results.

shows that an elasticity of -2 implies estimates of effects of
cost increases on new vehicle sales that are about 70 percent
larger than corresponding estimates based on assuming an
elasticity of -1. Thus, Sierra's choice of a demand elasticity
would tend to underestimate the fleet-turnover effect.

- The price increase assumed by Sierra ($850 per vehicle) is
  higher than any of the price increases we calculated to
  represent potential effects of the new hardware regulations
  (see Table 7.2-1); smaller price increases would lead to
  smaller estimates of the fleet-turnover effect on emissions,
  other things equal.

- The fact that both Gruenspecht and Sierra estimate that the
  fleet-turnover effect is attenuated over time makes sense
  because price increases for new vehicles can be expected to
  slow the retirement of older vehicles, but older vehicles will
  be retired eventually.

In sum, the stakes in the disagreement about the direct costs of
the new ICEV hardware regulations include the air quality effects of the
regulations. To the extent that the new ICEV hardware regulations
increase ICEV prices, other things equal, they will tend to be less
attractive than suggested by the analysis of narrow cost effectiveness
in Section 6.3. However, we do not have sufficient information to
adjust the narrow cost effectiveness estimates developed there to
account for price and fleet-turnover effects.

7.5 CONCLUSIONS

The analysis here illustrates the potential value of considering
market effects of policies to reduce ozone. On the cost side, we
developed information about important issues that seem not to have been
analyzed in the context of the California LDV strategy. On the benefit
side, we explained why consideration of market effects may be crucial to
accurate estimation of emissions reductions.

On the cost side, analysts of the new ICEV hardware regulations
have emphasized additional vehicle production costs required for
compliance. Little analytic attention has been paid to who will bear

these costs. We have shown how estimates of additional production costs of new California LDVs can be used to predict resulting increases in their prices. Predicted price increases can, in turn, be used to analyze the distribution of costs between new car buyers--virtually all of whom are Californians--and owners of vehicle manufacturing companies and California vehicle dealers, some of whom are Californians.

On the emissions side, price increases for new vehicles--and consequent changes in the age composition of the vehicle fleet--may have substantial implications for the emission reductions that can actually be expected from policies that increase the costs of producing new vehicles. We have not attempted to quantify these effects, but previous analyses suggest that if price increases are near the high end of the range we estimated (see Table 7.2-2), such indirect effects on emissions could nullify the direct emissions benefits of the regulations for a period of at least a few years and substantially attenuate the total emission benefits of the regulations for several more years.

There is a wide range of disagreement about the size of the production cost increases that drive the market-mediated effects. We are unable to narrow this range. At the very least, we hope to have clarified--in the case of the new regulations that require hardware improvements in new California ICEVs--the potential stakes for Californians, and how the actual stakes depend on the actual size of the production cost increases. We have also shown how someone with an estimate for marginal production cost increases could go about developing estimates of the effects of the new hardware regulations on average prices and annual sales of new ICEVs in California and the annual dollar costs to consumers and producers.

8. DIRECT COSTS AND BENEFITS OF NON-HARDWARE BASED ICEV ELEMENTS

OVERVIEW AND PREVIEW OF FINDINGS

In this section, we examine the direct costs and emission reductions of the non-hardware based elements of California's LDV strategy. We first consider California's Phase 2 gasoline (CP2G). We then turn to the elements of the strategy that attempt to limit the deterioration of emission control systems. Smog Check II is designed to identify and require repair of all vehicles, new and old, whose emissions systems are working improperly. On-board Diagnostics (OBD II) is designed to detect improperly functioning emission control systems and aid in their repair. The accelerated vehicle retirement (AVR) program for the South Coast attempts to remove older, high polluting vehicles from the fleet.

After discussing the direct costs, emission reductions, and narrow cost effectiveness of these elements, we consider--in Section 9--market responses to these programs.

To preview the findings of this section:

(1) The direct costs of CP2G will likely be between 7 and 19 cents a gallon, which includes the cost of a slight reduction in gas mileage. CP2G may also reduce the costs of vehicle emission control systems, but there appear to be no estimates of the magnitude of this effect. The studies reviewed suggest that CP2G will reduce ROG and NOx emissions up to 25 percent for some vehicles currently on the road, but because the percent reductions appear to vary substantially depending on model year and mileage, the percentage reduction for the entire fleet may be significantly less. Because CP2G will probably eliminate the discrepancy between the fuel used for certification and the fuel actually used by drivers, the CP2G may also substantially reduce emissions of new vehicles certified on CP2G. The reduction may be about 20 percent.

(2) Narrow cost-effectiveness ratios for CP2G vary from $9,000 to $46,500 per ton of ROG plus NOx, depending on what cost and emission

reduction estimates are used. This range may overstate true narrow cost effectiveness because the estimates do not include any cost saving in ICEV hardware and do not appear to include emission reductions for vehicles certified on CP2G.

(3) Smog Check II attempts to fix many of the suspected problems with the current inspection and maintenance program. However, it is highly uncertain whether the new program will be substantially more effective than the current one. In part because repair costs are uncertain, the incremental costs of the program are also uncertain. NCERs estimated for programs similar to Smog Check II run from $500 to $5,500 per ton ROG plus NOx, but given the uncertainty over emission reductions, we are not at all confident that the actual NCER will fall in or near this range.

(4) OBD II may already have had a major effect on how manufacturers design and build emissions control systems. It may reduce the number of malfunctioning emission control systems in use, but more information is needed on how drivers respond to the check-engine light both when the vehicle is under warranty and when it is not. OBD II has great potential to improve the inspection and maintenance process, but how much it will do so remains uncertain because it is still easy for a smog-check technician to overlook a check-engine light.

(5) Existing studies put the NCER for OBD II anywhere from $2,000 to $15,000 per ton ROG plus NOx. But, given that the studies reviewed do not appear to include the repair costs induced by OBD II or address the issues concerning driver response to the check-engine light, it is highly speculative whether or not the NCER will fall in this range.

(6) The direct costs of the accelerated vehicle retirement (AVR) program proposed for the South Coast--which include transportation services lost from scrapped vehicles and program administration costs-- are likely to be in the range of $700-$1,000 per vehicle scrapped. Direct emissions benefits are quite uncertain because it is very difficult to predict the emission levels of retired vehicles and the replacement transportation. NCERs for AVR programs estimated in studies we reviewed range from $2,000-$10,000 per ton of ROG + NOx. Potentially important considerations not accounted for in these NCERs include

potentially beneficial interactions with I&M, migration of older vehicles into the South Coast, and incentives for owners of older vehicles to delay scrapping or emission repairs or to tamper with vehicles to make them dirtier.

8.1 REFORMULATED GASOLINE

Starting on January 1, 1996, all gasoline sold in California was required to meet California Phase 2 reformulated gasoline (CP2G) specifications. CCP2G has tremendous potential for reducing emissions from in-use vehicles because it will very quickly be used by all vehicles in the fleet.

The principal studies we reviewed in evaluating this element of the LDV strategy are Battelle (1995), Burns et al. (1995), CARB (1991), CARB (1995d) and Sierra (1994a). We first discuss estimates of the direct costs of CP2G before turning to estimates of emission reductions.

8.1.1 Direct Costs

There is consensus about the direct resource costs of CP2G. CARB initially estimated that CP2G would increase gasoline production costs from 12 to 16 cents per gallon between 1996 and 2005 depending on the refiner (CARB, 1991, p. 134). CARB is not explicit about what type of gasoline it is using for comparison, but given that the study was conducted in 1991, the gasoline was probably RF-A, the industry average gas in 1989. CARB's estimate includes variable and fixed production costs, but it does not include a fuel mileage penalty. CARB reports that some refiners estimate decreased fuel economy will cost consumers 2 to 4 cents per gallon (CARB, 1991, p. 134).[121] CARB also does not include additional costs that may be incurred by gasoline retailers, such as higher inventory carrying costs. It seems unlikely, however, that these costs would be significant on a cents per gallon basis.

CARB (1995d) more recently estimated that CP2G would increase the average cost of gasoline 10 cents per gallon relative to Phase 1 gasoline, with the increase varying from 5 to 15 cents depending on

---

[121]CARB's estimate is consistent with more recent studies on CP2G. Burns et. al. (1995, p. 147) show fuel efficiency declining 2 to 4 percent when CP2G is compared with RF-A.

refiner. Part of the difference from its earlier estimate is due to the change in baseline (recall that Phase 1 gasoline is thought to cost 2 to 3 cents more than RF-A), but part represents a decrease in the lower end of the initial estimate.

Sierra puts the incremental cost of CP2G at approximately 11 cents per gallon, although Sierra does not state precisely what fuel is being used for comparison (Sierra, 1994a, p. 108). In addition to fixed and variable costs, Sierra's estimate appears to include a fuel economy penalty. Sierra does not indicate what, if any, additional retail costs are included.

When auto manufacturers start certifying vehicles on CP2G, the costs of their emission control systems may decline. This is because less emission control hardware, and perhaps a smaller investment in software, may be necessary to achieve the certification standards. For example, the lower Reid Vapor Pressure of CP2G may decrease the size of the charcoal canister needed for the evaporative emission control system, and lower sulfur content may extend the life of the oxygen sensors or the efficiency of catalysts.[122] The magnitude of these effects will depend not on the comparison of CP2G and current in-use fuel, but on the comparison between CP2G and the certification fuel.

We have seen little information comparing the emission characteristics of CP2G and the certification fuel. In the one study we found where the two fuels were compared, ROG and CO emissions were 31 and 24 percent lower when CP2G rather than the certification fuel was used in low-emission vehicles, but emissions were 11 percent higher for NOx (Lippincott, Segal, and Wang, 1993). How these differences will affect manufacturer emission control costs is unknown.

To the extent that the CP2G regulation lowers emission control costs of auto manufacturers, the overall resource costs of CP2G will be lower than the direct costs per gallon cited above.

_____

[122]Indeed, OBD II systems as currently designed may not even work with high sulfur fuels.

8.1.2 Direct Emission Benefits

In our analysis of CP2G, we define direct emission benefits as the change in emissions caused by CP2G, assuming there is no change in vehicle miles traveled or other driver response such as increased use of fuel additives. Changes in VMT due to higher prices of gasoline to consumers will be discussed in Section 9.1.

The direct emission benefits generated by CP2G will differ depending on whether the vehicle was certified on indolene or on CP2G. Vehicles currently on the road were certified on indolene. It is likely that models introduced in the future will be certified on CP2G. For vehicles certified on indolene, emission reductions can be estimated by comparing emissions using the baseline fuel (California Phase 1 RFG in our analysis) and CP2G. For vehicles certified on CP2G, the emission reductions depend not only on the properties of CP2G and the baseline fuel, but also on the certification fuel.

We first discuss emission reductions in vehicles not certified on CP2G, which are all vehicles on the road today. We then consider emission reductions from vehicles certified on CP2G. We do not know when manufacturers will shift to CP2G for certification, but it will likely be soon after CP2G is introduced in June 1996.

Emission Reductions in Existing Vehicles. Table 8.1-1 summarizes the results of three studies that compare emissions from vehicles using CP2G with those using the industry average gasoline in 1989 (RF-A). None of the studies we reviewed compared CP2G emissions with California Phase 1 RFG emissions. The estimates reviewed here may thus overstate the difference between CP2G and Phase 1 RFG, but by how much is unknown.

The studies reviewed generally find that CP2G substantially reduces emissions, but the estimates vary across studies and across vehicle model year and mileage within individual studies. As shown in Table 8.1-1, the results are based on small numbers of vehicles, so the statistical confidence intervals around the estimates are relatively large. The studies suggest that NMOG exhaust reductions are smaller for older vehicles (Burns et al., and CARB) and decline as vehicle mileage increases (Battelle and Burns et al.). The decline for older vehicles may be because these vehicle have higher mileage or perhaps because emission control technology differs. Note, however, that absolute emission reductions may not be lower for older and higher mileage cars because baseline emission levels increase with mileage.

CP2G also appears to reduce NOx emissions, but the reductions are less in percentage terms than for ROG. There is also no clear relationship between vehicle age and mileage and the percent NOx reduction.

The studies generally show substantial reductions in evaporative emissions, although in one study (Burns et al.) the percentage reductions are small for some model years. The specific reactivity of CP2G is also lower than RF-A. Specific reactivity is analogous to the reactivity adjustment factors discussed in Section 4.1. The values reported in the last column of Table 8.1-1 are consistent with the reactivity adjustment factors established by CARB for CP2G--0.98 for TLEVs and 0.94 for LEVs (Battelle, 1995, p. 77).

Emission Reductions in New Vehicles. California Phase 2 reformulated gasoline is carefully specified in CARB regulations so it is likely that when CP2G is used for certification, the certification fuel will be very similar to the in-use fuel. This will eliminate the discrepancy between the emission characteristics of the fuel currently used in certification (indolene) and that actually used (RF-A). As discussed in Section 4.2, Lippincott, Segal, and Wang (1993) estimate that exhaust emissions for ROG and NOx are 23 and 19 percent lower, respectively, when indolene is used rather than RF-A. Thus, the CP2G rule may result in approximately a 20 percent reduction in exhaust emissions by eliminating the discrepancy between the certification fuel and the in-use fuel. In its analysis, CARB assumes that CP2G will produce no emission benefits in 1996 and later vehicles (see Table 8.1-1). This is because they assume that vehicles will continue to just meet the certification standard with or without CP2G (although perhaps more cheaply with CP2G) and apparently do not consider the current discrepancy between certification fuel and in-use fuel.

Table 8.1-1

Direct Emission Reductions of California Phase 2 Gasoline in Existing Vehicles

Study	Type of Vehicle	Vehicle Model Year	Number of Vehicles Tested	Mileage (1000s)	Percent Reduction of CP2G Relative to RF-A			
					Exhaust NMOG (gm/mi)	NOx (gm/mi)	Diurnal Evap. (gm/test)	Specific Reactivity (gm ozone/ gm NMOG)
Battelle (1995, pp. H-2,3)[a]	Medium- and heavy-duty vans	1992	48[b]	5	-22	2	--	--
				15	-20	-13	-14	-2
				25	-15	-19	--	--
CARB (1991, pp. 59, 61)	Light-duty vehicles	1996+	--[c]	--	0	0	0	--
		1986-95	--	--	-27	-20	-15	--
		1981-85			-7	1	-23	--
		1975-80	--	--	2	0	-27	--
		Pre 1975	--	--	-10	2	-29	--
Burns et al. (1995, p. 147)	Light-duty vehicles	1994	6[d]	>4	-27	-16	-16	-3
		1989	10[d]	16-33	-22	-7	-4	-6
		1983-85	7[d]	46-79	-12	-9	-5	-9

[a] Battelle separately reports results for the vehicles of three different manufacturers. We average the percentage difference for the three manufacturers.

[b] 21 vehicles were fueled with Phase 2 RFG and 27 were control vans fueled with RF-A.

[c] CARB built an emission model based on data on emissions from vehicles using several different types of fuel. CARB did not provide information on the number of vehicles tested.

[d] Each vehicle tested both on Phase 2 RFG and RF-A.

CARB calculates the total ROG plus NOx emission reductions due to CP2G in tons per day. In its 1991 study, it predicts total reductions in 1996 on-road emissions will be 158 tons per day in ozone non-attainment areas with the reductions declining over time (CARB, 1991, p. 139).[123] Estimated emission reductions rose to 300 tons per day in a 1994 CARB Fact Sheet on CP2G, but no explanation for the difference was provided (CARB, 1995d).

8.1.3 Narrow Cost-Effectiveness Ratios

CARB's revised estimates of direct costs and its 1991 estimates of direct emissions reductions between 1996 and 2005 for ROG and NOx (CARB, 1991, p. 139), imply NCERs of $17,200 to $46,500 per ton of ROG plus NOx.[124] (The range is due to a 7 to 19 cent per gallon variation in cost, which includes a 2 to 4 cent per gallon fuel economy cost). NCERs decrease from to $9,000 to $24,490 using CARB's 1994 emission reduction estimates.[125] Setting aside the uncertainty over emissions reductions in existing vehicles, both these ranges may be too high because they do not consider any reductions in the cost of vehicle emission control systems made possible by CP2G. The $17,200 to $46,500 range may also be too high because CARB attributes no emission reductions to newly produced vehicles. This caveat may apply to the $9,000 to $24,490 range as well, but we do not know what assumptions were made about newly produced vehicles when the emission reductions behind these numbers were calculated.

These NCERs are narrow because they do not include effects such as the change in VMT induced by higher gasoline prices or reductions in emissions other than ROG and NOx.

---

[123]Emission reductions decline over time because vehicles certified on CP2G (which CARB assumes generate no emission reductions) make up an increasing proportion of the fleet.

[124]This range is much higher than the $10,800 to $14,400 estimated by CARB because (1) CARB included tons of CO and SO_2 reduced, and we do not, and (2) CARB allocated 20 percent of the costs to toxic pollutant reduction, and we do not.

[125]The ranges are calculated based on the ratio between the emission reductions in CARB's initial and subsequent estimates.

8.2 SMOG CHECK II

A smoothly functioning inspection and maintenance program has significant potential for reducing emissions. If, as previous studies have suggested, 10 percent of the vehicles emit 50 percent of the emissions, merely cleaning up these vehicles to the average of the remaining fleet would reduce LDV emissions by 40 percent. Even though the effectiveness of Smog Check II (SC II) is central to an effective ICEV emission control strategy, the costs and emissions reductions it will generate remain unclear.

The principal studies of Smog Check II that we reviewed are Aroesty et al. (1994), Glazer et al. (1995), Klausmeier (1995), McConnell and Harrington (1992), and the California I/M Review Committee in Sommerville (1993).

8.2.1 Direct Costs

McConnell and Harrington (1992, p. 37) identify four major components of the direct costs of inspection and maintenance programs: inspection costs, driver costs, net repair costs, and oversight and enforcement costs. *Inspection costs* are the annualized sum of labor, test equipment, land, and building costs. *Driver costs* are the value of driver time spent on vehicle inspection and repair and the costs of replacement transportation. *Net repair costs* are the costs of repairing the vehicle, net of any reduction in fuel costs due to an increase in gas mileage resulting from repairs. *Enforcement and oversight costs* are the costs incurred by BAR and CARB to administer and enforce the program.

There have been no studies that have directly estimated the costs of SC II. In their Fourth Report to the California legislature, the California I/M Review Committee (Review Committee) estimated the costs of various changes to the then existing inspection and maintenance program (Sommerville, 1993). Although the alternatives analyzed were not identical to SC II, the Review Committee's estimates can give a sense of how the costs of the program might change. We draw on this information to examine each of the four cost components identified above.

Inspection Costs. As shown in Table 8.2-1, the Review Committee estimates that inspections cost about $21 per test under the current system (Sommerville, 1993, p. 94). The Review Committee estimated that new constant-speed dynamometers[126] testing equipment required for SC II would cost about $40,000 per test lane, and that if all tests were done as they are today in many low volume test-and-repair stations, the cost per test would rise to $33 (Sommerville, 1995, pp. 82, 94). In contrast, if tests were done in a relatively small number of test-only facilities, the Review Committee estimated that the cost per test would actually fall to $15 (Sommerville, 1993, p. 88). The main reasons given by Sommerville for this difference are (1) high cost mechanics perform smog-checks in many of the test-and-repair stations but lower skilled labor is adequate in the test-only stations, and (2) test-only stations end up testing more vehicles per hour per test lane than test-and-repair stations.

Table 8.2-1

Costs of Current Smog-Check Program Estimated by California I&M Review Committee[a]

Cost per vehicle inspected ($/vehicle)	56
Inspection	21
Net repair	14
Oversight and enforcement	7
Driver costs	14
Number of inspections (millions)	9
Annual costs ($ millions)	504[b]

[a]Sommerville (1993).

[b]Assumes 9 million vehicles inspected per year.

The average test cost in SC II will presumably fall between these two estimates. Exactly where will depend on the percent of tests done in each type of station. As discussed in Section 5.5, SC II requires approximately 15 percent of vehicles to be tested in test-only stations. If only the required percentage is tested in test-only stations, the average cost per test would be $30. However, if costs and prices in

---

[126]Vehicles are tested under load at constant speed.

test-only stations are lower, consumers may migrate to these stations if there is sufficient capacity. BAR policy on licensing test-only station will, in part, determine what the test-only capacity will be. It is thus hard to predict how the average test cost in SC II will differ from that today, but the available data suggest that the difference may be small.

Driver Costs. The Review Committee predicted that driver costs would be less in a test-only system than in the current system, although the difference was small--$12.67 versus $13.87 per driver (Sommerville, 1993, p. 103).[127] They reasoned that drivers spend more time driving between the test-only and repair stations in a test-only setup, but the time is more than offset by shorter test time and a shorter waiting period. We find this conclusion counterintuitive and suggest it warrants further investigation. The current program allows test-only stations, and there are currently many stations that have no or only limited repair capability. It would seem that taking an option away, the test-and-repair station, would make drivers worse off. In addition, if the program becomes more effective, presumably more repairs will be required, thereby increasing the time drivers spend on inspection and repair activities. Thus, it seems likely that driver costs would be higher under SC II, but how much higher is uncertain.

Net Repair Costs. The Review Committee estimated that repair costs are about $60 per failed vehicle, which amounts to $12 per vehicle inspected because about 20 percent of vehicles inspected fail under the current program. The Review Committee assumed that repair costs will increase in proportion to the additional emissions reduced (Sommerville, 1993, pp. 107-108). However, they do not present any data on the relationship between emission reduction and repair costs. As we will see shortly, there is a great deal of uncertainty about what the emission reductions of SC II will be; consequently, even if the Review Committee's method for scaling up repair cost is accurate, how much to scale it up is uncertain.

---

[127]The driver cost magnitudes are similar to those reported in McConnell and Harrington (1992, p. 43).

Oversight and Enforcement Costs. Oversight and enforcement costs are funded by a fee levied on every inspection. The fee is $7.00 under the current system, which, multiplied by the approximately 9 million inspections per year, implies an annual budget of $63 million. The fee has recently gone up to $7.75, suggesting that enforcement costs of the new program may be at most 10 percent higher than the current program. However, it is possible that the fee would have been raised even if there had been no new program.

As shown in Table 8.2-1, the current program costs approximately one-half billion dollars per year based on the Review Committee estimates. There is considerable uncertainty about how costs will change under SC II. The costs will depend critically on how many inspections per year are required and on how effective the program is in detecting high emitters and requiring repair of inspected vehicles-- subjects to which we now turn.

8.2.2 Direct Emission Reductions

Most of the studies reviewed recognize that the behavioral responses of drivers and smog-check technicians are central to the emission reductions produced by the smog-check program. Thus, to varying degrees, they attempt to incorporate these responses in their analyses of the program. We follow suit and, in our analysis of Smog Check II, define direct emission reductions to include the effects of behavioral responses.

To evaluate the potential emission reductions from Smog Check II, we start by assessing how the program addresses the weaknesses of the existing program identified in Section 4.5: inadequate tests, low cost ceilings for waivers, predictable tests, technician fraud, and inability of technicians to fix vehicles. We then evaluate quantitative estimates of the emission reductions predicted for SC II.

How Smog Check II Addresses Weaknesses of Existing Program

Inadequate Test Procedures. Overall, SC II makes some improvement in test procedures, but important gaps remain. On the positive side, SC II will measure NOx using a constant speed dynamometer. This may improve identification of high NOx emitters. On the negative side, SC

II does not fix many of the weakness of the current test procedure. Cold-start emissions will still not be directly tested in Smog Check II. Thus a vehicle may pass an inspection even if the emission control system is not properly functioning during this critical period. Tests of evaporative emissions will still not be very thorough. A gas-cap pressure test will be used to test for leaks in the fuel system, but important parts of the evaporative control system will not be tested.[128] It is also unlikely that the new test procedure will solve problems of detecting vehicles with high, but variable, emissions. Even U.S. EPA's more sophisticated test, the IM240, does not seem to solve this problem.[129]

Low Cost Ceilings for Waivers. SC II requires repair costs to exceed $450 before a waiver can be issued and does not allow waivers in two consecutive years. In principle, these changes should result in more vehicles being fixed. There is some evidence to support this assumption. In the third quarter of 1994, when the waiver threshold varied from $50 to $350, approximately 6 percent of vehicles that failed their initial inspection received waivers. That percentage fell to about 2 percent in 1995, the first quarter after the threshold was raised to $450.

However, the decrease in waiver rates cannot be translated directly into emission reductions. The size of the effect depends critically on how many vehicles are falsely passed. The higher repair limit in SC II

---

[128]For example, purging of the evaporative canister is not tested. CARB is experimenting with an innovative test of the entire evaporative system (helium-gas tests) but its effectiveness has not yet been demonstrated.

[129]The General Accounting Office reports: "We reviewed U.S. EPA data on vehicles that were initially tested at the Hammond, Indiana, testing site and subsequently tested at U.S. EPA's contractor laboratory facility in New Carlisle, Indiana. We found that test results can vary substantially from one location to the other. We identified 64 vehicles--1986 models year or newer--that failed the IM240 test at the Hammond testing site and were sent for further test and repair services at the contractor's laboratory. Eighteen of the 64 vehicles, or 28 percent, that initially failed on IM240 test at the Hammond testing site passed a second IM240 test at the laboratory in New Carlisle, even though no repairs were made to the 18 vehicles" (cited in Small and Kazimi, 1995, p. 90).

may have induced drivers to look more vigorously for smog-check stations that will falsely pass them. The same effect may result from disallowing waivers in consecutive years. This feedback is complex and difficult to model. But, it does raise questions about the ultimate effect of tightening waiver requirements if mechanic fraud is not controlled.

Predictable Tests. With remote sensing, SC II introduces an element of uncertainty about when vehicles will be tested. By requiring annual tests for vehicles previously identified as high emitters, SC II also increases the test frequency for high emitting vehicles. These measures may deter drivers from tampering.[130] Vehicles identified as high-emitters with remote sensing must be tested within 30 days and repaired if necessary within another 30 days. They will then be tested annually for 2 to 5 years.

However, it is difficult to assess what the ultimate effects on tampering will be, for two reasons. First, even though remote sensing is a promising technology, its effectiveness has yet to be determined. In the evaluation of a 1994 pilot remote sensing program in Sacramento, Klausmeier et al., (1995, pp. 3-63, 3-68) found that remote sensors identified 11 percent of the fleet as high emitters and that these emitters accounted for 40 percent of excess fleet emissions. Unfortunately, 25 percent of the vehicles identified did not fail a smog check test. This false failure rate may be too high to make remote sensing politically acceptable. Second, even if detected, drivers will have plenty of time before testing to undo any tampering.[131]

Through remote sensing, SC II may also reduce the amount of time that high emitters are on the road. High emitters will be subject to

----

[130]Some argue that new car technology will make it very difficult to tamper with vehicles (see Ross et al., 1995, p. 16), regardless of the type of I&M program. So far, the data do not support this view. Aroesty et al. (1994, Figure 3.1) show that tampering rates have not declined for more recent model year vehicles. Advertisements and articles on aftermarket computer engine control chips suggest that such customizations are popular. Tampering may well continue but evolve into different forms.

[131]Although drivers may give up tampering if the expected time between inspections is low.

inspection and repair soon after they are identified by remote sensing, rather than at the next biennial review. This is a sensible strategy, but again depends both on the effectiveness of remote sensing and on the test and repair process. We now turn to the latter topic.

Technician Fraud. SC II attempts to reduce fraud by installing real-time data links between test stations and BAR, increasing enforcement, and requiring a proportion of the fleet to be tested in test-only facilities. These changes may well significantly reduce false passes; but it is not obvious that this will happen. The issues we discuss below should make policy makers wary of claims that fraud in the new system will be much lower than in the old.

Real-time data links are intended to aid enforcement. For example, with real time data links, enforcement agents will be able to retest a suspected high emitter immediately after it has received a smog certificate. Some aspects of the new data links may have unintended effects, however. For example, the computer system will notify mechanics if a car has recently failed tests and may be shopping for a certificate. This may make the mechanic wary of falsely passing this vehicle, but may give him the green light to falsely pass others.

The increased data available from remote sensing and the increased investment in training and test equipment required of smog-check stations may also provide important deterrents to fraud. Data from remote sensing devices could be used to identify stations that regularly passed vehicles identified as high emitters. The new testing equipment will cost $20,000 to $40,000, and smog-check stations may not want to risk their investment in equipment or training by having their license revoked due to fraud convictions. The effectiveness of these incentives depends on the effectiveness of enforcement.

Many assert that fraud will be less in test-only stations than in test and repair stations,[132] and SC II hopes to reduce fraud by requiring 15 percent of vehicles to be tested in test-only stations. It is not obvious that mechanics' incentives to falsely pass vehicles are

---

[132]U.S. EPA, for example, assumes that emission reductions in systems that separate test from repair are twice as great as those that allow combined test and repair.

less in test-only stations,[133] but it may be easier to monitor the 50 to 75 test-only stations planned than the approximately 10,000 test-and-repair stations. Thus the effectiveness of the system still depends on enforcement. BAR staff suggested that inspectors may be permanently stationed at test-only stations, but this will not reduce fraud if, for example, inspectors are not thorough or turn a blind eye to infractions.

Past experience with test-only programs provides little evidence that programs that require testing in relatively few test-only stations perform any better than programs with test-and-repair stations. After reviewing the literature, Aroesty et al. (1994, p. 32) conclude that tampering and overall failure rates do not differ significantly between regions that utilize centralized, decentralized, or no I&M program. Glazer (1995, p. 92) cite a study of a centralized program targeting CO emission in Minneapolis/St.Paul (Scherrer and Kittelson, 1994). The study found that CO levels fell only 1.3 percent (plus or minus 1.4 percent) more than they would have with no program--hardly an impressive showing.

Inability to Fix Vehicles. The new system will strengthen mechanic training requirements, thus potentially increasing the ability of mechanics to diagnose and repair vehicles. This may well be the case, but the continuing pressure from drivers to control costs may limit the consequent emission reductions.

Quantitative Estimates of Effectiveness of Smog Check II

In a March 1995 report, Radian simulated the effectiveness of a biennial inspection and maintenance program very similar to SC II (Klausmeier, 1995, Section 5). The program Radian simulated sent 18 percent of the fleet tested each year to test-only stations. The vehicles required to go to test-only stations included

- A 2 percent random sample of all vehicles due for inspection (one percent of the fleet in a biennial inspection program),

_____

[133]Mechanics in test-only stations may face similar pressures to keep customers coming back that mechanics in test-and-repair stations face.

- Vehicles identified as high-emitters in current or recent inspections (percent unspecified),
- Approximately 25 percent of vehicles due for inspection that were identified as possible high emitters using Radian's high emitter profile,[134] and
- Vehicles not due for inspection identified by remote sensing as high emitters (the number of vehicles is not disclosed, but it was no more than 5 percent of fleet).

Radian used California's I&M model, CALIMFAC, to simulate the effects of the program.[135] They modified the model to incorporate features of the new program and the new data on high emitter identification rates and repair effectiveness analyzed in their report. Radian (Klausmeier, 1995, p. 5-34) estimated that ROG and NOx emissions would be 22 and 14 percent lower respectively in the year 2000 than they would have been had there been no I&M program. These reductions compare to the 18 percent and 7 percent reductions for ROG and NOx respectively estimated by the Review Committee for the current program (see Section 4.5). Radian's simulations thus imply that SC II will eliminate substantially more emissions than the current program.

We are uncertain about the reliability of these estimates. Several assumptions may cause the Radian model to overstate the actual emission reductions:

- Identification rates for vehicles that should fail inspection in test-only stations are based on data on emissions tests by CARB mechanics. Zero mechanic fraud is assumed.

_____

[134]The high emitter profile uses past smog check data to identify those vehicles most likely to fail (Klausmeier, 1995, p. 4-2). The profile Radian developed ends up targeting very few cars that are less than 7 years old and 70 to 80 percent of cars greater than 12 years old (Klausmeier, 1995, p. 4-16).

[135]CALIMFAC is similar in data and structure to the EMFAC models discussed previously, but has been extended to include I&M program features.

- Repair rates are based on how well CARB mechanics can repair vehicles, not on the performance of real world mechanics who face pressures from customers to control costs.[136]

- Radian appears to assume that full pressure and purge tests of the evaporative system are done, but SC II requires only gas cap pressure tests.

We also do not know if remote sensing will turn out to be a workable technology, and there is considerable uncertainty about how well the inspection and maintenance models that Radian modified represent the real world.[137]

Smog Check II is a ambitious effort to make California's inspection and maintenance program more effective. However, the program's effects are very uncertain. If enforcement reduces mechanic fraud, and if remote sensing is successful in identifying high-emitters on the road, it is quite possible that the reductions may match Radian's predictions. However, we also think it quite possible that the improvements may be minimal.

8.2.3 Narrow Cost-Effectiveness Ratio

There are no NCER estimates specifically for Smog Check II. The Review Committee did calculate NCERs for various changes to the current Smog Check program, many of which shared features with Smog Check II. Their estimated NCERs ranged from approximately $500 to $5,500 per ton of ROG plus NOx removed for different program options (Sommerville, 1993, p. 115).[138] We do not know whether the NCER for Smog Check II

---

[136]Radian does assume the repair effectiveness in test-and-repair stations is half that of test-only stations. This is in keeping with assumptions (that are hotly contested) used in U.S. EPA models.

[137]For example, U.S. EPA's MOBILE model predicted 25 percent reduction in CO emission for the Minneapolis/St. Paul program discussed above when a study that measured changes in ambient air concentrations found emission reductions of only 1.3 percent (Aroesty et al., 1994, Figure 3.6). The discrepancy between some empirical evidence that Smog Check is having little effect and the model-based predictions of Review Committee also provides reason for pause.

[138]The lower estimate is for a centralized program with no cost limit, improved inspection quality, and steady-state dynamometer test. The higher estimate is for a decentralized program with improved inspection quality, and steady-state dynamometer test. The Review

will end up in this range. Most fundamentally, one can reasonably wonder whether the new program will reduce emissions much more than the old.

8.3 ON-BOARD DIAGNOSTICS II

We discussed the direct costs of OBD II in Section 6.1.2. Estimates of direct variable costs ranged from $45 to $111 per vehicle; including fixed costs and dealer margin increased the upper bound to $157 (see Table 6.1-3). In this section we examine how OBD II may affect LDV emissions. The principal studies we reviewed are Albu et al. (1992), CARB (1989b), and Sierra (1994a). In our analysis of OBD II, we define direct emission reductions to include the behavioral responses of drivers and smog-check technicians to the system.

8.3.1 Direct Emission Reductions

The OBD II system will monitor each component of the vehicle emission control system. When the OBD II system detects a fault, a light on the vehicle dashboard (the "check-engine" light) is supposed to illuminate. The system is designed so that when it detects a fault, the emissions of the vehicle would be above certification standards with high probability.[139]

However, even if vehicle emissions are above certification standards, the OBD II system will not necessarily detect a fault. For example, the performance of each emission control component could be within its allowed range, but the combined effect of several poorly performing components could cause the vehicle to fail a certification test (CARB, 1989b, p. 32).

CARB and Sierra both estimate the emission reduction effects of OBD II. CARB (1989b, Attachment I) first predicted what type of malfunctions OBD II would detect. Then, using estimates of how often these malfunctions occur in the fleet and on the reduction in emissions

---

Committee estimates the NCER for the current program is $7,560 per ton ROG plus NOx. In all cases we have allocated all costs to ROG and NOx (and none to CO reduction).

[139]In most cases a malfunction is determined to occur if the deteriorated or failed component causes emission to exceed 1.5 times the applicable emission standard (Albu, Kao, and Cackette, 1992, p.22).

when they were repaired by CARB mechanics, CARB estimated how much emissions would fall.[140] In effect, CARB removes the emissions of a certain set of malfunctions from the fleet. Sierra, on the other hand, estimates emission reductions by assuming that OBD II will increase the identification rates for vehicles that should fail their smog check inspections (Sierra, 1994a, p. 55). Sierra is vague about exactly how much higher the identification rates would be.

Some technical questions remain about both of these estimates, but technical concerns pale in comparison to uncertainties around the institutional and behavioral responses to OBD II.[141] The main oversight in both the CARB and Sierra studies is that they do not consider the institutions or the behavior needed for OBD II to actually reduce emissions. CARB basically assumes that people will take their vehicles in for repair if the check-engine light comes on. However, drivers may not take their cars in for repair if they detect no change in performance and believe that the check-engine light only indicates problems with the emission system. Sierra assumes that if the check-engine light is on, a smog-check mechanic is more likely to identify an emission system problem. Since 1990 a vehicle is not supposed to pass a smog check if the check-engine light is on. But whether this requirement has made any difference on the identification of emission system problems depends on the efficacy of the Smog Check program.

To illustrate how pervasive these issues are, we briefly examine how the response of manufacturers and drivers and the performance of the inspection and maintenance program might influence the effectiveness of OBD II.

---

[140]CARB uses data from its surveillance program (see Section 3) to determine the prevalence of various malfunctions in the on-road population.

[141]See Albu, Kao, and Cackette (1992 pp. 25-29) for a discussion of some potential problems OBD II may not detect. Potential problems that might not be detected include malfunctions of mechanical/pneumatic systems (such as variable valve timing mechanisms) because they are generally not monitored. Also, even though OBD II can monitor whether some components are operating within their normal range, it often cannot tell how well they are operating in that range. For example, coolant temperature sensors may generate readings that are in the range of plausible coolant temperatures, but may not be correct.

Manufacturers. We have not been able to review in detail how tight the emission system component performance tolerances will be under OBD II. However, our discussions with manufacturers suggest that they are very concerned about keeping the check-engine light from illuminating because they are worried about warranty costs, reputation effects, and emission system recalls. These possible costs give manufacturers powerful incentives to install durable emission control equipment--a real benefit of OBD II. It also gives firms powerful incentives to design an OBD II system that is as forgiving as possible. For example, manufacturers could conceivably program the system to loosen the performance tolerances once the vehicle is no longer subject to recall (100,000 miles). It will be up to CARB staff to enforce the required OBD II system performance.

Drivers. Whether a driver brings a car with an illuminated check-engine light in for repair depends on the costs and the benefits to the driver. The costs are the vehicle repair costs and the time and inconvenience involved. The benefits are possibly better vehicle performance, possibly higher resale value, and as will be discussed below, possibly lower inspection and maintenance costs.[142] As long as the vehicle is under warranty, there would be no repair costs, but the time and inconvenience of taking the car for repair remain. If emission system failures do not affect vehicle performance, drivers may ignore the check-engine light for long periods of time, particularly once the vehicle is off warranty.[143,144]

Inspection and Maintenance. There are important interactions between the inspection and maintenance and OBD II. As discussed above, if Smog Check II is completely ineffective, OBD II may have little

---

[142]Some consumers may also consider the environmental benefits of repairing the vehicle.

[143]CARB staff believe that 67 to 75 percent of drivers take the vehicle in for repair when the light comes on. We have not seen any studies on this issue. Before interpreting such figures, one would want to know how long drivers waited before bringing in their vehicles and whether the vehicles were still under warranty.

[144]Emission control is becoming increasingly integrated into overall powertrain design, and there may be little separation between vehicle performance and emission system performance in the future.

effect on emissions, particularly after the warranty has expired. Conversely, if SC II is very effective without OBD II, then the added benefits of OBD II may be minimal. Given the past performance of Smog Check and our concerns about how much Smog Check II will improve upon it, the former situation seems more relevant than the latter.

Integration of the OBD II and the inspection and maintenance program has great potential for reducing emissions due to component aging, improper maintenance, and tampering. OBD II monitors the emission control components that control cold-start emissions, something that it is difficult for inspection and maintenance programs to do.[145] The OBD II system is designed so that it can be directly linked to smog-check computers. The OBD II computer could be queried and any faults required to be fixed before a vehicle passes.

Indeed, OBD II could conceivably make emissions tests in inspection and maintenance programs unnecessary, but this appears unlikely in the near future. More needs to be learned about how OBD II status correlates with actual vehicle emissions and how easily the OBD II system can be bypassed.[146] The state has directed BAR to investigate the role OBD II could have in the smog check program (California Assembly Bill No. 2018, Chapter 27, p.18)

OBD II may turn out to be the most effective element of California's ozone control strategy, but a great deal of uncertainty about its performance remains. It has probably already had a major effect on how manufacturers design and build emissions control systems. It may reduce malfunction rates in vehicles still under warranty, but more information is needed on how drivers respond to the check-engine light. It has great potential to improve the inspection and maintenance process, but how much it will do so remains uncertain because it is

---

[145]Testing cold start emissions in an inspection and maintenance setting would require letting the car cool down for a considerable amount of time before testing.

[146]For example, it may not be difficult to develop computer chips that mimic a vehicle's OBD II chip, even down to the vehicle identification number, and never report emission system faults. CARB has developed detailed regulations that attempt to make this very hard to do (for example requiring vehicle-specific encryption codes), but we do not have a good sense of how foolproof these systems are.

still easy for a smog-check technician to overlook a check-engine light. It is very difficult to reduce these uncertainties, and we do not believe that the existing studies are sufficiently comprehensive to provide meaningful estimates of emission reductions.

8.3.2 Narrow Cost-Effectiveness Ratio

CARB projects that the NCER for OBD II will be approximately $2,000 to $2,500 per ton ROG plus NOx (CARB, 1989, p. 19)[147]. Sierra estimates that it will be approximately $7,000 with basic I&M and $15,000 with enhanced I&M (Sierra, 1994c, p.20).[148] We believe that these numbers provide little information about what the NCER for OBD II will actually turn out to be. As discussed in Section 6.1.2, there is not a great deal of disagreement on the hardware cost, but neither CARB nor Sierra appears to include repair costs induced by OBD II in their cost estimates. The uncertainties discussed above about how drivers will respond to the check-engine light and the effectiveness of the I&M program make the emission reduction estimates on which these NCERs are based highly speculative.

8.4 DIRECT COSTS AND EMISSION BENEFITS OF THE AVR PROGRAM

The state implementation plan includes--as measure M-1--a program to purchase and scrap up to 75,000 older, high-emitting LDVs per year in the South Coast starting in 1999, and smaller numbers each year from 1996 to 1998 to gain experience.[149] The program is projected in the SIP to reduce emissions in the South Coast by an increasing number of tons per day over time.[150] The program was enacted into law by SB 501, signed by Governor Wilson on October 14, 1995.

In this section we discuss what is known about the direct costs and direct emission reductions that would actually result from such an

---

[147]CARB estimates of variable production costs ($45 per vehicle) have been adjusted upwards to account for fixed and dealer margin as discussed in Section 6.1-3.

[148]The emission reductions for ROG plus NOx cited in Sierra (1994c, p. 20) are combined with the OBD II hardware costs in Table 6.1-3.

[149]CARB (1994d, Volume II, p. B-2).

[150]ROG emissions reduced per day are estimated at 5 tons in 1999 growing to 14 tons in 2010. The corresponding figures for NOx are 4 and 11 tons per day. (CARB, 1994d, Volume II, p. B-2.)

accelerated vehicle retirement (AVR) program. We conclude that while the existing estimates of narrow cost-effectiveness are quite encouraging, projection of costs and benefits involves some very formidable complexities and there is considerable uncertainty about these quantities.[151]

There has never been an AVR program nearly as large or long-lived as the one proposed for the South Coast. SB 501 seems to recognize that there are difficult design, implementation and evaluation issues to be addressed,[152] but leaves--quite wisely, it seems--many features of the program to be determined by CARB or other state agencies, and directs CARB to make recommendations for future program strategy and funding levels, drawing on analysis of experience in the first two years of the program. Biennial reports are also required, addressing various issues including assessments of "[w]hether the M-1 strategy of the 1994 SIP can reasonably be expected to yield the required emission reductions."

Thus we have no analogous historical experience to analyze.[153] We can, however, analyze key issues that are likely to arise in the evaluation, design, and implementation of programs that conform to what has been specified in the SIP and SB 501. To do so, we rely on analyses and discussions of actual AVR programs, analyses of hypothetical large-scale programs, and microeconomic reasoning.

Generally stated, in an AVR program owners of vehicles that meet some eligibility criteria are offered a certain amount of money (often called the "bounty") in exchange for their vehicles, which are then retired (scrapped) if the offer is accepted. Usually, bounties are the same for all vehicles purchased in the program, but sometimes offers differ over vehicles. Within this general framework, there are numerous decisions to be made including the size of the program, how large a bounty to offer, the eligibility criteria (usually a minimum vehicle

---

[151]Market-mediated effects--which could have important implications for actual (direct plus indirect) emission reductions--are analyzed in some detail in the next section.

[152]Many of these are discussed below.

[153]There have been several short-lived programs involving many fewer vehicles. As discussed below, these provide information useful for analyzing some, but not all, of the analytic issues posed by the SIP measure.

age, and, often, additional requirements), how to screen and recruit potential participants, and which eligible owners will receive offers. Another key issue is whether the acquisition plan of the program will be implemented only once or repeated every year for several years as is the case with the SIP measure.

AVR programs that have been implemented in the United States have been one-time programs and involved many fewer vehicles than the 75,000 per year that has been proposed for the South Coast. They include a program instituted by UNOCAL in the South Coast Air Basin in 1990 involving more than 8,000 vehicles, and subsequent programs involving fewer than 500 vehicles each in Kern County (California), Chicago, Delaware, and Sacramento.[154]

In our discussion of AVR programs, we emphasize three recent analyses: Alberini, Edelstein, Harrington and McConnell (1994), henceforth cited as AEHM (1994); Sierra Research (1995a); and Hahn (1995). The first of these, an extensive analysis of the Delaware program, is reviewed in detail--despite the fact that it involves a small-scale, one-time program--because it includes much more sophisticated empirical analyses of some crucial issues than do other evaluations, and it contains insightful discussion of issues pertaining to evaluation of AVR programs and design of larger or on-going programs.[155] Sierra (1995a) is a detailed analysis of AVR scenarios similar to the state implementation plan measure, the only such analysis we have been able to review.[156] Hahn (1995) is an analysis of costs and benefits of a large, but one-time, AVR program in Los Angeles County. We also refer repeatedly to Engineering-Science (1994), an evaluation of

---

[154]See Alberini, Edelstein, Harrington and McConnell (1994, pp. 2-7) for an overview of the Kern County and Chicago programs and Alberini, Edelstein, Harrington and McConnell (1994) and Alberini, Harrington and McConnell (1993, 1994, 1995) for extensive discussion and analysis of the Delaware program. Engineering-Science (1994) evaluates and provides details of the Sacramento program.

[155]See also Alberini, Harrington and McConnell (1993, 1994, 1995), and Alberini, Edelstein, and McConnell (1994).

[156]Carl Moyer of Acurex has told us that he has done such an analysis-- and that an account exists in draft form--but to date we have been unable to obtain a copy. We have, however, benefited from discussions with Moyer concerning some of the issues we consider here.

the Sacramento Vehicle Emission Reduction Studies (VERS) program, and to Office of Technology Assessment (OTA, 1992) and to Hsu and Sperling (1994), both of which provide insights into the difficulty of evaluating AVR programs and the sensitivity of results to varying assumptions within plausible ranges.

Table 8.4-1 summarizes the features of the AVR programs addressed in AEHM (1994), Sierra (1995a), and Hahn (1995). Besides establishing the context for understanding the estimates developed, the table provides examples of eligibility criteria, target populations of vehicles, strategies for recruiting vehicles, methods for identifying target vehicles, and bounty levels that are typically considered.[157]

_____

[157]SB 501 specifies that to be eligible for the South Coast program, a vehicle must have been registered in the air district for at least the past 24 months and qualify as a high emitter. (The definition of high emitter is left to the agency--to be determined by the Governor--that will oversee the program.) The Sacramento-area program evaluated by Engineering-Science (1994)--which was part of the "Vehicle Emission Reduction Studies" (VERS) sponsored by the state Bureau of Automotive Repair (BAR)--involved two groups of 75 vehicles each, recruited in different ways. Almost all of the owners of the vehicles in one group were referred to a VERS test center after being identified as a potential high emitter at a smog-check center and tested at a VERS test center. A purchase offer (of an appraised value-- not to exceed $1000--plus $40) was made if the levels of measured emissions were sufficiently high relative to the appraised value of the vehicle (pp. 15-16). Owners of vehicles in the second group responded to one of three newspaper ads offering a flat price of $500.

Table 8.4-1

Features of AVR Programs Considered in Recent Empirical Analyses

	AEHM (1994)	Sierra (1995a)	Hahn (1995)
Actual or hypothetical program?	Actual	Hypothetical	Hypothetical
Types of vehicles	Passenger vehicles, light-duty trucks and vans	Passenger vehicles and light-duty trucks	Passenger vehicles and light-duty trucks
Geographic location	Delaware	South Coast (Los Angeles) Air Basin	Los Angeles County (p. 226)
Duration and time period of program	One time: 1992 (p. 12)	Ongoing: 1996 to 2010	One time (1991 implicit in construction of supply curve)
Number of vehicles scrapped	125 in actual program	1996 to 1998: 36,000/year 1999 to 2010: 75,000/year (Scenario 4, p. A-23)	Various, determined by bounty and constructed vehicle supply curve
Ages of vehicles eligible for scrapping	12+ years old (i.e., pre-1980 vehicle in 1992) (p. 12)	8+ years old (some scenarios involve 12+ years old)	Base case: Pre-1980 vehicles (p. 230) (Pre-1978 in sensitivity analysis; p. 237)
Other eligibility criteria	Must receive offer letter. Vehicle continuously registered in DE for one year at time of offer, vehicle operational and regularly used (p. 13)	Program design not addressed explicitly. Implicitly, eligibility requires high ROG emission rate (see below)	None

Table 8.4-1 (cont'd.)

Vehicle identifica- tion, targeting or recruiting strategy	Offer letters sent to 1,034 owners of vehicles with I&M waivers (p. 12) and a random sample of 3,294 other owners (p. 20). First come, first served, up to 125 vehicles	Assume program successfully targeted on high emitters. Method for doing so not addressed	Bounty offered to all owners of age- eligible vehicles
Bounty level (dollars offered for each vehicle)	$500 (p. 12)	Not explicit. Financial cost of $1,000/vehicle implicitly includes bounty and administrative costs	$250, $500, $750, $1,000 (Table 3)

8.4.1 Direct Costs of the Proposed AVR Program

In discussing the "costs" of an AVR program, we must distinguish between

- *Resource* or *economic* costs: the value of the resources used up or absorbed because of the program, and

- *Financial* or *program* costs: the number of dollars that must be expended to implement the program

The former concept is the one relevant to an economic (i.e., social cost and benefit) evaluation, and we focus on it. The latter is undoubtedly crucial for the prospects for implementing an AVR program.

Components of resource costs. The resources absorbed by an AVR program include the transportation services lost from vehicles that are destroyed (scrapped)[158] and the resources involved in administration: program design; recruiting, receiving, testing and disposing of vehicles. Economic costs can vary greatly on a per-vehicle basis, depending on program design. The value of the transportation services lost when vehicles are taken off the road depends on the characteristics

---

[158]We may want these vehicles off the road, but that's not to say that they have no economic value (i.e., before netting out their emission costs).

of these vehicles: their condition, remaining miles, fuel economy, etc., which themselves depend on the size of the bounty, the eligibility criteria, the recruitment procedures, etc. The administrative cost per vehicle can also vary considerably, depending on whether emission tests are performed on scrapped vehicles, how vehicles are recruited (e.g., placing an ad in a newspaper, using Department of Motor Vehicles records and sending letters to owners of vehicles with I&M waivers, identifying vehicles that appear to be high emitters from remote sensing and contacting their owners).

Surplus benefits to participants are financial, but not resource, costs. A bounty accepted by a participant in an AVR program could substantially overstate the resource costs involved in retiring the vehicle. The entire bounty is part of the financial costs of a program, but the part of this payment that exceeds the value of the lost services of the vehicle is not part of resource costs. Economists generally assume that the value of the lost services would be well measured by the value of those services to the vehicle's owner, which itself would be well measured by the minimum amount of money the owner would be willing to accept (WTA) to give up the vehicle. The difference between the bounty paid and the WTA accrues as a net benefit to participating owners. Economists call this the surplus benefit to participants.[159] The surplus represents neither a net (i.e., societal-level) economic cost nor a benefit because no resources are used up.[160]

Estimating costs. For actual AVR programs, administrative costs are not especially difficult to estimate, at least after the fact. Accurately estimating the economic costs of an actual program--even after the fact--requires assessing the value of the lost transportation services, which economists conceptualize as the WTA of the owner for his or her vehicle. The amount of the bounty gives us an upper bound on the WTA of an owner who accepts the bounty--because an owner won't accept an

---

[159]This concept is analogous to consumers' surplus (discussed in Section 7.2). They both involve differences between payments and latent economic values.

[160]Surpluses are transfers of money from those who finance the AVR program to participants who receive more for their vehicles than the values they actually place on them.

offer less than his or her WTA--but the owner's (minimum) WTA could be substantially less than the bounty. (E.g., an owner who accepts an offer of $700 might have been willing to accept $200.)

Estimating the resource or financial costs of a hypothetical or proposed program is even more difficult. It requires predicting administrative costs, the bounty level required to attract the target number of vehicles to be scrapped, and the distribution of WTAs or average WTA of the actual participants (to estimate the value of the lost transportation services).[161]

Methods used to estimate costs. Table 8.4-2 summarizes the methods used to address or estimate costs in the recent three studies that we emphasize. AEHM (1994) and Hahn (1995) emphasize the distinction between financial and economic cost, while Sierra (1995a) does not. Perhaps more important, both AEHM (1994) and Hahn (1995) analyze the participation decision, thus providing some insight into how the number and characteristics of vehicles scrapped would depend on features of the program.[162]

---

[161]Such estimation must take account of other air pollution programs that affect participation decisions in the proposed AVR program. For example, an I&M program that was effective in requiring owners of older vehicles to spend whatever is necessary to reduce their emissions could increase greatly the number of owners who would accept an AVR bounty offer of any particular amount. This observation may be even more important on the emission side; see below.

[162]AEHM (1994) and Alberini, Harrington, and McConnell (1993, 1995) provide detailed empirical analysis of data from the Delaware program. Hahn (1995)--who analyzes a hypothetical program in Los Angeles County-- has no such data to analyze. He constructs a supply curve (of vehicles that would be made available for scrappage) from registration data and used-vehicle prices, assuming that all cars of a make, model year, and general condition category would accept any bounty greater than or equal to the average selling price of such cars. We expect that this assumption leads to substantial overestimation of the number of vehicles that would be supplied to the program at each bounty level: If there is much variation across owners in the valuation of cars of the same make, model year, and general condition category, then many owners would not be willing to accept the average selling price for vehicles in the group to which Hahn assigns their vehicles. Thus Hahn's assumption overestimates the supply of vehicles at any bounty price. Hahn acknowledges the problematic nature of this assumption (1995, p. 240).

Table 8.4-2

Direct Costs of AVR Programs: Methods and Estimates in Recent Empirical Studies

	AEHM (1994)	Sierra (1995a)	Hahn (1995)
Methods:			
Bounty level (dollars offered for each vehicle)	$500 (p. 12)	Not made explicit. Financial cost of $1,000/vehicle implicitly includes bounty plus direct program costs	$250, $500, $750, $1,000 (Table 3)
Financial cost of program	$600/vehicle ($500 bounty plus $100 assumed for administration, testing, disposal) (p. 75)	In all years $1,000/vehicle (not split between bounty and administration) (Table A-15)	Second cost measure (p. 227): bounty times number of vehicles purchased
Economic cost of program	Financial cost minus surplus to participants	Not addressed	First cost measure (p. 227): Area under vehicle supply curve up to bounty level
Surplus benefit to participants	Bounty ($500) minus claimed WTA (p. 83)	Not addressed	Referred to as "transfer" and netted out of first cost measure
Vehicles that would be scrapped	Econometric analysis relating bounties accepted and claimed WTA to vehicle use, and vehicle and owner characteristics. (See also AHM, 1993, 1995.)	Target number of vehicles with ROG emission rates above .82g/mi ("high emitters") assumed scrapped each year. (p. A-14)	Vehicle supply function constructed using data on 1991 fleet composition by make, model and model year (p. 226) and prices of vehicles in fair or good condition (p. 227)
Discounting?	No--Costs all incurred in first year	No	No--Costs all incurred in first year

Table 8.4-2 (cont'd.)

Selected Estimates:

Number of vehicles scrapped	Simulated program targeted at waivered vehicles, $500 bounty: 77 vehicles	Assumed in construction of scenarios	Base case, as function of bounty: $500: 243,000 $750: 475,000 $1,000: 653,000 (Table 3)
Financial cost of program	Simulated program: $46,200 (i.e., 77 vehicles, with bounty $500/vehicle and assumed administration cost of $100/vehicle)	Assumed: $35M/yr 1996-1999 $75M/yr 2000-2010	In base case, as function of bounty: $500: $121M $750: $356M $1,000: $653M (Table 3)
Surplus benefit to participants	Simulated program: $8,764 (Table 27; see also Table 28)	Not considered	Base case, as function of bounty: $500: $31M $750: $118M $1,000: $259M (Derived from Table 3)
Economic cost of program (financial cost minus surplus)	Simulated program: $37,436	Not considered	Base case, as function of bounty: $500: $90M $750: $238M $1,000: $394M (Derived from Table 3)

Sierra (1995a), the only study we have seen that considers quantitatively a program similar to the SIP measure, assumes a financial cost of $1,000 per vehicle without providing an explanation. We have been informed that the reasoning behind choice of this figure is as follows.[163] The 75,000 vehicle-per-year scale of the South Coast program requires purchase of roughly 3 percent of the assumed-

[163]Personal communication to L. Dixon from Charles T. Walz, Texaco, October 20, 1995. (Texaco sponsored the Sierra study.)

eligible[164] vehicles in the South Coast annually; thus purchase prices similar to the bounties paid in the Delaware ($800) and Illinois programs ($856) were believed to be conservative.[165] Administrative costs per vehicle were assumed to be similar to those in the VERS program ($150).[166] This is a plausible basis for estimating per-vehicle *financial* costs in the absence of any historical experience with a program resembling the one in the SIP. What would such an estimate imply about per-vehicle *economic* costs?

Suppose that the (implicit) Sierra (1995a) assumptions about purchase prices and administrative costs are accurate. How much might their resulting estimates of *financial* costs overstate the *economic* costs of the program? Conceptually, the overstatement per vehicle is the average surplus benefit received by each program participant. Results from AEHM (1994) and Hahn (1995) reported in Table 8.4-2, all based on assuming a fixed bounty offer to each potential vehicle seller, provide information on this score. For example, in AEHM's simulated program, surplus benefits to participants ($8,764) represent about 23 percent of total purchase payments (total financial cost of $46,200 minus administrative costs of $7,700). Hahn (1995) incorporates no administrative costs.[167] In this case, then, the surpluses (at various assumed bounty levels), divided by Hahn's measure of the financial cost of the program, represent the percentages of payments that are surplus benefits to participants, not resource costs of the program. The estimates reported in Table 8.4-2 yield percentages of roughly 26, 33, and 40 corresponding to bounty levels $500, $750 and $1,000, respectively. Thus if the Sierra figure for financial cost per vehicle of $1,000 is assumed to reflect a purchase price of $850, we might conclude that $200-$300 of this should be interpreted as surplus benefits to program participants.

---

[164]High-emitters, about ten years old or more. Such high emitters include roughly 50 percent of the age-eligible vehicles in the South Coast.

[165]For example, AEHM (1994, Table 17, p. 59) report an estimated 25 percent offer-acceptance rate among waivered vehicles at a bounty of $800.

[166]Engineering-Science (1994, p. 2).

[167]See description of the two cost measures, p. 227 and Table 3.

8.4.2 Direct Emissions Effects of the Proposed AVR Program

Direct emission reductions are defined as those that would occur if there were no market or behavioral adjustments that would affect emissions.[168]

Conceptually, direct emission effects are the

- emissions avoided on scrapped vehicles, minus
- emissions generated by vehicles or trips that replace transportation services of scrapped vehicles.

Emissions avoided on a scrapped vehicle can be decomposed as the product of: a) the vehicle's emission rate (g/mi); b) number of years it would have remained on the road in the absence of the program; and c) its miles driven per year in the absence of the program.

The issue of emissions from vehicles or trips that replace transportation services of scrapped vehicles is *extremely* complex. As has been recognized by several analysts--but may not be sufficiently widely appreciated--it involves much more than the characteristics and use of the vehicle that a program participant purchases after turning in his or her vehicle to the program; it also involves what the seller of the replacement vehicle does, and the person who sells the seller a vehicle, etc. (See AEHM, 1994, pp. 70-71 for a discussion.)[169]

How Direct Emissions Effects Are Typically Estimated

To estimate emissions avoided and replacement emissions in a hypothetical program, it is often assumed that:

---

[168]Potentially important market adjustments affecting emissions include in-migration of older vehicles to the geographic area in which vehicles are being scrapped. Potentially important behavioral adjustments include delays in scrapping or repairing vehicles or vehicle tampering (and increases in emissions) induced by incentives that might be built into a large, on-going AVR program. Both issues are considered in Section 9.

[169]Engineering-Science (1994, p. 22) also recognizes the complexity of this issue, but (as is the case in every study we have reviewed) does not have a means of directly dealing with it.

- Emission rates for scrapped vehicles are average emissions for their age classes (e.g., using emissions factors from some version of EMFAC or MOBILE);[170]
- Scrapped vehicles would have stayed on the road three (sometimes two or four) years;[171]
- Replacement vehicles or trips emit at fleet average rates;[172]
- Total vehicle miles traveled is unchanged by AVR program.

Such assumptions are largely driven by U.S. EPA and CARB guidance on how to evaluate AVR programs, but they don't have much empirical basis. For regulatory purposes--e.g., design of emission trading programs, preparation of a state implementation plan--decisions must be made about how these quantities are to estimated. Lack of reliable empirical information about such issues means that the actual emission benefits of an AVR program (even after the fact) are likely to remain a matter of guesswork for the foreseeable future.[173]

How AVR Interacts with Other Elements of the Strategy

In addition to the uncertainty surrounding the key assumptions discussed above, estimating the direct emission effects of the AVR

---

[170]Evaluations of actual programs generally base their estimates of emission rates for scrapped vehicles on (laboratory) testing of all or a sample of the purchased vehicles.

[171]Hsu and Sperling (1994, p. 91) report that CARB uses three years, a figure which is "not, as CARB admits, supported by data." Evaluation of the VERS AVR program estimates remaining lifetimes by having mechanics inspect vehicles and make judgments. (Engineering-Science, 1994, p. 20.) AEHM (1994) surveyed participants and asked when they intended to *sell* their vehicles. They may have the only estimates of how remaining lifetimes of vehicles sold to an AVR program depend on the bounty level (albeit from responses to when an owner planned to *sell*, rather than *scrap*, a vehicle). As economic theory strongly suggests, remaining lifetimes of vehicles of owners accepting an offer from an AVR program are higher the higher is the bounty. (AEHM, 1994, Table 19, p. 65.)

[172]Hsu and Sperling (1994, pp. 93-94) report that CARB uses average emissions, but "with no empirical basis." Some studies of actual programs contain test-cycle measurements of emissions of some of the vehicles purchased to replace retired vehicles.

[173]See, for example, OTA (1992), AEHM (1994), Hsu and Sperling (1994) for more extensive discussions of various sources of difficulty. Some of the difficulties are discussed below.

program is complicated by the program's interactions with I&M and with
Phase 2 RFG effects on older vehicles.

AVR emissions benefits depend on how well I&M works. The
interactions with I&M should be considered in evaluating or designing an
AVR program, but this is hard to do because of the complexity
involved.[174] A more effective smog check program would make AVR
programs more effective in reducing emissions under some conditions but
less effective under others. For example, an I&M program that was
extremely effective (presumably involving high dollar limits for
waivers, or no waivers at all, and very vigorous and effective
enforcement) would lead to the clean-up or scrappage of high emitters
even without an AVR program. Such a successful I&M program would leave
little for AVR programs to accomplish.

Alternatively, if I&M were substantially, but incompletely,
effective, AVR programs might be expected to be more effective than they
would be with the current I&M situation. Making I&M more effective
would make owners of dirty vehicles who would not be induced to scrap
their vehicles by I&M alone (i.e., given the commercial scrap values of
their vehicles) more receptive to offers from an AVR program. This
would tend to make AVR programs better at attracting relatively dirty

---

[174]In cases where there is synergy (positive interaction) between
program elements--I&M and AVR programs for example--an issue that often
arises is which program element should "get SIP credit" for the emission
reductions that are produced through the interaction of the programs.
This question can be of substantial concern to participants in the
policy process, but is of little concern for program evaluation
purposes. For evaluation purposes, the issue is making sure that when
costs and benefits are compared with and without a program element or
set of elements, adequate analytic account is taken of the (assumed or
actual) situation concerning other program elements that interact with
the ones under study. As a purely logical matter, there is no correct
allocation of total emission reductions between program elements that
interact. For example, when effective I&M helps get more dirty vehicles
off the road because there is a relatively generous AVR program in
place, it seems there are emission reductions that would not occur
unless both programs were in place. Strictly, when an emission
reduction would be lost if *either* element is removed--the key test for
an incremental effect--this reduction cannot be causally attributed to
one element or the other, and any allocation rule must be somewhat
arbitrary. SB 501 directs CARB to develop procedures to deal with this
issue.

vehicles among program-eligible vehicles (and for this reason tend to increase emissions avoided).

Interactions with RFG. RFG can be expected to lower emission rates of both scrapped and replacement vehicles. Actual benefits of an AVR program depend on the relative effectiveness of RFG in vehicles of different ages and vintages. As discussed in Section 8.1.2, some data suggest that RFG reduces emissions more effectively for newer vehicles. To the extent that these data are revealing and the pattern reflects vehicle age rather than vehicle vintage, replacing older vehicles with newer vehicles through an AVR program would tend to be more effective in the presence of RFG.

Information on Direct Emissions Benefits of the Planned AVR Program

What empirical information is available and applicable to predicting the direct emission effects of an AVR program like the SIP measure? There is a lot of information, but after sifting through it, we are left with considerable uncertainty.

Table 8.4-3 summarizes the approaches and results of AEHM (1994), Sierra (1995a) and Hahn (1995). The estimates of AEHM (1994) may well be very informative about the small, one-time program in Delaware that they study. It is no criticism of that work that it hasn't answered a question that wasn't addressed, and, as the authors repeatedly caution, their results should not be extrapolated to a large, on-going program.

Hahn (1995) uses data from Los Angeles County to model a large, but one-time, program. His results might be more informative about the state implementation plan program than those of AEHM (1994).[175] As we discussed above, we suspect that the way Hahn constructs his supply function leads to substantial overestimation of the number of vehicles that would be scrapped for each bounty level.

Sierra (1995a) sets out to estimate the direct emission effects of an AVR program very much like the SIP program. We are unable to judge whether their estimates are likely to be too high or too low. Sierra makes some assumptions--for example, how they take account of enhanced

---

[175]However, there should be very important differences in behavior between one-time and ongoing programs.

I&M and RFG--that seem to work against crediting the AVR program with as much emission reduction as would be appropriate. However, the Sierra estimates also rest on some assumptions that may well work in the opposite direction.

The direct emission effects of an AVR program depend crucially on the emission rates of vehicles that are retired by the program. Fundamentally, this depends on the vehicle characteristics of owners who receive offers above their WTAs.[176] Without describing (at least to some extent) the rules and procedures of the program (for example, eligibility criteria, how vehicles in the target population of high-emitters would be identified and recruited, who will receive offers, the size of the offers)--which Sierra (1995a) does not do--one cannot *analyze* (theoretically or empirically) what types of vehicles will be surrendered in response to offers.[177] Instead, Sierra makes assumptions that may or may not be reasonable.

For example, Sierra (1995a) makes an assumption that conflicts with economic common sense and may lead both to implausibly high implicit

---

[176]No matter what other program features one has in mind for the AVR program in the SIP, everyone assumes (and SB 501 stipulates) that participation by vehicle owners will be voluntary. What this implies is that no matter how owners are recruited or how it is decided whether or how much to offer, the vehicle owner must decide whether to accept an offer.

[177]For example, one phase of the VERS AVR program involved pre-screening for high-emitters at I&M facilities, offers being made only after testing at a VERS testing center indicated that emission levels were high relative to the appraised value of the vehicle, and offers being based on the appraised value. Different procedures for pre-screening, recruiting and determining offers to owners of high emitters can be expected to have very different effects on emissions. For example, in the VERS program, letters were also sent to 268 owners of vehicles identified through remote sensing as potential high emitters, requesting them to bring their vehicles in for testing; only 36 responded by bringing in their vehicles; and of those only one qualified as a high-emitter and was purchased. (Engineering-Science, 1994, p. 15.) The responses to mail recruitment, for example, of potential high emitters is likely to depend crucially on whether recipients of letters consider that the letter might be the first step to offers to purchase their vehicles (which seems much more likely in a large, on-going AVR program than in a one-time, small-scale program like VERS), how likely they think they are to receive offers if the letter is part of an AVR program, how much they think they might be offered, etc.

estimates of remaining lifetimes of scrapped vehicles and
underestimation of the average emission rates of scrapped vehicles. (We
are unable to judge whether the net effect of these factors is to
understate or overstate emission reductions.) The assumption is that
the numbers of vehicles of each eligible vehicle age that would be
scrapped under the program would be proportional to their numbers in the
fleet. Economic logic--bolstered by AEHM (1994)--suggests that the
fraction of owners who accept a bounty offer of a given size will
increase with the age of the vehicle.[178]

Even defining direct emission reductions--as we have--to exclude
emissions effects of potential behavioral responses like delaying of
scrapping or emissions repairs or tampering and potential market
responses like in-migration of older vehicles, at least one very
formidable estimation challenge remains: the emissions associated with
replacement transportation. No study has a good analytic handle on this
issue because of the extreme complexity of the chain of responses
triggered when a vehicle is retired. The kinds of assumptions that are
typically made--for example that retirement doesn't affect total VMT and
that the replacement transportation emits at the average rate of the
fleet--may yield results that are largely revealing of the actual
effects. However, we find it difficult to be confident on that score.

----

[178]This is because a bounty offer will be accepted only if it
exceeds the value of a vehicle, and vehicle values tend to decline with
vehicle age, holding other factors constant. AEHM (1994) provide
indirect evidence on this point in their Table 19, which shows that the
average remaining lifetimes of vehicles that would be sold to the
program increase as the level of the bounty increases.

Table 8.4-3

Direct Emission Effects of AVR Programs: Approaches and Estimates from Recent Empirical Studies

	AEHM (1994)	Sierra (1995a)	Hahn (1995)
Methods:			
Vehicles that would be scrapped (i.e., whose owners who accept bounty offer)	Econometric analysis relating bounties accepted and claimed WTA to vehicle use, and vehicle and owner characteristics. (See also AHM, 1993, 1995.)	Target number of vehicles with ROG emission rates above 0.82g/mi ("high emitters") assumed scrapped each year (p. A-14) in proportion to numbers registered in South Coast (p. A-16). Vehicles newer than MY1997 never scrapped. (p. A-16)	vehicle supply function constructed using data on 1991 fleet composition by make, model and model year (p. 226) and prices of cars in fair or good condition (p. 227)
Pollutants considered	ROG, NOx, CO (p. 35)	ROG, NOx	ROG, NOx
Emission rates of scrapped vehicles	63 vehicles tested (tailpipe and evaporation) with IM240; 20 of these also tested with FTP (pp. 22-23)	ROG emission rates for high emitters estimated for years 2000, 2010, 2015, and 2020 from regression using average ROG emissions and odometer readings (from CARB surveillance data) for three vehicle groups (p. A-15)	Based on estimated odometer readings from MOBILE4 and emission factors from EMFAC7E (p. 228). Evaporative emissions added (p. 228)
Miles per year of scrapped vehicles	Three methods produce similar averages across vehicles (pp. 67-69). Program evaluation assumes mileage the same for all vehicles (p. 69)	Not calculated explicitly. Determined implicitly by distribution of vehicles of different ages assumed scrapped by program (see above)	Based on MOBILE4 (p. 228)
Remaining lifetime of scrapped vehicles	Econometric analysis of owners' responses to when they expected to have sold vehicle (p. 63)	Not calculated explicitly. Determined implicitly by age distribution of vehicles of different ages assumed scrapped by program (see above)	Base case: three years for all scrapped vehicles. (p. 230) (Two and four years considered in sensitivity analysis; p. 236)

Table 8.4.3 (cont'd.)

Methods:

	AEHM (1994b)	Sierra (1995a)	Hahn (1995)
Emission rates of replacement vehicles	Average of all vehicles on road (p. 70). Arbitrariness of assumption and alternatives discussed (pp. 70-71)	Determined implicitly by modification of registration distribution based on vehicles scrapped by program and assumption that vehicles not scrapped in program are scrapped at historical rate for vehicles of that age. (pp. A-16-A-17)	Base case: Average tailpipe emission rate for fleet (p. 230) using EMFAC7E (p. 228). (Sensitivity analysis considers emission rates of 1983 MY, new, and average pre-1980 vehicles.)
Effect of program on total VMT	No effect, as suggested by follow up survey information (p. 70)	Assumed not affected by program. (p. 19)	Base case: No effect. (p. 230)
Interaction with I&M	Different emission rates calculated for vehicles with and without I&M waivers (Tables 12-15)	EMFAC7F emission factors adjusted. E.g., in 2000 assume enhanced I&M reduces tailpipe ROG, evap ROG and NOx about 50%, 40%, and 110% more than current I&M. (p. A-7)	Base case: 1990 California program (p. 230). In separate scenario, enhanced I&M reduces WTA by estimated cost of enhanced I&M (pp. 237-238)
Interaction with RFG	Not considered.	Baseline total organic gas (TOG) emission factors reduced by about 27% (p. A-12)	Not considered
Discounting?	No (emissions benefits incurred over only a few years)	No	Base case: emission reduction discounted at 5% per year
Uncertainty quantified?	Calculated confidence intervals and sensitivity analyses for emissions reductions as function of bounty level (p. 85)	Sensitivity analysis over program scenarios varying program size, timing, vehicle-age eligibility (p. A-23)	Sensitivity analysis over (e.g.) fractions of vehicles in good and fair condition, replacement vehicle, remaining lives

Table 8.4.3 (cont'd.)

Selected estimates:

	AEHM (1994b)	Sierra (1995a)	Hahn (1995)
Average remaining vehicle life of scrapped vehicles	$500 offer: 1.7 years $1,000 offer: 2.5 years (p. 65)	Not estimated explicitly or reported.	By assumption
Number of vehicles scrapped	125 (Determined by program construction.)	Assumed in construction of scenarios	In base case, as function of bounty: $500: 243,000 $750: 475,000 $1,000: 653,000 (Table 3)
Emission reductions (emissions avoided on scrapped vehicles minus emissions generated by replacement vehicles)	In 1992: 14.8 tons ROG 1.1 tons NOx 68.9 tons CO (Derived from Table 23)	In 2010: Reductions (tons/day) Scenario 4: ROG=13.8, NOx=10.7 (Table A-15) (Fleet average ROG emissions of catalyst-equipped vehicles reduced from 0.131 to 0.108 g/mi--Table A-10)	In base case, as function of bounty (thousands of tons): $500: 18 ROG, 6 NOx $750: 35 ROG, 12 NOx $1,000 48 ROG, 16 NOx (Table 3)

8.4.3 Estimates of Narrow Cost Effectiveness for the Proposed AVR Program

Table 8.4-4 reports selected estimates of the narrow cost-effectiveness ratios (NCERs) for AVR programs from the three recent analyses we have emphasized. All are in the general range of $4,000 to $10,000 per ton of ROG + NOx.[179] These figures compare favorably to NCERs typically calculated for many other elements of the California LDV strategy. We have argued that the relevance of the AEHM (1994) and Hahn (1995) estimates to an large, on-going AVR program like the one in the SIP is equivocal (and reported that AEHM caution against presuming that their results are relevant to predicting effects for such programs).

The Sierra estimates are based on analysis of a program like the one in the SIP. We have discussed the basis for their estimates of financial costs, suggested that the assumed figure of $1,000 per vehicle of financial cost may well be close to the mark, and argued that basing cost estimates on financial cost tends to overstate economic costs per vehicle scrapped by perhaps $200-$300 (because it doesn't net out surplus benefits to program participants). We have discussed the Sierra methods for estimating direct emission benefits and highlighted some aspects that may tend substantially to understate these benefits and another that may tend substantially to overstate them. Thus, we have no basis for judging whether the net effect is to yield overestimates or underestimates of NCERs of an AVR program like the one in the SIP.

As we discuss at length in Section 2 and emphasize repeatedly throughout this report, even accurate NCERs are typically not a reliable, complete guide to policy choices because they usually fail to account at all for potentially important social costs and benefits. What indirect effects of an AVR program like the one in the SIP (i.e., costs and benefits not accounted for in the definition of narrow cost effectiveness) seem potentially most important?

---

[179]The VERS program developed estimated NCERs of about $2,000 per ton of ROG + NOx for vehicles that were pre-screened on emissions and about $5,000 for vehicles that were not. (Engineering-Science, 1994, p. 4.)

Table 8.4-4

Narrow Cost-Effectiveness Estimates from Recent Studies of AVR Programs

	AEHM (1994)	Sierra (1995a)	Hahn (1995)
Selected estimates:			
Number of vehicles scrapped	125 in actual program by design	Assumed in construction of scenarios	Base case, as function of bounty: $500: 243,000 $750: 475,000 $1,000: 653,000 (Table 3)
Emission reductions	In 1992: 14.8 tons ROG 1.1 tons NOx 68.9 tons CO (Derived from Table 23)	In 2010: Reductions (tons/day) Scenario 4: ROG = 13.8, NOx = 10.7 (Tbl. A-15) (Fleet (with catalysts) average ROG reduced from .131 to .108g/mi; Table A-10)	In base case, as function of bounty (thousands of tons): $500: 18 ROG, 6 NOx $750: 35 ROG, 12 NOx $1,000 48 ROG, 16 NOx (Table 3)
Cost effectiveness	a) Actual program, ignoring surplus benefits: $5,057/ton HC ($4,000 and $6,000 for waivered and non-waivered vehicles). Sensitivity analyses (Table 24). b) Simulated program for waivered vehicles, $500 bounty, 77 vehicles, net of surplus benefits: $3,457/ton of ROG (Table 27; see also Table 28)	Through 2020, ranges over 6 scenarios in financial cost/ton, ($000s); (Scenario 4 in parens): ROG: 11.8 to 19.3 (14.5); NOx: 16.8 to 22.9 (19.0); ROG+NOx: 6.9 to 10.5 (8.2) (Tables A-12 to A-17)	Base case, as function of bounty, dollars per ton of ROG+NOx (surplus benefits not in cost): $500: $3,800 $750: $5,100 $1,000: $6,100 (Table 3)

We think at least three merit the attention of policymakers:

First, by providing a way that the owner of a high emitter can sell his or her vehicle, an AVR program *well-designed for this purpose* may reduce fraud and evasion in, and hence complement, Smog Check II. For a vehicle owner to prefer vehicle retirement to smog check non-compliance, the bounty offered must be higher than the value that the vehicle owner attaches to the vehicle in its current condition, including any imputed costs of smog-check non-compliance. Thus, the size of the bounty and how it relates to the condition of the vehicle's emission system could be a critical factor in designing an AVR program that would provide an attractive alternative to non-compliance with I&M.[180]

Second, large-scale, on-going AVR programs like the one in the SIP are recognized to have the potential of drawing older vehicles into the air district that is attempting to reduce the stock of older vehicles.[181] This issue is analyzed at length in the next section.

Third, depending on various aspects of program design, large-scale, on-going AVR programs may provide incentives for vehicle owners to keep their vehicles dirty, to keep dirty vehicles on the road, or to make vehicles dirtier.[182] Emissions increases due to such effects, if any, would not be captured in NCERs as calculated in existing studies (and, indeed, have been defined here as outside the scope of the definition of *direct* emissions effects). We return to this issue in the next section.

---

[180]For example, if offered bounties are to be based on market values of particular vehicles, these markets values might best be determined by *not* deducting for the emission control problems of the vehicle.

[181]SB 501 recognizes this as an issue, referring to it as "in-migration."

[182]For example, the VERS program involves a specific screening procedure for targeting high emitters, but great pains were taken to avoid tampering in response to incentives from the program. (Engineering-Science (1994, pp. 6, 15, 36.) SB 501 acknowledges the importance of avoiding perverse incentives, for example by directing that the AVR program be "...designed insofar as possible to eliminate any benefit to any participants from vehicle tampering..." The EDF-GM Mobile Emissions Reduction Credit Program also involves elements designed to attenuate perverse incentives. (Environmental Defense Fund and General Motors, no date.)

9. MARKET-MEDIATED EFFECTS OF ICEV NON-HARDWARE ELEMENTS

OVERVIEW AND PREVIEW OF FINDINGS

In this section we briefly consider how markets could react to California Phase 2 reformulated gasoline (CP2G) and Smog Check II and what those responses imply for emission reductions. We then analyze how vehicle markets are likely to respond to an AVR program like that proposed for the South Coast and what such responses imply for emission reductions and for the design of AVR programs.

To preview our findings:

(1) Gasoline price increases from CP2G can be expected to reduce total vehicle miles traveled (VMT) by LDVs by 1.5 to 4 percent. If VMT reductions are spread evenly over the fleet, then comparable percentage decreases in emissions would result. If drivers of older, dirtier vehicles are more responsive to gasoline price increases, emission reductions could exceed 4 percent of total LDV emissions.

(2) Market-mediated effects may dramatically influence the emission reductions of the AVR program planned for the South Coast. The program can be expected to cause migration of older vehicles into the South Coast *and* to increase prices of older vehicles. In fact, if prices do not rise, that would indicate a troubling degree of in-migration.

(3) The keys to getting substantial emission benefits from the AVR program are raising barriers to in-migration and designing the program to avoid incentives for drivers of older vehicles to delay scrapping or emission repairs or to tamper with their vehicles to make them dirtier. Avoiding such perverse incentives while limiting scrapping through the program to high emitters may prove extremely difficult. Making I&M more effective--to lower the market value of vehicles needing emission repairs--could help substantially.

9.1 MARKET-MEDIATED EFFECTS OF RFG

As discussed in Section 8.1.1, California Phase 2 reformulated gasoline is widely expected to increase gasoline prices by 7 to 19 cents per gallon. These increases should reduce the sales of gasoline, miles driven, and thereby emissions. In the short-run, a period too short-run for the composition of the vehicle fleet to respond very much, almost all of the response to higher gasoline prices is the quantity of driving (reductions in VMT). In the longer run, decreases in gasoline purchases due to higher gasoline prices reflect both more fuel-efficient vehicles and fewer miles driven.[183] How much would an increase in gasoline prices in the range of 7 to 19 cents per gallon be expected to affect emissions?

We use estimated elasticities of demand for gasoline in the short and long runs to consider this question. Recall that a price elasticity of demand measures the percentage change in quantities purchased for each one-percent increase in price. Assuming a consumer price for gasoline of roughly $1.20 per gallon, the range of price increases due to CP2G converts to 6 to 16 percent. Estimates of short-run price elasticities of demand for gasoline vary from study to study, but generally are not far from -0.25.[184] Thus, over the course of a few years or less, we might expect price increases due to CP2G to decrease VMT--and total emissions from vehicles using CP2G--by 1.5 to 4 percent. Long-run price elasticities are larger, most often estimated in the range of -0.8 to -1.0.[185] The long-run elasticity of VMT with respect to gasoline prices is often estimated at about -0.25 or larger (absolutely).[186] In sum, we might expect the market-mediated effects of CP2G to include reductions of VMT in the range of 1.5 to 4 percent.

If the VMT responses are distributed evenly over all vehicles, then we would expect this market-mediated response to CP2G to reduce LDV emissions by 1.5 to 4 percent. However, if drivers of older, and (on average) dirtier vehicles, are more responsive to price than are owners of newer vehicles, the marketed-mediated effect on emissions would tend

---

[183]Note that the portion of decrease in fuel use due to increased fuel efficiency will tend not to decrease emissions because emissions standards are set on a g/mile not a g/gallon basis.

[184]See Dahl and Sterner (1991, Tables 1, 2).

[185]See Dahl and Sterner (1991, Tables 1, 2).

[186]Personal communications to authors by Alan F. Eisenberg (Ford) and Harry L. Foster (GM).

to be larger. The market-mediated effects of CP2G add on to the direct emission reduction discussed in Section 8.1.

9.2 MARKET-MEDIATED EFFECTS OF SMOG CHECK II

Smog Check II is designed to get high emitting vehicles repaired or off the road. By increasing the cost of keeping a dirty vehicle on the road, Smog Check II--if effective--would tend to induce earlier retirement of high-emitting vehicles that cannot be repaired at a cost that is worthwhile, given the value of the transportation services provided by the vehicle. Reducing stocks (or supply) of older vehicles can be expected to increase the price of older vehicles and will tend to delay retirement of vehicles not scraped because of the smog check program. The increase in prices of older cars will also tend to increase the demand for newer cars.

9.3 MARKET-MEDIATED EFFECTS OF ACCELERATED VEHICLE RETIREMENT PROGRAMS

9.3.1 Overview of Analysis

The market-mediated effects of the non-hardware regulations that seem most important and difficult to analyze are those associated with the AVR program. An AVR program of the scale and duration proposed for the South Coast is likely to have major effects on markets for used vehicles. Depending on the design of the AVR program, its market-mediated effects could call for major adjustments in estimates of direct cost and emission effects. The reasons for this provide some lessons for those who will be responsible for designing the AVR program established by SB 501.

Table 9.3-1 summarizes the (quite limited) extent to which the three recent AVR studies address the kinds of market effects analyzed here.

Table 9.3-1

How Recent Analyses of AVR Programs Address Market Effects

Issue	AEHM (1994)	Sierra (1995a)	Hahn (1995)
Effects of program on prices of vehicles of age-eligible vehicles	Potential discussed (p. 91). Unlikely to be important in this small program. Issue analyzed briefly, but not quantitatively	Not considered	Mentioned (p. 225, 226); not analyzed. (sensitivity analysis--not detailed--described in footnote 8, p. 226)
Effects of program on prices of vehicles ineligible for scrappage	Alluded to (p. 81)? Unlikely to be important in this small program	Not considered	Mentioned (p. 226); not analyzed
Inflow of vehicles to region	Mentioned (p. 81); unlikely to be important in this small program	Not considered	Mentioned (p. 238); tax-based countermeasures suggested
Effects of perverse incentives in ongoing programs	Discussed (p. 92-93); not relevant to program being evaluated	Not considered	Alluded to (p. 239) in reference to "moral hazard"?

We use a competitive (supply and demand) framework to model and analyze a market for older vehicles in the geographic region targeted by the AVR program, in particular, the South Coast (see Appendix 9.A for details). The analysis emphasizes the potential for price increases of older vehicles and for vehicles to be drawn into the South Coast as a result of the proposed AVR program. It leads us to the following conclusions:

- Large-scale AVRs should be expected to increase the prices of older vehicles, which would tend to reduce the rate at which they are scrapped outside of the AVR program. Such price increases also have distributional implications for owners and potential buyers of older vehicles. Price increases for older vehicles can be expected to lead to (perhaps small) price increases for newer used vehicles and, to a lesser and perhaps trivial extent, new vehicles.

- An AVR program like the one being developed for the South Coast will tend to draw older vehicles into the South Coast from outside the region, not to be scrapped but to replace (some of) the vehicles that are scrapped. To the extent that such in-migration occurs, the number of older vehicles in the region will not decline as much as the number of vehicles purchased and scrapped through the AVR program.[187] Price effects can be expected to become more pronounced over time in an ongoing program like that proposed for the South Coast.

- Key determinants of the emission effects of an AVR program like the one in the SIP are the extent to which older vehicles are drawn into the region and the emission rates of vehicles that are drawn in compared with the emission rates of vehicles that are scrapped through the program.

Neither the possibility of price increases nor the possibility of in-migration is a novel suggestion.[188] However, some participants in the policy debate have suggested that both effects might be absent, or at least trivial. Perhaps the most important lesson to be drawn from the analysis detailed in Appendix 9.A is that such suggestions do not hold up under the most basic economic scrutiny. Merely positing a supply curve for vehicles of the ages eligible for AVR program participation and viewing the program as increasing the demand for such vehicles leads immediately to the conclusion that either the quantity of such vehicles in the region (those in service plus those that are

---

[187]AVR programs can be designed to control *program participation and scrapping* of vehicles from outside the region. For example, SB 501 stipulates that vehicles purchased in the SIP program must be registered in the South Coast for at least 24 months. However, stipulations like this cannot prevent the inflow of similar vehicles to *replace* vehicles that are scrapped.

[188]For example, SB 501 requires assessments of net emission benefits to consider "...in-migration of other vehicles into the area and any tendencies to increased market value of used vehicles and prolonged useful life of existing vehicles, if any."

scrapped) will increase (from in-migration), their prices will rise, or both. An increase in demand must increase quantity or price; in general, it will do some of both.

Most participants in the policy debate view the possibility of increased prices for older vehicles as an undesirable outcome. The analysis detailed in the appendix suggests a very different perspective: The *lack* of price increases would imply that the program is failing to reduce the stock of vehicles in the region that are old enough to qualify for participation in the AVR program. As the appendix details, for there to be no price effect, the number of vehicles drawn into the region because of the AVR program must equal the number vehicles scrapped in the program.[189]

We have no quantitative information to offer concerning how large the price effects might be or the extent to which vehicles that are scrapped by an AVR program will be replaced by vehicles from outside the region. We emphasize, however, that buying and destroying 75,000 older vehicles per year that would not have been scrapped anyway must appreciably increase prices, attract substantial numbers of vehicles into the region, or both. For reasons detailed in the appendix, we anticipate that both types of effects will occur, with price effects getting larger relative to in-migration effects in later years.

9.3.2 Implications for Policy

A natural, and perhaps very desirable, response to the potential for in-migration is to raise barriers to in-migration. Some barriers currently exist; for example, used vehicles brought in from outside the state are required to pay an additional fee of $300 to register the vehicle and to pass a smog check. Additional barriers might be erected and might substantially stem in-migration. However, a necessary side-effect of successfully stemming in-migration is increased prices.

If policymakers cannot or choose not to restrict in-migration, a key to AVR program effectiveness is trying to make sure that vehicles

---

[189]Another way to appreciate the beneficial effects of an increase in prices for older vehicles is to view them as an inducement for drivers to replace them with newer vehicles.

drawn into the region have lower emission rates than vehicles scrapped in the AVR program. This might be done by targeting especially high emitters in the AVR program--for example, by limiting eligibility to vehicles that have recently failed the initial I&M test, have received waivers, or have triggered high readings on remote sensors. But as we suggested above, attempts to target high emitters might, if not designed very cleverly, backfire because of perverse incentives that are especially difficult to avoid in large, on-going AVR programs.

Targeting offers to high emitters and a large-scale, ongoing program is a dangerous combination. If AVR program offers are to be accepted at a reasonably high rate, they must be somewhat generous in comparison with market values of at least many age-eligible vehicles.[190] If offers are generous, many owners of older vehicles will be anxious to receive an AVR program offer. If vehicles have to be especially dirty to receive an offer, and offers are desirable, then owners have incentives to keep dirty vehicles in service, to keep their vehicles dirty, or to make their vehicles dirtier. The larger the program, the more likely it is that a dirty vehicle will lead to an offer, and the stronger this perverse incentive.

In the extreme, trying to target especially dirty vehicles in a large, ongoing AVR program could make matters worse. (Emission increases caused by perverse incentives are not accounted for at all in the NCERs reviewed above or any we have seen.) At the very least, targeting may be much less effective than would be suggested by an analysis that ignored potential responses to perverse incentives.[191]

There may be a more promising way to induce owners of dirtier vehicles to participate in the AVR program: rather than making offers only to such owners, make offers of any given size more attractive to them by reducing the values of their vehicles and thereby their WTAs. We should anticipate that an offer to buy a vehicle is more likely to be

---

[190]Note that attempting to tailor AVR offers to the market values of vehicles will directly increase the costs of program design and administration as well as reducing participation rates.

[191]AEHM (1994, pp. 92-93) provide an especially useful discussion of potential sources of and vehicle-owner responses to perverse incentives in AVR programs.

accepted the higher is the offer relative to the value of the vehicle to the owner. If Smog Check II is as ineffective as some estimates suggest, there is little reason to think that two otherwise identical vehicles, one of which is a high emitter, will have very different values to their owners. In contrast, if Smog Check II were reasonably-- but not nearly perfectly--effective, then high emitters will be worth less, and their owners, other things equal, will be more receptive to an offer from the AVR program. Thus, a key to making an AVR program effective may be an effective I&M program, but not so effective that nearly all high emitters would be fixed or scrapped even in the absence of an AVR program.[192]

---

[192]See AEHM (1994, pp. 94-97) for a very useful discussion of potential interactions between AVR and I&M programs and implications for the design of AVR programs.

10. DIRECT COSTS AND BENEFITS OF THE ZERO-EMISSION VEHICLE MANDATE

OVERVIEW AND PREVIEW OF FINDINGS

The zero emission vehicle (ZEV) mandate is a controversial element of the California LDV strategy. The mandate requires seven large automobile manufacturers to produce ZEVs for sale starting in 1998. The required number is 2 percent of annual LDV sales in 1998, rising to 5 percent in 2001 and 10 percent in 2003. Starting in 2003, the 10 percent EV requirement also applies to intermediate volume manufacturers (see Section 5.8).

Although the ZEV mandate does not specify what technology must be used, it is widely accepted that an electric vehicle (EV), powered by batteries, will be the only means available over the next decade for meeting the mandate.[193] Therefore, our evaluation focuses on battery-powered EVs.

In this section, we consider the direct cost and emission reduction of the ZEV mandate and the implications for narrow cost effectiveness. In the context of EVs, *direct costs* mean the production cost of an electric vehicle produced because of the mandate and the lifetime operating cost of the vehicle. We review and assess studies that provide estimates of these costs. The studies generally construct estimates of EV production costs by comparing them to the costs of an ICEV of similar size and body style. The costs of battery charging infrastructure, either in homes, work sites, or public places, are also direct resource costs of electric vehicles. However, we do not address infrastructure costs in this report.

In the context of EVs, *direct emission* reductions mean the decrease in tons of ROG and NOx emissions that would result from fulfilling the ZEV mandate if the only effect of the mandate were to replace ICEVs one for one with EVs driven the same number of miles. As in previous

---

[193]Fly-wheels and fuel cells are other potential power sources, but they appear to be many years away from commercialization.

chapters, we gauge *narrow cost-effectiveness* in terms of the ratio of direct costs to direct emission reductions.

In Section 11, we consider how the California EV and ICEV markets will respond to the ZEV mandate during its first five years. Understanding *market-mediated effects* is crucial to evaluating the costs and benefits of the mandate, including how costs are distributed and how the mandate may affect the price of new ICEVs and thus the age composition of the ICEV fleet.

To preview our findings on direct costs emission reductions and narrow cost effectiveness ratios of the ZEV mandate:

(1) The battery is the key source of uncertainty about EV operating cost, range, and consumer acceptance. The first electric vehicles are expected to use lead-acid batteries, but these batteries will allow very limited driving range. Lead-acid batteries are viewed as a transitional technology by almost everyone.

(2) Considerable effort is underway to develop better batteries. Optimistic estimates are that advanced batteries that would double or triple the range possible with lead-acid batteries could be available in the year 2000. However, these estimates assume no unforeseen technical difficulties are encountered in battery development, evaluation, or manufacturing.

(3) The direct resource costs of EVs will likely be considerably more than those for comparable ICEVs during the first five years of the mandate (1998-2002). Judging by studies that we review, $3,300 and $15,000 are lower and upper bounds for the incremental variable production costs per vehicle during that period. Discounted lifetime EV operating costs (including all batteries) will likely exceed those of comparable ICEVs by $3,000 to $13,000 per vehicle, and incremental fixed costs may well fall between $1.0 billion and $4.2 billion. Overall, the ZEV mandate will likely cost from $2.9 to $12.3 billion between 1998 and 2002 if the mandates in California, New York, and Massachusetts remain in place.

(4) The production costs of EVs are likely to fall as production volumes grow. We think it reasonable to believe that production costs, excluding the battery, can approach those of ICEVs, but the questions are when and under what conditions. Past data on how product prices change as cumulative output doubles suggest that EV production costs may drop 10 to 25 percent with each doubling of output. We adopt this range in our analysis of the long-term costs and benefits of EVs, but further work is needed to better understand what rates are most likely for EVs.

(5) As battery costs fall and EV technology matures, the incremental EV lifetime operating costs, including all batteries, will likely decline as well. Our analysis suggests that the range into which incremental operating costs will likely fall will decrease from $3,000 and $13,000 per vehicle during the first five years of the mandate to $1,000 and $6,500 in the long run.

(6) Emission reductions of EVs depend on the effectiveness of the ICEV control program and how manufacturers adjust their mix of TLEVs, LEVs, and ULEVs to continue meeting the NMOG standard when EVs are included in their fleets. We estimate the emission reductions of EVs under a variety of scenarios. First, we assume that the ICEV control program is effective, and second, that it is ineffective. We also evaluate two extreme scenarios of how manufacturers remix their sales of ICEVs. In the first, EVs produce no NOx benefits; in the second, they produce the maximum possible NOx benefits. We estimate that each EV will reduce emissions by as little as 51 pounds of ROG plus NOx over the life of the vehicle if the ICEV program is effective and there are no NOx reductions, and by as much as 579 pounds if the ICEV program is ineffective and there are maximum NOx reductions.

(7) We calculate EV narrow cost-effectiveness ratios using different assumptions about the key parameters that determine these NCERs: initial EV production and operating costs, rates

of decrease in production and operating costs over time, emission reductions per EV, fleet penetration of EVs, the time horizon over which costs and benefits are considered, and the discount rate. These cost-effectiveness ratios are narrow because they ignore factors such emission reductions other than ROG and NOx, non-emission related improvements in well being such as the added convenience of home EV refueling, EV infrastructure costs, and the effects of possibly higher ICEV prices on fleet turnover. Using upper and lower bounds that we develop for each parameter, we find that the NCER could be just about anything. The long-term NCER is $5,000 per ton of ROG plus NOx when initial EV costs are low, costs decline quickly, emission reductions are large, fleet penetration remains at 10 percent, and the discount rate is 3 percent. Long-term cost effectiveness is $850,000 per ton ROG plus NOx when initial costs are high and decline slowly, emission reductions are low, fleet penetration remains at 10 percent, and the discount rate is 5 percent. The NCERs we calculate range between $10,000 and $1.2 million per ton when the costs and benefits of vehicles sold only through 2010 are considered.

10.1 ELECTRIC VEHICLE TECHNOLOGY

In reviewing the current state of electric vehicle technology, we rely primarily on the following studies: Abacus (1994), Adams (1995), CARB (1994b), Doddapaneni et al. (1994), Haines (1995), Kalhammer et al. (1995), and Sony (1995).

The key components of the electric vehicle drive train are the battery charger, the battery pack, the controller, and the electric motor.[194] Battery chargers convert AC power from an electric outlet to the DC power required for charging the batteries. The location of the charger can vary from vehicle to vehicle--some are placed in the vehicle itself while others are off-board. Chargers are usually designed to run on either standard household outlets (110 volts/15 amperes) or higher power outlets (220 volts/30 amperes, the power supply for an electric

---

[194]The following description draws from CARB (1994b, pp. 22-26).

clothes dryer for example). Using a standard outlet, a charger can recharge a typical battery pack in eight to 10 hours; a higher power outlet can accomplish recharging in two to four hours.

The battery pack stores energy for use by the electric vehicle. The battery pack is made up of a number of individual battery cells.[195] We use the terms "battery pack" and "battery" interchangeably. How much energy the battery can store and how quickly it can be discharged are the critical factors that determine the range and acceleration of an electric vehicle. Developing high-energy battery packs is the principal technological challenge. We return to current and expected battery performance shortly.

The controller regulates the flow of electricity from the battery pack. For AC motors, the controller also converts the pack's DC current to the AC current used by the motor. Many electric vehicles also have regenerative braking. During braking, the electric motor, working as a generator, helps slow the vehicle, and the power generated this way is transferred through the controller back to the batteries.

The electric motor converts the electrical energy (supplied by the battery pack through the controller) to the mechanical energy that turns the wheels. Both DC and AC motors are used today. Most DC motors require a transmission, but AC motors can operate over a sufficiently wide range of revolutions per minute that they require only a simple reduction gear.

Electric vehicles typically have many accessories. Some, such as window defogging and defrosting, are required for safety. Others, such as heating, air conditioning, and power steering, provide comfort or driving ease. Accessories can consume a considerable amount of energy and thus reduce the vehicle's range--that is, how far it can travel on a single battery charge. Manufacturers and components suppliers are devoting substantial effort to developing more energy-efficient accessories.

---

[195]The battery pack is made up of battery modules, which are in turn made up of battery cells. There can be hundreds of battery cells in a battery pack.

10.1.1 Battery Technology

The battery is central to the range and performance of an electric vehicle and is a major component of cost. In this section we explain the critical attributes of batteries and then briefly describe the current state of battery technology and developments that may occur over the next 5 or 10 years.

The key attributes of the battery in an electric vehicles are its

- **Energy density.** Energy density is the amount of energy the battery stores per unit of battery mass. It is usually measured in watt-hours per kilogram (wh/kg).

- **Cycle life.** Cycle life is the number of times that a battery can be discharged and recharged. Batteries are usually discharged to 20 percent of capacity, and the end of battery life is generally considered to be the point when the battery can hold only 80 percent of the original charge. Battery life is sometimes reported as the numbers of years that the battery will last in operation or the number of miles that the battery pack can power the vehicle.

- **Pack size.** Pack size is the amount of energy that can be stored in the battery pack at any one time, measured in kilowatt-hours (kwh).

- **Cost.** We use two measures of cost. The first is the cost per kwh of energy storage ($/kwh). This is the cost of producing a battery pack of a given size. The second is cost per kwh of energy delivered ($/kwh delivered), which measures the cost of energy delivered during the lifetime of the battery. It is cost per kwh storage divided by cycle life; a longer battery life spreads the production cost over more energy delivered by the battery. We distinguish between battery production cost and purchase price.

- **Pack weight.** The weight of the battery pack is measured in pounds (lbs) or kilograms (kg).

In addition to the characteristics defined above, features such as specific power, battery efficiency, safety, durability, maintenance requirements, and toxicity are also important. Specific power (measured in watts per kilogram) determines how much power the battery can deliver at a particular time. It is the key factor in determining vehicle acceleration. Battery efficiency refers to the extent of energy losses within the battery during charging or discharging. Many batteries also contain toxic materials that may be released into the environment during battery manufacture, use, disposal, or recycling.

The range of an electric vehicle depends fundamentally on the efficiency of the vehicle (the miles/kwh used by the vehicle--analogous to miles per gallon for ICEVs) and battery capacity. Due to battery cost considerations, space limitations in the vehicle, and requirements for suspension and handling, there are practical limits on the size and weight of the battery that can be put in a vehicle. Also, increasing battery weight decreases the vehicle efficiency. Thus, increasing energy density is a key goal of battery development.

The cost to the consumer of all the battery packs required during the lifetime of the electric vehicle depends on purchase price, vehicle efficiency, pack size, battery cost, and cycle life, plus total VMT. The latter three determine the number of packs needed during the life of the vehicle. Battery development efforts have thus emphasized increasing cycle life as well as reducing production cost.

Current State of Battery Technology

In this section we review the current status of the following electric vehicle battery technologies: lead-acid, nickel-cadmium, nickel metal hydride, sodium nickel chloride, lithium ion, and lithium polymer.

Lead-Acid. Conventional and advanced lead-acid (PbA) battery packs are currently available for use in electric vehicles. As summarized in Table 10.1-1, conventional lead-acid batteries typically have energy densities of approximately 35 wh/kg, accept 500 recharging cycles, and last in a vehicle for approximately 3 to 4 years (CARB, 1994b, p. 15, and Abacus, 1994, p. B-3). It is difficult to pinpoint actual purchase prices and production costs, but, currently, standard lead-acid batteries appear to sell for between \$125 and \$200 per kwh.[196] As a result of these attributes, the lifetime operating costs of PbA batteries currently run between \$0.25 and \$0.40 per kwh delivered over the life of the battery.

Table 10.1-1

Current Battery Technologies

Battery Type	Energy Density (wh/kg)	Cycle Life (cycles)	Stage of Development	Price (\$/kwh)	Lifetime Cost (\$/kwh delivered)
Lead acid	35	500	Production	125-200	0.25-0.40
Advanced lead acid	42	500	Pilot Prod.	400	0.80
Nickel Cadmium	50-55	800-1,000	Production	600-800	0.60-1.00
Nickel Metal Hydride	70-80	600	Prototype packs	>1,000	>1.67
Sodium Nickel Chloride	80	>1,000	Pilot Prod.	\$1,000 -\$3,000	1.00-3.00
Lithium Ion	100	1,000 -1,200	Prototype modules	>1,000	0.83-1.00
Lithium Polymer	150-200	?	Cell development	?	?

Electrosource Inc. in Austin, Texas is currently manufacturing an advanced lead-acid battery on a pilot production line. Its energy density is 42 wh/kg, and it has a cycle life similar to or perhaps slightly greater than that of conventional lead-acid batteries (Abacus, 1994 p. B-3). Advanced lead-acid batteries have recently come on the market, and Chrysler Corporation has signed a major purchase contract with Electrosource (New York Times, 4/6/95). The batteries are reportedly selling for approximately \$400 per kwh.

---

[196]1994 lead-acid battery prices range from \$121-\$272 in Abacus cost simulations (1994, p. B-3). CALSTART staff estimated that lead-acid batteries were currently selling for about \$200 per kwh. Note that the lead-acid starter batteries in ICEVs are much cheaper--from \$70 to \$100 per kwh--but are a different type of battery from those used in electric vehicles.

Nickel-cadmium. Nickel-cadmium (NiCd) batteries are also used in electric vehicles and are particularly popular among European manufacturers. NiCd energy density is typically about 50-55 wh/kg. With a life upwards of 800 to 1,000 cycles, NiCd batteries will last substantially longer than PbA batteries. However, NiCd batteries are expensive in terms of $/kwh storage (Kalhammer et al., 1995, p. III-10). Abacus (1994, p. B-3) assumes that NiCd batteries can be bought for $500 per kwh, but others we interviewed during the course of this project thought $600-$800 was more accurate. At $600 to $800 per kwh storage, lifetime battery operating cost ranges from $0.60 to $1.00 per kwh delivered.

Range with current batteries. The vehicle range possible with batteries currently available on commercial scales is quite limited. Vehicles powered by lead-acid batteries can typically travel 50 to 90 miles on a single charge, assuming that accessories are not used (see Moomaw et al., 1994, pp. 3-13 to 3-17). Using air conditioning reduces range by roughly 20 percent; high speeds, hard accelerations, heating, and hill climbing reduce it further. Because of these range limitations, it is widely believed that electric vehicles powered by lead-acid or even nickel cadmium batteries will achieve very limited consumer acceptance, and that such batteries are a transitional technology. Thus, considerable effort has been devoted to developing batteries that store more energy per unit mass, last longer, and cost less.

Nickel Metal Hydride. Nickel Metal Hydride (NiMH) batteries are currently used in many consumer electronic devices, and substantial progress has been made in scaling the batteries up in size for use in electric vehicles. Ovonic Battery Company, Inc., in Michigan appears furthest along in the process, although other battery manufacturers, such as Saft, appear to be close behind. Ovonic packs are currently being tested by vehicle manufacturers. NiMH energy density ranges from 70 to 80 wh/kg (see Table 10.1-1), roughly doubling the range possible with lead-acid battery packs of the same weight.

Considerable uncertainty remains over the cycle life of NiMH battery packs. In a presentation at a 1995 CARB workshop, Ovonic claimed that its battery module lasted 600 cycles (Adams, 1995). The Ovonic tests were apparently not done on full battery packs, however, and the cycle life of the full pack could be lower.[197] At the same workshop, Toyota raised questions about the cycle life and performance of NiMH batteries at high temperatures (Haines, 1995). Some tests have shown reduced cycle life and a high self-discharge rate at high ambient air temperatures (over 100 degrees F), and further evaluation of the batteries in such conditions is needed.

In March 1994, General Motors and Ovonic formed a joint venture to commercially produce an NiMH battery. The new firm, GM Ovonic, expects to build a pilot production plant in 1996.

Sodium Nickel Chloride. AEG Anglo Batteries in Germany is currently testing and developing a Sodium Nickel Chloride (NaNiCl) battery. The so-called ZEBRA battery is being produced on a pilot production line and tested in 70 EVs in Europe. The energy density is 80 wh/kg, and several batteries have delivered more than 1,000 cycles in actual use (Kalhammer et al., 1995, p. III-37). The batteries operate at approximately 600 degrees F, and even though they have passed crash tests, safety remains an issue.

Lithium Ion. Lithium Ion (LiIon) batteries have recently started to be used in consumer electronics products, currently accounting for perhaps 10 percent of that market (Michael Fetcenko, personal communication, 1995). In consumer electronics applications, lithium ion batteries have energy densities of over 100 wh/kg and can last up to 1,200 cycles (Kalhammer et al., 1995, p. III-22; Doddapaneni et al., 1994, p. 5). Sony has recently announced development of a LiIon battery module for electric vehicles with an energy density of 100 wh/kg and a cycle life of 1,200 cycles and good performance over a very wide range of ambient temperatures (Sony, 1995).

At approximately $1,000 per kwh even for small consumer electronics cells, LiIon battery are currently very expensive (Steve Albu, CARB, personal communication, 1995). One of the reasons for the high cost is that LiIon batteries currently contain cobalt, a precious metal.

---

[197]There are 13 cells in an Ovonic module and approximately 25 modules in a 30 kwh battery pack (Adams, 1995).

Research is focusing on replacing cobalt with much less expensive materials, such as manganese, but researchers are just learning how this will affect energy density and cycle life.

Lithium Polymer. This solid state battery may be safer than the liquid-electrolyte LiIon battery. It also promises to have even higher energy density (150 to 200 wh/kg). However, the battery is still in the early stages of development (Kalhammer et al., 1995, p. III-28), and estimates of in-use performance, availability and cost are highly speculative.

Expected Battery Development Through 2002

The California Battery Technical Advisory Panel (BTAP) recently completed an assessment of the expected performance and availability of batteries for electric vehicles that could be offered commercially between 1998 and 2003 (Kalhammer et al., 1995). The BTAP based its analysis on information supplied by battery developers and auto makers and on its own knowledge.

The BTAP estimated when batteries *could* be available in commercial volumes (>10,000 battery packs a year). The Panel's estimates assume that there are no unforeseen technical issues encountered in battery development, evaluation, or manufacturing that would require battery developers to return to earlier development stages. The Battery Panel was explicit in explaining that its estimates of availability should be interpreted as the *earliest* dates at which the batteries might be available. The Panel's estimates are presented in Table 10.1-2 and summarized graphically in Figure 10.1-1.

As can be seen by comparing Tables 10.1-1 and 10.1-2, the BTAP concludes that, if all goes well, there could be substantial technological improvements over the next several years. For example, the BTAP estimates that the cycle life of NiMH batteries may increase from perhaps 600 cycles today to 800 to 1,000 cycles for NiMH type AB5 and 1,000 to 2,000 cycles for type AB2.[198] Similarly, LiIon cycle life is expected not to decline below 1,000 as the batteries are scaled up from modules to full battery packs.

---

[198]AB2 and AB5 are two different types of NiMH batteries.

Table 10.1-2

California Battery Technical Advisory Panel Projections of Battery Performance and Availability

	1995	1996	1997	1998	1999	2000	2001	2002
			Earliest Date Commercially Available					
PbA								
wh/kg	35			50				
cycles	400-600			400-600				
Prdcost	125-175			120-150				
Lifcost	0.26-0.55			0.25-0.47				
NiCd								
wh/kg		50		55-60				
cycles		800-1,000		1,500-2,000				
Prdcost		300-350		300-350				
Lifcost		0.38-0.55		0.19-0.29				
NiMH, type AB2								
wh/kg						70-80		
cycles						1,000-2,000		
Prdcost						225-500		
Ult prdcost						150		
Lifcost						0.14-0.63		
Ult lifcost						0.09-0.19		
NiMH, type AB5								
wh/kg						80-90		
cycles						800-1,000		
Prdcost						230-250		
Ult prdcost						150		
Lifcost						0.29-0.39		
Ult lifcost						0.19-0.23		

Table 10.1-2 (Cont'd.)

					Earliest Date Commercially Available			
	1995	1996	1997	1998	1999	2000	2001	2002
NaNiCl								
wh/kg						90-100		
cycles						1,000-1,200		
Prdcost						230-345		
Ult prdcost						175		
Lifcost						0.24-0.43		
Ult lifcost						0.18-0.22		
LiIon								
wh/kg								120-140
cycles								1,000-1,200
Prdcost								200-500
Ult prdcost								165
Lifcost								0.21-0.63
Ult lifcost								0.17-0.21

cycles = cycle life when batteries drawn down to 80 percent depth of discharge.

Prdcost = battery production cost when battery first produced in commercial volumes.($/kwh).

Ult prdcost = ultimate learned-out production cost ($/kwh).

Lifcost = battery cost per kwh delivered over lifetime of one battery when battery first produced in commercial volumes ($/kwh delivered). Lifcost = prdcost/(cycles*0.8). The 0.8 factor is necessary because cycle life is usually measured using 80 percent depth of discharge.

Ult lifcost = ultimate battery cost per kwh delivered with learned out production cost ($/kwh).

The nature of the BTAP's information casts some doubt on their estimates of battery performance. The BTAP generally "accepted performance information from battery developers without adjustment if the information seemed plausible given the Panel's knowledge base," (Kalhammer et al., 1995, p. I-5). Because one expects that battery developers have an optimistic view of the potential of their technology, it is likely that the battery performance specifications are optimistic even if all goes well.

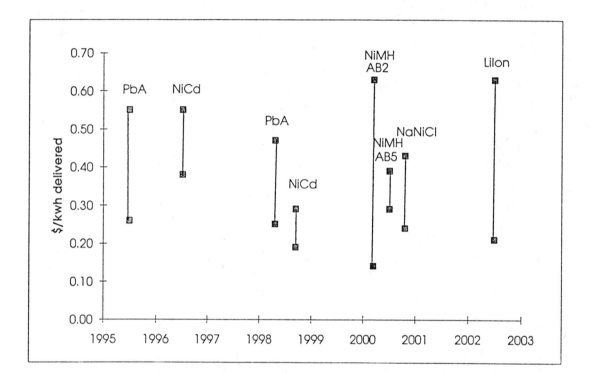

Figure 10.1-1 Battery Panel Estimates of Potential Battery Costs per Kilowatt Hour Delivered

The BTAP cost estimates are also likely optimistic. The Panel did not develop its own estimates but "relied almost entirely on the battery cost information provided by developers," (Kalhammer et al., 1995, p. III-47). The Panel believed that the cost estimates from different developers vary in degrees of certainty and optimism, and that developers may have provided estimates that approximated generally accepted cost *targets* rather than well-grounded, realistic predictions. The cost estimates should thus be interpreted cautiously. For example, BTAP accepts the Ovonic estimate that NiMH batteries (type AB5) will cost $230 to $250 per kwh in 2000. Not only is this range remarkably narrow, but others we interviewed are skeptical that the price will fall below $350 per kwh, reasoning that because the battery contains both nickel and precious metals, NiMH production cost will not fall much below that of the NiCd battery. Similarly, the cost projection for LiIon batteries assumes that developers are successful in replacing high-cost cobalt with manganese, which is far from certain.

10.2 DIRECT COSTS OF ELECTRIC VEHICLES

We now consider what is known about the direct costs of electric vehicles. In this case direct costs are the costs of producing and operating an electric vehicle and the infrastructure required. We review the available information on (1) the production cost of an electric vehicle excluding the first battery, and (2) the lifetime operating costs of the vehicles. EV operating costs include the cost of all batteries required during the life of the vehicle including the first one, electricity, and repair and maintenance.[199]

Using available information, we develop lower and upper bound estimates of (1) average production and operating costs for the vehicles sold during the first five years of the mandate and (2) how costs might decline after 2002. These estimates are used later to calculate narrow cost effectiveness ratios for electric vehicles.

10.2.1 Production Costs of an EV Excluding the Battery

We first review and critique studies of the production costs of electric vehicles that are similar in size, body style, and performance (except for range) to ICEVs on the road today. As discussed below, the

---

[199]We do not address the infrastructure costs of electric vehicles, such as the cost of installing 220 volt residential outlets, in this report.

Big 7--the seven companies subject to the mandate in 1998--apparently intend to produce such vehicles.[200]

The Big 7 may also meet the mandate by purchasing ZEV credits from other companies that produce electric vehicles. We thus examine the production costs of two types of vehicles that may be less costly to produce: conversions and small non-traditional vehicles. Conversions are ICEVs from which internal combustion engine components have been removed (or have not been installed in the first place--so-called gliders) and electric vehicle components installed. Small non-traditional vehicles are vehicles that have relatively poor acceleration or limited top speed that might be demanded in market niches where freeway capability is not required.

Production Costs of EVs Similar to ICEVs on the Road Today

We have reviewed in detail four studies on the production costs of electric vehicles that are similar in size, styling, and performance (except for range) as ICEVs on the road today. These are Sierra (1994a), Abacus Technology Corporation (1994), General Accounting Office (1995), and Booz, Allen & Hamilton, Inc. (1995). They appear to span the range of production cost estimates for these types of vehicles.[201,202] Below, we summarize and interpret their findings and also summarize information on EV production costs provided us by the three major American automobile manufacturers during confidential interviews in July 1995.

In most of the studies, the estimated total cost per vehicle depends on the number of vehicles produced, and the figures presented

---

[200]The seven are: General Motors, Ford, Chrysler, Toyota, Nissan, Honda, and Mazda.

[201]We also reviewed Delucchi (1992). However, we do not summarize his findings because they appear to be illustrations of cost conditions under which EV technology might succeed rather than projections of what costs will actually be. Delucchi (1992, p. 19) writes: "I think it is more useful to show the conditions under which a technology might succeed, than to say that if technologies do not develop as hoped then they will fail."

[202]CARB does not estimate electric vehicle production costs. In its evaluation of the ZEV mandate, it assumes that electric vehicle production costs will be similar to ICEV production costs after 2002, but provides no analysis to support this assumption.

below are associated with particular production volumes. Recall from
Table 5.8-1 that, if manufacturers meet their mandate quantities
entirely by producing EVs, the California mandate requires each of the
Big 7 to produce approximately 3,500 vehicles on average between 1998
and 2000, rising to nearly 9,000 in 2001 and approximately 17,500 in
2003. These volumes roughly double if the mandates in New York and
Massachusetts remain in place.[203]

The studies reviewed typically express EV costs by comparison with
the costs of a comparable ICEV. For example, an electric pickup with
power steering and air conditioning is compared to a gasoline-powered
pickup of similar size, power, and with similar options. Where
possible, we separately report the incremental variable production costs
in excess of that for a comparable ICEV and the total fixed costs
required for the EV program.[204]

Sierra (1994a). Sierra Research, Inc., estimates EV production
costs using confidential data collected from five large manufacturers on
fixed, variable, and dealer costs--the same basic method used to
estimate the costs of ICEV emissions control hardware-based regulations
discussed in Section 6. Sierra estimates the costs of producing the
volumes required by the California mandate between 1998 and 2010 as well
as producing twice the California volume over the same period (see Table
10.2-1).[205] As it did for ICEV emissions control costs, Sierra presents
both the average of costs reported by the manufacturers and its own
"best-case" estimate. The Sierra estimates include adjustments for

---

[203]Also recall that the required volumes vary significantly by
manufacturer. In 1998, the volume required for California varies from
900 to 6,600; in 2003 it varies from 4,500 to 33,000.

[204]Some studies report average fixed costs (fixed costs per
vehicle), but because the proportionate changes in EV production volumes
possible are so large (going from hundreds to tens of thousands of
units, for example) we think it more useful to report total fixed costs
for the EVs produced, rather than fixed costs per vehicle.

[205]Sierra is not explicit about the production volumes assumed in
its various scenarios. But to give a sense of the magnitudes involved,
in the simulations below, we assume the cumulative production volumes
required of all manufacturers through 2010 at twice the California
mandate is 2.6 million.

dealer markup and costs of capital, but as with ICEV hardware analysis, the magnitudes of these adjustments are not directly reported.

Sierra estimates costs for a small passenger car, specifically designed as an electric vehicle.[206] Sierra gives no description of the performance or features of this hypothetical vehicle.[207] Based on detailed discussions with the three American automobile manufacturers that provided data to Sierra, it appears that the vehicle was comparable in all respects except range to a fully equipped ICEV of similar body size and styling.

Using manufacturer data, Sierra estimates that each electric vehicle will cost approximately $53,000 more than a comparable ICEV between 1998 and 2010 for California mandate volumes (see Table 10.2-2). The cost per vehicle is approximately 45 percent less for twice the California volume. Sierra does not report data that allow us to determine how incremental costs might change between 1998 and 2010 or what they would be in any subperiod of this time interval.

Sierra's best-case estimates are substantially lower than the average of those reported by the five manufacturers. The estimated total incremental cost per vehicle is approximately $17,000 at the volumes required by the California mandate. The cost per vehicle falls by roughly half for twice the California volume. This is curious: Although average fixed costs might be expected to drop by 50 percent when volume doubles, it seems implausible that average variable costs would also halve, since that would require that there be no added variable costs from doubling volume.[208] We would expect economies of scale to reduce the variable costs per vehicle, but as noted in Table 10.2-1, Sierra does not discuss economies of scale. This raises some questions about Sierra's costing methodology that we have not resolved.

---

[206]These are often referred to as "purpose-built vehicles". Manufacturers, in contrast, may also adapt existing ICEVs to be electric.

[207]In personal interviews, Sierra provided us with some information not contained in the report. What Sierra could tell us, however, was limited by confidentiality agreements with the companies who supplied data.

[208]Put another way, doubling volume can halve average total costs only if all costs are fixed.

Sierra does report that 63 percent of ZEV total costs per vehicle are fixed, 29 percent are variable, and 8 percent represent dealer margin (Sierra, 1994a, p. A-10). We applied these percentages to the total cost estimates; our derived figures for variable costs are shown in Table 10.2-2. Incremental variable costs range from approximately $2,500 to $4,900 in the best-case estimate and from $8,700 to $15,300 for the manufacturer estimates. These numbers should be interpreted cautiously, however, because Sierra reports only one percentage breakdown of total costs, and the percentage breakdown must vary with production volume if there are any variable costs.

The derived values for variable production costs imply fixed costs of between $6,000 and $21,000 per vehicle for twice California volumes.[209] Assuming that approximately 2.6 million EVs are required to meet twice the California mandate between 1998 and 2010, these average fixed costs translate into approximately $16 billion to $56 billion in fixed costs between 1998 and 2010 (discounted to 1993).

Sierra's estimates are difficult to evaluate because little information is provided on what is driving costs. As discussed presently, the Sierra manufacturer estimates for incremental variable costs appear consistent with the data that Chrysler, Ford, and General Motors (hereafter, the Big 3) provided us in interviews, but we do not know how to interpret the Sierra best-case estimates.

---

[209]Sierra's estimate for dealer costs are included in these totals.

Table 10.2-1

**Summary of Studies Comparing Production Costs of Electric Vehicles
(Excluding Battery Pack) and ICEVs**

	Sierra (1994a)	Abacus (1994)	GAO (1994)	Booz·Allen (1995)
Type of EV	Small purpose built passenger car	Adaptation of Ford Aerostar	Adaptation of VW Citistromer (4 seat, passenger)	Four-passenger, commuter car: adaptation of ICEV initially, then purpose-built
Comparable ICEV	Not specified	Ford Aerostar	VW Citistromer	Ford Escort
Basis for estimate	Data provided by 5 large manufacturers	Costs of adding EV components to ICEV shell	Selling prices projected by large European manufacturer	Build of cost of EV based on component prices provided by EV component suppliers
Annual production volume	Volumes required by CA mandate and twice CA mandate	10,000 in 1998 and 100,000 in 2005 per vehicle model	1,000 and 100,000 per vehicle model	Twice CA mandate
Production date	1998 to 2010	1998 and 2005	Not specified	1998, 2000, 2002, 2004
Fixed costs estimated?	Yes	Not addressed	Not addressed	Yes
Dealer markup included?	50% of standard markup, but standard markup not reported	Not addressed	Not addressed	10 percent for selling costs and 3 percent for dealer profit added to production cost
Manufacturer profit	Included but magnitude not reported separately	Not addressed	Not addressed	5 percent added to production cost

Table 10.2-1 (Cont'd.)

	Sierra (1994a)	Abacus (1994)	GAO (1994)	Booz·Allen (1995)
Economies of scale	Not addressed	25% from 1,000 to 10,000 units 50% from 10,000 to 100,000 units	25% from 1,000 to 10,000 units 31% from 10,000 to 100,000 units	Included by not specified separately
Learning over time	50% reduction in fixed costs each 5-year product cycle; 5% reduction in variable costs a year	Costs fall 1% a year (p. A-4)	Not addressed	Included, but not specified separately

Table 10.2-2

**Estimates of Additional Cost of an Electric Vehicle Without the Battery
Compared with a Comparable ICEV
(dollars per vehicle)**

	Type of Car	Variable Cost	Total Cost
Sierra Manufacturer[a] (discounted to 1993, 1993 dollars)	small passenger		
CA mandate volume (1998-2010)		15,266	52,641
Twice CA mandate volume (1998-2010)		8,742	30,145
Sierra Best Case[a] (discounted to 1993, 1993 dollars)	small passenger		
CA mandate volume (1998-2010)		4,940	17,034
Twice CA mandate volume (1998-2010)		2,490	8,588
Big 3 (1995 dollars)			
CA mandate volume (1998-2002)	various	15,000	
Abacus[b] (1994 dollars)	minivan		
10,000 vehicles (1998)			57
100,000 vehicles (2005)			-5,561
GAO[b] (1992 dollars[c])	midsize passenger		
1,000 vehicles			15,050
100,000 vehicles			-1,290
CA volume (1998-2002)[d]			7,497
Twice CA volume (1998-2002)[d]			6,066
Booz·Allen (1994 dollars, twice CA volume)	Ford Escort		
1998		4,829	
2000		3,529	
2002		1,829	
2004		329	

[a]Sierra estimates were reduced by $4,000 to remove the approximate cost of the first battery.

[b]Whether and how fixed costs are included in total cost not addressed. Sierra variable costs imputed from data provided on breakdown of total costs.

[c]Base year for dollars not specified explicitly. Assumed to be year of study on vehicle costs cited by GAO.

[d]Imputed.

Data Supplied by the Big 3. To help us interpret the costs in the Sierra report and provide more up-to-date information, we interviewed technical staff at the three American manufacturers' electric vehicle programs in late July 1995. Two of the three companies described the electric vehicles they plan to produce to meet the 1998 mandate and provided cost estimates. The third manufacturer would not reveal plans for 1998, but provided a detailed qualitative discussion of cost issues.[210]

The Big 3 estimated that the variable production costs of the EVs they would produce between 1998 and 2002 would be approximately $15,000 more per vehicle than the comparable ICEV.[211] These costs reflect average costs during the five year period, assuming California mandate volumes.[212] As was the case for the ICEV control cost estimates discussed in Section 6, the electric vehicle cost estimates appeared to result from detailed costing exercises and be based on actual purchase agreements that manufacturers had negotiated or were in the process of negotiating with suppliers. We were not able to audit the numbers they supplied, but view them as credible estimates of their projections of costs for the vehicles they currently plan to supply during the first five years of the mandate.

The manufacturers provided no estimates of variable costs for volumes twice the California mandate, but some said that even at double the California mandate, volumes were still very low and incremental costs would change little.

---

[210]These data were provided on a confidential basis.

[211]Individual company data did not vary a great deal around this value. Confidentiality concerns prohibit us from being more specific.

[212]Care should be taken in comparing the data provided us with the numbers reported by Sierra because: (1) the number of firms in the two samples differs (three in our sample, five in Sierra's); (2) Sierra projected costs from 1998 to 2010, the firms we interviewed were looking at much shorter time horizons--three to five years in two cases and 10 years in the third; (3) Sierra's data are two years older. Both the type of electric vehicle planned and the costs of components may have changed; and (4) Sierra's costs are discounted and the costs we were given are not.

Our discussions with the manufacturers suggest at least two reasons why their incremental electric vehicle estimates are so high relative to the Sierra best-case estimate. First, the manufacturers plan to produce high quality electric vehicles that, except for range, give performance similar to comparable ICEVs. Second, high costs are due to low production levels and new components. We discuss each in turn.

It was clear that the three manufacturers plan to produce high quality, reliable electric vehicles with performance and features similar to those of their ICEV counterparts: comparable acceleration, handling, braking, power steering, air conditioning, heating, and defrosting. Warranties will also be similar to those for ICEVs, and the vehicle will be required to meet the same safety standards.[213] This is not the only approach to meeting the mandate, but it appears to make good business sense to these large companies. Companies are apparently unwilling to risk letting a production run of several thousand electric vehicles negatively affect company reputation and consequently the sales of the millions of ICEVs they annually produce.

The required EV components will be expensive at first because they are being produced in such small numbers. One manufacturer told us they had trouble even convincing suppliers to sell various types of components to them in such small quantities. (An order of several thousand units is very small in an industry accustomed to thinking of orders in the hundreds of thousands or even millions.) In addition to the low production volumes, EV components are expensive because many are new, and the manufacturers or suppliers have not yet learned how best to make them.[214] An example is the power steering unit for electric vehicles. This is a relatively new product that has so far been made only in very small numbers.

We received only sketchy information from the Big 3 on the fixed costs for the electric vehicles they plan to produce to meet the mandate. Fixed costs were in the hundreds of millions of dollars per

---

[213]Warranty costs are included with the production cost of the vehicles. These are repair costs that are actually incurred after the vehicle is produced, but will be borne by producers, not by consumers.

[214]Economies due to learning are usually thought of as depending on cumulative production to date.

manufacturer. They include the cost of vehicle design, building prototypes, performance and safety testing, vehicle assembly lines, and overhead costs directly attributable to the vehicle. The fixed cost numbers were nowhere near as large as those reported in the press for some major ICEV models,[215] but are spread over a much smaller number of vehicles.

Abacus Technology Corporation (1994). In a report recently produced for the U.S. Department of Energy, Abacus Technology Corporation (Abacus) estimates the purchase price of an electric minivan by subtracting the cost of the ICEV drive train, fuel system, and accessories such as air conditioning and power steering from the manufacturer's suggested retail price of a Ford Aerostar (Abacus, 1995, p. A-7).[216] The combined cost of the ICEV components is based on internal Department of Energy estimates, but the basis for these estimates is not discussed. Abacus then adds the prices of electric vehicle components--including motor, controller, transmission, high power charger, and air conditioner--as quoted to Abacus by component suppliers or electric vehicle conversion companies (Abacus, 1995, p. A-8).

The electric vehicle priced by Abacus appears to have reasonable acceleration (powered by a 60 kilowatt motor, equivalent to approximately 80 horsepower), although it may still be less than the Ford Aerostar used for comparison (which has 135 horsepower). The electric vehicle has air conditioning, but not power steering.

Abacus estimates the EV purchase prices for 1998 and 2005. The production volumes assumed in the two years are different. For 1998 Abacus assumes industry-wide production of approximately 65,000 vehicles (approximately twice the volume required by the California EV mandate) so that the Big 7 will make on average about 10,000 vehicles each. Using government projections that are not detailed, it assumes that

---

[215]For example Ford reportedly spent $6 billion to develop its Mystique/Contour line and Chrysler spent $1.3 billion on its Neon project (cited from *Automotive Engineering*, October 1994 by Booz·Allen, 1995, p. 7-10)

[216]The manufacturer's suggested retail price includes dealer markup and presumably some recovery of fixed cost.

2,000,000 electric vehicles will be sold in 2005 so that each manufacturer will produce 100,000 units of several different models.[217] Thus, Abacus' second estimate of the price of an electric minivan assumes annual production of 100,000 in 2005 (see Table 10.2-1).

Abacus estimates that the purchase price of an electric minivan without the battery will be $57 more than a comparable ICEV in 1998.[218] This is dramatically below both the estimates provided us by the Big 3 and the Sierra's manufacturer estimate. The primary reason for the difference appears to be that many electric vehicle components included by the automobile makers we interviewed were missing from the Abacus report. For example, Abacus does not include costs for battery tray, heavy duty wiring, and power steering. Also, in contrast to the auto makers we interviewed, no additional costs for tires, warranty, assembly, or the heavy duty suspension needed to support the batteries are included. Given these significant omissions we think it likely that Abacus seriously underestimates electric vehicle costs.

Abacus does not discuss fixed costs in its report. Abacus may be assuming that fixed costs of suppliers are included in supplier price quotes, but manufacturer costs to design and test components and prototype vehicles and to modify assembly lines are apparently not included (or are assumed to be zero). It may thus be reasonable to interpret the change in purchase price to reflect change in variable costs of the vehicle.

Abacus estimates that when EV production reaches 100,000 units per model in 2005, the purchase price of EVs without the battery will be $5,561 below that of a comparable ICEV. The main factor driving this decline is the increase in scale of production. Abacus assumes that electric vehicle component prices it was quoted in 1994 (when production was assumed to be around 1,000 units) will fall by 25 percent by 1998 and 50 percent between 1994 and 2005. These percentage declines were based on a study by the Japanese Institute of Applied Energy that showed

---

[217]For comparison, twice the California mandate requires that approximately 275,000 vehicles be produced in 2005.

[218]We have excluded taxes and title cost from the purchase prices of both the EV and the ICEV.

battery production cost per unit falling 25 percent as battery production increases from 1,000 units in 1994 to 10,000 units in 1998 and falling 50 percent as production increases to 100,000 units in 2005 (cited in Abacus, 1995, p. A-4). We have not reviewed the Japanese study, but based on Abacus' account, we infer that it was done only for batteries and not for other electric vehicle components. It may therefore not be appropriate for predicting changes in production costs of electric vehicles. In addition, even if the scale economies do reduce costs and selling prices in 2005 relative to 1998, the level of the price in 2005 is still low to the extent that the 1998 price is low.

General Accounting Office (GAO, 1994). GAO estimated the purchase price of a mid-sized four passenger electric vehicle at production volumes of 1,000 and 100,000 units.[219] As indicated in Table 10.2-1, GAO was not explicit about the time frame assumed. GAO based its estimates on the findings of a report prepared by the German Ministry of Transportation on the expected percent change in purchase price of a Volkswagen Citistromer (mid-sized, 4 passenger vehicle) as annual production volumes vary.[220] The Citistromer is an adaptation of the Volkswagen Golf/Jetta model and has a top speed of approximately 65 miles per hour (GAO, 1994, p. 53). It also presumably has performance, handling, and safety features comparable to the ICEV counterpart.

Using data provided by Volkswagen, the Ministry of Transportation estimated that the price would fall approximately 27 percent as the annual production rate rose from 1,000 to 10,000 units and would fall 50 percent as production levels increased from 1,000 to 100,000 units annually (cited in GAO, 1994, p. 75).[221] The declines in price appear

---

[219]GAO says that it is estimating the "purchase cost" of an electric vehicle. It appears to be thinking in terms of a purchase price. A conversation with the author failed to clarify this issue.

[220]Volkswagen is not subject to the ZEV mandate in 1998, but is subject to it in 2003 and is apparently considering selling a version of the vehicle in 1998 (Booz·Allen, 1995, p. 3-16).

[221]The price of the vehicle excluding the battery was approximately $40,000 when production was 1,000 units annually. According to GAO, Volkswagen has "relatively extensive experience producing EVs" (GAO, 1994, p. 74).

to be due solely to the scale of production. No learning economies are discussed.

GAO reports estimates of purchase price but does not discuss how they relate to production cost. In particular, there is no discussion of how and whether fixed costs are included in the price. It would appear from the relationship between price and volume reported that fixed costs are either small or are not fully amortized over each of the volumes examined (see GAO, 1994, p. 75).[222] Dealer markups may also be included in the price, but this is not discussed by GAO.

GAO concludes that the purchase price of an electric vehicle without the battery will remain significantly above that of a comparable ICEV at low production volumes. As shown in Table 10.2-2, cost is $15,050 higher at 1,000 units a year, but is $1,290 dollars lower when production levels reach 100,000 units (GAO, 1994, p. 81).[223] GAO does not directly estimate what the purchase price would be at volumes sufficient to meet the California mandate or twice those volumes. A summary of the German study that does report changes in purchase price at these volumes (GAO, 1994, p. 75) suggests that the incremental price of an EV excluding the battery over an ICEV would be approximately $7,500 at the volume required on average per firm during the first five years of the mandate and $6,000 at twice that volume.

Booz, Allen & Hamilton, Inc. (1995). In a report produced for the New York State Energy Research and Development Authority, Booz, Allen & Hamilton, Inc. (Booz·Allen) estimates the production cost of a four-passenger commuter car similar to the Ford Escort. Booz·Allen estimates production costs in 1998, 2000, 2002, and 2004 when overall industry output levels of electric vehicles are twice the levels required by the California mandate. They estimate costs for a vehicle with acceleration, comfort and safety similar to a small ICEV (Booz·Allen, 1995, p. 7-15). In contrast to the estimates provided by the Big 3,

---

[222]If substantial fixed costs are included in the price and were amortized over each of the volumes reported, the declines in per unit price should be much larger than reported.

[223]According to the project manager for the GAO study, the prices in the GAO study included a 14 percent tax. Both the EV and comparable ICEV costs were adjusted downward to remove this tax.

however, they do not include air conditioning and power steering, which, of course, tends to lower estimated incremental EV costs.

Costs are estimated from price data collected from electric vehicle component suppliers, small electric vehicle manufacturers, and the automotive industry press. Booz·Allen apparently assumes the prices quoted are equal to production costs. They report estimates for marketing costs and manufacturer and dealer profit separately, and the numbers reported here exclude these costs.

Booz·Allen estimates that the incremental variable cost of an EV, excluding the battery, is approximately $4,800 in 1998 and $329 in 2004 (see Table 10.2-2). The cost reductions are driven by predictions made by component suppliers of how costs will decline because of learning and increased volumes.

The Booz·Allen estimates appear to miss many important costs of producing an EV. Costs for the battery tray, heavy duty wiring, and warranty are not included. Also, at $3,500 per vehicle in 1998, the cost of the AC induction or DC permanent magnet powertrain assumed in the analysis is very low. This is significantly below the prices quoted in the report for drivetrains that are currently available, and based on their own discussion, appears to be an optimistic assumption for just the cost of the motor by 1998, let alone the charger, controller, and transmission (see Booz·Allen, 1995, p. 7-8, 7-9).[224]

The projected declines in incremental variable costs over time are large, and the declines appear to based on optimistic assumptions. Labor costs per vehicle drop 50 percent from $2,000 (approximately the labor costs of an ICEV, according to Booz·Allen) to $1,000 between 1998 and 2004. Apparently, this assumption is made because Booz·Allen believes that EVs will have fewer moving parts and should ultimately be easier to assemble. However, no quantitative basis is given for the assumption. Powertrain costs drop roughly 40 percent to $2,000 per

---

[224]For example Booz·Allen cites a motor supplier projection that motors currently selling for $24,000 will sell for $2,000 at production volumes of 30,000 a year. For production volume of one manufacturer to be near this level by 1998, about three-fifths of all electric vehicles produced (approximately 50,000 at twice California mandate levels) would have to use motors from the same manufacturer.

vehicle in 2004, which is the cost projection of learned-out costs provided by one small motor manufacturer. Once weighted by the number of vehicles required for twice the mandate in each year, the Booz·Allen estimates for costs between 1998 and 2002 imply an average incremental cost of $3,320 between 1998 and 2002.

Booz·Allen (1995, pp. 7-16, 7-17) estimates that the fixed costs of producing the electric vehicles will be between $150 million and $600 million per manufacturer and will be amortized over the 7 year period. Their estimates are of the same order of magnitude as the fixed cost estimates provided to us by the Big 3.

Costs of Converting ICEVs to Electric Vehicles

Electric vehicle converters, such as BAT and Solectria, also produce electric vehicles. They currently sell small numbers of vehicles. When the mandate takes effect, they may also be a source of electric vehicle credits. In this section, we briefly summarize current information on the costs and characteristics of these converted vehicles.

In comparison with the vehicles that the Big 7 apparently intend to produce during the first years of the mandate, converted vehicles may be of lesser quality than most ICEVs on the road today. Handling and braking may be worse because the ICEV chassis is not designed for the weight and location of the battery pack. Converted vehicles may not have the same road clearance or be designed to withstand hazardous driving conditions such as heavy rains. Converters do not have to crash test vehicles, and the safety of conversions may not be a high as ICEVs currently produced by large manufacturers. Also, the converters do not appear to offer the same bumper to bumper warranties expected of the Big 7 (see Moomaw et al., 1994, pp. 3-12 to 3-17), and service support may not be as good.

In a report prepared for the Northeast Alternative Vehicle Consortium, researchers at the International Environment and Resource Program at Tufts University assembled information on the prices and specifications of electric vehicle conversions currently available on the market (Moomaw et al., 1994). Sales prices from many different converters were compared to the sales prices of the conventional gasoline vehicles that were converted. Table 10.2-3 presents several examples that span the range of differences in price between the conversions and comparable ICEVs reported in the study. Incremental prices for EVs excluding the battery range from about $5,000 and $15,000 for passenger vehicles and from $6,000 to $23,000 for utility vehicles. One important reason for the difference is the type of electric motor used. BAT uses direct current (DC) motors while Solectria uses more expensive alternating current (AC) motors that also require more expensive controllers and converters.

We first note that the figures reported by Moomaw et al. are prices, not costs of production. The prices may not necessarily be closely linked to production costs. For example, a converter might set price below cost initially if it were trying to get a foothold in the market. We thus have little information about what the production costs of conversions are and how the costs break down into fixed and variable costs.

Second, the converter prices reflect production at very low levels using very labor intensive processes with little specialization. Conversion prices would likely decline as production levels increase. Moomaw et al. (1994, p. 4-5) estimates that, as the production goes from 1,000 units per year to 20,000 units per year, prices will fall 43.4 percent (which means for the Solectria Chevrolet S-10 the incremental price over the ICEV would fall from approximately $23,000 to $5,000 and the Solectria Geo Metro price would fall from approximately $15,000 to approximately $7,500).[225]

---

[225]Part of this decline results from the assumption that converters are able to obtain gliders when their production volumes increase. Gliders are ICEV vehicles into which the ICEV powertrain and emission control system have never been installed.

Table 10.2-3

Prices of Electric Vehicle Conversions Excluding the Battery
(dollars per vehicle)

| | Passenger Vehicles | | Utility Vehicles | |
	BAT	Solectria	BAT	Solectria
ICEV	Geo Metro	Geo Metro	Ford Ranger	Chevrolet S-10
EV Range	60-100	60	50-80	70
Top Speed	80	60	75	60
Passengers	2	4	2	2
EV Price	15,900	26,050	24,100	42,370
ICEV Price	7,295	7,295	11,868	15,641
Difference	8,605	18,755	9,822	26,729
Difference Excluding Battery[a]	4,606	14,755	5,822	22,729

[a]Battery assumed to cost $4,000.
SOURCE: Moomaw et al. (1994), pp. 3-9 to 3-13.

Niche-Market Vehicles

There are a number of electric vehicles being introduced or developed that are smaller or have lower top speed or acceleration than ICEVs on the road today. Such vehicles might be demanded in niche markets where freeway capability is not required. Examples include

- A very small 2-passenger electric vehicle produced by the Personal Independent Vehicle Company (PIVCO), a Norwegian company. PIVCO plans to introduce this vehicle in European and American markets by early 1997. Current models have a top speed of 45 miles per hour, but 1997 models are designed to go 65-70 miles per hour. The range is 50 miles and the price is projected to be $10,000 including lead acid batteries (CALSTART, 1995).

- The "Smart" vehicle produced by Mercedes-Benz and Swatch. The Smart vehicle is also a very small two-seater and will reportedly sell for $10,000 to $13,000 in 1997 (CALSTART, 1995).

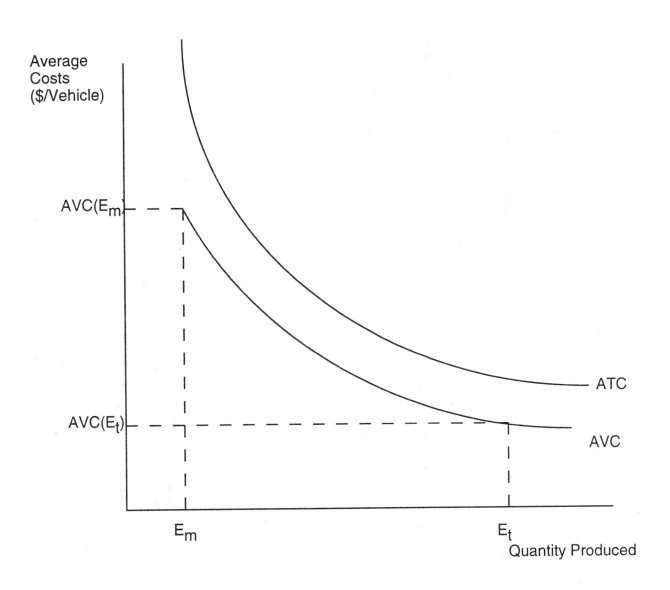

Figure 10.2-1

General Depiction of the Cost Characteristics of EV Production

ATC = average total cost of producing EVs during 1998 to 2002
AVC = average variable cost of producing EVs during 1998 to 2002
E_m = quantity of EVs required to be offered for sale in California under the mandate
E_t = quantity of EVs that would be comparable to production level of typical ICEVs for California and other markets

Decline in Production Costs After 2002

We now turn to how electric vehicle production costs might change after the first five years of the mandate. In its analysis of the electric vehicle mandate, CARB concludes that

> Initially electric vehicles will cost more than conventional gasoline-powered vehicles. ... Over the long-term, however, electric vehicles [excluding the battery] are expected to cost about the same as a conventional vehicle (1994a, p.60).

CARB thinks this is a reasonable conclusion because electric vehicles have fewer moving parts and have drive trains that can by easily adapted to many different types of vehicles (CARB, 1994a, p. 60). In support of its position, CARB cites an often-used statement by John Wallace, Director of Ford's Electric Vehicle Planning and Program Office, that Ford could build an electric vehicle, without the battery, at as low a cost or even at slightly lower cost than an ICEV (CARB, 1994a, p. 60). We think it reasonable to believe that as annual production volumes increase and manufacturers learn how to produce EVs more cheaply, the EV production costs excluding the battery could eventually approach those of ICEVs, but the questions are when and under what conditions.

Few studies have been done to date to examine how EV production costs might fall over time. In this section we review historical information on how prices for other products have declined over extended periods of time as cumulative output grows. We review three studies of the so-called experience curve--Dino (1984), Abernathy and Wayne (1974), and Moomaw et al. (1994)--and consider whether these studies may be relevant to EVs.

The experience curve relates the product *price* and cumulative output, and the sensitivity of price to cumulative output is commonly measured as the percent reduction in price, subtracted from 100, associated with a doubling of cumulative output. Thus, prices following an 85 percent experience curve decrease 15 percent each time cumulative output doubles.

Dino. Dino (1984) analyzes the experience curves for radios, monochrome TVs, color TVs, and VCRs. He finds that the slope of the experience curve changes according to the stage of the product life cycle. Price on a constant dollar basis is level sometimes, but generally drifts upward in the introduction stage, falls significantly during the take-off and growth stage, and stabilizes during the mature phase of the product's life cycle (p. 59).

Dino finds that the experience curve for the products examined ranged from 73 to 88 percent during the take-off and growth stage. The art in the analysis is determining when one stage ends and another begins. In Dino's analysis the level of cumulative output at the point separating the introduction stage and the take-off and growth stages varies a great deal. For radios, monochrome TVs, and color TVs the take-off and growth stage starts when cumulative output reaches approximately 10 million units industry wide. For VCRs, take-off and growth starts at 1 million units.

Abernathy and Wayne. Abernathy and Wayne (1974) report an experience curve for Ford's Model T. They find that average list prices of Ford vehicles followed an 85 percent experience curve between 1908 and 1926 when cumulative output of Ford vehicles grew from approximately 40,000 units to 15 million units. The decline stopped when Ford introduced the Model A to improve product performance.

Moomaw et al. Moomaw et al. (1994, pp. 5-7 to 5-9) report the price changes for Volkswagen Beetles in Brazil between 1960 and 1968 and prices of Nissan vehicles between 1955 and 1970.[231] Their figures imply experience curves of approximately 90 percent for both the VW Beetle and Nissan vehicles. The data on production quantities are reported only as indices, so the cumulative output over which the experience curves apply cannot be determined. Moomaw et al. do not discuss why they ended their analysis of the VW Beetle in 1968. After 1970, the prices of Nissan vehicles began to rise, which Moomaw et al. attribute to a decision by Nissan to produce more upscale products.

Summary. The experience curves in the studies reviewed range from approximately 75 to 90 percent. This suggests bounds for the rate of EV

---

[231]Moomaw et al. do not specify the price index they are using for Nissan vehicles--presumably it is the average prices of Nissan vehicles weighted by the number of vehicles sold.

cost decline after 2002, but a great deal of uncertainty remains over whether the decline in electric vehicles costs will be similar to that of other products at other times:

- **Relevance of experience of industries and products studied to EVs.** For example, the high power electronics in EVs are not necessary in the consumer electronics equipment studied by Dino. EVs contain many different types of components, and they may follow very different types of experience curves. A more detailed analysis that matches the EV components to the experience curves of comparable products would be useful.

- **Stage in the product cycle.** When does the product introduction phase end and the take-off and growth stage begin? In the case of EVs, the analysis is further complicated because some components of EVs may already have reached the mature phase of their product cycle. Examples include the components in EVs similar to those in ICEVs and low-power electronics.

- **Industry output versus firm output as the measure of cumulative output.** Dino uses industry output, Abernathy and Wayne and Moomaw et al. use firm output. Further work is needed on whether this is an important distinction and, if so, whether firm or industry output is more relevant to EV cost decline.[232] If advances by one firm are quickly reverse engineered or imitated by others, industry output may be more relevant. If, in contrast, there are many firms in the industry and little information flow between them, firm output may be more relevant.

- **Price decreases versus cost decreases.** The studies reviewed analyze changes in retail price. As discussed above, these may not closely reflect production costs; studies of price will be revealing about cost to the extent that the rate of price to cost is stable over time.

---

[232]Strictly interpreted, it should not matter whether the experience curve applies to industry or firm output: doubling industry output or the outputs of the individual firms that make up the industry should have the same effect on product price, if market shares remain constant.

- **Spillover of EV technological developments to ICEVs.** Improved EV technology may also be used in ICEVs and may decrease the costs of ICEVs. Thus, the cost difference between ZEVs and ICEVs may not fall as fast as otherwise expected (Moss et al., 1995, p. 30).

Thus, the evolution of future EV costs remains highly speculative. How costs decline, however, is central to developing some feel for the long-term cost effectiveness of EVs. In the analysis of narrow cost effectiveness that follows, we construct and use fast and slow scenarios for the decline in EV costs after 2002. In both scenarios, we assume that costs depend on industry, rather than on firm output. We also assume that the Massachusetts and New York mandates remain in place and that EV output levels are twice those required by the California mandate. In the fast cost-decline scenario, costs follow a 75 percent experience curve (decline 25 percent each time cumulative output doubles). In the slow cost-decline scenario, costs follow a 90 percent experience curve.

We interpret the cost estimates for 1998-2002 to incorporate learning during that period. In both post-2002 scenarios, learning according to the experience curves is first applied to the average production cost assumed during the first five years of the mandate.

Because there is uncertainty in the cumulative output at which learning begins, we vary the cumulative output at which the learning curves are anchored across the two scenarios. In the fast scenario, learning starts when cumulative output reaches approximately 150,000 units (the amount required through 2000 in California, Massachusetts, and New York). In the slow scenario learning starts when output reaches approximately 400,000 units (the amount required through 2002).

10.2.2 Incremental Lifetime Operating Costs of Electric Vehicles

We now turn to lifetime operating costs. The principal studies we rely on are CARB (1994a, 1994b), GAO (1994), Abacus (1994), Moomaw et al. (1994), and Booz·Allen (1995). The incremental lifetime costs of operating EVs consist of:

- All batteries required during the life of the vehicle, including the first one;
- EV fuel costs relative to ICEVs;
- EV repair and maintenance costs relative to ICEVs.[233]

For an ICEV, the fuel tank is analogous to the batteries, but the fuel tank's cost is small and included in the cost of the ICEV. Incremental fuel costs are the difference between the cost of electricity used in an EV and cost of the gasoline used in an ICEV. Some aspects of repair and maintenance costs are very similar for ICEVs and EVs--for example, tires wear out on both. Others are very different. For example, ICEVs require replacement of air filters and spark plugs and timing adjustments that EVs do not even have. In contrast, EV controllers, motors, or battery packs may need periodic maintenance (battery watering, for example), repair, or replacement.

Battery costs are the largest component of total (as opposed to incremental) lifetime electric vehicle operating costs. In the studies we reviewed (discussed shortly) batteries accounted for 50 to 65 percent of lifetime operating costs, electricity accounted for 10 to 20 percent, and repair and maintenance accounted for 25 to 35 percent. Tires accounted for about one-third of the repair and maintenance costs. For internal combustion engines, operating costs were roughly evenly split between (1) gasoline and oil costs and (2) repair and maintenance costs.

Our analysis of incremental lifetime operating costs is based on the literature as well as on a model we construct and simulate. We do not rely exclusively on a literature review for several reasons. First, new information on battery cost and availability from California's Battery Technical Advisory Panel has become available since the cost studies reviewed were completed. Second, we want to construct upper and lower bounds for the difference between EV and ICEV operating costs, but the studies reviewed combine to varying degrees assumptions that are optimistic and pessimistic in terms of the difference in EV and ICEV operating costs. As a result, we find it difficult to judge directly whether a given estimate is very likely too high or too low. Simulating

---

[233]Repair costs covered under warranty are included in production costs for both EVs and ICEVs.

our own model allows us to choose different combinations of parameter values and construct upper and lower bounds. Third, the studies reviewed all include gasoline taxes as part of the operating costs of ICEVs, but these taxes should be excluded when comparing the resource costs of EV with those of ICEVs.[234]

We first review the assumptions used by CARB, GAO, Abacus, Moomaw et al., and Booz, Allen & Hamilton (Booz•Allen) in their calculations of incremental operating costs during the first five years of the mandate. These five studies appear to span the range of available estimates. As we review the assumptions used in these studies, we specify the sets of assumptions that we use in our simulations of operating costs during the first five years of the mandate. We compare the predictions of our model for operating costs during the first five years with the estimates in the studies. We then consider how operating costs may change after 2002. We simulate our model using parameter ranges developed for the years after 2002 and compare them to predictions in the studies for operating costs after 2002.

Incremental EV Operating Costs Between 1998 and 2002

The three components of incremental operating costs are addressed in turn: lifetime battery cost, incremental fuel cost, and incremental repair and maintenance cost.

Lifetime Battery Cost. We measure lifetime battery cost in dollars per kilowatt-hour delivered. This combines both battery storage cost per kwh and cycle life.[235,236] As shown in Table 10.2-4, battery costs per kwh hour delivered vary from $0.12 to $0.78 in the studies reviewed,

---

[234]When we revisit the operating cost issue in Section 11 to consider consumer choice between EVs and ICEVs, we include gasoline taxes because they should be considered in that choice.

[235]Because battery cycle life is usually calculated using 80 percent depth of discharge, we calculate cost per kilowatt delivered using 0.8 times cycle life.

[236]The driving range of the vehicle on a single charge determines the size of the battery pack needed. This influences the number and timing of battery pack purchases and affects discounted lifetime operating costs. As shown in Appendix 10.A, however, the effect of the timing of battery pack purchases does not affect discounted operating costs a great deal (less than 15 percent), and we abstract from it.

but if the highest value--apparently corresponding to NiMH in pilot production--is excluded, the range runs is $0.12 to $0.42. This range appears optimistic for battery costs during the first five years of the mandate. Recall from Section 10.1.1 that the Battery Panel projected battery costs between $0.14 and $0.63 during that period, and there is considerable reason to conclude that the Panel's projections are optimistic.

In our simulations of EV operating costs below, we vary battery costs between $0.20 and $0.55 per kwh delivered. The lower number is the lowest of the Battery Panel's projections for the first five years, excluding one extremely optimistic projection (a NiMH battery that costs $225 per kwh and lasts 2,000 cycles). The upper is the high estimate for currently available lead acid batteries. Although more expensive batteries than this may clearly be developed, we question whether they would be used in large numbers if they were so expensive. Assuming vehicle lifetime of 130,000 miles and vehicle efficiency of 4 miles per kwh, a battery costing $0.55 per kwh delivered would cost $17,875 (undiscounted) over the lifetime of the vehicle. It is hard to imagine a commercially viable vehicle with battery costs much higher than this.[237]

---

[237]Higher costs of batteries that allow higher EV range illustrate one of the limitations of narrow cost effectiveness for policy analysis. These batteries will increase the EV cost effectiveness ratio and thus make EV look worse, but consumers may be willing to pay for the long range.

Table 10.2-4

Summary of Studies Comparing Lifetime Operating Costs of Electric Vehicles and ICEVs

	CARB (1994a, 1994b)				GAO (1994)	
	(1)	(2)	(3)	(4)	(1)	(2)
Production date	?	?	?	?	?	?
EV production level	?	?	?	?	1,000	100,000
Battery						
Type	PbA	PbA	NiMH	NiMH	PbA	PbA
wh/kg	50	50	80	80	119	89
$/kwh	120	120	150	150		
Life (cycles)	1,000	1,000	1,000	1,000	500	500
Lifetime cost ($/kwh delivered)	0.12	0.12	0.15	0.15	0.24	0.18
Electric Vehicle						
Type of vehicle	Escort	Escort	Escort	Escort	Citistromer	Citistromer
Efficiency (mi/kwh)	4	3	4	3	2	2
Range (mi)	131	95	131	96	55	55
Life (miles)	129,000	95,000	129,000	95,000	100,000	100,000
Maintenance (percent of ICEV)	66	66	66	66	67	67
Electricity ($/kwh)	0.065	0.065	0.065	0.065	33% less than peak	33% less than peak
ICEV						
Miles per gallon	27.5	27.5	27.5	27.5	?	?
Gas cost	$1.25	$1.25	$1.25	$1.25	?	?
Discount rate	8.00	8.00	8.00	8.00	?	?
Inflation rate	4.00	4.00	4.00	4.00	?	?
Operating cost						
EV ($/mi)	0.052	0.068	0.059	0.077	0.20	0.17
ICEV ($/mi)	0.061	0.061	0.061	0.061	0.10	0.10
EV-ICEV lifetime costs (dollars)	-1,161	665	-258	380	10,000	7,000

Table 10.2-4 (Cont'd.)

	Abacus (1994)				Moomaw et al. (1994)	
	(1)	(2)	(3)	(4)	(1)	(2)
Production date	1998	1998	2005	2005	1998	1998
EV production level (per manufacturer)	10,000	10,000	100,000	100,000	20,000	20,000
Battery						
Type	PbA	NiMH	PbA	NiMH	PbA	NiCd
wh/kg	52	80	52	80	?	?
$/kwh	167	450	136	195	150	500
Life (years)	4	5	5	8	3	10
Lifetime cost ($/kwh delivered)	0.36[a]	0.78[a]	0.24[a]	0.21[a]	0.42[a]	0.25[a]
Electric Vehicle						
Type of vehicle	Minivan	Minivan	Minivan	Minivan	Pickup	Commuter
Efficiency (mi/kwh)	3	3	3	3	4	4
Range (mi)	94	94	94	94	84	50
Life (miles)	130,000	130,000	130,000	130,000	120,000	120,000
Maintenance (percent of ICEV)	63	63	63	63	50	50
Electricity ($/kwh)	0.12	0.12	0.12	0.12	0.05	0.05
ICEV						
Miles per gallon	18	18	18	18	16	46
Gas cost	$1.38	$1.38	$1.38	$1.38	1.20	1.20
Discount rate	7.00	7.00	7.00	7.00	7.00	7.00
Inflation rate	4.18	4.18	4.18	4.18	4.00	4.00
Operating cost						
EV ($/mi)	0.19	0.25	0.21	0.21	0.142	0.101
ICEV ($/mi)	0.16	0.16	0.22	0.22	0.147	0.100
EV-ICEV lifetime costs (dollars)	3,128	10,722	-1,660	-1,452	-600	120

Table 10.2-4 (Cont'd.)

	Booz·Allen (1995)			
	(1)	(2)	(3)	(4)
Production date	1998	2000	2002	2004
EV production level (per manufacturer)	6,000	6,000	15,000	30,000
Battery				
Type	PbA	NiMH	NiMH	NiMH
wh/kg	?	?	?	?
$/kwh	175	175	150	150
Life (years)	4	5	5	7
Lifetime cost ($/kwh delivered)	0.35[a]	0.25[a]	0.25[a]	0.18[a]
Electric Vehicle				
Type of vehicle	Escort	Escort	Escort	Escort
Efficiency (mi/kwh)	4	4.5	5.2	5.2
Range (mi)	100	90	104	104
Life (miles)	150,000	150,000	150,000	150,000
Maintenance (percent of ICEV)	100	100	100	100
Electricity ($/kwh)	0.085	0.086	0.086	0.087
ICEV				
Miles per gallon	27.5	27.5	27.5	27.5
Gas cost	$1.20	$1.20	$1.20	$1.20
Discount rate[b]	6.00	6.00	6.00	6.00
Inflation rate	?	?	?	?
Operating cost				
EV ($/mi)	0.13	0.12	0.11	0.09
ICEV ($/mi)	0.08	0.08	0.09	0.09
EV-ICEV lifetime costs (dollars)	7,500	6,000	3,000	0

[a] Imputed from other parameter values. Cycle life in cycles determined by dividing annual mileage by range and multiplying by battery life in year assumed in study. Annual mileage calculated assuming 12 year vehicle life. $/kwh delivered then determined by dividing battery cost by cycle life.

[b] Unclear whether this is real or nominal discount rate.

Vehicle efficiencies range between 2 and 5.2 miles per kwh in the studies reviewed for passenger cars and between 3 and 4 miles per kwh for pickups and minivans.[238] Five or so is an apparent upper bound for passenger car efficiency under actual operating conditions. The GM Impact has efficiency of roughly 5 (excluding accessories), and it appears to be pushing lightweight construction, drive train efficiency, and aerodynamic technologies quite hard. Two miles per kwh appears too low for passenger car efficiency. This value is used by GAO in its study of VW Citistromer costs, but a close reading of the report suggests that the vehicle efficiency is based on a minivan (GAO, 1994, p. 77). In our analysis below, we allow for passenger car efficiency of 3 to 5 miles per kwh. Both the GAO study and data available for Ford Ranger suggest pickups and minivans may get only 2 miles per kwh. Thus in the analysis below, we vary pickup and minivan efficiency between 2 and 4.

Incremental Fuel Cost. Undiscounted lifetime fuel costs for EVs or ICEVs are the product of

- Miles traveled,
- The inverse of vehicle efficiency (kwh per mile for EVs, gallons per mile for ICEVs), and
- Unit fuel cost ($/kwh for electricity and $/gallon for gasoline).

Unit electricity costs in the studies reviewed vary between $0.05 and $0.12 per kwh. The low costs are in line with the rates utilities such as Los Angeles Department of Water and Power and Sacramento Municipal Utility districts are offering customers for off-peak EV charging. The high rate is comparable to current domestic electricity rates (excluding taxes) in much of Southern California.[239] The range of $0.05 to $0.12 per kwh thus seems to be an appropriate range for

---

[238]These efficiencies are from the electrical wall outlet to the wheels. Because 10 to 20 percent of power is lost during the charging process between the wall and the battery, the efficiencies from the battery to the wheel are 10 to 20 percent higher.

[239]Southern California Edison's domestic rate is $0.124 per kwh hour in the first block (354 kwh per month) and $0.143 per kwh for additional monthly usage. Rates for typical domestic service do not vary by time of day.

electricity cost. There are two important caveats. First, we are interested in the incremental production cost, not sales price, of electricity. Further work would be needed to judge how closely these sales prices correspond to off-peak and average production costs.[240] For example, any subsidy (i.e., price below actual incremental cost of the electricity) embedded in the off-peak EV rate should be excluded. Second, it is unlikely that all EV charging will be done at off peak hours; to the degree that EVs are charged at other times, the $0.05 per kwh figure will understate EV electricity costs.

Gasoline costs vary between $1.20 and $1.38 per gallon in the studies reviewed. This seems like a reasonable range for current prices of gasoline to the consumer. But, all these prices include gasoline taxes. When comparing the resource costs of EVs to the resource costs of ICEVs, gasoline taxes should not be included in the costs of gasoline because they represent transfers from consumers and producers to the government rather than costs to society as a whole.[241] When federal, state, and local taxes are deducted, the $1.20 to $1.38 range drops to $0.75 to $0.91 per gallon.[242] This adjustment increases incremental EV operating costs $1,000 to $3,000 depending on the other parameter values. In our analysis of operating costs, gasoline costs range from $0.75 to $0.91 per gallon, but as in the case of electricity costs, further investigation of any discrepancy between gasoline price and cost is needed.[243]

Increasing ICEV fuel efficiency will increase incremental EV operating costs, other parameters held constant. Gas mileage for pickups and minivans varies in the studies from 16 to 18 miles per

---

[240]Some of the studies focus on sales price because they attempt to estimate the cost to the consumer of operating an electric vehicle. Here we are interested in resource cost.

[241]Gasoline taxes are relevant in determining the demand for electric vehicles. EV demand depends on the cost *to the consumer* of operating EVs.

[242]In Los Angeles the federal tax is $0.184 per gallon, state and local gasoline taxes are $0.18 per gallon, and sales tax is 8.25 percent.

[243]Because we are comparing gasoline and electricity costs, the same percentage difference between electricity cost and price and gasoline cost and price would net out in the analysis.

gallon, which seems reasonable. Most studies set passenger car efficiency at 27.5 miles per gallon, although Moomaw et al. put it at 46 for a very small commuter car. Because we are focusing on EVs likely to be produced by the Big 7, we restrict our attention to more conventionally sized passenger cars, assuming throughout that passenger car fuel efficiency is 27.5 miles per gallon.

Repair and Maintenance Costs. As shown in Table 10.2-4, four of the five studies estimate that repair and maintenance costs (including tire replacement) will be between 33 and 50 percent lower for EVs than for ICEVs. Booz•Allen, in contrast, assumes no difference in repair and maintenance costs.

The argument usually used to support the contention that EVs will have lower repair and maintenance costs is that electric vehicles have fewer components and fewer moving parts than ICEVs.[244] This is true, and perhaps repair and maintenance costs will be lower for EVs in the long run. However, there are three reasons to be skeptical that they will be lower than those for ICEVs, particularly during the first 5 years

- EV technology is evolving rapidly, but the projections of repair and maintenance costs may be implicitly based on those of a stable technology. Reliability of components in the early years of commercial scale production will also probably be lower than that in later years.

- There is no discussion of the labor cost of battery maintenance and replacement in the studies reviewed. Some batteries must be regularly watered, and the process of removing and installing new battery packs may be time consuming and costly.

- Repair and maintenance costs of ICEVs appear to be declining. Engines that require no scheduled maintenance other than

---

[244]Most studies assume that tire replacement costs will be higher for EVs than ICEVs. This is because EVs often use low rolling resistance tires that are more expensive than conventional tires, and tires on EVs must be replaced more often due to the higher weight of an EV relative to an ICEV. Higher tire costs thus decrease the overall reduction in EV repair and maintenance costs relative to ICEVs to some extent.

routine oil and fluid changes for 100,000 miles are now being
introduced.

We thus view estimates that EVs will have lower repair and
maintenance costs with some skepticism, at least for the first five
years of the program. Consequently, in our analysis we discard the most
optimistic assumption on EV operating costs and vary EV operating cost
from 67 percent to 100 percent of ICEV costs.

Synthesis. Table 10.2-5 summarizes the findings of the studies
reviewed on incremental lifetime operating costs including the costs of
all batteries. Except for Moomaw et al., EV lifetime operating costs
are projected to be between $3,000 and $10,722 more than those of an
ICEV for electric vehicles produced between 1998 and 2002 (see Panel A
of Table 10.2-5). When gas taxes are excluded, incremental EV operating
costs rise to between $5,021 and $13,643. The low incremental costs for
Moomaw et al. are due to several factors. They assume low electricity
costs ($0.05 per kilowatt-hour) and a large difference in EV and ICEV
repair and maintenance costs.[245] For pickups they assume high EV
efficiency, and for their commuter car, a relatively low battery cost.

---

[245]Moomaw et al. assume high repair and maintenance costs for ICEVs
and then that EVs repair and maintenance costs are 50 percent lower.

Table 10.2-5

Summary of Findings of Studies on Incremental Lifetime Operating Costs for EVs Produced Between 1998 and 2002 and After 2002

Study (scenario)	Year	Vehicle Type	Battery	Difference in Lifetime Costs (Dollars)	
				Including Gas Taxes	Excluding Gas Taxes
A. EVs Produced Between 1998 and 2002					
Moomaw (2)	1998	passenger	NiCd	120	1,135
Booz•Allen (3)	2002	passenger	NiMH	3,000	5,021
Booz•Allen (2)	2000	passenger	NiMH	6,000	8,021
GAO (2)	?	passenger	PbA	7,000	8,347
Booz•Allen (1)	1998	passenger	PbA	7,500	9,521
GAO (1)	?	passenger	PbA	10,000	11,347
Moomaw (1)	1998	pickup	PbA	-600	2,319
Abacus (1)	1998	minivan	PbA	3,128	6,049
Abacus (2)	1998	minivan	NiMH	10,722	13,643
Abacus (2)	1998	minivan	NiMH	10,722	13,643
B. EVs Produced After 2002					
CARB (1)	?	passenger	PbA	-1,161	591
CARB (3)	?	passenger	NiMH	-258	1,494
CARB (4)	?	passenger	NiMH	380	1,670
CARB (2)	?	passenger	PbA	665	1,955
Booz•Allen (4)	2004	passenger	NiMH	0	2,021
Abacus (3)	2005	minivan	PbA	-1,660	1,261
Abacus (4)	2005	minivan	NiMH	-1,452	1,469

NOTE: Scenarios defined in Table 10.2-4.

Upper and Lower Bounds for Lifetime Operating Costs. Table 10.2-6 summarizes the parameter ranges developed above that we use in our simulations of incremental operating cost. (The model and our methods are described in Appendix 10.A). Separate scenarios are run for passenger cars and pickup trucks and minivans.

Table 10.2-6

Parameter Ranges Used in Simulations of Lifetime Operating Costs
1998-2002

	Optimistic	Pessimistic
EV Efficiency		
Passenger cars	5 mi/kwh	3 mi/kwh
Pickups/minivans	4 mi/kwh	2 mi/kwh
ICEV Efficiency		
Passenger cars	27.5 mi/gallon	27.5 mi/gallon
Pickups/minivans	18 mi/gallon	18 mi/gallon
Battery cost per kwh delivered	$0.20 per kwh	$0.55 per kwh
EV repair and maintenance costs	67 percent of ICEV	100 percent of ICEV
Electricity cost	$0.05 per kwh	$0.12 per kwh
Gasoline cost		
Including taxes	$1.20 per gallon	$1.38 per gallon
Excluding taxes	$0.91 per gallon	$0.75 per gallon

Table 10.2-7 summarizes the distribution of the difference between EV and ICEV operating costs when the true values of the individual parameter values are assumed independent and uniformly distributed in the ranges listed in Table 10.2-6. That is, we assume that the parameters are statistically independent and that each parameter has equal probability of being in any interval of fixed width within its assumed range. We present the results both including and excluding gasoline taxes. Our interest in this section is on the results when gasoline taxes are excluded. We use the distribution of incremental EV operating costs when gasoline taxes are included in the discussion of consumer demand for EVs in Section 11. We also estimate the distribution for operating costs when the parameters are assumed to follow normal and triangular distributions (see Appendix 10.A). The results for the normal case are very similar to those for the uniform case. The operating cost distribution is more concentrated toward the middle of its range for the triangular assumption.

Table 10.2-7

**Distribution of Incremental EV Operating Costs for EVs Produced
Between 1998 and 2002 Assuming Uniform Distribution for
Individual Parameter Values
(dollars per vehicle)**

| | Including Gasoline Taxes | | Excluding Gasoline Taxes | |
| | Passenger | Pickup or | Passenger | Pickup or |
Percentile	Car	Minivan	Car	Minivan
5	1,316	608	3,085	3,352
10	1,992	1,582	3,766	4,316
15	2,536	2,363	4,315	5,093
20	3,017	3,061	4,800	5,817
25	3,463	3,701	5,252	6,455
30	3,890	4,329	5,683	7,077
50	5,537	6,615	7,339	9,352
70	7,249	9,175	9,064	11,935
75	7,767	9,920	9,583	12,660
80	8,377	11,013	10,183	13,758
85	9,052	12,142	10,903	14,873
90	10,004	13,742	11,806	16,484
95	11,251	15,799	13,084	18,552

With the exception of the Moomaw et al. study, the incremental
lifetime operating costs for passenger cars when gasoline taxes are
excluded in the studies reviewed fall between approximately the 20th and
90th percentiles of our projected distribution for operating costs. For
minivans and trucks the incremental operating costs fall between the
20th and 80th percentiles. The Moomaw et al. study is the outlier,
falling below the 5th percentile for both passenger cars and pickups and
minivans.

We conclude that it is highly likely that incremental lifetime
operating costs excluding gasoline taxes during the first five years of
the mandate will fall between the 5th and 95th percentiles of the
operating cost distribution presented in Table 10.2-7. This provides
quite optimistic and pessimistic estimates. Using our uniform
probability distributions, there is only a 5 percent probability that
the parameters will jointly take values that produce operating costs
below the 5th percentile. Likewise there is only a 5 percent

probability that the parameters will jointly take values that produce operating costs above the 5th percentile.

The 5th and 95th percentiles for operating costs excluding gasoline taxes using the uniform assumption are approximately $3,000 and $13,000, respectively. For pickups and minivans, they are approximately $3,400 and $18,600. We restrict our attention to incremental operating costs between $3,000 and $13,000 because it is hard to imagine that if the incremental operating costs for pickups and minivans are substantially higher than $13,000 they will play on important role in the mandate (i.e., companies will market cars to satisfy the mandate rather than pickups or minivans).

The 5th percentiles for incremental operating costs including gasoline are $1,316 for passenger cars and $608 for pickups and minivans. In our analysis of consumer demand for EVs in Section 11, we use $1,000 as the lower bound for incremental EV operating costs to consumers during the first five years of the mandate, which is the average of the two numbers rounded to the nearest $500. Because we think it likely that manufacturers will focus their attention on passenger cars if the lifetime incremental cost of pickups and minivans is significantly higher than that for passenger cars, we base our upper bound on the 95th percentile for passenger cars. We therefore set our upper bound for lifetime operating costs including gasoline taxes at $11,000--the 95th percentile for passenger cars rounded to the nearest $500.

Changes in Incremental Lifetime Operating Costs After 2002

Because EVs are an immature technology and ICEVs are a mature one, incremental EV lifetime operating costs may decline after 2002 due to improvements in battery cost and performance, EV efficiency, and perhaps lower repair and maintenance costs of EVs relative to ICEVs. To provide a sense of how much incremental costs excluding gasoline taxes might fall, we adjust the parameter ranges to reflect these potential improvements and repeat our modeling exercise. We then compare the results to estimates in the studies reviewed of incremental lifetime operating costs for vehicles produced after 2002. After determining levels to which incremental operating costs may fall after 2002, we then discuss how quickly they might fall to those levels.

Table 10.2-8 reports the ranges for parameter values used in the simulations of long-run incremental operating costs. The lower bounds for EV efficiency are raised for the simulations of long-run incremental operating costs. We think it quite likely that over time the least efficient vehicles will be weeded out. Specifically, the range for passenger car efficiency is now 4 to 5 miles per kwh rather than 3 to 5 in the simulations for 1998 to 2002. Similarly, the efficiency range for pickups and minivans is 3 to 4 rather than 2 to 4 miles per kwh.[246]

Table 10.2-8

Parameter Values Used in Simulations of Long-Run Lifetime Operating Costs

	Optimistic	Pessimistic
EV Efficiency		
Passenger cars	5 mi/kwh	4 mi/kwh
Pickups/minivans	4 mi/kwh	3 mi/kwh
ICEV Efficiency		
Passenger cars	27.5 mi/gallon	27.5 mi/gallon
Pickups/minivans	18 mi/gallon	18 mi/gallon
Battery cost per kwh		
delivered	$0.16 per kwh	$0.39 per kwh
EV repair and		
maintenance costs	50 percent of ICEV	100 percent of ICEV
Electricity cost	$0.05 per kwh	$0.12 per kwh
Gasoline cost		
excluding taxes	$0.91 per gallon	$0.75 per gallon

Battery costs per kwh delivered are reduced from the $0.20 to $0.55 range used between 1998 and 2002 to $0.16 to $0.39. The new lower bound is the average of the Battery Panel's low estimates for the ultimate "learned-out" costs of advanced batteries (see Table 10.1-2). The learned-out costs are the lowest battery costs are expected to go after all economies of scale and learning to manufacture more efficiently have been exhausted. We think it likely that the Battery Panel's estimates

---

[246]We considered increasing the upper bound for EV efficiency. Note, however, that ICEV efficiency (gas mileage) may also increase in the future, and we do not change our assumption concerning miles per gallon.

are optimistic, so this average seems like an appropriate lower bound for the future. As shown in Table 10.1-2, $0.39 is the lowest high estimate made by the Battery Panel for advanced batteries that go into commercial production between 1998 and 2002. This value corresponds to a NiMH battery that costs $250 per kwh to produce and lasts 800 cycles. A battery with such attributes seems quite possible in the future, so we view freezing battery performance at these levels as pessimistic and hence use it as an upper bound.

We have also reduced the lower bound for EV repair and maintenance costs relative to ICEVs in the long-run simulations to 50 percent. This allows the possibility that the large advantages for EVs in repair and maintenance that some predict will materialize.

As can be seen by comparing Tables 10.2-9 with 10.2-7, the distribution of lifetime operating costs excluding gasoline taxes shifts considerably downward from that between 1998 and 2002. Now the 5th and 95th percentiles for passengers cars are $1,234 and $6,459, approximately half the $3,085 and $13,084 previously. Only from the most optimistic combinations of parameter values will EV operating cost drop below ICEV operating costs--and our simulations suggests that this will occur with very low probability.

We now compare the results of our simulations of long-run EV operating costs with estimates for operating costs after 2002 in the studies reviewed. As shown in Panel B of Table 10.2-5, estimates of EV incremental operating costs after 2002 are all positive when gasoline taxes are excluded, but fall at the lower end of our projected distribution for long-run operating costs. Except for CARB's lowest estimate, the incremental operating costs range from approximately $1,500 to approximately $2,000 for passenger cars and $1,300 and $1,500 for pickups and minivans. CARB does not explicitly date its estimates, but given the assumptions on battery costs and cycle life and the discussion in the text, it seems clear that CARB is thinking of battery characteristics well into the future.[247] The $1,500 and $2,000 for

---

[247]CARB (1994b, p. 32) comes to the conclusion that "*In the future operating costs plus the battery costs will be approximately equal to*

passenger cars correspond to approximately the 10th and 20th percentiles in our distribution. The range in the studies for pickups and minivans is between the 5th and 10th percentiles for pickups and minivans. CARB's lowest estimate appears highly unlikely based on the range of parameter values used in our simulations.

Table 10.2-9

Distribution of Incremental Long-Run EV Operating Costs Excluding Gasoline Assuming Uniform Distribution for Individual Parameter Values (dollars per vehicle)

Percentile	Passenger Car	Pickup or Minivan
5	1,234	1,023
10	1,669	1,570
15	1,991	1,990
20	2,271	2,361
25	2,531	2,694
30	2,781	3,018
50	3,751	4,267
70	4,723	5,526
75	4,984	5,867
80	5,266	6,241
85	5,575	6,667
90	5,947	7,188
95	6,459	7,920

All of these studies have incremental costs at the lower end of our simulated distribution. But, in developing upper and lower bounds for these costs, we want a balanced range--that is, an upper bound as pessimistic as the lower bound is optimistic. Therefore, as we did in our analysis of incremental operating costs during the first five years of the mandate, we base our lower and upper bounds for long-run incremental EV operating costs on the 5th and 95th percentiles of the projected distribution for incremental operating costs. For passenger cars the respective percentiles are approximately $1,200 and $6,500; for pickups and minivans approximately $1,000 and $7,900. We settle on a

the operating costs of conventional gasoline-powered vehicles" (emphasis added).

range of $1,000 to $6,500. The $1,000 figure is the average of the two 5th percentile estimates rounded to the nearest $500. If the incremental operating costs of pickups and minivans turn out to be substantially higher than passenger cars, their numbers may be small, suggesting that $6,500 is a reasonable upper bound for incremental lifetime operating costs after 2002.

We assume the same rates of learning as we did for production costs to project how quickly operating costs will decline from their average level between 1998 and 2002 to their long-run levels. In the optimistic scenario, we assume that EV operating costs fall from an $3,000 during the first five years of the mandate along a 75 percent experience curve until they reach $1,000. In the pessimistic scenario, we assume they follow a 90 percent experience curve and decline from $13,000 to $6,500.[248]

10.2.3 Incremental Cost of the ZEV Mandate Between 1998 and 2002

Having completed our analysis of incremental EV costs, we pause to note that it appears that the ZEV mandate will be costly during its first five years. Table 10.2-10 reports estimates of the total incremental production and lifetime operating costs attributable to the ZEV mandate between 1998 and 2002 alternatively assuming that the mandate applies in California only and that it applies in California, Massachusetts, and New York. Using the high and low estimates developed in the previous sections, we estimate that the ZEV mandate will cost between $1.9 billion and $7.9 billion for California alone and $2.9 billion to $12.3 billion if New York and Massachusetts join in. These costs must be evaluated with the emission reductions caused by EVs. This is the subject to which we now turn.

---

[248]As we did for production costs, we base learning on cumulative output at the end of 2000 in the optimistic scenario and at the end of 2002 in the pessimistic scenario.

Table 10.2-10

Costs of the ZEV Mandate Between 1998 and 2002

	Lower Bound	Upper Bound
Production cost		
Variable ($/vehicle)	3,320	15,000
Fixed ($ billions)	1.050	4.200
Operating cost ($/vehicle)	3,000	13,000
Total cost ($ billions)[a]		
Calif. volume (198,400)	1.858	7.864
Twice Calif. volume (396,800)	2.859	12.298

[a]Discounted using 4 percent real discount rate.

10.3 DIRECT EMISSION REDUCTIONS

We seek to analyze the effect of the ZEV mandate on emissions by comparing emissions when all elements of California's ozone reduction strategy are in place except the ZEV mandate with emissions when the ZEV mandate is included. This is the same approach taken in Sections 7 and 8 and can be thought of as adding the ZEV mandate to the remaining elements of the California strategy. In this section, we assume that manufacturers actually sell the electric vehicles, not merely offer them for sale, and that electric vehicles displace the sales of comparable new ICEVs one for one. Thus, we assume that electric vehicle sales do not change the overall number of new vehicles sold each year. We also assume that the purchase of electric vehicles does not affect the miles driven by the vehicles already in the fleet and that electric vehicles are driven the same amount as the ICEVs they displace. This implies that the electric vehicle mandate does not cause total vehicle miles traveled to change. Below, we relax some of these assumptions.

The direct emissions reductions of the ZEV mandate depend on the emissions of the ICEVs they displace, and consequently, depend on the effectiveness of California's ICEV emission control strategy.[249] As

---

[249]We do not consider the power plant emissions of ROG and NOx emissions due to ZEVs. These appear to be small, particularly in the current non-attainment areas in California (see CARB, 1994a, p. 72). We also do not consider emissions from battery production or recycling in this analysis. A recent study by Lave, Hendrickson, and McMichael (1995), which has received substantial public attention, has suggested

discussed in Sections 7 and 8, there is a great deal of uncertainty over how well the ICEV elements of the strategy will work. To account for this uncertainty, we estimate the emissions reductions caused by the ZEV mandate under two different scenarios: (1) California's ICEV program is effective, and (2) the ICEV program is ineffective. In the "Effective Scenario", TLEVs, LEVs, and ULEVs are assumed to emit at levels predicted by the EMFAC models with enhanced I&M and EEE controls in place. The ICEV program is successful in that EMFAC assumes low zero-mile emission and deterioration rates for TLEV, LEV, and ULEVs (see Section 7.2). In the "Ineffective Scenario", future ICEVs are assumed to emit at the rates currently estimated for CA93 vehicles. This might be the case if the new elements of the ICEV control strategy are partially effective, and if, as many believe, the actual in-use emissions of 1993 vehicles are substantially higher than current estimates (see Section 3).

In the Effective Scenario, we assume that manufacturers meet the NMOG standard with or without the ZEV mandate because the NMOG standard applies in both cases. In the absence of the ZEV mandate, manufacturers would presumably attempt to pick the most profitable mix of TLEVs, LEVs, and ULEVs that will just satisfy the NMOG requirement.[250] When a manufacturer sells EVs to meet the mandate, it can then slightly increase the ROG exhaust emissions of its ICEVs (by changing the mix of TLEVs, LEVs, and ULEVs) and still meet the NMOG requirement. Thus, the ZEV mandate will tend not to affect tailpipe ROG emissions of new ICEVs. It will reduce evaporative emissions, however.[251] Evaporative emission

---

that EVs will have extremely costly environmental impacts because use of lead-acid batteries will lead to very high and dangerous levels of human exposure to lead. This study has triggered much controversy and criticism. We have not reviewed the study or the criticism of it in detail. An initial reading of the study and the criticisms of it suggests one should be cautious about accepting the Lave, Hendrickson, and McMichael (1995) conclusions at face value.

[250]Vehicles that meet CA93 exhaust standards and the more stringent requirements of EEE, ORVR, and OBD II can also be used to meet the NMOG standard. To simplify the discussion, however, we ignore this complication.

[251]This argument does not require that vehicles emit at their certification requirement, but rather that the ratio of certification requirements for different vehicle categories equal the ratio of

standards do not differ for TLEVs, LEVs, and ULEVs. Thus, the ROG emission reductions generated by an EV will not depend on whether a TLEV, LEV, or ULEV is displaced when an EV is sold.

Because the NOx standards are 0.4 grams per mile for TLEVs and 0.2 grams per mile for LEVs and ULEVs, remixing of the ICEV fleet may also change overall NOx emissions of the new ICEVs sold. To illustrate the potential range of such an effect, we consider two extremes. In the "No-NOx Reduction" case, ZEVs produce no change in overall NOx emissions from new vehicles sold. This would be the case if, for example, the manufacturer remixes the fleet by (1) increasing the number of TLEVs by the number of ZEVs sold and (2) slightly increasing the ratio of ULEVs to LEVs.[252] Table 10.3-1 illustrates this possibility with an example in which 1,000 vehicles are sold with and without the ZEV mandate.

Table 10.3-1

**Illustration of How Remixing TLEVs, LEVs, and ULEVs Can Affect
NOx Emissions (assuming 1,000 vehicles sold)**

| | Number of Vehicles Sold | | | | Average Fleet Exhaust Emissions (gm/mi) | |
	TLEV	LEV	ULEV	ZEV	ROG	NOx
No-NOx Reduction Case						
Without ZEVs	25	580	395	0	0.0624	0.205
With ZEVs	75	515	360	50	0.0624	0.205
Full-NOx Reduction Case						
Without ZEVs	25	580	395	0	0.0624	0.205
With ZEVs	25	635	290	50	0.0624	0.195

lifetime vehicle emissions. The latter is very close to the case for CARB's estimates of CA93, TLEV, LEV, and ULEV exhaust emissions (CARB, 1994a, p. 46).

[252]Some argue that manufacturers will produce no TLEVs after, say, 1996 (CARB makes this assumption). However, it may be profitable to continue producing high-power cars that emit at TLEV levels. How manufacturers will rebalance their fleets depends on the profitability of selling different types of vehicles--thus on both the cost of the emission control equipment and the selling price.

The "Full-NOx Reduction" case results in the largest reasonable reduction in NOx. This would be the case, as illustrated in the bottom rows of Table 10.3-1, if the manufacturer remixed the fleet by (1) leaving the number of TLEVs unchanged and (2) reducing the ratio of ULEVs to LEVs.[253] The result is that each ZEV displaces the NOx emissions of one LEV or ULEV.

We now calculate the emission effect of selling one EV, with all the ICEV-related elements of the California strategy in place.

The logic for the Ineffective Scenario is straightforward: the EV reduces emissions by the lifetime emissions of a CA93 vehicle. Table 10.3-2 presents the Sierra (1995c) and Hwang et al. (1994) estimates for the emissions of a CA93 vehicle. These are based on the data presented in Table 3.3-1 and assume that vehicles travel 130,000 miles during their lifetimes. For the Ineffective Scenario, we use the (CA93 vehicle) estimates from Hwang, et al.(1994) rather than Sierra's for two reasons. First, they are based in a more recent version of CARB's EMFAC model. Second, using the higher estimates is in keeping with the intent of the Ineffective Scenario to be optimistic about the emission benefits that could be generated by ZEVs. The ROG and NOx emission reductions used in the Ineffective Scenario are summarized in Table 10.3-3.

_____

[253]NOx emission reductions would be greater if manufacturers reduced the number of TLEVs (which have higher NOx emissions than LEVs and ULEVs) when ZEVs are introduced. However, it does not seem likely that a manufacturer would produce fewer TLEVs in response to a relaxing of the NMOG requirement on its ICEVs.

Table 10.3-2

ICEV Emission Estimates Used to Project Direct Emission Benefits of Electric Vehicles
(pounds per vehicle over 130,000 mile vehicle life)

| | ULEV | | CA93 Vehicle | |
	Sierra[a]	Hwang et al.[b]	Sierra[c]	Hwang et al.[b]
ROG				
Exhaust	17	25	123	152
Evaporative	33[d]	51	210[d]	210[e]
Total	50	76	333	362
NOx	91	107	196	217
ROG + NOx	141	183	512	579

[a]Sierra (1995c), Tier 1 emissions (with EEE) calculated from difference between ZEV and Tier 1 vehicle (with EEE), then ULEV benefit subtracted to determine ULEV emissions with EEE. Enhanced I&M scenarios used.

[b]Hwang et al. (1994), p.11, and letter to authors.

[c]Sierra (1995c), Tier 1 emissions without EEE calculated as in table note a, then EEE benefit added. Basic I&M scenarios used.

[d]It is unclear what parts of marketing emissions Sierra includes in its evaporative emission estimate.

[e]Sierra estimate used.

The emission reductions in the Effective Scenario are based on the evaporative and NOx emissions for a ULEV presented in Table 10.3-2. Again, we use the estimates of Hwang et al. (1994) because they are based on more recent emission models than the Sierra numbers. Lifetime ROG emission reductions are 51 pounds per vehicle in the Effective scenario (see Table 10.3-3). NOx reductions are zero in the No-NOx reduction case and 107 pounds in the Full-NOx reduction case. The concern of many that even the latest revisions of these models may understate in-use emissions (see Section 3) reinforces the pessimism of these estimates about the emission benefits of ZEVs.

Table 10.3-3

**Projected Emission Reductions for Each Additional EV
Sold Under Different Scenarios
(pounds per vehicle lifetime)**

	Effective Scenario		Ineffective Scenario
	No-NOx Reduction	Full-NOx Reduction	
ROG	51	51	362
NOx	0	107	217
ROG+NOx	51	158	579

10.4 NARROW COST-EFFECTIVENESS RATIOS FOR THE ZEV MANDATE

We now combine our estimates of costs and emission reductions to calculate narrow cost-effectiveness ratios for electric vehicles. We project the streams of costs and emission reductions over time, discount them to 1995, and take the ratio of discounted costs to discounted emission reductions. We first discuss how these ratios should be interpreted and used to evaluate the desirability of EVs. We then discuss the assumptions and methods we used to calculate the narrow cost-effectiveness ratios and finally present the results.

10.4.1 Usefulness and Limitations of Narrow Cost Effectiveness

As discussed in Section 2, the narrow cost-effectiveness ratio (NCER) includes the direct costs and emission reductions that have been quantified. Narrow cost-effectiveness ratios inevitably miss important costs and important benefits. Our calculation of EV NCERs below excludes factors that may make EVs look more or less desirable than the a calculated NCER would indicate. Factors excluded that would make EVs look more desirable than suggested by the NCER include:

- Other emission benefits. EVs also reduce emissions of CO, CO_2, and air toxics.

- Non-emission related improvements in well-being. EVs would reduce urban noise and afford the convenience of home refueling.

- Incidence of costs. The NCERs below are calculated from a national perspective. EV NCERs to Californians will be lower to the extent that EV costs are shifted to those outside California.

- Technology spillovers. The technologies developed for EVs may have useful applications in ICEVs and in other products.

Factors excluded that would tend to make EVs look less desirable than suggested by the NCER include:

- Effect on fleet turnover. If the ZEV mandate causes ICEV prices to rise, an issue analyzed in Section 11, fleet turnover may slow and ICEV fleet emissions may rise.

- EV infrastructure costs. We have not included EV infrastructure costs in our analysis.

- Inconvenience to consumers of reduced range. This potentially reduces consumer well-being.

- Location and time of emission reductions. All ROG and NOx emission reductions, wherever and whenever they occur, are included in the NCERs below. However, some reductions will undoubtedly be in areas where and at times when pollution levels are low and thus may be of little value.

As discussed in Section 2.6, when comparing different ozone-control measures, policymakers should consider both the costs and benefits that have been included in the NCER and the costs and benefits that have not. If the NCER ratio is low, for example, a measure may be economically advantageous if the uncounted net costs (costs less benefits) are not large relative to the uncounted net costs of other measures with higher NCERs. If NCER is high relative to those of other alternatives, the measure may be economically advantageous only if there are substantial uncounted net benefits (benefits minus cost) relative to the net benefits of other measures.

10.4.2 Calculation of Narrow Cost-Effectiveness Ratio

The narrow cost effectiveness ratio for EVs depends many parameters:

- Initial level of incremental production and operating costs,
- Rate of decline in production and operating costs over time,
- Emission reductions per EV,

- Number of EVs sold,
- Time horizon over which the NCER is calculated, and
- Discount rate.

We calculate NCERs for EVs under several different sets of assumptions about these parameters, which we now describe. Computational details are provided in Appendix 10.B.

Initial costs. Two different cases are modeled: low initial costs and high initial costs. The basis for these assumptions is detailed in Sections 10.2.1 and 10.2.2. In the low initial cost case, both EV incremental production and lifetime operating costs are set at the lower end of the ranges developed above. During the first five years of the mandate, incremental variable production costs are $3,320 per vehicle, fixed production costs are $1.05 billion, and incremental lifetime operating costs are $3,000 per vehicle. In the high initial cost case, these parameters are set to $15,000 per vehicle, $4.2 billion, and $13,000 per vehicle, respectively

Cost decline after the first five years. Each of the initial cost cases is paired with two different assumptions of how fast EV costs decline after the first five years. The basis for these assumptions is detailed in Sections 10.2.1 and 10.2.2. In the fast decline case both variable production and operating costs follow a 75 percent experience curve. EV variable production costs decline until they equal those of ICEVs, and then remain there. EV operating costs (including all batteries) decline until they are $1,000 above those of an ICEV (which is the optimistic assumption of eventual EV incremental operating costs). Incremental fixed costs fall by 50 percent in each successive 5-year product cycle, and are set to zero starting in the fourth product cycle.

In the slow decline case, variable production and operating costs follow a 90 percent experience curve. Variable costs again decline until they are equal to ICEV variable production costs, but operating costs decline only until they are $6,500 above ICEV operating costs. Incremental fixed costs again fall by 50 percent in each product cycle, but never (quite) reach zero.

Emission benefits. Each of the four initial cost-cost decline cases are combined with three different assumptions about the emission reductions due to EVs: (1) Ineffective ICEV control program, (2) Effective ICEV control program, full-NOx reduction, and (3) Effective ICEV control program no-NOx reduction. The basis for these assumptions is described in Section 10.3.

Number of EVs sold. Our analysis assumes that the EV mandates in Massachusetts and New York remain in place if and only if California's does. Thus, EV production volumes are tied to combined passenger car and light-duty truck sales in these three states. We set overall LDV sales in the three states at 2.48 million per year in all years. We calculate NCERs under three different patterns of EV fleet penetration. In all cases, fleet penetration follows the pattern required by the mandate through 2003 but it then either remains at 10 percent or increases linearly from 10 percent of new car sales in 2003 to 20 or 40 percent in 2020. Fleet penetration after 2020 remains at the 2020 level in all cases. Forty percent may or may not be a reasonable upper bound for EV fleet penetration in the foreseeable future. Simulated NCERs up through this percentage should give a sense of how NCERs vary with eventual fleet penetration.

Time horizon. Narrow cost-effectiveness ratios are calculated for EVs produced between 1998 and 2010, between 1998 and 2020, and from 1998 on into the indefinite future. We call the last the *long-term* narrow cost-effectiveness ratio. We chose the first interval because several other EV analyses calculate NCERs through 2010 and the goal of the State Implementation Plan for Ozone is compliance in 2010. We calculate long-term narrow cost effectiveness ratios because in principle cost-effectiveness should consider all future costs and emission reductions. We chose the intermediate interval (1998 to 2020) because of the possibility that the EV mandate may be irrelevant by a date in the future such as 2020. For example, there may other technologies, such as flywheels or fuel cells, that totally supplant battery powered electric vehicles after 2020. By comparing the NCERs through 2010 and 2020 and the long-term NCER, the reader can gain a sense of how NCER changes as the time horizon lengthens.

Discount rate. NCERs are calculated for 3 and 5 percent real discount rates. These roughly correspond to the range of rates used in the studies reviewed.

10.4.3 Results of EV Narrow-Cost Effectiveness Ratio Simulations

Table 10.4-1 presents the narrow cost-effectiveness ratios for the various sets of parameter assumptions examined. Table 10.4-2 shows the dates at which EV variable production costs and operating costs reach their long-run values in the different scenarios.

NCERs vary greatly over the different scenarios examined. The long-term NCER is estimated as $5,000 per ton ROG + NOx removed when initial EV costs are low, costs decline quickly, emission reductions are large, fleet penetration remains at 10 percent, and the discount rate is 3 percent (see Panel A). Long-term cost effectiveness is estimated as $845,000 per ton when initial costs are high and decline slowly, emission reductions are low, fleet penetration remains at 10 percent, and the discount rate is 5 percent (see Panel D). The NCER estimates vary between $10,000 per ton and $1.2 million per ton when calculated only through 2010.

The variations of individual parameters over their specified ranges have differing effects on NCER. The variations in emission reductions and initial costs cause the largest changes in the NCER. Smaller, but still substantial variations, are caused by changes in the time horizon considered, the fleet penetration of EVs, the rate of cost decline, and the discount rate. We review each of these factors in turn.

Emission reductions. What is assumed about the emission reductions generated by ZEVs makes a large difference in the NCER: the factor of 10 variation in the emission reductions examined results in roughly a factor of 10 variation in NCER.

Initial costs. The range of initial incremental EV costs simulated also has large impact on the long-term NCER. Our lower and upper bounds for incremental variable production, operating, and fixed costs during the first five years vary by roughly a factor of four, which translate into variation by factors of 6 to 9 in long-term NCERs (compare Panels A and C or Panels B and D).

Table 10.4-1

Narrow Cost-Effectiveness Ratios for Electric Vehicles Under Various Assumptions

Fleet Penetration in 2020 (percent)	Emissions Avoided per Vehicle (lbs ROG + NOx)	Narrow Cost Effectiveness at 3 Percent Discount Rate ($1000/ton ROG + NOx)			Narrow Cost Effectiveness at 5 Percent Discount Rate ($1000/ton ROG + NOx)		
		Through 2010	Through 2020	Long-term	Through 2010	Through 2020	Long-term

A. Low Initial Cost, Fast Cost Decline

(Initial incremental variable costs = $3,320 per vehicle; initial fixed cost = $1.050 billion; initial incremental operating cost = $3,000 per vehicle; 75 percent learning rate; ultimate incremental operating costs = $1,000 per vehicle)

Fleet Penetration	Emissions Avoided	Through 2010	Through 2020	Long-term	Through 2010	Through 2020	Long-term
10	579	10	8	5	12	9	7
10	158	38	28	20	44	33	26
10	51	119	87	62	135	102	81
10	368	16	12	9	19	14	11
20	368	15	10	7	17	12	9
40	368	13	9	7	15	10	8

B. Low Initial Cost, Slow Cost Decline

(Initial incremental variable costs = $3,320 per vehicle; initial fixed cost = $1.050 billion; initial incremental operating cost = $3,000 per vehicle; 90 percent learning rate; ultimate incremental operating costs = $1,000 per vehicle)

Fleet Penetration	Emissions Avoided	Through 2010	Through 2020	Long-term	Through 2010	Through 2020	Long-term
10	579	15	10	7	17	12	9
10	158	54	37	24	61	44	33
10	51	168	116	75	189	136	102
10	368	23	16	10	26	19	14
20	368	21	13	8	24	15	11
40	368	17	11	7	20	12	9

Table 10.4-1 (Cont'd.)

Fleet Penetration in 2020 (percent)	Emissions Avoided per Vehicle (lbs ROG + NOx)	Narrow Cost Effectiveness at 3 Percent Discount Rate ($1000/ton ROG + NOx)			Narrow Cost Effectiveness at 5 Percent Discount Rate ($1000/ton ROG + NOx)		
		Through 2010	Through 2020	Long-term	Through 2010	Through 2020	Long-term

C. High Initial Cost, Fast Cost Decline

(Initial incremental variable costs = $15,000 per vehicle; initial fixed cost = $4.200 billion; initial incremental operating cost = $13,000 per vehicle; 75 percent learning rate; ultimate incremental operating costs = $6,500 per vehicle)

Fleet	Emissions	Through 2010	Through 2020	Long-term	Through 2010	Through 2020	Long-term
10	579	54	42	32	61	48	40
10	158	199	153	117	224	176	147
10	51	615	475	364	693	547	456
10	368	85	66	50	96	76	63
20	368	79	58	45	89	67	56
40	368	70	52	42	79	59	50

D. High Initial Cost, Slow Cost Decline

(Initial incremental variable costs = $15,000 per vehicle; initial fixed cost = $4.200 billion; initial incremental operating cost = $13,000 per vehicle; 90 percent learning rate; ultimate incremental operating costs = $6,500 per vehicle)

Fleet	Emissions	Through 2010	Through 2020	Long-term	Through 2010	Through 2020	Long-term
10	579	96	80	59	105	90	74
10	158	351	293	217	386	328	273
10	51	1,088	909	673	1,197	1,017	845
10	368	151	126	93	166	141	117
20	368	143	112	79	158	126	100
40	368	132	98	67	146	110	84

Table 10.4-2

**Dates When Incremental Variable Production and Operating
Costs Reach Their Long-Run Values**

	Eventual EV Fleet Penetration (percent)		
	10	20	40
A. Low initial cost, fast cost decline			
Variable production costs	2003	2003	2003
Operating costs	2003	2003	2003
B. Low initial cost, slow cost decline			
Variable production costs	2011	2009	2008
Operating costs	2008	2007	2006
C. High initial cost, fast cost decline			
Variable production costs	2006	2006	2005
Operating costs	2003	2003	2003
D. High initial cost, slow cost decline			
Variable production costs	>2100[a]	>2100[b]	>2100[c]
Operating costs	2022	2016	2012

[a]The incremental variable production cost is $3,133 in 2100.
[b]The incremental variable production cost is $1,917 in 2100.
[c]The incremental variable production cost is $771 in 2100.

Time horizon. With a longer time horizon, fixed costs can be spread over more vehicles, and higher cumulative production leads to lower variable EV production cost and operating cost. Thus, NCERs decline as the time horizon grows over which costs and emission reductions are calculated. The long-term NCERs are approximately 50 percent of those through 2010. This illustrates that the benefits of ZEVs after 2010 may be important and that the ZEV mandate may be viewed as economical only if the costs and benefits over the long run are included.

Fleet penetration. The NCER falls as fleet penetration rises. This is because the fixed costs can be spread out over more vehicles as fleet penetration increases, and a faster increase in cumulative output causes EV production and operating costs to fall more rapidly through the experience curve effect. The change of NCER over the range of eventual fleet penetration examined (10 to 40 percent) is not that large, however. Long-term NCERs drop 15 to 35 percent when eventual fleet penetration increases from 10 to 40 percent.

Cost decline. The different rates of cost decline that we have used in the simulations also have a relatively moderate impact on NCER. The long-term NCER increases by roughly 20 to 40 percent when cost decline is slow rather than fast and initial incremental cost is low (compare Panels A and B). As one would expect, the effect is larger when initial costs are high. Comparing Panels C and D demonstrates that long-term NCERs are 80 to 90 percent higher in the slow decline case when initial costs are high.

Discount rate. Increasing the discount rate raises the NCER because EV costs are distributed more toward the beginning of the period than are emission reductions. Varying the discount rate between 3 and 5 percent does not make a large difference, however. In Panels A and B when initial costs are low, long-term NCERs are 15 to 30 percent higher when the discount rate is 5 percent rather than 3 percent. The difference approaches 50 percent in Panels C and D when initial costs are high.

Varying all parameters simultaneously. To provide another perspective on how the NCER for EVs varies with parameter values, we calculate the NCER when all parameters (except fleet penetration) are moved a given percentage of their specified ranges from the values most favorable to EVs. Fleet penetration is held at 10 percent. The NCER is $5,000 per ton of ROG plus NOx in the best case for EVs (as discussed above), $17,000 per ton when all parameters are moved 25 percent of their specified ranges, $43,000 when moved 50 percent (the interval midpoints), $135,000 when moved 75 percent, and $845,000 in the worst case for EVs.

11. MARKET-MEDIATED EFFECTS OF THE ZEV MANDATE 1998 TO 2002

OVERVIEW AND PREVIEW OF FINDINGS

As we have emphasized throughout our analysis, narrow cost-effectiveness analyses typically ignore effects mediated through markets and thereby may fail to consider crucial economic effects of the policy under study. The ZEV mandate is no exception. In this section, we analyze some effects of the ZEV mandate that operate through markets for LDVs. Understanding market-mediated effects is crucial to understanding the costs and benefits of the mandate, including the distribution of costs among various groups, and feedback effects on emissions due to potential increases in the prices of new LDVs.

Market effects of the mandate both through 2002 and after 2002 may be very important. Because of extreme uncertainties about market developments after 2002 (due to extreme uncertainties about the development of EV technology--especially battery technology), we attempt to quantify market effects only for the period 1998 to 2002.

To preview our findings:

(1) Demand for EVs that will actually be produced by the companies obligated by the mandate is very uncertain. The key issue is the price at which companies could sell enough EVs to satisfy the mandate. Taking account of EV operating cost disadvantages and the federal tax credit for EV purchases, we conclude that--if EV infrastructure and range improve according to somewhat optimistic assumptions--during 1998 to 2002 EVs excluding any battery are likely to sell for as much as the price of comparable ICEVs to as little as $10,000 below the prices of comparable ICEVs.

(2) During 1998 to 2002, the ZEV mandate may or may not increase average prices of new ICEVs in California. Price increases could be as large as $550 per vehicle.

(3) The ZEV mandate will have major impacts on profits of vehicle manufacturers during 1998 to 2002:

a) in the EV market, the seven manufacturers subject to the ZEV mandate in its first five years and their California dealers may gain up to $350 million per year or lose up to $1.5 billion;

b) in the ICEV market, the ZEV mandate may cost the seven manufacturers subject to the mandate between $100 million and $800 million per year. Other ICEV companies may lose up to $60 million per year, but they could gain up to $550 million per year.

(4) The ZEV mandate could have major impacts on buyers of new LDVs in California during 1998 to 2002:

a) buyers of EVs stand to gain $20 million to $200 million per year;

b) buyers of new ICEVs may be unaffected, but they may lose up to $800 million per year;

c) if EV production and operating costs turn out to be at the low ends of the ranges developed in Section 10, California consumers in the aggregate may gain up to $200 million per year;

d) if EV production and operating costs turn out to be at the high ends of the ranges developed in Section 10, then losses to ICEV buyers could far exceed gains to EV buyers, and the total loss to California consumers might be as high as $750 million per year.

(5) If ICEV prices do increase by hundreds of dollars per vehicle-- which would cause declines in new car sales and delays in the retirement of older vehicles--the ZEV mandate could increase LDV emissions for roughly three to five years and reduce the direct emission benefits of ZEVs for several more years.

11.1 QUANTIFYING THE MARKET EFFECTS OF THE ZEV MANDATE: OVERVIEW

Market effects of the ZEV mandate are relevant to an economic evaluation of the mandate *no matter when* they occur. We attempt to quantify these effects, but only for the first five years of the mandate period, 1998 to 2002. We think it crucial to explain why we focus on only the first five years of the mandate, and what this analytic choice does *not* imply about the market effects of the ZEV mandate and their relevance to policy decisionmaking.

Why quantify only for 1998 to 2002? The market effects of the ZEV mandate are driven by cost and demand (or marketability) conditions for EVs. As discussed above, there is a very wide range of reasonable disagreement about future EV production costs, operating costs and performance characteristics, especially as we look several years into the future. Since operating costs and performance characteristics are key determinants of EV demand, we should anticipate that there are very wide ranges of reasonable disagreement about both cost and demand conditions for EVs, especially if we look several years into the future.

This uncertainty implies a very wide range of reasonable disagreement about market effects of the ZEV mandate.[254] Our analysis above indicates that, when we look several years into the future, EVs costs might or might not turn out to be competitive on cost and performance dimensions with ICEVs of comparable size and body style. Thus, the market effects of the ZEV mandate may be very minor or very large. As a consequence, we conclude that there is little point in developing quantitative estimates of long-term market effects of the ZEV mandate.

What the lack of quantification beyond 2002 does not mean. The analytic choice to quantify only for the period 1998 to 2002 reflects the state of current knowledge about the factors relevant to quantification for the longer term. However, the fact that we lack information for quantifying the market effects of the ZEV mandate for the longer term does not imply that these effects are likely to be large or small; it simply means that in our judgment they can't be quantified with sufficient precision for such quantification to be useful (or even responsible).[255]

What the choice to quantify for 1998 to 2002 does not mean. Our decision to examine the first five years quantitatively--despite the

---

[254]Such extreme degrees of uncertainty are very common when--as is the case here--key economic outcomes are driven by long-term developments involving currently nascent technologies.

[255]Recall that in the cases of some other elements of the California LDV strategy, we judged the available information inadequate to support quantification of any of the key effects; for example, the smog check and vehicle scrappage programs.

fact that we cannot informatively analyze later years quantitatively--
should not be interpreted to imply that the ZEV mandate can be sensibly
evaluated by focusing on only the near term. As exemplified in our
analysis of narrow cost effectiveness above, the ZEV mandate might be
expected to involve more costs than benefits in the near term, and these
net costs may or may not be sufficiently rewarded by benefits in the
longer term. Hence, the ZEV mandate can be viewed as an investment
(requiring sacrifice in the near term) that we might make in hopes of a
(highly uncertain) payoff in the longer term. The question, of course,
is not whether such a long-term investment will pay off in the short-
term; rather, it is what the prospects are for the benefits--most of
which may be reaped only after 2002--to be large enough to justify the
costs. What we quantify in this section is helpful in understanding some
of the costs.

The value of quantifying for 1998 to 2002. Our quantitative
analysis of market effects of the ZEV mandate for the years 1998 to 2002
is done in terms of average vehicles, prices, etc., and focuses on
market-level effects. It serves several purposes.

First, and most important, it provides information about the
potential near-term stakes of the mandate in terms that policymakers and
the public care about and are not addressed by narrow cost-effectiveness
calculations: vehicle prices and total dollar costs to different groups
within and outside California. Our analysis of near-term market effects
provides information relevant to analyzing the ZEV mandate as a long-
term investment, in particular, information about the potential sizes of
the near-term costs required to find out what the eventual benefits will
be. This is important for the obvious reason that prudent investors
should consider the costs of investing in making investment decisions.
It is also important for a more subtle reason: If we undertake the
investment required by the ZEV mandate without recognizing how high the
near-term costs *might* be, there is a danger that we will embark on the
course set by the mandate, pay substantial investment costs, then repeal
the mandate in the face of surprisingly high costs and be left with
substantial investment costs and little or no investment benefits.

Second, our quantitative analyses provide insight about how sensitive the estimates of market-mediated effects are to varying assumptions about some key determinants of these effects.

Third, by developing and illustrating a method for estimating market effects, we provide readers with a basis for developing their own estimates for the near or longer terms.

The analysis is structured as follows. To predict market effects for the first five years of the mandate, we must first characterize the demand for EVs during the early years of the mandate, especially the kinds of EVs that the Big 7 companies are likely to market in during 1998 to 2002 (Sections 11.2 and 11.3). We then analyze the California market for EVs during 1998 to 2002, without and with the mandate (Section 11.4). This analysis culminates in estimates of ranges for dollar gains to EV buyers and dollar losses to Big 7 companies in the EV market (Section 11.5). We then consider how the ZEV mandate might affect the market for new ICEVs in California (Section 11.6). We develop ranges of estimates of increases in ICEV prices and annual dollar gains and losses to various groups. We then draw on all these results to analyze how the gains to EV buyers from the first five years of the ZEV mandate compare to the losses to ICEV buyers and subsidy payments from U.S. taxpayers to EV buyers (Section 11.7). We conclude by considering quantitatively how the price effects of the mandate could affect the composition of the vehicle fleet and its implications for emissions during the short-term (Section 11.8).

11.2 CONCEPTUALIZING THE DEMAND FOR EVS FROM 1998 TO 2002

The public discussion of EV demand is very confusing. For example, at the recent CARB "Workshop on EV Marketability" in July 1995, various speakers seemed to be talking about entirely different phenomena while using the same words.

To set the context for our discussion, we briefly review standard principles from the economics of product demand as they apply to the demand for EVs. We need to distinguish between market demand for EVs (i.e., the total quantity of EVs that would be purchased from all EV sellers) and demand for EVs from individual companies. At either the market or company level, the "demand for EVs" refers to a relationship between price(s) and the numbers of EVs buyers would choose to buy at each price (or set of prices), *holding constant various other factors* that affect how many EVs buyers would wish to purchase at that price (or those prices).

In particular, the demand for EVs at the market level depends on what potential EV buyers know or anticipate about the performance characteristics of the EVs offered for sale, their operating costs, the availability of EV infrastructure, and the prices and operating costs of ICEVs (the primary substitutes for EVs). For example, other things equal, more EVs will be demanded at any set of EV prices (from the various sellers) for the EVs offered for sale:

- The higher the quality of the EVs offered for sale (e.g., the better their range, acceleration, top speed, interior space, reliability);

- The lower the lifetime operating costs that EV buyers expect to incur (e.g., the lower the prices; the better the technical performance and the longer lasting are the available batteries; the lower the price to consumers (including taxes) of electricity used for recharging; the lower EV repair and maintenance costs);

- The greater the availability and the lower the price of using EV infrastructure (e.g., the more convenient and less expensive to consumers the equipment for home recharging, the more conveniently located and the lower the price of fast-recharging services);

- The higher the prices and operating costs of ICEVs (e.g., the more expensive gasoline (including taxes) is, the higher ICEV repair and maintenance costs are).

How the demand for the EVs offered by an individual company depends on the price of those EVs--i.e., a company-level demand curve--depends on market-wide factors (such as what consumers know or anticipate about electricity and gasoline prices and taxes, EV infrastructure, performance and operating costs of ICEVs), what consumers know or anticipate about the performance of this company's EVs in comparison with the performance of EVs offered by other companies, the prices of EVs offered by other companies, etc.

Thus the "demand for EVs" could refer to any of a diverse range of often hypothetical products at various times during the next 15 or more years. This leaves much room for large differences in *implicit* assumptions about many of the factors mentioned above.

11.3 DEMAND FOR EVS THAT COULD BE MARKETED DURING 1998 TO 2002

In this section we analyze demand for EVs at the market and firm levels. We quantify only for the first five years of the mandate. The major studies we reviewed are Hill (1987), Turrentine and Kurani (1995), Greene (1985), Henderson and Rusin (1994), Beggs et al., (1981), Calfee (1985), Bunch et al., (1993), and Nesbitt, Kurani and DeLuchi (1992). We also attended the CARB workshop on EV marketability and reviewed handouts.

During the years 1998 to 2002, with the ZEV mandate in effect, we anticipate that some EVs sold in California will be produced by Big 7 companies and other EVs will be produced and sold by non-Big 7 companies.[256] The Big 7 apparently plan to meet large portions, and perhaps virtually all, of their mandated EV quantities by manufacturing and marketing vehicles under their own brand names. We expect, however, that some EVs will be produced by other companies from whom Big 7 companies will buy credits that can be used to meet part of their obligations under the mandate.

For reasons developed at some length below,[257] we expect that Big 7 EVs, that is the kinds of EVs that the Big 7 are likely to market under their own brand names during the first five years of the ZEV mandate, will account for the predominant share of EVs marketed in California during 1998 to 2002. Moreover, there seems to be much more information available about the characteristics and markets for these vehicles than for EVs that will be offered by other companies. Thus, we first consider demand for Big 7 EVs. Analyzing demand for EVs produced by

---

[256]Such as EV conversion companies, producers of niche vehicles such as PIVCO, and non-Big 7 ICEV producers.

[257]See Section 11.4.2 and Appendix 11.C.

other companies during 1998 to 2002 requires considering the performance and prices of Big 7 EVs, which are key determinants of demand for EVs of other companies. Thus consideration of demand for non-Big 7 EVs is deferred until we have discussed the pricing and performance of Big 7 EVs.

11.3.1 Demand for EVs Marketed by Big 7 Companies.

The Big 7 seem to be committed to making their EVs as comparable as possible in terms of performance characteristics other than range to their ICEVs of similar size and body styles. We proceed under the assumption that this will be the case. We do so not only because of the supporting empirical evidence, but because--as discussed in Section 10.2--producing these kinds of vehicles seems to make good business sense for these companies.

There are two primary sources of information about the demand for Big 7 EVs: marketing surveys done by private companies and research studies in the public domain. We discuss each below.

Proprietary Marketing Surveys

Most--if not all--of the Big 7 companies have done marketing surveys in the course of preparing for the EV mandate.[258] Such work is generally proprietary, and we have no access to it. What we know about these studies is almost entirely from oral presentations made publicly by company representatives of five of the Big 7 companies at the CARB "Workshop on EV Marketability." At the workshop, presenters made it clear that a motivation for presenting results of their proprietary marketing research was to encourage CARB to consider a delay in implementation--if not an outright repeal--of the ZEV mandate.

We presume that major vehicle manufacturers are quite good at assessing demand for their products. Nonetheless, assessing the demand for EVs is likely to be much more difficult than the market research that companies generally undertake because potential customers are much less familiar with EVs than with ICEVs. A major difficulty for us, as

---

[258]For example, to understand how many vehicles of different types they can anticipate selling at different prices as part of their efforts to decide what types of vehicles to market in 1998, to whom, and how.

we interpret the findings presented by companies at the CARB workshop, is that we do not have access to written accounts of the research. Because we do not have the kind of information generally used to assess the meaning and reliability of research, we cannot describe very precisely the prima facie interpretation of their reported results or evaluate them critically.

With these caveats in mind, we summarize what seemed to be the main points made by the Big 7 companies at the CARB workshop. Independent information--primarily, results reported by Turrentine and Kurani (1995)--allows us to consider the plausibility of various company claims as we interpret them.

Companies uniformly reported that their market research indicates demand for EVs will be far short of what is needed to meet the ZEV mandate in 1998. However, as is clear from the principles of demand analysis enumerated above, such a statement might mean many different things. In fact, similar statements by different companies may really have meant quite different things. For example, it was generally unclear to us what types of vehicles were described to survey participants, what performance characteristics were assumed, how the state of the EV infrastructure was characterized, what respondents were told about the characteristics and prices of EVs offered by competitors, etc.

It did seem clear, however, that the five companies making presentations were referring to EV quantities demanded at prices in the general range of their projections of average variable production costs of vehicles they are considering for marketing in 1998. As discussed in Section 10.2 above, these vehicles are expected to be as comparable as possible to ICEVs of similar size and body style, and the costs involved could be much higher than the costs of the most comparable ICEVs.[259] Given the levels of average variable costs that the companies project to

---

[259]Recall from Section 10.2 that our review of the evidence suggests that the EVs marketed by the Big 7 during 1998 to 2002 are likely to involve average variable production costs (excluding the battery) of $3,300 to $15,000 more than the corresponding costs of comparable ICEVs. Moreover, some Big 7 companies seem to think that even the high end of this range is too low.

produce EVs at the scale required by the mandate, we find entirely plausible the companies' claim that prices in this range will not result in sufficient demand to satisfy the mandate.

Companies also claimed that consumer interest in hypothetical EVs was markedly higher, other things equal, when range was assumed to be 100 miles or more. As we discuss below, this claim seems consistent with evidence from other sources.

Studies in the Public Domain

The other general source of information about EV demand is research studies in the public domain. These include studies of potential household demand for EVs, a study of fleet demand, and the study we think provides most relevant information about household demand for our purposes, Turrentine and Kurani (1995).

In Appendix 11.A we describe two general approaches to gauging demand for EVs and review several studies applying them. Regarding household demand for EVs, we conclude that:

a) Studies of *potential* demand for EVs, based on counting households with travel patterns and lifestyles compatible with EV ownership, provide almost no information about how many households would actually buy an EV and under what conditions;

b) Analyses of survey responses to questions about willingness to buy an EV contain very little information about the demand for Big 7 EVs because they characterize average tastes and not the fraction of households that would be unusually amenable to an EV purchase, and the respondents did not know nearly as much about EVs as potential buyers will when EVs are actually marketed.[260]

The Turrentine and Kurani study. Turrentine and Kurani (1995), referred to below as TK, build on earlier work by these researchers (e.g., Kurani, Turrentine, and Sperling, 1994.) It involves eliciting vehicle preferences or buying intentions from 454 California households chosen because they were expected by the researchers to be especially

---

[260]A key aspect of this conclusion is the fact that many consumers know very little about performance characteristics and advantages of EVs and that stated interest in EVs often increases markedly after information is presented or a test drive is taken.

receptive to purchasing an EV. The study design is based on two useful
and powerful premises:

- Eliciting preferences from respondents with very little
information about EVs is likely to be quite unrevealing about
the demand for EVs in a real market setting in which sellers
can be expected to make major efforts to inform buyers.

- A substantial--if not predominant--proportion of the household
demand for EVs can be expected to come from "hybrid
households"--households that have more than one LDV and can use
EVs as part of a household fleet that also includes at least
one ICEV.

TK provide information on the fraction of respondents who state
that they would buy an EV under various conditions embedded in
hypothetical choice scenarios. Such fractions are revealing of points
on demand curves. The questions are: *What* points on *what* demand curves?

The TK survey assesses quantities demanded of EVs--including the
first battery pack--only at prices to households equal to the prices of
ICEVs that are comparable in size, body style, styling, optional
features, etc.[261] The remaining questions focus on what the respondents
assume about the various factors that affect demand--for example,
vehicle performance characteristics, mechanical reliability, operating
costs, and availability of infrastructure.

TK present subjects (households) with two sets of choices, referred
to as Choice Situations One and Two. Each subject is asked to choose
one vehicle in each situation. In Choice Situation One, respondents
were asked to choose either a gasoline vehicle or an EV, based on
written and video descriptions, with each vehicle having several body

---

[261]More specifically, the scenarios they present to respondents
involve a price charged by sellers for various EVs of $4000 more than
for comparable ICEVs, which after the deduction of government supported
EV-purchase subsidies of $4000 make the prices of EVs and comparable
ICEVs identical. Neighborhood electric vehicles--very small vehicles
with two, three or four seats that are not freeway capable and have no
comparable ICEV (an example of what we have called "niche vehicles")--
were assumed to be priced between $5,500 and $10,000 and qualify for a
$2000 purchase subsidy.

styles and options.[262]   In Choice Situation Two, respondents were asked to make choices among six vehicle types--three pure EVs, one hybrid EV, a gasoline vehicle and a natural gas vehicle.

To characterize demand for EVs in the years 1998 to 2002, we rely on TK results for Situation One because this allows us to construct a more informative bound than if we use of results from Situation Two.[263]

In many respects, the TK scenario in Choice Situation One corresponds reasonably well to what can be expected from the average Big 7 EVs during 1998 to 2002. For example:

- Acceleration (0-60 mph in 13 seconds)
- Top speed (80 mph)
- Portrayal of general advantages of home recharging
- Promise of no smog check
- Availability of seven different EV body styles
- Battery life of 25,000 miles or 2 to 3 years

However, several other features of the TK hypothetical Choice Situation One make EVs more attractive to respondents than the average Big 7 EVs that will be available during 1998 to 2002. Such features include:

- Optimistic range from battery pack option Type 1 (80-100 miles);[264]

---

[262]We have not reviewed the video materials used in the TK study.

[263]The scenarios in Situation One are more compatible with the information reviewed in Section 10.1 on EV and battery performance during 1998 to 2002. In Situation Two respondents are asked to select from many more kinds of EVs (multiple body styles of each of four EV types) than will plausibly be available during 1998 to 2002. Moreover, more than 70 percent of households choosing pure EVs (and more than 55 percent of those choosing a pure EV or hybrid EV) chose the Regional EV, which is described as having a range of 120-150 miles. As discussed in Section 10.1, The advanced batteries that would make this range possible will be available in 2000 at the *earliest*. This vehicle is portrayed by the authors as part of "one plausible future market" (TK, p. 57).

[264]While this range may be only moderately optimistic, the fact that it includes 100 miles could have dramatic implications for respondent choices.

- Optimistic implicit lifetime operating costs for battery pack option Type 1;[265]
- Availability of an even better battery pack (option Type 2) that will allow range of 100-120 miles;[266]
- An assumed replacement cost of battery Type 2 ($2,000) much lower than implied by even the most optimistic projections for a battery with its assumed capabilities;[267]
- An optimistic view of the costs of installing a 220 line for faster home recharging;[268]
- An optimistic view of the availability of fast recharging.[269]

---

[265]For Battery pack option Type 1, EVs have essentially no operating-cost disadvantage relative to gasoline vehicles. This is due largely to the assumed performance and cost of the battery pack: The replacement cost ($1,200) seems much too low for the assumed range of 80 to 100 miles. To achieve this range, an EV would require 16 to 25 kwh of energy storage (even assuming that the battery is fully discharged in each cycle--the usual assumption is 80 percent discharge). Thus the assumed $1,200 per battery pack implies $48 to $75 per kwh, while lead acid batteries are currently priced at $125 to $175 per kwh, and the most optimistic estimates suggest that this will fall only to $120 to $150.

[266]Battery Type 2 is especially important because 63 percent of respondents who chose an EV in Situation One chose to pay extra for the Type 2 battery option. (TK, 1995, p. 50.) To achieve the assumed range of 100-120 miles using accessories seems likely only with batteries that will be available no earlier than 2000.

[267]The TK assumptions imply a cost of $67 to $100 per kwh, while optimistic estimates for advanced batteries are over $230 per kwh when they are first commercially available. At roughly $150 per kwh, even the "learned-out" costs of advanced batteries are substantially above the TK assumptions.

[268]The promotional information for EVs incorporated in the experiment states "Utility rebates available for installing a new circuit." This raises the question of whether respondents who would need to install a 220 line to take advantage of faster home recharging were unduly optimistic about the costs to them of doing so.

[269]The fast-charging issue is important because a substantial number of respondents expressed a willingness to pay $900 for this option, which was described to respondents as delivering an 80 percent charge in 20 minutes. Those who chose the option were asked to indicate on a map where they would like to have a station located; this raises the issue of what the respondents assumed about the locational convenience of fast-charge stations and whether respondents were likely to be optimistic about this relative to the availability of such infrastructure in the 1998 to 2002 period.

In addition, TK (pp. 91-92) discuss--but fail to dispel--concerns that stated preferences for EVs elicited in their survey could overstate actual demand even under real-world conditions identical to the hypothetical conditions.[270] This fact, coupled with the features of the scenario highlighted above, cause us to conclude that the demand curve about which we learn from the TK results is a different demand curve-- involving higher quantities demanded at every price--than the demand curve relevant to forecasting Big 7 EV sales during the 1998 to 2002 period.[271]

11.3.2 Synthesis: Demand for Big 7 EVs in California During 1998 to 2002

The available information doesn't reveal much about the demand at *various* prices for Big 7 EVs during the first five years of the ZEV mandate. However, we have sufficient information to develop an informative range for what turns out to be the critical issue: At what prices--net of any purchase subsidies[272]--can we expect the Big 7 companies to be able to sell enough EVs during 1998 to 2002 to satisfy the mandate? Our conclusion--which we explain presently--is that, if potential EV purchasers consider the full cost of owning and operating EVs, we can expect them to demand enough EVs to satisfy the mandate at prices to them (i.e., net of any subsidies and excluding the battery) of

---

[270]In conceding that the survey responses could substantially overestimate "real" purchase intentions of EVs, TK argue--quite plausibly--that their results should be taken to signify more than "feel good" answers, including, for example, political opinion in support of EVs. They also argue that what would prevent buying behavior from matching stated preferences is "budget" not "sincerity." We find these comments quite reasonable. However, they merely reinforce our concerns that the fraction of respondents choosing EVs in the TK survey could greatly overestimate the fraction of hybrid households that would actually buy EVs of the quality postulated in the survey at prices equal to those of comparable ICEVs.

[271]Thus, we are also skeptical of TK's fundamental conclusion: "The results of this study give strong evidence of a market for EVs large enough to fulfill the year 1998 and 2001 mandates with current electric vehicle and battery technologies." (Turrentine and Kurani, 1995, p. 10.)

[272]The willingness of households or fleet managers to purchase an EV should depend on the net price to them of doing so. Subsidies for EV purchases are described and incorporated in the analysis below.

between $1,000 and $11,000 less than the price of an ICEV of comparable size and body style. After explaining this conclusion we incorporate subsidies into the analysis.

Household demand. We first consider the price to households at which we can expect households to demand enough EVs during 1998 to 2002 to contribute substantially to the ability of the Big 7 companies to meet their mandated quantities. We base our conclusions primarily on (1) Turrentine and Kurani (1995), and (2) our analysis in Section 10.2 of the lifetime operating costs of an EV relative to those of a comparable ICEV.

In considering an EV purchase, we assume that most potential EV buyers would compare the performance and full life-cycle costs (i.e., purchase prices plus present values of lifetime operating costs) of an EV with those of an ICEV of comparable size and body style. In terms of performance, EVs have some clear disadvantages--range being the most important for most buyers--and some clear advantages--the convenience of home refueling is probably the most important. We interpret Turrentine and Kurani's (1995) results to indicate that most, if not all, of the mandated quantities could be satisfied by household purchases if:

a) the performance of the average Big 7 EV is as good as portrayed in their Choice Situation One,

b) the price of the EV to households is the same as that of a comparable ICEV, *and*

c) the lifetime operating costs of EVs are the same as those of ICEVs.

Suppose we assume, as is optimistic but not inconceivable, that EV battery technology, manufacturing capability, and infrastructure advance rapidly enough that a substantial number of households view the performance of the *average* Big 7 EV during 1998 to 2002 as comparable that to ICEVs.[273] How much would such consumers be willing to pay for a

---

[273]While this seems optimistic, a factor that we haven't discussed tends to increase demand for EVs: subsidies for *use* of EVs, such as rebates for the installation of 220 lines for home charging, preferential parking or use of carpool lanes for EVs, and discounted electricity rates for EV recharging (which were taken into account in the analysis of EV operating costs). Following standard demand theory,

Big 7 EV *without a battery pack*? That depends on what they anticipate about the lifetime operating costs on the EV relative to a comparable ICEV. We concluded in Section 10.2 that, for EVs purchased during 1998 to 2002, the present value of lifetime operating costs--including all EV battery packs and including gasoline taxes in ICEV operating costs--can be expected to be $1,000 to $11,000 more than the present value of the lifetime operating costs of a comparable ICEV (see the discussion of Table 10.2-7). Consequently, we expect there would be enough household demand to meet a sizable proportion of the mandated quantities during 1998 to 2002, if EVs are viewed by many households as comparable in performance to ICEVs of similar size and body style and EVs--without any battery packs--are priced (to households) at $1,000 to $11,000 less than such ICEVs.

TK provide no direct information for Situation One concerning the quantities demanded at prices above those of comparable ICEVs; none of their choice experiments considered prices in that range. However, they do write that "Our previous research, though informal, seems to confirm the opinion that not many consumers will pay extra for electric vehicles." (Turrentine and Kurani, 1995, p. 9.)

Fleet demand. We have relatively little empirical information about potential fleet demand for Big 7 EVs. The key conclusion from Hill (1987, p. 284) is: "Our analysis provides strong evidence that firms would be willing to cope with the limited range of electric vehicles *if* these vehicles were able to provide a less costly means of doing business." Combining this conclusion with our range of lifetime operating cost disadvantages of EVs relative to comparable ICEVs for vehicles purchased during 1998 to 2002, we conclude that there would be considerable EV demand from fleets--perhaps even enough to meet the mandate quantities with no EV sales to households--at prices for EVs without any batteries of between $1,000 to $11,000 less than the prices of comparable ICEVs. The existence of *any* fleet demand for EVs at

---

use subsidies enter the analysis differently than purchase subsidies because subsidies for EV use tend to increase (shift outward) EV demand curves, while subsidies for EV purchases lower prices to the demanders and hence move them down the relevant demand curve.

prices higher than this would be doubtful (given Hill's key conclusion), except for a factor that we have not been able to quantify: Fleet demand for EVs driven by the federal Energy Policy Act of 1992, which requires fleets to purchase alternatively fueled vehicles (AFVs), which would include EVs and many other AFVs.[274] Despite the existence of this factor, however, almost everyone we interviewed expressed considerable pessimism about fleet demand as the key to Big 7 EV sales during the early years of the mandate.

Subsidies for EV purchases. Currently subsidies for EV purchases are available from the U.S. and California governments and the South Coast Air Quality Management District (SCAQMD). We incorporate the federal subsidy in our analysis of 1998 to 2002, but not the other two, for reasons we explain presently.

The federal program is in effect through 2002. It provides tax credits of 10 percent of the purchase price of an EV up to a maximum of $4,000 per vehicle. We incorporate this subsidy into our analyses of demand and market effects of the ZEV mandate because it is substantial in size and enacted for the time period we analyze.

The SCAQMD program (the "ZEV Incentive Program") provides for purchase subsidies to South Coast EV buyers of up to $5,000 per vehicle. A total of $6 million has been allocated for the years 1996 and 1997. There is also a small program of state tax credits administered by the California Energy Commission, operative only until December 1, 1996, involving no more than $750,000 in credits annually. We do not incorporate a district-level or state-level subsidy in our analysis because we cannot predict whether such subsidies will be available after 1997.[275]

Summary interpretation. The available information suggests the following conclusions about the demand for Big 7 EVs:

- If companies price EVs near the average variable costs of
  producing EVs that *they* project (i.e., near the high end of our

---

[274]See GAO (1994, pp. 42-43) for a summary of the National Policy Act requirements for purchase of AFVs and other programs bearing on the demand for EVs for fleet use.

[275]We do explain our methods in sufficient detail to allow readers to adjust our estimates using their own projections or after future subsidies are enacted.

range of $3,320 to $15,000 more than comparable ICEVs), they will likely fall far short of selling the quantities required under the mandate.

- Companies will be able to reach the quantities required under the mandate only by pricing EVs--without any batteries--so that they cost purchasers (after the federal subsidy is deducted) $1,000 to $11,000 less than the prices of ICEVs of comparable size and body style.[276]

- For EV prices to buyers involving any substantial premium over the price of a comparable ICEV, quantities of the EVs demanded will be much lower than mandated quantities.

Figure 11.3-1 summarizes these conclusions by sketching the demand curve facing a typical Big 7 company for its EVs during 1998 to 2002. The figure pertains to each company individually.[277] In the figure, E, which is measured on the horizontal axis, denotes the number of EVs--without a battery pack--demanded from one of the Big 7 companies. Measured on the vertical axis is P^-, which denotes the price paid by EV buyers, net of any government purchase subsidy. At a price like P_C-- which is in the range of average variable cost of producing EVs that the company projects--a company will not be able to sell its mandated quantity (E_m).[278] The price at which they can sell their mandated

---

[276]Note that the $11,000 figure is not a worst-plausible case because it doesn't factor in pessimistic scenarios about average EV performance characteristics during 1998 to 2002. Suppose, for example, that advancement in battery technology is disappointing over the next few years in terms of range in actual use. If the operating cost disadvantage of EVs turns out to be near the $11,000 figure, it is unlikely that the Big 7 companies will be able to sell their mandated quantities even charging $11,000 less than the price of a comparable ICEV because it is likely that not enough potential buyers will view EVs as comparable in performance (for their purposes) to ICEVs, and they will require price discounts relative to ICEVs to compensate for more than the operating cost disadvantage.

[277]Implicit in the construction of the demand curve for the EVs of a single company are the operating costs of the EV, availability and price of EV infrastructure, and quality and prices of the EVs offered by the other six companies.

[278]Note that the scales of the horizontal axes on Figures 10.2-1 and 11.3-1 are very different. In particular, the mandated quantity E_m-- which is the same number in each figure--is much farther to the left in the former figure than the latter.

quantities (P_m) is below the price of a comparable ICEV (P_{ice}); according to our analyses the difference between P_{ice} and P_m is likely to be in the range of $1,000 and $11,000.

Having characterized the costs and demand for EVs, we are prepared to analyze how the ZEV mandate will affect market outcomes during the years 1998 to 2002.

11.4 THE CALIFORNIA EV MARKET IN 1998 TO 2002 WITH AND WITHOUT THE ZEV MANDATE

In this section, we analyze the potential effects of the ZEV mandate that operate through the ZEV market. As in the case of EV demand, we quantify only for the first five years of the mandate.

By definition, the market effects of the ZEV mandate are the differences in market outcomes with and without the mandate.[279]

11.4.1 Behavior of Big 7 Companies Without the ZEV Mandate

Without the EV mandate--and without subsidies to EV purchase or use much larger than currently in place--the numbers of EVs sold in California during the years 1998 to 2002 would be nowhere near the numbers that are required under the mandate. This proposition does not seem controversial. But considering its underpinnings provides context for our discussion of how the Big 7 companies are likely to behave with the mandate in place.

---

[279]The effects of interest are those of policy decisions that have yet to be made. For example, policymakers can now decide whether to *continue* the mandate, but not whether to institute it (as they did in 1990). Effects of instituting the mandate can no longer be altered. These effects include the costs of and knowledge gained from R&D on EV technology already spurred by the mandate.

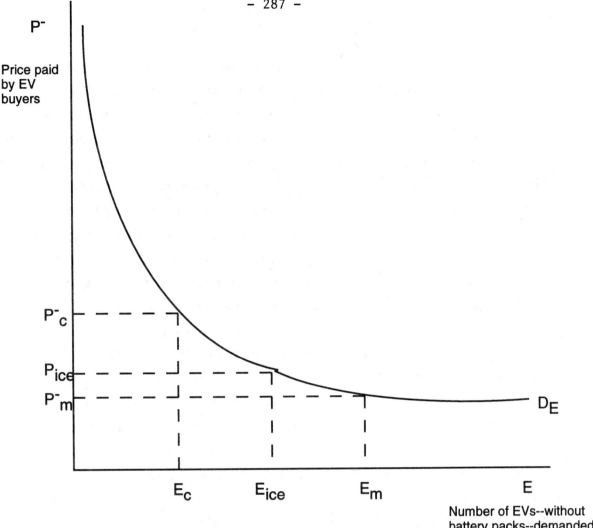

Figure 11.3-1

Demand for a Big 7 Company's EVs During 1998 to 2002:
Summary Interpretation of Available Information

Notes:

P⁻ = price paid by buyers for EVs without a battery pack; i.e., price charged by company minus 10% federal tax credit (the purchase subsidy)

E = number of EVs demanded from company

D_E is demand curve for EVs without battery packs offered by a single Big 7 company

P^-_c = price in range of company's projected unit cost of manufacturing EVs, without battery packs, minus subsidy

P_{ice} = price of ICEVs comparable to company's EV

P^-_m = price at which company could sell the mandated number of its EVs without battery packs

E_c = number of company EVs without battery packs that would be demanded at net price near company's unit cost of manufacturing EVs without battery packs

E_{ice} = number of company EVs without battery packs that would be demanded at a net price equal to price of comparable ICEVs

E_m = number of EVs company is mandated to offer for sale

EV demand, cost, and profitability for Big 7 companies. During 1998 to 2002, in the absence of the ZEV mandate, major vehicle manufacturers are unlikely to offer EVs for sale on more than a very limited basis, if at all. This conclusion follows from our conclusions about Big 7 projections of EV production costs and EV demand depicted in Figures 10.2-1 and 11.3-1, respectively. Figure 11.4-1 depicts the EV production cost conditions projected by a Big 7 company and demand facing that company during the period 1998 to 2002, assuming EV purchase subsidies of 10 percent of purchase price (as authorized through 2002 under the federal tax-credit program). In particular, the demand curve, labeled D_{Es} in Figure 11.4-1, is the demand curve in Figure 11.3-1 shifted upward by the amount of the subsidy.[280]

The key feature of the figure is that the (projected) demand curve (even with the subsidy) lies entirely below the company's (projected) average variable and marginal cost curves (AVC_p and MC_p). This means that there is no quantity of EVs for which companies anticipate being able to price EVs high enough to cover even marginal and average variable costs. Under such conditions, companies anticipate that they would lose money in the short-run marketing *any* quantity of EVs during the 1998 to 2002 period (even ignoring the fixed costs involved).

Big 7 company sales of EVs during 1998 to 2002 without the mandate. The conclusion that Big 7 companies do not anticipate being able to market EVs profitably during 1998 to 2002 results largely from their projections that their average variable production costs for EVs in that time period are likely to be much higher than those of comparable ICEVs and the likelihood that EVs will have substantial operating cost disadvantages relative to ICEVs.

---

[280]The (standard economic) argument is that if a consumer is willing to pay up to $X to buy a good in the absence of any purchase subsidy, that consumer would pay up to $X plus the amount of an available subsidy for the same good.

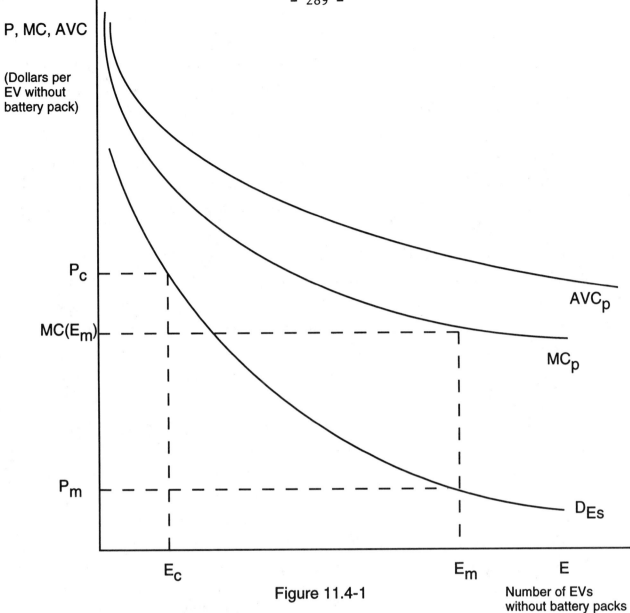

Figure 11.4-1

Number of EVs
without battery packs

EV Cost and Demand Conditions Projected by an Individual Big 7 Company
During One of the Years 1998 to 2002 with Federal Purchase Subsidy

Notes:

D_{Es} is demand curve for EVs without battery packs offered by the company (10% higher than unsubsidized D_E in Figure 11.3-1)

MC_p = marginal cost of producing a company EV without a battery pack, as projected by company

AVC_p = average variable cost of producing company's EVs without battery packs, as projected by company

P = price paid by EV buyers with no purchase subsidy

P_c = price in range of MC_p and AVC_p at production levels near mandated quantity

P_m = price at which company could sell the mandated number of its EVs without battery packs

E = number of company EVs

E_c = number of company EVs that would be demanded at a price near company's projected unit cost of manufacturing EVs at production levels near mandated quantity

E_m = number of EVs company is mandated to offer for sale

Companies often accept losses in the early years of marketing a new product. Might they be willing to do so to introduce EVs during 1998 to 2002? Companies voluntarily market products at a loss during introductory periods because they expect the long-term gains to outweigh the short-term losses. Should we expect that long-term considerations would make Big 7 companies willing to sell substantial numbers of EVs in 1998 to 2002 even in the absence of the ZEV mandate? An analysis, detailed in Appendix 11.B, leads to the conclusion that this is plausible only for companies that have developed EVs that could be expected to generate substantial buyer enthusiasm and thereby enhance the reputation of the company. Publicly available information indicates that there might be only one existing EV that fits this description: the General Motors Impact. Woodruff (1995) reports on the very positive response of participants in GM's PrEView Drive campaign. In January, 1996, GM announced plans to market the EV1--which is almost identical to the Impact--in California and Arizona later in the year (*Automotive News,* January 8, 1996). GM is hopeful that the EV1 will provide major benefits to their corporate image (*Automotive News,* February 12, 1996).

In sum, our analysis suggests that, without the mandate, the Big 7 companies would not choose to sell anything close to the quantities of EVs required under the mandate because doing so will involve short-term losses that they don't expect to be outweighed by the long-term gains.

11.4.2 Behavior of Big 7 Companies with the ZEV Mandate

The California market for EVs will be very different in the presence of the ZEV mandate.

Pricing of EVs offered by Big 7 companies. At what prices will the Big 7 offer EVs that they produce? Profit maximization suggests that they will charge the highest price at which they can sell their mandated quantities. As we noted in our discussion of Fig. 11.4-1, selling at this price implies that Big 7 companies would expect to lose money on every additional EV they sell.

Big 7 alternatives under the mandate. Under the ZEV mandate, a Big 7 company isn't required to meet its obligations by producing for sale its total mandated quantities of EVs (i.e., 2 percent or 5 percent of its total LDV sales). There are two other alternatives:

- Acquire credits from another company that sells EVs but isn't using its credits to satisfy its own obligation under the mandate[281]
- Pay fines of $5,000 for every unit of shortfall between its mandated quantity and the total of the number of EVs produced and offered for sale and EV credits purchased

We now consider the likelihood that companies will choose one of these two alternatives. Our most fundamental conclusions are:

a) the alternatives can be expected to involve relatively high costs for each unit of the mandate satisfied, and

b) most, if not almost all, of the mandated quantities are likely to be met by production and sale of EVs by Big 7 companies.

Will Big 7 companies merely pay the fines? If Big 7 companies anticipate that they will lose more than $5,000 on every additional EV they produce and sell, the option of paying the fine might seem preferable. We cannot rule out the possibility that they will choose to pay fines to satisfy large portions of their mandated quantities, but there is good reason to be skeptical.

Paying the fine may be viewed by companies as involving costs of more than $5,000 per unit. Such costs include adverse publicity--and damage to the company's reputation--if companies that pay the fine are viewed by the public as evading the mandate or unsympathetic to California's efforts to improve air quality. Moreover, managers of Big 7 companies may fear that paying the fine--which involves a failure to comply with government regulations--will subject the company's officers and directors to lawsuits by stockholders. Finally, companies have told us that they expect that if they choose to pay fines rather than producing and selling EVs the size of the fine is likely to be increased.

---

[281]For example, the other company might be a conversion company that agrees to provide EV credits in exchange for access to gliders, a manufacturer of niche vehicles such as the PIVCO, or another ICEV manufacturer that isn't subject to the mandate until 2003, but sells some EVs in California before 2003.

Note that much of these extra costs might be avoided if companies are viewed as using the payment of fines as a fallback--rather than a primary--strategy, and do not use fines to cover large fractions of their mandated quantities. For example, the risks of bad publicity, stockholders' suits and regulatory reaction might be relatively minor if companies are viewed as making good faith efforts to comply with the mandate by selling large numbers of EVs or buying substantial numbers of credits and using the payment of fines only if their efforts to produce and sell EVs or buy credits fail to meet their mandated quantities.

In sum, we expect that companies will not pay fines to cover large fractions of their mandated quantities. Moreover, if they do, it will be because they project losses substantially more than $5,000 for every additional EV they produce and credits are either not available or sell for even higher prices.

Our analysis of market effects is structured to allow for the possibilities that (1) companies pay small numbers of fines as a fallback strategy and (2) they pay large numbers of fines and perceive high costs of doing so.

Will credits account for a substantial fraction of mandated quantities? It is very hard to predict what fraction of the mandated quantities will be met by purchasing credits. Nothing we have read and no one that we interviewed has led us to expect that this fraction will be very large (e.g., even as large as 10 percent).

There is no direct empirical evidence to draw on. A theoretical analysis detailed in Appendix 11.C probes the questions:

- Under what conditions would companies cover substantial fractions of the mandated quantities with credits?
- If large numbers of credits are sold, what companies are the mostly likely sources of these credits?

That analysis reinforces the view that vehicles produced by non-Big 7 companies (i.e., other ICEV companies, converters, niche-vehicle producers) are unlikely to account for a substantial fraction (e.g., more than 10 percent) of the EVs produced during 1998 to 2002 because of the ZEV mandate. Some other central implications are:

- If Big 7 companies do buy substantial numbers of credits, the most likely source of credits is ICEV companies that become subject to the mandate in 2003;[282]
- Credits will not sell for substantially less than the costs to companies of meeting the mandate by producing EVs or paying fines.

The discussion here provides a non-technical overview of the analysis detailed in Appendix 11.C and explains these conclusions.

The analysis uses supply and demand models of the market for credits and the market for EVs produced by non-Big 7 companies. The demand for EV credits comes from Big 7 companies. How much would they be willing to pay for an EV credit? Up to the cost avoided on the best alternative--either the cost they attribute to paying a fine or the additional amount they would lose by producing and selling an additional EV.

The supply of EV credits comes from non-Big 7 companies. The price at which a company would be willing to supply a credit depends on the cost of producing a credit. To produce a credit, a company has to produce and sell an EV; this is costly (and credits will command a positive price) if the price at which a non-Big 7 EV can be sold is less than the marginal cost of producing the vehicle.

The analysis thus suggests that a non-Big 7 company will produce an EV and sell a credit only if it can do so at losses at the margin that are smaller than both the extra losses Big 7 companies incur from producing and selling an additional EV and the costs Big 7 companies perceive in paying fines. It may seem plausible that this will be the case for large numbers of non-Big 7 EVs until one considers an important fact: the relevant demand for non-Big 7 EVs is the demand in the presence of Big 7 companies marketing their EVs under pressure from the mandate.

The analysis suggests strong doubts that during the period 1998 to 2002 credits will account for thousands of EVs per year, as would be required to account for more than 10 percent of the total mandate

---

[282]We argue below that these other ICEV companies are likely to have EV production costs as high as or higher than those of the Big 7.

quantities.[283]   Because non-Big 7 EVs can be expected to be competing
with Big 7 EVs priced to sell large quantities, we expect that non-Big 7
EVs can be sold in large quantities only at quite low prices: Why, for
example, would many EV buyers be willing to pay anywhere near the price
of an ICEV for a non-Big 7 EV when they are likely to be able to buy
very high quality EVs from the Big 7 for prices below--and perhaps far
below--the price of comparable ICEVs?[284]   Under these circumstances, the
prices that non-Big 7 EVs can command if large numbers (e.g., more than
10 percent of mandated quantities) are to be sold are likely very low
relative to their marginal production costs.   If so, the cost of
generating credits can be expected to be very high.   Thus we are
doubtful that credits will account for even as much as 10 percent of the
EVs produced during 1998 to 2002 because of the mandate.[285]

A central lesson of the analysis is that credits will be produced
only if non-Big 7 companies can produce EVs with lower marginal losses
than Big 7 companies can.   The most likely source of large numbers of
credits seems to be the ICEV companies that are not subject to the ZEV
mandate until 2003.   These companies--faced with a 10 percent mandate
level in 2003--may perceive substantial benefits to selling some EVs in

---

[283]As discussed in Appendix 11.C, converters and niche EV producers
may sell substantial numbers of EVs during 1998 to 2002; the argument
here is that they are unlikely to sell thousands per year.

[284]The idea that non-Big 7 vehicles would command a lower price does
not imply that they are *economically* inferior; for example, it is also
expected some of them will cost less to produce. In fact, some EV
enthusiasts believe that the best transition path to the development of
a long-term market for EVs involves a major, if not predominant, role in
the near term for vehicles that do not compete directly with ICEVs, such
as neighborhood EVs. (See, for example, Sperling, 1995.) Our analysis
suggests that the mandate may be an impediment to such a transition path
by greatly depressing the demand for such vehicles.

[285]Moreover, under these conditions, for thousands of EV credits to
be generated and sold annually, marginal losses on production and sale
of Big 7 EVs would need to be very high and Big 7 companies would have
to attribute very high costs to paying the fine. This is worth
emphasizing because some have argued: a) Big 7 losses on EVs won't be
large, b) Big 7 companies would be willing to pay the fine without
attributing costs above the $5000, and c) non-Big 7 companies will
produce a lot of EVs because of the ability to sell credits. The
analysis here suggests that, as a matter of economic logic, these three
premises do not comfortably coexist.

California before 2002. If so, such benefits would compensate somewhat for their marginal losses from selling EVs, and make these companies more willing to sell EVs--and produce EV credits--than other EV companies.

Suppose the Big 7 do purchase large numbers of EV credits from ICEV companies that become subject to the mandate in 2003. How would that affect our quantitative analyses? In general, it would affect the interpretation, but not the basic thrust, of our results. This is because we would expect EVs produced by other ICEV companies also to be as similar as possible to comparable ICEVs[286] and thus have similar prices and similar, if not higher, costs.[287] For example, in Section 10.4, to calculate narrow cost-effectiveness ratios, we relied heavily on estimated ranges of the production costs of Big 7 EVs. The possibility that large numbers of EVs are produced by other ICEV companies would not lead us to reduce the cost estimates, but would require us to alter our interpretation of the source of the vehicles.

Might the Big 7 produce EVs, but not sell them? It has been suggested that--since the mandate does not require sales of EVs, but "merely" production and offer for sale of EVs--companies might produce the vehicles, offer them at very high prices and not sell them at all. Such a strategy would be sensible from the company's point of view only if the costs of selling EVs *that have already been produced* are higher than the benefits to the company of selling those vehicles. The benefits of selling the vehicles (rather than merely letting them sit somewhere) include: a) the extra revenue that could be gained; b) the value of the additional knowledge the company would gain; and c) the value of avoiding the adverse publicity that would result from failing to sell the mandated quantity. Failing to sell EVs that are already produced (rather than selling them for whatever the market will bear) seems implausible, then, unless the best EV a company can market would perform so poorly that the reputation costs of selling it would be quite

---

[286]Such a product strategy makes sense for the non-Big 7 *ICEV companies* for the same reasons it does for the Big 7.

[287]Production costs might be higher because of even smaller scales of production.

high. We cannot totally dismiss this possibility, but we do not explicitly consider it further.

Where does this leave us? We expect that the mandate will cause all of the Big 7 companies to produce substantial numbers of EVs during the years 1998 to 2002. If credits (i.e., non-Big 7 EVs) will account for even 10 percent of the EVs produced because of the mandate (i.e., more than 2,500 during each year from 1998 to 2000 or more than 6,200 per year during 2001 and 2002--see Table 5.8-1) we expect that the predominant source of credits will be non-Big 7 ICEV companies preparing for 2003 when they will face the 10 percent mandate level. Since we expect that EVs built by these other ICEV companies will have costs similar, if not higher, than those of the Big 7, we emphasize cost and demand conditions for the Big 7 EVs. Note further that no matter what one believes about the prevalence of credits or fines, or even production of EVs that aren't sold, one key conclusion is unaffected: For every additional EV in a Big 7 company's mandated quantity, the company is likely to perceive a cost.

11.5 EFFECTS OF THE ZEV MANDATE ON THE CALIFORNIA EV MARKET

To recap, the available studies of EV cost and demand conditions and basic economic models and reasoning have led us to conclude that with the ZEV mandate during the period 1998 to 2002, the Big 7:

- Can be expected to produce EVs as comparable as possible to their ICEVs of similar size and body style
- Will meet most--if not virtually all--of their mandated EV quantities by selling such EVs or buying credits from other ICEV companies that aren't subject to the mandate until 2003[288]
- Are likely to incur incremental variable production costs of $3,320 to $15,000 per EV relative to comparable ICEVs
- Will be able to sell their EVs for $1,000 to $11,000 less than the prices of comparable ICEVs plus the amount available to buyers because of the 10 percent federal tax credit.

---

[288]In addition, we have concluded that if part of the mandated quantity is met by paying fines, it would only be because marginal losses from buying EV credits or selling EVs would be high.

11.5.1 An Overview of the Stakes in the EV Market

Table 11.5-1 draws on these conclusions to develop a sense of the range of numbers likely to be involved. All of the figures are constructed and interpreted as averages across companies and over the five-year period.

Price and cost of comparable ICEVs. Since much of the information on cost and demand for EVs is expressed relative to costs and prices for comparable ICEVs, we need to put numbers on these quantities. In Table 11.5-1 we consider only one ICEV, which we think of as the average comparable ICEV. This ICEV is assumed to sell for $20,000, which is roughly the average selling price of ICEVs. We chose this number because it is also within the price range of ICEVs comparable to the EVs that the Big 7 are likely to market during 1998 to 2002.[289] We assume that the average variable cost of this comparable ICEV is half of the selling price, or $10,000.[290]

---

[289]For example, Ford has announced plans to market an electric version of its Ranger ICEV (pick-up truck), which sells for roughly $11,000, Chrysler has announced plans to market an electric version of its next-generation mini-van, which we would expect to sell for somewhat more than $20,000, and GM has recently announced plans to market the Impact (a two-seater sports car) that is expected to sell for $30,000, or more.

[290]This is a ballpark estimate (companies do not report production costs of vehicles). It is based on recognizing that prices must cover all costs for manufacturers and dealers to be profitable and that costs of design, plant and equipment, marketing, selling, and warranty are very considerable.

Table 11.5-1

Illustrative Costs, Prices and Profit Margins for Big 7 EVs--Without Battery Packs--During 1998 to 2002
(dollars per vehicle unless otherwise specified)

	EV Market Scenario			
	Low Cost High Price	Low Cost Low Price	High Cost High Price	High Cost Low Price
COMPARABLE ICEV:				
Price of ICEV	20,000	20,000	20,000	20,000
Average variable cost of ICEV	10,000	10,000	10,000	10,000
BIG 7 EV:				
Incremental average variable cost	3,320	3,320	15,000	15,000
Average variable cost of EV	13,320	13,320	25,000	25,000
Total EV fixed costs ($ millions)	1,050	1,050	4,200	4,200
Average fixed costs of EVs (assuming twice CA volume)	2,646	2,646	10,585	10,585
Average total costs of EVs (assuming twice CA volume)	15,966	15,966	35,585	35,585
Lifetime EV operating cost disadvantage	1,000	11,000	1,000	11,000
EV price to sellers without subsidy	19,000	9,000	19,000	9,000
EV price to sellers with subsidy (10% federal tax credit)	21,411	10,300	21,411	10,300
Average profit per EV with tax credit	5,445	-5,666	-14,174	-25,285
Operating profit per EV with tax credit	8,091	-3,020	-3,589	-14,700

Notes:

Average fixed and total costs calculated using total 3-state EV volume 1998-2002 of 396,800.

EV price without subsidy calculated as ICEV price minus EV operating cost disadvantage.

EV price with 10% federal tax credit is price without subsidy divided by 0.9 plus $300 to incorporate subsidy on first battery pack.

Average profit per EV with tax credit is price with subsidy minus average total cost.

Operating profit per EV with tax credit is price with subsidy minus average variable cost.

Costs of a Big 7 EV without battery pack. In Section 10.2, we
concluded that EVs marketed by Big 7 companies during the early years of
the mandate are likely to involve average variable costs per EV--without
a battery pack--of $3,320 to $15,000 more than the average variable
costs of a comparable ICEV. Combining these figures with the assumed
$10,000 average variable cost of the comparable ICEV, Table 11.5-1
provides a range of $13,320 to $25,000 for the variable cost per EV in
the low- and high-cost EV scenarios, respectively. We also concluded
that fixed costs of EVs (e.g., design, plant and equipment) over the
first five years of the mandate are likely to be in the range of $1.05
billion to $4.2 billion.[291] Thus we settle on a range for average total
costs per EV of just less than $16,000 to just more than $35,500 per
EV.[292]

Prices for Big 7 EVs. The range of prices at which the Big 7 could
sell their mandated quantities of EVs--without any purchase subsidies--
reported in Table 11.5-1 is $9,000 to $19,000. This corresponds to the
assumed price of $20,000 for a comparable ICEV and our conclusion that--
because of operating cost disadvantages of EVs during 1998 to 2002--Big
7 companies will be able to sell the mandated quantities of EVs without
battery packs at a price *to buyers* of between $1,000 and $11,000 less
than the price of comparable ICEVs. The range of prices with a 10
percent federal tax credit in place--$10,300 to $21,411--represents the
prices that Big 7 companies can charge for their EVs and still have

---

[291]Some of these fixed costs--e.g., for design of EVs--have
undoubtedly already been incurred by companies and, therefore, can no
longer be recovered. Such costs are not part of the economic costs of
keeping the mandate. The extent to which companies have already incurred
costs of plant and equipment for producing EVs under the mandate is
unclear.

[292]These calculations illustrate a factor to keep in mind when
interpreting ranges constructed by combining ranges of multiple factors.
For example, note that the almost $20,000 range for average total
production costs per EV in Table 11.5-1 results from combining the low
ends of the ranges for variable and fixed costs and combining the high
ends of those ranges. Since it is not a forgone conclusion that
variable costs at the low end would be accompanied by fixed costs at the
low end, etc., ranges constructed by combining low ends with low ends
and high ends with high ends are likely to be considerably more
conservative than the ranges from which they are constructed.

- 300 -

buyers facing net prices of $9,000 to $19,000 allowing for an extra $300
in willingness to pay sellers to account for a 10 percent subsidy on an
approximate price of $3,000 for the first battery pack.[293]

Implications for profit margins. The wide ranges of prices and
production costs leave open the possibility that Big 7 companies earn
gains of more than $5,000 per EV (in the low-cost, high-price scenario)
or losses of just over $25,000 per EV (in the high-cost, low-price
scenario).[294] Even more important for what follows, note that profit
margins excluding all fixed costs--what we refer to as operating profit
margins in the table--range from gains of more than $8,000 per EV (in
the low-cost, high-price scenario) to losses of almost $15,000 per EV
(in the high-cost, low-price scenario).

**Illustrative values of total dollar gains and losses to Big 7
companies in the EV market.** What do these figures imply about total
dollar profits or losses of Big 7 companies in the California EV market
due to the EV mandate? Another very wide range. Assuming that the Big
7 sell 198,400 EVs in California during 1998 to 2002 implies dollar
profits of more than $1 billion in the low-cost, high-price scenario but
dollar losses of more than five times that in the high-cost, low-price
scenario. We emphasize that these calculations ignore a potentially

---

[293]Our analysis of cost was done--following the cost studies
reviewed--in terms of an EV without a battery pack. We expect, however,
that EVs will be sold with battery packs and that the purchase price of
the EV including the battery pack will qualify for the federal tax
credit. The $300 allowance for the battery subsidy is based on an
approximate price of $3,000 for the first battery pack, based on our
review of the likely availability and costs of batteries during the 1998
to 2002 period. (Section 10.1). A sample calculation is $10,300 =
$9,000/0.9 + $300.

[294]These calculations assume production volumes of twice the
California mandate levels (to allow for the mandates in New York and
Massachusetts), or a total of 396,800 EVs over the 1998 to 2002 period
and allocate all fixed costs to the first five years of the mandate.
Note again that some of the fixed costs are now sunk, and are
economically irrelevant for future policy decisions. Note also that
allocating all of the fixed costs to the five-year period seems
reasonable, but is controversial. Finally, note that to the extent that
Big 7 companies choose to meet some of their mandates by paying fines or
buying credits, the fixed costs will be spread over fewer than the
assumed numbers of EVs and fixed costs per vehicle will tend to be
higher.

important effect on Big 7 company profits: If EV sales displace ICEV sales, company profits in the ICEV market will tend to decrease for that reason.[295]

EV buyers stand to gain. While the Big 7 companies may or may not suffer losses in the EV market due to the mandate, there will be some gainers in the EV market: many of the consumers who purchase EVs.

11.5.2 Estimating Annual Dollar Gains and Losses in the EV Market: Methods

We now develop some quantitative information concerning the sizes of the annual gains to California EV buyers and gains or losses to Big 7 companies and their dealers in the California EV market under the mandate. In interpreting these as gains and losses due to the mandate, we are assuming that without the mandate the Big 7 would not sell any EVs in the California market during the years 1998 to 2002.[296] We also assume that the Big 7 companies meet their mandate quantities by producing and selling EVs; to the extent that credits or fines are used, the numbers presented here require adjustment.[297]

We also emphasize, as discussed in Section 10.4, that there are other costs and gains to Californians to be considered in a complete accounting of the social costs and benefits due to the EV mandate. Some them are analyzed in the next section.[298]

---

[295]For example, even if companies earn a positive profit margin on EVs, company profits will fall due to the mandate if ICEV sales are displaced one-for-one by EV sales and ICEV operating margins are higher than EV operating margins. We consider displacement of ICEV sales by EV sales in our analysis of the effects of the ZEV mandate that operate through the ICEV market.

[296]As the above discussion indicates, we think this is plausible, with a single potential exception: General Motors and the Impact.

[297]Note, for example, that if companies pay fines to meet a substantial part of their mandate quantities, companies will incur extra costs of at least the dollar payments for fines but will avoid some variable production costs because they produce fewer EVs, while EV buyers will tend to gain less because of higher prices (at which companies can sell the reduced quantities of EVs) and fewer EVs purchased.

[298]Specifically, below we estimate gains and losses in the ICEV market attributable to the mandate. Note that a full accounting of social costs would also have to include the costs of providing

Table 11.5-2 details calculations designed to illuminate the potential sizes of the gains to consumers and effects on producers in the EV market due to the mandate. Different columns of the table show calculations for different sets of assumptions or cases. The assumptions considered in the various cases correspond to ranges of values for key parameters that have been presented above or are explained presently.

First we explain the assumptions made in the various cases, then discuss the results.

Case assumptions. We discuss our case assumptions in the order in which they are entered into the table (i.e., row by row, with descriptions in the first column). Most of the values assumed in calculating gains and losses were introduced--and their rationales provided--in the discussion of Table 11.5-1. Note particularly that the Big 7 are expected to market EVs of very different body types, costs, performance, and prices during 1998 to 2002, and that the numbers used here are intended to present the typical (or average across companies) cost and demand conditions of an EV produced and sold by a Big 7 company and thereby enable estimation of market-level effects.

---

infrastructure to support EV use and a full accounting of benefits would have to account for effects on air quality.

Table 11.5-2

Projected Annual Gains and Losses in California EV Market from ZEV Mandate
(Ignores Benefits of Emission Reductions)

Case assumptions:	Low EV costs:				Medium EV costs:				High EV costs:			
Variable cost without a battery ($/EV)	13320	13320	13320	13320	19160	19160	19160	19160	25000	25000	25000	25000
EV average fixed costs ($/EV)	2646	2646	2646	2646	6616	6616	6616	6616	10585	10585	10585	10585
Mandate percentage	0.05	0.05	0.02	0.02	0.05	0.05	0.02	0.02	0.05	0.05	0.02	0.02
ICEV sales of Big 7 (M ICEV/yr)	1.24	1.24	1.24	1.24	1.24	1.24	1.24	1.24	1.24	1.24	1.24	1.24
EV price to sellers (10% subsidy)	21411	10300	21411	10300	21411	10300	21411	10300	21411	10300	21411	10300
Price of comparable ICEV	20000	20000	20000	20000	20000	20000	20000	20000	20000	20000	20000	20000
Variable cost per comparable ICEV	10000	10000	10000	10000	10000	10000	10000	10000	10000	10000	10000	10000
Net EV price to consumers	19000	9000	19000	9000	19000	9000	19000	9000	19000	9000	19000	9000
Implications:												
Quantity of EVs (EVs/yr)	62000	62000	24800	24800	62000	62000	24800	24800	62000	62000	24800	24800
Big 7 EV revenues ($M/yr)	1327	639	531	255	1327	639	531	255	1327	639	531	255
Big 7 variable costs ($M/yr)	826	826	330	330	1188	1188	475	475	1550	1550	620	620
EV profits to Big 7 and dealers ($M/year)	338	-351	135	-141	-271	-960	-108	-384	-879	-1568	-352	-627
Subsidy payments ($M/year)	136	72	54	29	136	72	54	29	136	72	54	29
Surplus to EV buyers: high ($M/year)	194	194	78	78	194	194	78	78	194	194	78	78
Surplus to EV buyers: low ($M/year)	39	39	16	16	39	39	16	16	39	39	16	16
High Surplus+.15*profits-.1*subsidies	231	134	92	54	140	43	56	17	48	-49	19	-19
Low Surplus+.15*profits-.1*subsidies	76	-21	30	-8	-15	-112	-6	-45	-107	-204	-43	-81

As detailed in the rows of Table 11.5-2,

- The range for the variable cost per EV produced by the Big 7 is $13,300 to $25,000 (see Table 11.5-1); we also consider the intermediate value of $19,160.

- EV fixed costs per vehicle--$2,646 to $10,585--are based on the range of $1.05 billion to $4.2 billion and the total number of EVs (in California, New York and Massachusetts combined) of 396,800 vehicles (see Table 11.5-1); we also consider the intermediate value of $6,616.[299]

- The fraction of the total number of Big 7 LDV sales used to calculate their mandated quantities (what we call the "mandate percentage") is either .02 or .05 corresponding to the first three years and next two years of the mandate.

- In all cases, we assume that the total number of LDVs (ICEVs plus EVs) sold in California by the Big 7 is 1.24 million per year[300] and that the Big 7 sell their mandated quantities in each year.[301]

- We consider two values for the price at which the Big 7 can sell their mandated quantities in the presence of the 10 percent federal tax credit: $21,411 and $10,300 (see Table 11.5-1).

- In all cases, the price of a comparable ICEV is taken to be $20,000 and its variable costs assumed to be half of that figure.

Implied values. The first row here uses the mandate percentage and the 1.24 million vehicles figure to calculate the total number of EVs that the Big 7 are assumed to produce and sell: 24,800 and 62,000 with

---

[299]Recall that fixed costs that have already been incurred are no longer relevant to future decisions, but that we have no basis for estimating how large these "sunk" costs are.

[300]This is based on the approximate California market share of the Big 7 companies and an assumed total of 1.5 million LDV sales in California annually.

[301]The estimates in Table 11.5-2 may be largely insensitive to the extent to which some of the mandated quantities are met by buying credits from other ICEV companies because we expect that the EVs produced by those other companies, and their costs and prices, would be similar to those of the Big 7.

mandate percentages of .02 and .05, respectively. The remaining rows of Table 11.5-2 report values--all expressed in millions of dollars per year--representing annual gains or losses.

Estimating profits or losses to Big 7 companies. Profits and losses to Big 7 companies from EV production and sale are calculated as follows:

- Big 7 EV revenues: the product of the quantity of EVs sold and the price per EV;

- Big 7 total costs from producing EVs: the product of the quantity of EVs sold and the sum of variable cost plus fixed cost per EV;

- EV profits of Big 7 companies: revenues minus total costs (a negative value indicates a loss).

Estimating the size of the subsidy payments. The next row of Table 11.5-2 presents the implied annual subsidy payments due to the federal tax credit. It is calculated as the difference in the subsidized and unsubsidized prices (from Table 11.5-1) multiplied by the quantity of EVs.

To interpret the results, it is important to understand who gains and who loses from the subsidy payments. First, the losers are federal taxpayers, of which roughly 10 percent are Californians.[302] Even though the subsidy *payments* are made to EV buyers, according to our assumptions the gainers are the Big 7 companies because the existence of the subsidy increases their profits by the amount of the subsidy.[303]

---

[302]Note that federal taxpayers outside of California may also benefit from the mandate, for example, if the mandate spurs development of technology that is used to reduce air pollution outside of California.

[303]To see this, recall that Big 7 companies set prices to achieve sales of their mandated quantities (E_m) and that subsidies increase buyers' willingness to pay for each EV by an amount equal to the subsidy per vehicle (because buyers make decisions based on the prices they pay net of subsidy). The availability of the subsidy, then, allows Big 7 companies to sell E_m EVs while charging a price that is higher by the amount of the (per EV) subsidy. The subsidy, then, has no effect on EV quantities sold--and thus has no effect on production costs--while raising revenues (and profits, since costs don't change) by the subsidy per EV multiplied by E_m, which is exactly equal to the size of the total subsidy payment.

Estimating gains to EV buyers. Recall from Section 7 that economists measure gains to consumers from buying some amount of a product using the concept of consumers' surplus. Consumers' surplus is calculated as the total value placed on the units of the product by the buyers (the gross value of the product to consumers) minus what the buyers had to pay (i.e., give up in money terms) to purchase the good. The value of a product consumed by an individual is taken to be the maximum amount that individual would have been willing to pay for that unit of the product.

The ZEV mandate essentially establishes the market for the product under consideration (EVs); i.e., we are assuming that without the mandate the Big 7 would offer no EVs in the California market in 1998 to 2002. Thus the aggregate gain to consumers in the EV market is taken to be the entire consumers' surplus in the EV market.[304]

Thus far, we have made assumptions about only one point on the EV demand curve: the price at which the companies could sell enough EVs to meet the mandate. To calculate total consumers' surplus, however, we need to represent the market demand curve for Big 7 EVs for all prices above the selling price. This is because we need to place a value on each EV that is actually purchased according to the maximum amount that the buyer of that EV would have been willing to pay for it. Because this cannot be done at all precisely, we construct two demand curves and perform the calculations in each case using each demand curve alternatively.

These demand curves are presented and discussed in Appendix 11.D. We view the calculated values for consumers' surplus in the EV market as upper and lower bounds given our other assumptions. The upper bounds are developed assuming that 25 percent of EV buyers would be willing to

---

[304]This measure represents aggregate surplus benefits to EV buyers in the EV market. Not all EV buyers are necessarily made better off by the mandate. In particular, as developed below, the EV mandate may lead to increases in ICEV prices. Consumers who buy EVs in the presence of the mandate but who would prefer to buy an ICEV at the price that would prevail in the absence of the mandate are made worse off by the mandate. Such potential welfare effects are taken into account in our analysis of gains and losses in the ICEV market. (See the discussion in Appendix 11.H.)

pay a premium of $5,000 for an EV in terms of the full life-cycle costs of the EV (purchase price plus present value of future operating costs) relative to those of a comparable ICEV. The lower bounds are developed assuming that 25 percent of EV buyers would be willing to pay a premium of $1,000.

Estimating effects on Californians. In Section 7, we calculated gains and losses to consumers and producers due to the new ICEV hardware regulations. As we discussed there, the total dollar effect of a policy change on Californians (ignoring effects on emissions) is taken to be the dollar effect on consumers (all of whom are assumed to be Californians) plus the portion of the losses to producers that is assumed to be borne by Californians. As we did in Section 7, our calculations in Table 11.5-2 are based on the rough guess that 15 percent of producer losses accrue to Californians who own stock in the vehicle manufacturers or share in the producer gains or losses as vehicle dealers. We also subtract 10 percent of subsidy payments to account (roughly) for the share of federal tax revenues raised from Californians. We consider the 15 and 10 percent figures as illustrative, and we provide enough detail in the table to adjust our calculations assuming any fractions the reader thinks are more accurate.

11.5.3 Annual Gains and Losses in the EV Market: Estimates

Profits and losses to Big 7 companies and dealers. The annual dollar losses range widely depending on the assumptions. The highest estimated Big 7 annual profit of $338 million (in the fourth column of Table 11.5-2) results from assuming the conditions most favorable to the companies: the lowest assumed values for EV fixed and variable costs, a 5 percent mandate level, and the high price for EVs. The largest estimated annual loss of more than $1.5 billion (in the second to last column) results from assuming conditions least favorable to the companies.

Subsidy payments. Estimates of total dollar subsidies (federal tax credits to EV buyers) range from $29 million to $136 million per year. Subsidy payments increase with the mandate quantity, holding EV price constant, and increase with the EV price (holding quantity constant) because the tax credit is calculated as a percentage of purchase price.

Gains to EV buyers. How much value would EV buyers combined put on their vehicles in excess of the amount they would have to pay for them? The estimated upper bounds for annual consumers' surplus are reported above those for the lower bounds.[305] The calculated values range (over cases and the two demand curves) from a low of $16 million per year to a high of $194 million.[306]

Consumers' surplus depends only on the assumed demand function and the mandate quantity. Thus, as can be seen in the table, the calculated values do not change with changes in assumptions about cost, and there are only two distinct values for consumers' surplus calculated for each demand curve.

Total effects on Californians through the EV market. The total estimated gains or losses to Californians in the EV market due to the ZEV mandate (assuming 15 percent of producer profits or losses and 10 percent of federal EV purchase subsidies are borne by Californians) are reported in the last two rows of Table 11.5-2. Whether Californians in the aggregate appear to gain or lose from activity in the EV market is determined almost entirely by whether we use the upper or lower bound estimates for consumers' surplus. Using the upper bounds (see the second to last row of the table), total gains to Californians are positive (i.e., consumers' surplus is more than 15 percent of any

---

[305]Note that the upper bounds are always five times the corresponding lower bound. This results from the way the demand curves are constructed and the alternative assumptions that 25 percent of EV buyers would be willing to pay a $5,000 premium or a $1,000 premium for an EV over a comparable ICEV in terms of full lifetime operating costs.

[306]Note that the consumers' surplus estimates don't vary with the cost scenario because neither willingness to pay for EVs nor EV prices are assumed to depend on cost. EV prices are entirely driven by demand because they are set to meet the mandated quantities. Moreover, the consumers' surplus values do not differ with changes in the price of EVs because price differences are attributed to differences in the levels of lifetime operating cost disadvantages of EVs and (as detailed in Appendix 11.D) the EV demand curves use (i.e., the assumed structures of willingness to pay are specified in terms of) premiums EV buyers are willing to pay, taking account of full life-cycle costs of EVs relative to ICEVs.

producer losses) except in the high-cost, low-price scenario. Using the lower bounds for consumers' surplus, the net effect on Californians is estimated to be positive only for the low-cost, high-price scenarios. The largest calculated net gain to Californians in the EV market (due to the ZEV mandate) is $231 million per year in the case (fourth column) where the mandate quantity is high, EV costs are low, EV prices are high, and the demand curve used to calculate consumers' surplus assumes a relatively high consumer willingness to pay for EVs. In this case, the largest calculated gains in consumers' surplus are combined with gains to producers. The largest calculated net loss to Californians is $204 million per year (second to last column), where the lower bound for consumers' surplus is combined with high cost, the 5 percent mandate level and low EV prices, and producer losses are almost $1.6 billion per year.

11.6   EFFECTS OF THE ZEV MANDATE ON THE CALIFORNIA ICEV MARKET

The ZEV mandate will affect the California ICEV market because:

a)   sales of EVs should displace at least some ICEV sales,[307] and

b)   for some plausible scenarios, the mandate creates an additional cost for Big 7 companies when they sell an additional ICEV in California.

In this section, we analyze the potential effects of the ZEV mandate that operate through the ICEV market. As in the cases of EV demand and the effects of the ZEV mandate on the EV market, we quantify only for the first five years of the mandate.

We begin by considering the displacement issue. We then explain how the ZEV mandate may increase the costs of selling ICEVs in California, discuss a major controversy about the relevance of these costs for ICEV pricing, and analyze factors determining the extent to which such additional costs will increase ICEV prices. We then explain how we develop estimates of the potential sizes of effects of the ZEV mandate on prices and sales of ICEVs and the dollar values of potential

---

[307]In Section 10.4, to calculate NCERs, we assumed one for one displacement of ICEV sales by EV sales.

gains and losses in the ICEV market attributable to the ZEV mandate. We close the section by presenting a range of estimates.

11.6.1 Displacement of ICEV Sales by EV Sales

As analyzed just above, the ZEV mandate can be expected to cause EV sales in California to increase on the order of 25,000 EVs per year during 1998 to 2000 and by roughly 60,000 EVs during 2001 and 2002. Presumably, some of the projected buyers of new EVs would buy a new ICEV if it were not for the mandate and some EVs buyers would not buy a new ICEV in the absence of the mandate. EV buyers who would have bought new ICEVs might include, for example, consumers who buy EVs to replace an existing vehicle because they view EVs as good substitutes for the ICEVs they displace.[308] Other EV buyers might buy a Big 7 EV because of a commitment to environmental protection or to be a consumer pioneer. Many such EV buyers might not have bought a new vehicle in the absence of the ZEV mandate. We expect that both groups could account for a substantial fraction of EV sales, but have no basis for estimating the fractions. We account for this uncertainty below by considering the entire range of possibilities and considering the sensitivity of estimated market-mediated effects to the actual fraction.

11.6.2 Additional Costs of Selling ICEVs in California Due to the ZEV Mandate

The effect of the ZEV mandate on costs of selling ICEVs in California is more subtle than the effect of ICEV regulations on ICEV costs, but is no less real. Under the ZEV mandate, whenever a Big 7 company sells additional ICEVs, its mandate quantity increases, i.e., the company incurs a legal obligation to sell more EVs, buy more EV credits, pay more in fines or some combination of the three. Buying credits involves an extra cost, as does paying a fine. If selling additional EVs increases losses in the EV market, as the analyses above suggests is quite possible, then an increase in the mandate quantity for

---

[308]Perhaps because they recognize or discover ways to use an EV as part of a household fleet along the lines discussed by Turrentine and Kurani (1995).

a Big 7 company--caused, as it is, by selling more ICEVs--represents a cost of selling additional ICEVs in California.

11.6.3 Will Costs of the Mandate Be Spread Outside California?

This logic bears directly on an issue that has widely discussed in the debate over the ZEV mandate. Some have claimed that losses in the California EV market may not lead to appreciable price effects in the California ICEV market because the Big 7 companies may "spread" their EV losses over ICEV sales throughout the country. As we explain presently, this claim cannot be proven false, but we are somewhat skeptical of it. However, because some people take the claim very seriously, we allow for the possibility that it is valid in how we structure the analysis. We do this in the spirit of accommodating wide ranges of opinions about issues relevant to the effects of the ZEV mandate and helping readers understand the implications of various views.

We are skeptical that additional costs of ICEVs due to the ZEV mandate will be spread nationally for the following reasons. First, it does not stand up to some very fundamental economic logic. However, empirical information suggests that this economic logic is not compelling in some other contexts. Finally, we see no strategic economic advantage to Big 7 companies spreading costs nationally but we do see a major, political disadvantage of doing so.

Economic logic of assigning costs to their actual causes. Companies don't arbitrarily choose to spread costs over different product lines or increase prices capriciously: prices have important implications for their bottom lines and capriciousness can be very costly. Companies set prices for products according to the costs of those products and market conditions as part of their pursuit of maximum profits. The reason that we believe the ZEV mandate may increase prices in the California ICEV market is that under various plausible cost and demand scenarios the ZEV mandate imposes additional costs of selling ICEVs in California. The reason we are skeptical of claims that the ZEV mandate will increase prices of ICEVs outside of California is that the ZEV mandate does not impose additional costs of selling ICEVs outside California or otherwise affect market conditions outside California.

Do automobile companies always assign costs to their actual causes?
Actual pricing practice in the automobile industry seems to be closely
guarded within companies, and we have found no published studies that
bear directly on the issue of spreading costs. It does seem, however,
that companies sometimes do not assign costs to their actual causes for
pricing purposes, even when there is no apparent strategic purpose for
failing to do so. In particular, we have been told by people outside
and inside the automobile industry that in the case of vehicle
transportation and delivery costs, companies typically average or spread
cost differences over geographic markets. The delivered cost of a
particular kind of vehicle is said to be the same throughout the country
even though the cost of transporting the vehicle to different locations
may vary substantially depending on distance from the assembly plant and
how far the vehicle must be trucked to the dealership.[309] This practice
seems to conflict with the economic logic described above.

**Are there strategic advantages to spreading ZEV mandate costs
nationally?** It has also been argued in the ZEV debate that companies
often spread costs--e.g., across product lines--for various strategic
reasons such as meeting competition in different markets. In the
context of the ZEV mandate during 1998 to 2002, the issue of meeting
competition *within California* is salient because some companies that
sell LDVs in California (i.e., all but the Big 7) are not subject to the
mandate in those years.[310] However, we have identified no source of
strategic economic advantage to Big 7 companies to spreading costs
outside of California; for example, increasing prices in markets where
costs have *not* increased seems to conflict directly with the idea of
meeting competition.

---

[309]Moreover, in response to past California emissions regulations
that do not apply nationally and that appear to have increased hardware
costs of California vehicles, companies seem to have increased sticker
prices in California only to cover the costs of additional assembly-line
emission inspections required for California.

[310]We take account of this in our estimation procedure by using a
model that views the issue not as one of *spreading* costs outside of
California, but of *absorbing* costs that aren't incurred by competitors
within California.

Moreover, there seems to be an important strategic, albeit political rather than economic, reason for Big 7 companies not to spread costs nationally: Doing so might encourage policymakers in other states to infer that if they adopt a ZEV mandate, much of the resulting costs will be borne by people outside their own states. Since it seems clear that the Big 7 do not want to see ZEV mandates spread to other states, this seems to be a message the Big 7 would be loath to send.

11.6.4 Factors Determining the ICEV Price Effects of the ZEV Mandate

The implicit additional cost of selling ICEVs in California due to the ZEV mandate plays a key role in our analysis. We discuss the determinants of this cost conceptually, attach numbers to these concepts, then explain an estimation method that allows for the possibilities that the costs will be assigned to California for pricing purposes to varying degrees.

Effect of the mandate level on the costs of selling additional ICEVs. Under the 2 percent mandate applicable in 1998 to 2000, for every 49 ICEVs sold by a Big 7 company, the company is required to offer one EV additional for sale, buy an additional EV credit, or pay an additional $5,000 fine. If, for example, selling one more EV involves additional losses to the company of $4,900, then this $4,900 is a cost attributable to selling 49 ICEVs in California. Expressed per ICEV sold, in this example the ZEV mandate imposes additional costs of $100 per ICEV sold in California. Under the 5 percent mandate, the additional losses from selling one additional EV are incurred every time a Big 7 company sells an additional 19 ICEVs. Thus, in this case, the additional losses due to selling one more EV are spread over only 19 vehicles and the implicit cost per ICEV sold in California is about two and one-half times as large.

Marginal costs of a one-EV increase in the mandate quantity. How large would we expect the cost to a Big 7 company to be due to a one-unit increase in its mandate quantity? That depends on how that increment in the mandate quantity would be satisfied.

Suppose first that a company responds to the increase in the mandate quantity (due to selling an additional 49 or 19 ICEVs) by paying a $5,000 fine. The cost to the company of the increased mandate quantity is then the $5,000 plus any (e.g., reputation) cost the company perceives from doing so. Alternatively, if a company satisfies the additional mandate quantity by buying an additional EV credit, the cost of doing so is the price of the credit (plus any transaction cost of locating a seller, negotiating a price and making the purchase). The analysis of the credit market described above and detailed in Appendix 11.C indicates that Big 7 companies would pay for a credit up to the cost of the best alternative means of satisfying one unit of its mandate quantity.

What determines the cost of satisfying a one-unit increase in a company's mandate quantity by producing and selling an additional EV? As detailed in Appendix 11.E, our conclusion is that marginal losses on an EV--if any--are likely to be reasonably well approximated by the average variable cost of producing an EV minus its selling price. This is the negative of what we call the operating profit per EV in Table 11.5-1. As illustrated there, the operating profit per EV might be positive (e.g., in the low-cost, high-price scenario), in which case there is no cost to selling additional ICEVs and we would not expect the ZEV mandate to affect ICEV prices. On the other hand, Table 11.5-1 shows that the operating loss per EV might be as high as $14,700. Under these conditions, the effects of the ZEV mandate on ICEV prices might be considerable.

11.6.5 What Determines the ICEV Price Effects of These Costs?

In Section 7 we analyzed the effects of an increase in the costs of selling ICEVs in California due to the new regulations that require companies to upgrade ICEV hardware. What we saw there is that the extent to which price increases translate into cost increases depends on various factors such as the elasticities (responsiveness to price) of supply and demand, the extent to which different companies experience similar cost increases, and the ability of the companies experiencing relatively small cost increases to expand sales.

The issue of cost differences across companies--which we suggested could be important in the context of the ICEV hardware regulations--is more important in the context of the ZEV mandate, for two reasons:

- There is likely to be considerable variation across Big 7 companies in the price and average variable cost involved in selling an additional EV.

- Some companies that sell ICEVs--which we refer to as the *other ICEV companies*--are not obligated by the mandate to sell any EVs before the year 2003.

Differences in marginal losses among the Big 7 companies would result from differences in their efficiency in producing EVs, the marketability of their products, and the numbers of vehicles each company must sell under the mandate.[311] The fact that other ICEV companies are not obligated to sell EVs during 1998 to 2002 gives them a competitive advantage in relation to the Big 7 during those years.[312] How the other ICEV companies will respond is quite unclear. Will they match price increases of the Big 7 and benefit by being able to sell their vehicle at higher prices? Or will they not match price increases and benefit by picking up sales because of the price increases of the Big 7? In estimating the effects of the ZEV mandate on the ICEV market, we consider both possibilities.

Thus, actual price effects--and consequent gains and losses to various groups participating in the ICEV market--will depend on many complicated factors, some of which we can merely speculate about. One of the key issues is the behavior of the other ICEV companies.

11.6.6 Price Effects and Dollar Gains and Losses in the ICEV Market: Methods

Table 11.6-1 details calculations designed to indicate the potential sizes of the price effects and dollar gains and losses in the ICEV market due to the ZEV mandate. As with similar calculations above, we believe they highlight important sources of potential gains and

---

[311]For example, under the mandate, in 1998 Mazda is expected to sell roughly 1,000 EVs and Ford and General Motors roughly 6,500 each.

[312]The advantage is temporary; all but very small ICEV companies are subject to the mandate starting in 2003.

losses to Californians and provide a sense of the possible range of stakes. Once again, we explain our methods and present intermediate calculations in sufficient detail to enable readers to recalculate as they think appropriate.

The conceptual framework for pricing. To represent the effects of the ZEV mandate on the costs of the ICEVs sold by Big 7 companies, we ignore differences among them in the marginal losses of an EV or the prices of credits and consider ranges for the average across these companies. We assume that their prices are set competitively among themselves; i.e., that there is enough competition among the Big 7 in the typical market segment for their prices to be driven towards marginal production costs.[313]

Concerning the behavior of the other ICEV companies, we consider two possibilities:

- Hypothesis 1: the other ICEV companies match the prices set by the Big 7

- Hypothesis 2: the other ICEV companies do not raise their prices

We view these hypotheses as extreme or limiting cases: we would expect the other ICEV companies to respond to the mandate by neither lowering prices nor raising prices by more than the Big 7 do. Thus we interpret estimates alternatively based on Hypotheses 1 and 2--holding other parameter values constant--to indicate how sensitive conclusions might be to any behavioral assumption about how the other ICEVs companies will respond.

Case assumptions. Different columns of Table 11.6-1 detail calculations for different sets of assumptions or cases. The assumptions considered in the various cases correspond to what we consider likely ranges for key parameters. We discuss these in the order in which they appear in the table.

---

[313]As in the analysis in Section 7.2, we focus on pricing in the short run, i.e., any period of time shorter than it would take for companies to enter or leave the California ICEV market. In the short run, fixed costs do not affect prices.

- Three values are considered for the cost to a Big 7 company of a one-unit increase in its mandate quantity. The low value chosen--$500--is an arbitrary value chosen to consider the effects of the ZEV mandate on the ICEV market if the cost of a one-unit increase in the mandate quantity is small. In addition, some readers may wish to interpret the $500 figure as being the result of substantially higher costs, most of which are spread nationally so that they have little effect on ICEV prices in California. The intermediate value of $5,000 is chosen because this is the level of the fine for non-compliance. Recall, however, that there are likely to be additional costs to a company of paying the fine. The highest value--$14,700--corresponds to the largest operating loss per EV shown in Table 11.5-1.[314]

- The mandate percentages considered are .02 and .05.

- The next row uses the assumed marginal cost of a one-unit increase in the mandate quantity and mandate percentage to calculate the implied cost per ICEV caused by the mandate. The calculation merely divides the assumed marginal cost of a one-unit increase in the mandate quantity by 49 or 19 depending on whether the assumed mandate percentage is .02 or .05.

- The next three rows detail parameters values that are held constant in all cases. As in Section 7, we assume that the average price of an ICEV is $20,000. Big 7 and other ICEV company sales without the mandate are assumed to be 1.24 million and 0.26 million ICEVs per year, totaling the 1.5 million vehicles per year we assumed in Section 7.2.[315]

---

[314]Which results from the high-cost, low-price scenario for the EV market.

[315]We use the same baseline values for ICEV price and market-level sales here as in Section 7 where we estimated the price effects of increases in ICEV hardware costs. Thus, we are not explicitly evaluating the effects of the EV mandate assuming that all other elements of the California strategy are in place because we are not incorporating price effects of other elements of the strategy--most notably, the ICEV hardware elements--in our baseline assumptions. Likewise, in Section 7 we did not explicitly account for the effects of the EV mandate when estimating the price effects of the ICEV hardware

- The elasticity of demand for Big 7 ICEVs is assumed to be either -2 or -4 depending on which hypothesis about other ICEV behavior is used. The reasons for these choices are explained in Appendix 11.F.[316]

- The elasticity of supply for Big 7 ICEVs is assumed throughout to be 5, the same value that was used for all ICEV sellers together in predicting price effects of the ICEV hardware regulations in Table 7.2-2.

- The degree to which EV sales displace ICEV sales is initially assumed to equal one-half. What this means is that the demand for ICEVs falls (at prices near $20,000) by one-half the level of EV sales (or two EV sales displace one ICEV sale). We initially focus on the value of .5 because--as discussed above-- we expect that the true value is substantially different from both (its logical extremes of) 0 and 1. Because we have so little basis for assigning a value, all of the estimates in Table 11.6-1 were also calculated using displacement fractions of 1 ("full displacement") and 0 ("no displacement"). The resulting estimates (organized exactly as in Table 11.6-1) are presented in detail in Appendix 11.G. In the text, we first review estimates assuming 50 percent displacement and then collect results for all three cases to consider sensitivity of estimates to the degree of displacement.

---

elements. The reasons for not incorporating the effects of each element in the baseline for the other are twofold. First, doing so is extremely complicated given that we are estimating ranges of effects for each policy; evaluating each in the presence of the other would therefore call for use of a wide range of baselines to represent the effects of the other element in order to evaluate each of a wide range of cases. Second, it turns out that we would get similar answers if we were to do each evaluation taking explicit account of the presence of the other in the baseline; the changes in estimates are swamped by the variation in estimates across our cases. (This is because price and quantity effects of each set of policies are always substantially less than 10 percent of baseline levels, and estimated effects are not very sensitive to such small percentage changes in baseline levels.)

[316]The basic idea is that for any given price increase by the Big 7 companies, they will lose a smaller proportion of their sales if the other ICEV companies match the price increases than if they do not match them.

Table 11.6-1
Projected Gains and Losses in California ICEV Market from ZEV Mandate
Assuming 50% Displacement of ICEV Sales by EV Sales
(Ignores Benefits of Emission Reductions)

	Hypothesis 1 (prices matched):						Hypothesis 2 (prices not matched):					
Case assumptions:												
Cost to company of unit increase in mandate quantity	500	5000	14700	500	5000	14700	500	5000	14700	500	5000	14700
Mandate percentage	0.02	0.02	0.02	0.05	0.05	0.05	0.02	0.02	0.02	0.05	0.05	0.05
Implicit marginal cost of Big 7 ICEVs sold in CA ($/ICEV)	10	102	300	26	263	774	10	102	300	26	263	774
Average ICEV price without ZEV mandate ($ thousands)	20	20	20	20	20	20	20	20	20	20	20	20
Big 7 ICEV Sales without ZEV mandate (M vehicles/yr)	1.240	1.240	1.240	1.240	1.240	1.240	1.240	1.240	1.240	1.240	1.240	1.240
Other ICEV Sales without ZEV mandate (M vehicles/yr)	0.260	0.260	0.260	0.260	0.260	0.260	0.260	0.260	0.260	0.260	0.260	0.260
Elasticity of demand for Big 7 ICEVs	-2.0	-2.0	-2.0	-2.0	-2.0	-2.0	-4.0	-4.0	-4.0	-4.0	-4.0	-4.0
Elasticity of supply of ICEVs	5	5	5	5	5	5	5	5	5	5	5	5
Degree of ICEV demand displacement	0.50	0.50	0.50	0.50	0.50	0.50	0.50	0.50	0.50	0.50	0.50	0.50
Prices and quantities of Big 7 ICEVs:												
Big 7 price increase (dollars per ICEV)	7	73	214	19	188	553	6	57	167	15	146	430
Proportionate Big 7 price increase	0.000	0.004	0.011	0.001	0.009	0.028	0.000	0.003	0.008	0.001	0.007	0.021
Big 7 sales change (thousands of vehicles)	-11.1	-19.2	-36.6	-27.9	-48.5	-92.7	-11.6	-24.2	-51.2	-29.2	-61.1	-130.0
Proportionate Big 7 sales decrease	0.009	0.015	0.030	0.023	0.039	0.075	0.009	0.020	0.041	0.024	0.049	0.105
Big 7 sales with mandate (million vehicles/year)	1.2289	1.2208	1.2034	1.2121	1.1915	1.1473	1.2284	1.2158	1.1888	1.2108	1.1789	1.1100
Prices and quantities of other ICEV companies:												
Other ICEV companies price increase (dollars per ICEV)	7	73	214	19	188	553	0	0	0	0	0	0
Other ICEV companies sales change (thousands of vehicles)	-2.3	-4.0	-7.7	-5.9	-10.2	-19.4	-1.5	4.8	18.3	-3.6	12.4	46.8
Dollar gains and losses in ICEV market ($M/yr):												
Cost to California new ICEV buyers	11	108	317	28	276	798	7	70	202	18	177	505
Change in Big 7 revenues on ICEVs	-214	-295	-474	-535	-745	-1221	-226	-415	-827	-566	-1050	-2123
Change in Big 7 variable cost ($10K/ICEV)	-111	-192	-366	-279	-485	-927	-116	-242	-512	-292	-611	-1300
Change in Big 7 manufacturer and dealer profit in ICEVs	-103	-103	-108	-256	-261	-293	-109	-173	-314	-274	-439	-823
Change in other ICEV companies revenues	-45	-62	-99	-112	-156	-256	-29	96	367	-72	248	936
Change in other ICEV companies variable cost ($10K/ICEV)	-23	-40	-77	-59	-102	-194	-15	48	183	-36	124	468
Change in other ICEV companies and dealer profit	-21	-22	-23	-54	-55	-62	-15	48	183	-36	124	468
ICEV Cost to CA (Consumer loss-15% of profit change)	29	127	336	74	324	851	26	88	222	64	224	558

Prices and sales for Big 7 companies. The second panel of Table 11.6-1 reports predicted price increases and quantity decreases for Big 7 vehicles. As in Section 7.2, price increases are calculated from cost increases using the assumed elasticities of supply and demand.[317] The quantity decreases reflect two components: the shift in demand due to the displacement effect and the decrease in quantities purchased due to the increase in ICEV prices. The former component is calculated as one-half (i.e., the assumed degree of displacement) times the level of EV sales times the Big 7 ICEV market share (roughly 5/6). The price effects are then calculated, as in Section 7.2, from the percentage price increases and the assumed elasticity of demand.

Prices and sales quantities for other ICEV companies. The next panel of Table 11.6-1 reports price increases and quantity changes for other ICEV companies. The nature of these changes and how they are calculated differs under the two hypotheses about their pricing behavior. Production must decrease under Hypothesis 1 because both the displacement and price effects work in that direction. Under Hypothesis 2, production levels of the other ICEV companies may increase or decrease: production tends to fall because of the displacement effect, but tends to rise because sales are picked up from the Big 7 because they raise prices while the other ICEV companies don't.

Under Hypothesis 1, the price increases for other ICEV companies are assumed to equal those of the Big 7 companies. Quantity decreases due to the displacement effect are calculated as one-half (the assumed degree of displacement) times the level of EV sales times other ICEV company market share (roughly 1/6). Quantity decreases due to price increases are then calculated assuming that the other ICEV companies face a demand elasticity of -2 (when all ICEV prices rise together), the one assumed to apply at the market level. Under Hypothesis 2, the other

_____

[317] Using the formula given in Section 7.2: a) when the elasticity of demand is -2--i.e., under Hypothesis 1--and the elasticity of supply is 5, the price increase will be 5/7 of the implicit increase in the marginal cost of an ICEV; and b) when the elasticity of demand is -4--i.e., under Hypothesis 2--and the elasticity of supply is 5, the price increase will be 5/9 of the implicit increase in the marginal cost of an ICEV.

ICEV companies are assumed not to raise their prices at all. We calculate a decrease in sales due to the displacement effect as under Hypothesis 1. However, with the Big 7 raising prices, the other ICEV companies would be expected to gain sales from the Big 7. There doesn't seem to be any firm basis for pinning down the fraction of price-induced Big 7 sales losses that would be gained by the other ICEV companies.[318] We assume that this fraction is one half.

Gains and losses in the ICEV market. The last panel of Table 11.6-1 reports annual dollar gains and losses, all expressed in millions of dollars per year.

Estimating losses to ICEV buyers. Consumers suffer losses in the ICEV market if the ZEV mandate causes ICEV prices to increase.[319] Losses to consumers in the ICEV market are calculated as changes in consumers' surplus implied by the price increases and quantity decreases. Precisely how this is done--and the conceptual underpinnings--are detailed in Appendix 11.H.

Estimating changes in company profits. Changes in Big 7 company profits in the ICEV market are calculated from decreases in their ICEV revenue and their decreases in variable costs because production falls. The profit changes for the other ICEV companies are calculated from calculated changes in revenues and the changes in variable costs (production may rise of fall). For both sets of companies we assume that variable cost per ICEV is $10,000, or half the baseline price of ICEVs for the reasons given in discussing Table 11.5-1.

---

[318]The issue comes down to the extent to which (price-sensitive) buyers who would have bought from the Big 7 without the price increase view an ICEV from a non-Big 7 company as a reasonably close substitute for the Big 7 vehicle they would have bought.

[319]If there is no increase in ICEV prices, the consumption value that EV buyers give up by shifting from ICEV purchases to ZEV purchases is reflected in the consumers' surplus in the EV market (estimated above). More specifically, the surplus measure in the EV market takes account of the opportunities EV buyers give up in the ICEV market when they buy an EV (these opportunities are reflected in their willingness to pay for EVs). For discussions of how to take account of price changes induced in several markets by a policy change, see Sugden and Williams (1978, Ch. 10) or Just, Hueth and Schmitz (1982, Ch. 9).

Estimating effects on Californians. Total dollar losses to Californians in the ICEV market are calculated as losses to ICEV buyers plus 15 percent of losses to producers minus 15 percent of gains to other producers, if any. As we noted earlier, we consider the 15 percent figure to be illustrative, and we provide enough detail to adjust our calculations for this factor.

11.6.7 Gains and Losses in the ICEV Market: Results

Price effects. As we will see presently, dollar costs turn out to be somewhat sensitive to the pricing behavior of the other ICEV companies. A key reason is that Hypothesis 2, where the other ICEV companies do not increase prices, leads to smaller price increases for the Big 7 as well. The smaller price decreases for the Big 7 result from the assumption that if the other ICEV companies do not raise their prices, then Big 7 ICEVs sales will be especially sensitive to price increases. (This was built into the analysis with the assumed price elasticity of demand of -4.) This result may be thought of as reflecting the idea that companies will tend to absorb larger portions of their cost increases (i.e., not incorporate them in prices) the more competitive are market conditions.

Under Hypothesis 1, price increases calculated for the Big 7 range from $7 to $553 per vehicle. The smallest price increase occurs when we assume that the marginal cost of a one-unit increase in the mandate quantity is $500 and the mandate percentage is 2 percent, which together imply that the implicit marginal cost per ICEV due to the ZEV mandate is only $10. In contrast, if we assume that the marginal cost of a one-unit increase in the mandate quantity is $14,700--the other end of our wide range--and that costs are not spread outside California, and that the mandate percentage is 5 percent, then the implied price increase under Hypothesis 1 is $553 per ICEV.

Effects of the ZEV mandate on prices do not depend on the degree of displacement. This is because price effects are calculated from the cost increase and the elasticities of supply and demand and costs are assumed insensitive to variations in quantity levels (in the relevant ranges).

Effects on ICEV sales. The predicted sales declines of the Big 7--
assuming that two EV sales displace one ICEV sale--range from a low of
11,100 vehicles per year to a high of 130,000. The low figure (first
column) results from assuming that the mandate percentage is .02 and the
marginal loss per EV is small ($500). In this case, there is almost no
price increase ($7) and the sales decrease is almost entirely due to the
displacement effect: the Big 7's share (5/6) of the industry-wide
displacement (one half of the 24,800 EVs sold) or 10,333 vehicles.

Even though Big 7 price increases are lower when the other ICEV
companies are assumed not to match prices increases, Big 7 sales fall
more in this case because of the extra sensitivity of Big 7 sales to Big
7 price when the other ICEV companies do not raise their prices. Under
Hypothesis 1, sales of other ICEV companies fall by the same percentage
as those of the Big 7. Under Hypothesis 2, by assumption, the other
ICEV companies gain half of the sales that the Big 7 lose due to their
price increases. In percentage terms, the increase in other ICEV
company sales is as high as almost 19 percent; i.e., 46,800 vehicles
(compared with a baseline sales level of 260,000) in the case where
marginal cost of a one-unit increase in the mandate quantity is assumed
high, the mandate percentage is 5 percent, and as a result the Big 7
raise prices by $430 per vehicle.

Combining the predicted sales effects across the two groups of
companies, we estimate (as can be calculated from the table) decreases
in total sales in the ICEV market ranging from as little as 13,000
(seventh column) vehicles per year to a high of about 112,000 (sixth
column) in lost California ICEV sales.

Costs to new ICEV buyers. Dollar losses to consumers in the ICEV
market range widely, depending on the assumed marginal cost of a one-
unit increase in the mandate quantity and the level of the mandate
percentage. The range we calculate is annual losses of about $7 million
to almost $800 million. Assuming that the marginal cost of a one-unit
increase in the mandate quantity is $500, for the 5 percent mandate
level consumer losses in the ICEV market are predicted to be about $28
million per year if the other ICEV companies match the price increases
of the Big 7 and about $18 million per year if the Big 7 price increases

are not matched. If the marginal cost of a one-unit increase in the mandate quantity is assumed to be $5,000--which is a lower bound if Big 7 companies use payments of fines to satisfy their marginal increases in mandate quantities (induced by additional ICEV sales)--when the mandate level is 5 percent, the predicted consumer losses in the ICEV market are about $275 million per year if the other ICEV raise their prices and $177 million if they don't.

These estimates suggest that unless the actual marginal cost of a one-unit increase in the mandate quantity turns out to be near the low end of the range considered--and we cannot rule out that they are nil-- the costs of the EV mandate to California ICEV buyers may be very substantial.[320]

Effects on Big 7 profits in the ICEV market. The calculated range of effects of the ZEV mandate on the profits of the Big 7 and of other ICEV companies (and their California dealers) in the ICEV market is also very wide. (As discussed below, they are also *very* sensitive to the assumed degree of displacement.)

Holding the degree of displacement constant, the pricing behavior of the other ICEV companies is an important factor when cost changes-- and hence price changes--are relatively large. With 50 percent displacement (Table 11.6-1), under Hypothesis 1, where the other ICEV companies do raise their prices, predicted Big 7 losses range from $103 to $293 million per year. Under Hypothesis 2, where the other ICEV companies do not raise their prices, predicted Big 7 losses range from $109 to $823 million per year.

Effects on the profits of the other ICEV companies. The calculations assuming 50 percent displacement suggest that the ZEV mandate (in its first five years) will reduce the profits of the companies not subject to the mandate if they follow the price increases of the Big 7. Calculated values of lost profits under Hypothesis 1 range from about $20 million per year when the mandate percentage is .02 and about 2.5 times that value if the mandate percentage is .05. However, if the other ICEV companies do not raise their prices along

_____

[320]As will be seen shortly, the estimated effects on consumers are almost entirely insensitive to the degree of displacement.

with the Big 7, then--given our assumption that they pick up half of the sales that the Big 7 lose because of their price increases--the ZEV mandate is estimated to increase profits of other ICEV companies when the costs to the Big 7 are assumed to be large enough to involve substantial price increases. For example, under Hypothesis 2 the calculations suggest that when the mandate level is 5 percent the ZEV mandate could increase profits of other ICEV companies by up to almost $470 million per year, and $125 million per year if the marginal cost of a one-unit increase in the mandate quantity turns out to be $5,000 per EV.

Cost to Californians. Combining calculated annual losses to ICEV buyers with 15 percent of the annual gains or losses to all companies indicates how much the ZEV mandate may cost Californians in the ICEV market during 1998 to 2002. The range assuming 50 percent displacement is losses of $29 to $850 million. When price changes are small, most of the loss is due to lost profits (which result mostly from demand displacement). When price increases are large, most of the losses are due to losses of consumers' surplus.

What is sensitive to the degree of displacement? To get a better sense of how the degree of displacement affects these results, Table 11.6-2 collects results from Table 11.6-1 (which are based on assuming that one ICEV sale is displaced by every two EV sales) and Tables 11.G-1 and 11.G-2, which are based on assuming no and full displacement, respectively. (Price effects are not reported because they are totally insensitive to the degree of displacement.) The first panel of the table provides the values of the parameters that differ across cases.

As can be seen from Table 11.6-2, effects on consumers are almost entirely insensitive to the assumed degree of displacement. A larger degree of displacement leads to (slightly) lower estimated costs to consumers: With more displacement, there are fewer ICEV buyers to be adversely affected by increases in the prices of ICEVs.

Table 11.6-2

Sensitivity of Estimated Effects of ZEV Mandate in ICEV Market to Degree EV Sales Displace ICEV Sales

Case assumptions:	Hypothesis 1 (prices matched):						Hypothesis 2 (prices not matched):					
Cost to company of unit increase in mandate quantity	500	5000	14700	500	5000	14700	500	5000	14700	500	5000	14700
Mandate percentage	0.02	0.02	0.02	0.05	0.05	0.05	0.02	0.02	0.02	0.05	0.05	0.05
Implicit marginal cost of Big 7 ICEVs sold in CA ($/ICEV)	10	102	300	26	263	774	10	102	300	26	263	774
Elasticity of demand for Big 7 ICEVs	-2.0	-2.0	-2.0	-2.0	-2.0	-2.0	-4.0	-4.0	-4.0	-4.0	-4.0	-4.0
Cost to California new ICEV buyers												
No demand displacement	11	109	318	28	279	806	7	70	203	18	179	510
50% demand displacement	11	108	317	28	276	798	7	70	202	18	177	505
Full demand displacement	11	108	315	28	274	790	7	69	202	18	175	500
Big 7 sales change (thousands of vehicles)												
No demand displacement	-0.9	-9.0	-26.6	-2.3	-23.3	-68.5	-1.4	-14.1	-41.3	-3.6	-36.3	-106.6
50% demand displacement	-11.1	-19.2	-36.6	-27.9	-48.5	-92.7	-11.6	-24.2	-51.2	-29.2	-61.1	-130.0
Full demand displacement	-21.4	-29.4	-46.6	-53.5	-73.6	-116.9	-21.9	-34.3	-61.2	-54.7	-86.0	-153.4
Other ICEV companies sales change (thousands of vehicles)												
No demand displacement	-0.2	-1.9	-5.6	-0.5	-4.9	-14.4	0.7	7.0	20.7	1.8	18.1	53.3
50% demand displacement	-2.3	-4.0	-7.7	-5.9	-10.2	-19.4	-1.5	4.8	18.3	-3.6	12.4	46.8
Full demand displacement	-4.5	-6.2	-9.8	-11.2	-15.4	-24.5	-3.6	2.6	16.0	-9.0	6.6	40.3
Change in Big 7 manufacturer and dealer profit in ICEVs												
No demand displacement	0	-1	-6	0	-4	-38	-7	-71	-214	-18	-187	-579
50% demand displacement	-103	-103	-108	-256	-261	-293	-109	-173	-314	-274	-439	-823
Full demand displacement	-205	-206	-211	-513	-517	-549	-212	-275	-415	-530	-691	-1067
Change in other ICEV companies and dealer profit												
No demand displacement	0	0	-1	0	-1	-8	7	70	207	18	181	533
50% demand displacement	-21	-22	-23	-54	-55	-62	-15	48	183	-36	124	468
Full demand displacement	-43	-43	-44	-107	-108	-115	-36	26	160	-90	66	403
ICEV Cost to CA (Consumer loss-15% of profit change)												
No demand displacement	11	109	319	28	280	813	7	70	204	18	179	517
50% demand displacement	29	127	336	74	324	851	26	88	222	64	224	558
Full demand displacement	48	145	354	121	367	889	44	107	240	111	269	600

As would be expected, the estimated sales changes for both sets of companies are very sensitive to the degree of displacement. When the mandate percentage is 0.02, increasing the displacement fraction from 0 to 50 percent or from 50 percent to 100 percent costs the Big 7 companies about 10,000 vehicles in sales and costs the other companies about one-fifth that amount. When the mandate percentage is 0.05, rather than 0.02, the displacement effects on sales are (not surprisingly) 150 percent larger.

The table also reveals that the degree of displacement has very important implications for company profits. In fact, comparison of Table 11.6-2 and Table 11.5-2 indicates that if the degree of displacement is substantial, Big 7 companies may be expected to lose roughly as much in profits because of lost ICEV sales as their losses in producing and selling EVs.

To get an initial feel for the sensitivity of profits to the degree of displacement, recall that we are assuming that ICEVs have profit margins (price minus average variable cost) of $10,000 per vehicle. This implies, for example, that displacement of 20,000 ICEV sales by EV sales would cost the ICEV companies about $200 million in lost profits. As can be seen in Table 11.6-2, increasing the displacement fraction from 0 to 50 percent to 100 percent costs the Big 7 companies about $100 million per year when the mandate percentage is 0.02 and about $250 million per year when the mandate percentage is 0.05. The corresponding figures for the other ICEV companies are about $22 million (mandate percentage 0.02) and $55 million (mandate percentage 0.05)

We have estimated total costs to Californians in the ICEV market (due to the ZEV mandate) as consumer losses plus 15 percent of lost profits. Since consumer losses are insensitive to the degree of displacement, the effects of this factor on total costs to Californians is due entirely to effects on profits. As implied by the effects on profits described just above, estimated costs to Californians increase as the displacement fraction increases from 0 to 50 percent or from 50 percent to 100 percent by about $18 million per year if the mandate percentage is 0.02 (i.e., 15 percent of the extra losses of all companies combined of about $120 million) and by about $46 million per year if the mandate percentage is 0.05.

11.7 TOTAL EFFECTS ON CALIFORNIA CONSUMERS AND U.S. TAXPAYERS ACROSS THE TWO MARKETS

Our analysis of the effects of the ZEV mandate on the EV market indicates that EV buyers stand to gain tens or a few hundreds of millions of dollars per year. Our analysis of the effects of the ZEV mandate on the ICEV market indicates that ICEV buyers may lose nothing, but they may lose tens or even several hundreds of millions of dollars per year. Here we bring together the estimates of effects on consumers in the two markets to consider what determines whether all California new LDV buyers together are likely to gain or lose because of the ZEV mandate and how the estimated gains and losses compare with the costs to the U.S. taxpayer due to the 10 percent subsidy for EV purchases.

Table 11.7-1 reports estimated annual dollar gains and losses to consumers and subsidy payments from the analyses described above. The columns pertain to different cases created by combining (from Table 11.5-1) the low and high ends of our ranges for average variable costs of EVs ($13,320 and $25,000) and EV selling prices after accounting for the 10 percent federal tax credit ($10,300 and $21,411). Recall that the EV costs that help define the scenarios are production costs of EVs and that the key to the price scenarios is the lifetime operating cost disadvantages of EVs relative to ICEVs of comparable size and body style.

Estimates of gains to EV buyers and federal subsidy payments are taken from Table 11.5-2. Recall that these figures were calculated assuming that the Big 7 meet their entire mandated quantities by producing and selling EVs.

Estimates of losses to ICEV buyers are calculated using the implied marginal cost of satisfying a one-unit increase in the mandate quantity by producing and selling an additional EV. As in the construction of Table 11.6-1, estimates are based on assuming that all costs to the Big 7 of additional ICEV sales in California attributable to the mandate affect ICEV prices in California (but less than dollar-for-dollar). As before, readers who believe that significant spreading of such costs outside California will occur may use the results presented to get a sense of how an assumed degree of cost spreading would affect the conclusions here.

Regarding the costs of one-unit increases in the mandated quantities, in the case of the low-cost, high-price scenario, EV production is profitable at the margin. Under this scenario, then, it is not costly to companies to increase the mandated quantity, there is no effect on ICEV prices, and--as a result--there is no effect on consumers the ICEV market. The other three scenarios (reading across the column headings of Table 11.7-1) imply costs of a one-unit increase in the mandate quantity (MC stands for "marginal cost" in the column heading) of $3,020, $3,589 and $14,700. Estimates of effects on ICEV consumers in the first two of these cases are computed by rerunning the model used to construct Table 11.6-1 (using the values $3,020 and $3,589).[321] Estimates for the high-cost, low-price case are taken directly from Table 11.6-1.

The ranges within a cell of Table 11.7-1 correspond to the different assumptions about the form of the EV demand curve in the case of gains to EV buyers (i.e., they are the upper and lower bounds we calculated for consumers' surplus in the EV market) or the ICEV pricing behavior of the companies not subject to the mandate in the case of losses to ICEV buyers (i.e., they are based alternatively on pricing Hypotheses 1 and 2).

---

[321]The results in Table 11.6-1 are based on assuming 50 percent displacement of ICEV sales by EV sales, but recall from Table 11.6-2, that consumer losses are almost entirely insensitive to the degree of displacement assumed.

Table 11.7-1

Annual Gains and Losses to California Consumers and U.S. Taxpayers
1998 to 2003 Due to ZEV Mandate
(Millions of dollars, ignores benefits of emissions reductions)

	Low EV costs	Low EV costs	High EV costs	High EV costs
	High EV price	Low EV price	High EV price	Low EV price
	(EVs profitable)	(mandate MC = $3,020)	(mandate MC = $3,589)	(mandate MC = $14,700)
1998 to 2000 (2 percent):				
EV buyer gains	16-78	16-78	16-78	16-78
ICEV buyer losses	0	42-66	50-78	202-317
Subsidy payments	54	29	54	29
ICEV buyer losses plus subsidy payments	54	71-95	104-132	231-346
2001 and 2002 (5 percent):				
EV buyer gains	39-194	39-194	39-194	39-194
ICEV buyer losses	0	107-168	127-199	505-798
Subsidy payments	136	72	136	72
ICEV buyer losses plus subsidy payments	136	179-240	263-335	577-870

11.7.1 Effects on California Consumers in the Aggregate

First consider the estimated effects of the mandate on California consumers, ignoring the subsidy payments (and even California taxpayers' share of the subsidy payments). The relevant estimates are in the first two rows of each panel pertaining to the mandate percentages of .02 (upper panel) and .05 (lower panel). In the low-cost, high-price scenario, California consumers are projected to benefit from the ZEV mandate: they gain tens of millions of dollars in surplus in the EV market and there are no price effects (or losses to buyers) in the ICEV market. In low-cost, low-price and high-cost, high-price scenarios, the ranges of estimates of gains to EV buyers and costs to ICEV buyers overlap. This suggests that these effects may largely cancel out if both costs and prices turn out to be at the low--or both at the high-- end of the ranges were have considered. In the high-cost, low-price scenario, the estimates suggest that the costs to ICEV buyers in California could far exceed the gains to EV buyers. This is because under this scenario there is a potential for large price increases for ICEVs and the consumers' surplus in the EV market doesn't increase with decreases in EV prices.[322]

11.7.2 Effects on California Consumers and U.S. Taxpayers Combined

From a national, *consumer* perspective, costs to consumers outside of California are relevant. Adopting this broader perspective, here we bring into the analysis the subsidy payments for EVs from the 10 percent federal tax credit. Recall from Section 11.5.2 that these payments benefit the *sellers* of EVs, not the buyers, even though the payments are made to buyers.[323] Thus, when focusing on consumers, and adopting a national perspective, it is appropriate to view the subsidy payments as involving costs to consumers (that don't benefit other consumers).[324]

To see how consideration of subsidy payments might affect one's view of the effects on U.S. consumers of the ZEV mandate, compare the

---

[322]Recall from the discussion in Section 11.5.3, that the latter result, which is unusual, reflects: the unusual nature of pricing to meet a mandated (target quantity)--the prices that the Big 7 can charge and meet their mandated quantities increase with the willingness of all buyers to pay; and the willingness to pay of all buyers is linked to the lifetime operating costs of EVs which themselves drive the level of the price at which the mandated quantities can be sold.

[323]As detailed in Section 11.5.2, the effect of the subsidy is to make buyers willing to pay sellers more for EVs (because buyers care about the net price to them, not what the seller receives), but this leads sellers to charge correspondingly more for EVs (because they can do so and still meet their mandate quantities).

[324]Note that the costs of federal taxes are borne by consumers to the extent that they pay taxes directly and indirectly (through the effects of taxes on the prices of the goods and services they purchase). Note also that from a national, consumer *plus* producer perspective, the subsidy payments would not be considered a cost (i.e., to the economy as a whole).

top and bottom rows of each panel of Table 11.7-1. Moving across the
table from left to right, we see that:

a) the gain to California EV buyers in the low-cost, high-price
scenario may be entirely offset by the subsidy payments (which are
relatively high when prices are high because the tax credit is
determined as a percentage of purchase price).

b) in the low-cost, low-price and high-cost, high-price scenarios,
the gains to EV buyers may be swamped by the costs to other (California
and U.S.) consumers because once the subsidy payments are considered the
low ends of the cost ranges are just about the same as the high ends of
the estimated ranges of gains.

c) considering subsidies as representing an additional cost to
consumers makes the high-cost, low-price scenario somewhat more ominous.

The total effect of the ZEV mandate on California consumers and
consumers viewed nationally, then, depends crucially on how high
production and operating costs for EVs turn out to be during 1998 to
2002. The reason is that both higher production costs for EVs and
higher operating costs for EVs (the latter of which depress the prices
of EVs)--other things equal--may lead to higher prices for ICEVs and
larger losses for ICEV buyers, but would provide no offsetting benefits
to EV buyers.

11.8 MARKET-MEDIATED EFFECTS ON EMISSIONS

As illustrated in Tables 7.2-1, 7.2-2, and 11.6-1, increases in
prices for new ICEVs will tend to decrease sales of new vehicles. As
discussed in Section 7.4, decreases in new vehicle sales would tend to
slow the retirement of older vehicles, thus changing the age-composition
of the vehicle fleet. To the extent that older vehicles have higher
emissions rates per year, total emissions will be higher from a fleet
that is older on average.

In Section 7.4, we reviewed two studies that quantified the
emissions effects of an aging of the vehicle fleet due to costs of
emissions regulations. We concluded there that price increases for
ICEVs near the high end of the range of roughly $100 to $500--the range

of effects we estimated for the new ICEV hardware regulations--could
have a substantial effect on emissions reductions for a period of
several years. Available estimates of the sensitivity of emissions
levels to particular increases in vehicle prices (through fleet turnover
effects) are not directly applicable for our purposes, for reasons we
discussed earlier. However, these estimates were interpreted to suggest
that price increases of several hundred dollars per vehicle could
largely counteract, if not overwhelm, direct emissions reductions of the
new ICEV hardware regulations--such as those reported in Table 6.2-2--
for at least three to five years and attenuate them substantially for a
period of a decade or more.

In this section, we have seen the ZEV mandate may also cause
increases in ICEV prices. These price increases might be nil, but as
far as available information allows us to tell, they might be as large
as several hundred dollars per ICEV. (The largest projected price
increase reported in Table 11.6-1 is more than $500.) If the ZEV
mandate does result in ICEV price increases of several hundred dollars,
the emissions benefits of the mandate may be considerably less for a
period of several years--and even non-existent for a few years--than
would be suggested by the estimates of direct emissions effects
developed in Section 10.3. (See Tables 10.3-2 and 10.3-3.) Thus, the
stakes in the extent to which the mandate increases ICEV prices--which
is controversial--also include air quality.

In sum, to the extent that the mandate does increase ICEV prices,
other things equal, it will tend to be less attractive than suggested by
the analysis of narrow cost effectiveness in Section 10.4. We do not
have sufficient information, however, to adjust the narrow cost
effectiveness estimates developed there.

12. THINKING ABOUT POLICY OPTIONS

We have analyzed the social costs and benefits of many policy actions planned by California air-quality regulators to reduce ozone-producing emissions from light-duty vehicles (passenger cars, light-duty trucks). We have referred to these actions collectively as "California's LDV strategy."

In this concluding section, we review and integrate our findings to consider what our analyses suggest about future directions for ozone-reduction policies. (Readers wishing to review more detailed summaries of our findings might revisit the previews of findings at the beginnings of Sections 6 through 11.) We pay special attention to policies designed to encourage development and use of zero-emission vehicles (ZEVs).

12.1 OVERVIEW OF OUR ANALYSES AND MAJOR CONCLUSIONS

To analyze California's ozone reduction strategy, we

- Developed an economic framework for identifying costs and benefits that should be considered;
- Reviewed and critiqued the most informative or influential existing studies of various elements;
- Applied standard economic principles to interpret data and estimate effects;
- Characterized ranges of reasonable disagreement about key estimates;
- Developed models to predict the costs, emission reductions, cost effectiveness, and market effects of various components of the strategy;
- Identified major sources of uncertainty.

The results of our analyses are detailed in the preceding sections. Here, for the reader's convenience, we summarize the major components of our findings in three tables. Table 12.1-1 provides an overview of our analyses, listing the key studies of costs and/or emission reductions, describing how we examined some interdependencies between elements, and explaining how we examined market effects. Table 12.1-2 collects and explains the NCERs that we derived--in various ways--from these studies. Table 12.1-3 summarizes our findings on market-mediated effects.

Summarizing our findings in tabular form has both an advantage and a disadvantage.

The advantage is that the table facilitates a high-level view of the policy landscape. Looking across each row provides an overview of the information available for each element. Looking up and down the columns allows us to compare the kinds and quality of information available about different elements and easily identify similarities and differences in the sorts of factors that should enter the evaluation of each element.

The disadvantage is that the tables make all numbers appear to be equally reliable and comprehensive. We have used commentary in the table text and table notes to remind readers of some of the major reasons that values listed are not directly comparable. In addition, use of the tabular format obscures subtleties of meaning. To partially compensate for this limitation, we have provided a reference to the appropriate section or table in the body of this report.

Much of the analysis involved reviewing, interpreting and critiquing studies bearing on the costs and benefits of different parts of the California LDV strategy. The row headings in Table 12.1-1 list the policy elements we analyzed. The first column lists the major sources of information reviewed concerning costs, emission benefits and what we have called narrow cost-effectiveness ratios (NCERs). The effects--and especially emission benefits--of various elements depend on the effectiveness of other elements, and column (2) of the table highlights several interdependencies and describes how we analyzed them. The last column describes our analyses of market reactions to policy elements and how those reactions affect or distribute costs and benefits of the policies.

Table 12.1-1

Overview of Analyses Performed

Element of California Strategy	(1) Studies of Costs and/or Emission Reductions Reviewed	(2) Interdependencies Examined (Method)	(3) Market Effects Examined (Method)
ICEV Hardware			
TLEV, LEV, ULEV, EEE, ORVR, OBD II	CARB(1989a, 1990a, 1994a,b, 1995b), Sierra (1994a,c), Chrysler, Ford, GM, Honda[a]	I&M (sensitivity analysis), interaction of ORVR and Stage II vapor recovery nozzles (qualitative discussion)	Short-run effects on prices of ICEVs, losses to buyers, and lost profits (calibrated supply and demand models); effects on fleet turnover and emissions (qualitative analysis drawing on other empirical studies)
ICEV Non-Hardware			
CP2G	Battelle (1995), Burns, et al. (1995), CARB (1991, 1995d), Sierra (1994a)	ICEV hardware costs (qualitative discussion), certification standards (review of quantitative estimates)	Effects of gasoline price increase on vehicle miles traveled (estimated gas price increases combined with estimated demand elasticities)
Smog Check II	Aroesty et al. (1994), Glazer et al. (1995), Klausmeier et al. (1995), Sommerville (1993)	OBD II (qualitative discussion)	Effects on scrapping of older vehicles and prices of newer vehicles (qualitative discussion)

Table 12.1-1 (Cont'd.)

Element of California Strategy	(1) Studies of Costs and/or Emission Reductions Reviewed	(2) Interdependencies Examined (Method)	(3) Market Effects Examined (Method)
AVR	Alberini, Edelstein, and Harrington (1994), Alberini, Edelstein, and McConnell (1994), Alberini, Harrington, and McConnell (1994), Sierra (1995a), Hahn (1995), Engineering-Science (1994)	I&M (qualitative discussion)	In-migration and prices of older vehicles over time (qualitative supply and demand analysis)
ZEVs	Abacus (1994), Booz·Allen (1995), CARB (1994a,b), GAO (1994), Kalhammer et al. (1995), Moomaw et al. (1994), Sierra (1994a,c), Chrysler, Ford, GM[a]	Effectiveness of ICEV emission control program; NMOG standard (sensitivity analysis)	Short-run gains to EV buyers, price increases of ICEVs, losses to ICEV buyers, lost profits (calibrated supply and demand models), effects on fleet turnover and emissions (qualitative analysis drawing on other empirical studies)

aInterviews of motor vehicle manufacturers are listed separately because they provided estimates not reported in any written study cited. We also conducted interviews with authors of many written studies, such as CARB, Sierra Research, Inc., and GAO.

Table 12.1-2 provides information about the NCERs that we analyzed. Column (1) is a numerical summary of our information about the narrow cost-effectiveness of each element, and column (2) refers the reader to sections or tables above where details can be found. As indicated in column (3), the nature of these numbers varies a lot. In some cases, we took the NCERs directly from the studies reviewed or reexpressed them in a straightforward fashion. In others, the NCERs we report are based on adjusting NCERs that appear in other studies to make them more comparable to other NCERs or the precise concept of interest. In the case of the ZEV mandate, we used information from the studies and extensive modeling to examine important issues that no other studies address.

As we emphasize throughout the report, NCERs do not provide a complete basis for policy decisions, no matter how accurately they estimate what they set out to estimate. Thus the first step in using NCERs is being clear about what costs and benefits a particular NCER purports to estimate. Column (4) of Table 12.1-2 indicates, for each element, what costs and what benefits analysts have, in fact, attempted to account for in the NCERs they have developed.

No matter what the definition of an NCER includes, all estimated NCERs are subject to inaccuracies. In column (5) we list the major sources of uncertainty about the NCERs reported. To take two examples: Studies of the narrow cost-effectiveness of I&M programs attempt to incorporate behavioral responses such as fraud, and the accuracy with which they do so is dubious. In the case of the ZEV mandate, our sensitivity analyses highlight factors such as the magnitudes of incremental EV production and operating costs and the effectiveness of ICEV emission-control programs that dramatically affect the NCER.

For some elements, the most important reason that NCERs cannot provide a reliable guide to policy is that they don't even attempt to account for some possibly crucial costs and benefits of a policy. Column (6) of Table 12.1-2 lists costs and benefits we believe could be very important but are simply uncounted in any way in the NCERs we report.

Table 12.1-2

Narrow Cost-Effectiveness Ratios for Elements of California's LDV Strategy: Ranges, Sources, Definitions, Limitations

Element	(1) NCER ($1000s per ton of ROG+NOx)	(2) Where Discussed in Report	(3) Source	(4) Costs and Benefits Included in Definition of Narrow Cost Effectiveness[a]	(5) Key Uncertainties About NCER	(6) Key Uncounted Costs and Benefits[b]
ICEV Hardware						
TLEV	3-40	Sec. 6.3 Table 6.3-1	Derived from studies reviewed	Costs: R&D, production, and selling costs Benefits: emission reductions (both relative to next most stringent exhaust standard)	Accuracy of emission models, emission system deterioration rates, cost estimates	Effects on fleet turnover, location, and time of emission reductions
LEV	1-38					
ULEV	22-48					
EEE	0.5-3	Sec. 6.3 Table 6.3-1	Derived from studies reviewed	Costs: R&D, production, and selling costs Benefits: emission reduction relative to 1993 California vehicle	Accuracy of emission models, emission system deterioration rates, cost estimates	Location and time of emission reductions
ORVR	infinite	Sec. 6.3 Table 6.3-1	Derived from studies reviewed	Costs: R&D, production, and selling costs Benefits: emission reductions when Stage II vapor recovery nozzles also used	Interaction of ORVR and Stage II vapor recovery nozzles	Costs of modifications to underground storage tanks

Table 12.1-2 (Cont'd.)

Element	(1) NCER ($1000s per ton of ROG+NOx)	(2) Detailed In	(3) Source	(4) Costs and Benefits Included in Definition of Narrow Cost Effectiveness[a]	(5) Key Uncertainties About NCER	(6) Key Uncounted Costs and Benefits[b]
OBD II	2-15?[c]	Sec. 8.3.2	Taken directly from studies reviewed	Costs: R&D, production, and selling costs. Benefits: emission reductions with enhanced I&M	Behavioral response to check-engine light, effectiveness of Smog Check II	Repair costs, decreased time needed to diagnose malfunctions, costs and benefits of increased durability of emission-control system
ICEV Non-Hardware						
CP2G	9-46	Sec. 8.1.3	Derived from studies reviewed	Costs: R&D, production, and reduced fuel efficiency. Benefits: emission reductions given number of miles driven	Effects on vehicles certified on RFG, change in effectiveness as vehicles age	Reduced costs of ICEV hardware, emission reductions due to reduced driving
Smog Check II	0.5-5.5?[c]	Sec. 8.2.3	Taken directly from studies reviewed	Costs: inspection, repair, driver time, administration. Benefits: emission reductions of repaired vehicles	Extent of evasion, effectiveness of remote sensing, extent emission variability hinders identification of high emitters	Driver aggravation

Table 12.1-2, (Cont'd.)

Element	(1) NCER ($1000s per ton of ROG+NOx)	(2) Detailed In	(3) Source	(4) Costs and Benefits Included in Definition of Narrow Cost Effectiveness[a]	(5) Key Uncertainties About NCER	(6) Key Uncounted Costs and Benefits[b]
AVR	2-10[d]	Sec. 8.4.3, Table 8.4-4	Taken directly from studies reviewed	Costs: lost transportation services, program administration. Benefits: emissions avoided on scrapped vehicles net of emissions from replacement transportation	Emissions of replacement transportation, remaining lifetimes of scrapped vehicles	In-migration, responses to incentives for higher emissions, reductions in Smog Check evasion
ZEV	5-1,197	Sec. 10.4 Table 10.4-1	Modeling and sensitivity analysis based on data derived from studies reviewed	Costs: R&D, production, and lifetime operating costs in near- and long-term. Benefits: ICEV emissions directly displaced by EVs	Initial EV costs, decline in costs over time, effectiveness of ICEV emission control program, how manufacturers adjust ICEV fleet	Costs of managing reduced range, infrastructure costs, benefits of home refueling and quiet of EVs, effect on fleet turnover, ICEV mileage displaced per EV

[a]NCER includes costs borne both inside and outside California.

[b]In addition to the reductions of emissions other than ROG and NOx such as CO, air toxics, or particulates.

[c]We have very little confidence that the NCER is in or near this range.

[d]In contrast to other non-hardware elements of the California strategy, the NCER for AVR does not purport to incorporate behavioral effects.

Table 12.1-3

Summary of Market-Mediated Effects, 1998 to 2002

Element	(1) Findings on Market-Mediated Effects	(2) Where Discussed in Report	(3) Key Sources of Uncertainty
ICEV hardware	ICEV prices will increase $100-$500/vehicle ICEV sales will fall 10K-60K vehicles/year ICEV buyers will lose $150M-$700M/year Manufacturers and dealers will lose $100M- $800M/year	Table 7.2-2	Effects of regulations on variable production costs
	Emissions may increase in early years due to reduced fleet turnover	Sec. 7.4	Size of price effects
CP2G	Vehicle miles traveled will fall 1.5-4 percent Emissions will fall by comparable amounts or more	Sec. 9.1	Size of gasoline price increases
AVR	In-migration, price increases of older vehicles, or both will occur; lack of price increases would be a bad sign about in-migration	Sec. 9.3 Appendix 9.A	Barriers to in-migration, elasticity of demand for older vehicles

Table 12.1-3, (Cont'd.)

Element	(1) Findings on Market-Mediated Effects	(2) Where Discussed in Report	(3) Key Sources of Uncertainty
ZEVs	EV prices may be as much as $10,000 less than comparable ICEV	Table 11.5-1	Lifetime operating cost disadvantage of EVs
	EV buyers will gain $20M-$200M/year	Table 11.5-2	Willingness of EV buyers to pay premium over ICEV prices
	Producers may lose as much as $1.5B/year or profit as much as $350M/year in the EV market	Table 11.5-2	EV production costs, EV prices
	ICEV prices will increase $0-$550/vehicle	Table 11.6-1	Variable costs and prices of EVs, Big 7 pricing policies
	ICEV sales will fall 0-110K vehicles/year	Table 11.6-1	ICEV price increases, degree EV sales displace ICEV sales
	ICEV buyers will lose $0-$800M/year in the ICEV market	Table 11.6-1	Variable costs and prices of EVs, Big 7 pricing policies
	Big 7 will lose $100M-800M/year in the ICEV market	Table 11.6-1	Degree EV sales displace ICEV sales
	Other ICEV companies may lose up to $60M/year or gain $550M/year in the ICEV market	Table 11.6-1	Big 7 price increases, whether companies match Big 7 price increases
	California consumers may gain up to $200M/year or lose up to $750M/year	Table 11.7-1	Variable costs and prices of EVs, Big 7 pricing policies
	Emissions may increase in early years due to reduced fleet turnover	Sec. 11.8	Size of ICEV price effects

Studies purporting to estimate cost effectiveness for California ozone-reduction policies generally ignore how markets will react to the policy intervention. These reactions influence the actual costs of the policies, their distribution inside and outside California, and the actual emission benefits. Our analyses of the market-mediated effects of the various elements in the California strategy are summarized in Table 12.1-3. Column (1) summarizes key conclusions and column (2) indicates tables or sections where details can be found. The last column of the table indicates major sources of uncertainty about these market-mediated effects.

12.2 WHICH ELEMENTS MAKE GOOD ECONOMIC SENSE?

We have proposed economic efficiency as the policy goal of the California ozone-reduction strategy. Different policymakers have different amounts of freedom to pursue this goal. Those required to reduce emissions to comply with air-quality standards (e.g., CARB) would seek to achieve attainment in ways that are most efficient or least inefficient. Those who are free to change air-quality standards (e.g., the U.S. Congress) would seek to implement policies only if the benefits of doing so appear to exceed the costs.

We can't tell either kind of policymaker what to decide, but we attempt to help them by clarifying existing information, developing new information, and suggesting how best to use the limited information available.

In Section 2.6, we presented some rough rules of thumb for using NCERs to decide whether a policy element promotes economic efficiency in the South Coast, given the freedom available to the policymaker. These suggestions are replicated here, for the reader's convenience, as Table 12.2-1. The numerical values for NCERs shown in Table 12.2-1 are based on current estimates of benefits of emission reductions and are hardly definitive; we encourage policymakers to adjust them as they think appropriate.

Table 12.2-1

Illustrative Rules of Thumb for Using Narrow Cost-Effectiveness Ratios (NCERs) to Choose Ozone-Reduction Policies for the South Coast

If you think the NCER is about:	And you must find more tons of reductions, then:	And you are free to pursue economic efficiency, then:
$5,000/ton or less	Implement the policy unless uncounted costs appear to far outweigh uncounted benefits	Implement the policy unless uncounted costs appear to far outweigh uncounted benefits
$10,000/ton	Implement the policy unless uncounted costs appear to far outweigh uncounted benefits and alternative ways to reduce tons look even less promising	Implement the policy as long as uncounted costs appear not to much outweigh uncounted benefits
$25,000/ton	Don't implement the policy unless uncounted benefits appear to outweigh uncounted costs or alternative ways to reduce tons look even less promising	Don't implement the policy unless uncounted benefits appear to far outweigh uncounted costs
$50,000/ton or more	Don't implement the policy unless uncounted benefits appear to far outweigh uncounted costs and alternative ways to reduce tons look even less promising	Don't implement the policy unless uncounted benefits appear to outweigh uncounted costs by tens of thousands of dollars per ton

To implement these rules requires policymakers to interpret and combine the kinds of information summarized in Tables 12.1-1, 12.1-2, and 12.1-3. In our earlier discussion, we proposed three steps for proceeding systematically; here we quote the steps and suggest what we have contributed to implementing them:

> Step 1: *Use your beliefs about factors underlying the NCERs (based on information about the reliability of the data and methods used) to determine the narrowest range that you find plausible.*

We have contributed to this step by providing the kinds of information summarized in Columns (1), (4) and (5) of Table 12.1-2. Specifically, we have clarified what particular NCERs purport to measure, pointed out potential sources of inaccuracy, and analyzed what underlying conditions would be required for a true NCER to lie in a particular part of a range reported in Table 12.1-2.

> Step 2: *List the potentially important costs and benefits that are not accounted for in the NCERs you have, consider what you know about them, and form as precise a judgment as you can about the relative magnitudes of uncounted costs and uncounted benefits.*

We have contributed to this step by identifying uncounted costs and benefits (see column (6) of Table 12.1-2) and analyzing several of them, most notably market-mediated effects (see Table 12.1-3).

> Step 3: *Consult Table 12.2-1, perhaps modified to your liking, which provides some rough rules of thumb for the South Coast.*

We offer the following example of how we would implement these three steps if we were considering the incremental costs and benefits of producing ULEVs rather than LEVs.

Step 1. As shown in Table 12.1-2, the information we adapted from other studies leads us to a NCER range of $22,000 to $48,000 per ton of ROG + NOx from reducing exhaust emissions from LEV to ULEV levels. Recall that the NCERs include costs borne both inside and outside California. Uncertainty about the range reflects disagreement between CARB and Sierra studies of the incremental production cost of additional hardware to upgrade LEVs to ULEVs and, perhaps more important, uncertainties about levels of in-use emissions and the effectiveness of Smog-Check II. A policymaker who thinks the CARB cost estimates are more reliable and that ULEV deterioration rates will be lower than LEV deterioration rates might settle on a NCER near $25,000 per ton of ROG plus NOx. A policymaker who thinks the Sierra estimates are reliable and that ULEVs will deteriorate no less rapidly than LEVs might settle on a value near $50,000 per ton of ROG plus NOx as a good representation of the true NCER.

Step 2. Whatever value for the NCER you think most appropriate, consider what the NCER for the ULEV standard does not include--for example, as indicated in column (6) of Table 12.1-2, how market mediated effects could affect fleet turnover and emissions and the extent to which emission reductions will occur in non-attainment areas during times of the day and seasons when ozone levels are unlikely to cause damage. Consider how the incremental costs of ULEVs might affect prices and sales levels of ICEVs in California and the profits of manufacturers and their dealers. California policymakers are likely to emphasize the costs borne by Californians. Federal policymakers are likely to focus on costs to all Americans. Form a judgment about the factors that your NCER doesn't consider at all. Are the costs likely to outweigh the benefits, or vice versa? By a lot? A little?

Step 3. Suppose you are a California policymaker, needing to find tons of emissions to reduce, and you think that--after adjusting for costs borne outside California--$25,000 per ton is a reliable estimate of the NCER and that the price and fleet turnover effects of ULEVs rather than LEVs are very minor. Unless you have other ways to reduce the tons you think that ULEVs will provide, you may well conclude that ULEVs are an economical means of moving towards compliance. In contrast, suppose you are a federal policymaker, free to adjust the ozone standard, and you think that $50,000 per ton is a reliable estimate of the NCER and that the price and fleet turnover effects of ULEVs rather than LEVs are quite large. You might well conclude that ULEVs are economically inefficient and that if California doesn't have better options than this for achieving compliance with the federal ozone standards in the South Coast, then perhaps the standards should be relaxed in the South Coast.

12.3 WILL THE CALIFORNIA LDV STRATEGY REALLY CONTROL ICEV EMISSIONS?

The tables and discussion above focus on individual elements of the California strategy. Let's now step back and look across all the elements aimed at ICEVs. How far can we expect them to take us toward the state's ozone-reduction goals?

The key to getting benefits from our inevitably costly LDV strategy is controlling emissions in actual use. Historically, much of the emission problem from LDVs is attributable to vehicles whose emission control systems are not functioning properly and hence emit pollutants at very high rates. Is history "bunk" or are we "doomed to repeat it"?

As highlighted in our analyses and in Table 12.1-2, considerable uncertainty surrounds estimates of the future emission benefits of *all* of the elements of the strategy aimed at controlling emissions from ICEVs. For the regulations aimed at new vehicles, critical issues are the degree to which they will deteriorate and how much they will emit under driving conditions not reflected in certification tests. For the regulations aimed at vehicles already on the road, the critical issues are whether high emissions will be detected, whether owners will attempt to repair problems, and whether repairs will be effective.

Tailpipe and evaporative emission standards for new vehicles. New vehicles may or may not turn out to deteriorate much less than their predecessors. It is highly uncertain whether the rates of deterioration of new California LDVs will come close to those required to meet certification standards over the 50,000 and 100,000 miles required by the regulations, or what their emission rates might be beyond these mileage levels. We believe that the recall program, and perhaps the warranty regulations, provide companies with major incentives to produce very durable emission-control systems. Whether companies will succeed in making such systems and especially whether deterioration due to tampering or poor maintenance will be effectively reduced, are open questions. It is also uncertain how well new emission systems will control emissions under driving conditions not reflected in certification tests.

OBD II. The goal of OBD II--to detect malfunctioning emission-control systems and spur action to repair them--is crucial.

The extent to which OBD II will advance this goal is uncertain. Much of the technology is new, and the performance of new technologies generally disappoints optimists. There is also the crucial question of the behavior of drivers and mechanics when the system detects an emission problem (i.e., what happens after the light goes on?) The actual emission benefits of OBD II might be enhanced greatly by detailed attention to behavioral issues.

We view OBD II as an investment that could pay enormous dividends, but only if the behavioral issues are addressed successfully and perhaps only after the technology matures. Perhaps the most valuable payoff from OBD II will be the knowledge gained about the performance of early-generation on-board emission monitoring equipment in on-road use.

Smog Check II and AVR programs. If next-generation LDVs deteriorate much less than their predecessors, the regulations just discussed could make an enormous difference to aggregate emission levels once most existing vehicles are retired. But even if deterioration is not a problem for the next-generation vehicles, Californians will do a lot of breathing before these vehicles dominate the fleet. Reformulated gasoline seems to be part of the solution; what about inspection and maintenance and accelerated vehicle-retirement programs?

To date, California's experience with vehicle inspection and maintenance programs--like experience elsewhere--has been very disappointing. Smog-Check II is an aggressive attempt to identify and clean up vehicles with high emissions or get them off the road. The program could make a real difference. However, dramatic success of Smog-Check II is hardly assured. Past difficulties with I&M programs are indicative of major challenges to effectively implementing the new program.

Reducing emissions from existing high-emitters is such a high priority that Herculean efforts to make smog check work are warranted, but we should recognize that even Herculean efforts may fail. If Smog-

Check II does fail, policymakers should be mindful of the difference between tons of reductions projected in the State Implementation Plan-- which by themselves provide legal benefits but no health benefits--and actual emission reductions. The costs of Smog-Check II--including substantial time costs, enforcement costs, and inconvenience for motorists--will be real even if the emissions benefits are only theoretical.

Much of the design of the AVR program planned for the South Coast has yet to be done. Depending on the design, such programs could be a great success or a great failure. We have emphasized two serious pitfalls--in-migration and incentives for owners of vehicles to delay scrapping dirty vehicles, to keep vehicles dirty, or to tamper with them to make them dirtier. The program should be designed, implemented and enforced with potential pitfalls in mind. This will take substantial ingenuity, and efforts to achieve too much could backfire. If the AVR program is eviscerated by perverse incentives or in-migration, NCERs of less than $10,000 per ton (which ignore behavioral and market responses) will be of little consolation.

Our discussion, analyses, and conclusions pose a dilemma for California policymakers who must find a way to reduce emissions:

- Part of the emission reductions must come from LDVs;
- Vehicles with unusually high emissions are a key part of the problem;
- Efforts to control in-use emissions have not nearly eliminated emissions due to deterioration and aggressive driving;
- Dramatic future reduction in emissions from these sources is far from assured.

A dilemma like this calls for *consideration* of radical alternatives. One such alternative is mandating the commercialization of vehicles that don't emit directly. The ZEV mandate--which will lead to substantial sales of battery-powered electric vehicles in California starting in 1998--places California on such a course.

12.4 IMPROVING THE QUALITY OF THE DISCUSSION OF THE ZEV MANDATE

Like many high-stakes, polarized policy debates, the debate over the ZEV mandate includes many rallying cries that are more dramatic than insightful. Before we consider what economic analysis of the ZEV mandate tells policymakers, we think it is useful to discard this distracting rhetoric.

"Californians will pay the entire cost" or "Someone else will pay." When social costs are generated, someone must pay. Some people assert that all of the social costs of the California strategy will be borne by Californians. Others assert that the costs will be borne by others, e.g., automobile and oil companies, residents of other states. As our analyses of market-mediated effects illustrate, neither of these extreme views is plausible. Substantial portions of the costs of producing ICEVs with upgraded hardware or producing EVs can be expected to fall on both California consumers and on vehicle manufacturers and their California dealers.

"The market has spoken." Some argue that if EVs were a good idea then the market would reveal that fact in the form of numerous buyers willing to pay the cost of producing them. This argument should not be taken seriously. Current market-based incentives to abate pollution are well below the social benefits of reducing pollution. The environmental benefits of EVs would accrue almost entirely to people other than EV buyers, who would have to pay the price. The market that has been and is currently speaking cannot be relied upon to deliver economically efficient outcomes.

"We must do anything that will move us towards attainment." Some argue that at the rate we are going we will never achieve attainment in the South Coast and therefore that we must do anything that would move us along faster. This argument is also not to be taken seriously. Attainment would not be hard to achieve if we didn't care about costs. For example, we could ban LDVs from use in the South Coast or tax gasoline at $100 per gallon. Thus we have choices. The real issue is how to choose intelligently.

"We mustn't do anything that is very costly." This argument makes sense only if there are ways to achieve our air pollution goals that

aren't very costly or if there aren't major benefits to improving air
quality. We are skeptical of both propositions and think the burden of
proof lies with those who want Californians to accept one of them. The
real challenge is discovering and implementing approaches that achieve
real benefits at costs that are worth the benefits.

"Technology is the solution." This statement ignores an
uncomfortable fact that we have met several times in our analysis:
technology alone is unlikely to do the job, and human behavior is often
the key to getting the benefits out of a technology that "works." We
are inclined to believe that California will not make major progress in
reducing ozone without both improvements in technology and changes in
behavior. Moreover, looking to technology doesn't get us very far
unless we have a way to analyze: What technology is the solution? When
will that technology be the solution? Who can best develop that
technology? What can we do to make sure that the technology will be
used if it is developed?

12.5 WHAT DOES ECONOMIC ANALYSIS OF THE ZEV MANDATE TELL POLICYMAKERS?

As our analyses of the social costs and benefits of the ZEV mandate
make abundantly clear, its actual economic effects cannot be pinned down
at all precisely. The *long-term* NCERs we developed under various
assumptions are as low as $5,000 and as high as $850,000 per ton of ROG
plus NOx removed. Estimated NCERs depend on several controversial
factors: production and operating costs of EVs between now and 2002, how
quickly these costs could decline, the eventual fleet penetration of
EVs, and the effectiveness of policies to reduce emissions from ICEVs.
The narrow cost-effectiveness of the ZEV mandate could turn out to be
very low or very high. The market-mediated effects of the ZEV mandate
could be beneficial to Californians, but they could also be very
detrimental. In short, the ZEV mandate could turn out to be a great
success or a great failure.

This does not imply, however, that California policymakers should
forget about ZEVs; without ZEVs California might also face very
undesirable policy choices. To highlight this possibility consider the

following pessimistic--but not inconceivable--scenario as 2010 approaches.

Suppose California were to repeal the mandate and, as a--plausible, yet not inevitable--consequence, ZEV technology stagnates. Suppose further that the ICEV components of the current ozone-reduction strategy don't work very well, new cost-effective emission control options have not been discovered and that, a few years before 2010, California finds itself far short of meeting the current federal ozone standards. To make matters worse, suppose also that the health effects of ozone are found to be much worse than currently thought and as a result relaxing air quality standards appears reasonable to almost no one. Under these circumstances, and perhaps even some less extreme ones, California would find itself desperately seeking ways to reduce emissions of ozone precursors and finding only additional measures that are very expensive, such as very aggressive transportation control measures or even restrictions on industrial activity. In sum, there are great risks both to proceeding with the ZEV mandate in its current form and to repealing it and doing nothing else to encourage ZEV development.

How might we protect ourselves from such a situation?

It is crucial to recognize that now, in 1996, we need only decide how to proceed over the near term, until a few years into the next century, say. We need not decide whether or how California policy will address ZEVs beyond such a time horizon. We also think it crucial to proceed in ways that accommodate the realities: the environmental and economic stakes for Californians are high, the future is very uncertain, and we will learn more as time passes.

The uncertainties and risks involving ZEVs suggest that, in considering modifications to the ZEV mandate, we should be searching for near-term ZEV policies with three key characteristics.

- **Learning**. Policy should be designed with learning as an interim objective. As new information becomes available, the most promising set of policies should become better defined.

- **Robustness**. Near-term policy should be formulated while recognizing that very undesirable outcomes--economic, environmental, or both--are possible. Thus, policy should be formulated with specific attention to worst-case scenarios and policy paths that avoid the worst of the worst. Such policies are often referred to as "robust" policies.

- **Adaptability**. As we learn about various factors, we want to be in a position to use this information to improve policy. Policies that can be tailored as new information arrives are often referred to as "adaptive." In thinking about adaptation, it is important to recognize that flexibility in future policymaking brings with it costs of uncertainty to those who must anticipate future policy when they plan and invest.

We conclude by suggesting four principles that could help to shape ZEV policies along the lines suggested here. Strategically, policymakers should seek to improve the prospects of developing electric-drive technology; learning about, while at the same time preserving, its prospects; and avoiding unnecessarily large short-term costs.

First, ZEV policy should aim to determine whether EVs are a promising cornerstone of California's long-term ozone control strategy. Determining this requires learning about many different things, including:

- Performance, cost, and availability of EV technology;
- Consumer valuation of EV performance;
- Effectiveness of current ICEV control measures;
- Cost and effectiveness of alternative LDV emission control measures such as new transportation control measures or taxes aimed at vehicle-specific emission levels; and
- Cost and effectiveness of policies aimed at sources of emissions other than LDVs, such as heavy-duty vehicles and stationary sources.

Second, ZEV policy should protect the long-run prospects for ZEVs. While we are agnostic about whether EVs should be a cornerstone of California's LDV strategy, we think it very important to protect the long-run prospects for EVs. EVs may turn out to be attractive on cost and performance grounds, and for this reason it is critical to avoid near-term developments that would constrain our ability to rely on them in the long term. Both market and political factors are relevant here.

On the market side, we need to be concerned about how the mandate or its modification could affect behavior of both consumers and innovators over the long term.

ZEV policy should consider the potential for consumer disappointment with EVs due to limited range, reliability, or infrastructure. Such disappointment could give EVs a bad name and create long-term difficulties in marketing even EVs that would not disappoint consumers. If EVs do turn out to be economical, higher market penetration rates could be the key to getting large quantities of emission reductions from them. This underscores the importance of preserving the long-run marketability of EVs, and making sure they don't become the Edsel of the 1990s.

ZEV policy should also consider the impact of possible revisions in the mandate on the future willingness of innovators to invest. This calls for striking a careful balance between flexibility and predictability in policy formulation. For example, whatever the outcome of the current review of the mandate, it would be helpful if CARB would announce future times at which the policy will be reviewed and indicate the major factors that will be considered.

On the political front, it is also important to consider how the mandate might affect CARB's ability to adopt innovative policies in the future. If CARB promotes a policy now that turns out to be wasteful, it may not be able, for example, to promote EVs in the future even if technological developments make EVs a good bet.

Third, ZEV policy should also accommodate a broad range of vehicles and innovators because the most promising path to widespread EV use is far from clear. We should beware of policies that unduly emphasize one type of vehicle or one type of innovator. For example, some believe that the most promising path to major emission reductions from EVs involves important roles for small EVs (e.g., niche vehicles such as neighborhood electric vehicles). Apparently, these are not the type of vehicles that will be produced by the Big 7 in the early years of the mandate, however. While the right to sell EV credits will make non-Big

7 EVs more viable, other things equal, the mandate itself may stifle demand for non-Big 7 EVs by inducing the Big 7 to market very high-quality EVs at very low prices. The current mandate may thus give us little insight into what electric-drive transportation alternatives are most viable in the near term or the long-term viability of electric drive transportation generally.

Finally, ZEV policy should look for ways to lower the cost of achieving these objectives. For example, how can we learn more about the potential of advanced batteries while avoiding costs associated with commercialization of lead-acid batteries? What can we learn about consumer use of EVs and requirements for range without fielding a large fleet of EVs before the turn of the century? If the mandate is scaled back or delayed, are there cost-effective ways to make up any lost emission reductions? In view of potential market-mediated effects on fleet turnover and emissions, would there be any lost emission reductions?

Of course, such principles--if accepted--must be translated into policy actions. Doing so will require wisdom, energy, creativity, and cooperation.

Appendix

1.A NON-ECONOMIC UNCERTAINTIES

The following are examples of the non-economic uncertainties that permeate the search for policies that will achieve California's air quality goals most economically.

Links between emissions levels and ozone levels. The atmospheric chemistry of ozone formation is very complicated. Estimates of combinations of ROG and NOx emissions that would achieve the ozone standards are based on complex atmospheric models that are calibrated to current emission estimates and ozone readings. No one knows at all precisely which combinations of emission levels of ROG and NOx would achieve compliance with ozone standards.[325]

Current level of emissions. There is considerable uncertainty about the levels of emissions, especially from some sources. Emission levels from large stationary sources such as power plants are measured, and thus total emissions from these sources are reasonably accurately known. However, there is considerable uncertainty about the levels of emissions from mobile sources and from tens of thousand of small stationary sources. As Table 1.2-1 (in Section 1) shows, mobile sources are estimated to account for 56 percent of ROG emissions in the South Coast Basin and 82 percent of NOx emissions.

Proportionate emission reductions needed for compliance. Policy makers often think in terms of the proportionate reductions in emissions that appear to be necessary to attain our air-quality goals because doing so seems to ameliorate difficulties due to the uncertainties in

---

[325]In fact, some policies that reduce one precursor or the other might have no ozone-reduction benefits whatever. For example, how reducing ROG or NOx emissions affects ozone depends on the ratio of ROG and NOx present in the atmosphere. If the ratio of ROG to NOx is high, reducing ROG alone will have little impact on ozone. If the ratio is low, reducing NOx alone may even increase ozone (National Research Council, 1991, pp. 163-173). However, ambient measurements suggest that the ROG-NOx ratio in the South Coast basin is in an intermediate range where reductions in either ROG or NOx will reduce ozone (National Research Council, 1991, p. 301).

carrying capacities and emissions inventories.[326] However much thinking in proportionate terms helps, there is still substantial uncertainty about the proportionate reductions in emissions required for achieving our air quality goals.

_____

[326]Air-quality models are calibrated using measurements of actual ozone levels, and it is believed that this gives analysts a reasonably good fix on how far from required emission levels we are in proportionate terms.

2.A ESTIMATES OF EFFICIENT TAXES FOR DIFFERENT VEHICLES

We calculated the size of incentives that would encourage those who create pollution to make economically efficient decisions regarding the amount of pollution they generated. These emissions taxes would cause vehicle owners to pay the full social cost of their pollution and as a result lead them to give auto and oil companies efficient incentives to help them reduce their pollution.

There are many choices that drivers make that could affect the emissions, including what vehicle to use, how many miles to drive, and what gasoline to use. Thus, tax rates might be expressed in terms of the annual use of a vehicle (e.g., implemented with a surcharge upon registering the vehicle), cents per mile of driving, or a tax per gallon of gasoline used. We calculate efficient tax rates expressed in all three ways.

Tables 2.A-1, 2.A-2, and 2.A-3 compute efficient levels of taxes for different vehicles based on different assumed rates of emissions of ROG and NOx. Columns in the table pertain to vehicles with different emissions rates (g/mi) and rows to different estimates of pollution costs ($/ton) detailed in Table 2.B-1 in Appendix 2.B.

The different vehicles (and associated emissions rates) considered are as follows.

- The first five emissions rates are the certification emissions rates for ZEVs,[327] ULEVs, LEVs, TLEVs, and Tier 1 vehicles.
- The next two columns are based on 1992 and 2000 fleet-average emissions rates for gasoline vehicles in California based on EMFAC7F as adjusted and reported in Small and Kazimi (1995, Table 4).[328]

---

[327]We use a figure of .004 g/mi of HC emissions for ZEVs to represent one estimate of the emissions required to generate the electricity used to power an electric vehicle.

[328]After reviewing several studies suggesting that EMFAC7F underestimates ROG emission rates, Small and Kazimi multiply ROG emission rates in EMFAC7F by 2.1.

- The last two columns represent especially high emitters. The emissions rates are the average and maximum tailpipe emissions test results--as adjusted and reported in Hsu and Sperling (1994, Table 2)--for 74 vehicles scrapped as part of the 1990 UNOCAL scrappage program.

Using estimates of pollution costs ($/ton) and emissions rates (g/mi) for ROG and NOx, it is a matter of arithmetic to express emissions in terms of dollars per mile, per year (assuming 12,000 miles driven), or per gallon (assuming fuel economy of 23 miles per gallon), as we do in Tables 2.A-1, 2.A-2, and 2.A-3 respectively.[329]

To illustrate the construction of the tables, consider a vehicle that emits at the average rate of the California fleet in 1992: 3.76 g/mi of ROG and 1.26 g/mi of NOx. The tables show that efficient taxes for such a vehicle operated in the South Coast would be of the order of: 2 to 13 cents per mile (Table 2.A-1), or $230 to over $1500 per year assuming 12,000 miles driven (Table 2.A-2), or 45 cents to almost $3 per gallon of gasoline assuming fuel efficiency of 23 miles per gallon.

Note especially that efficient taxes in the South Coast vary enormously--from almost trivial to almost astounding levels--over vehicles with different emissions rates. Compare, for example, ULEVs to the 1992 fleet average to the worst emitters tested in the UNOCAL program based on damage-cost estimates. In terms of dollars per year (Table 2.A-2), for example, the taxes are less than $50 (ULEVs), roughly $235 to $675 (1992 fleet average), and $4000 to $15,000 (highest emitters tested by UNOCAL).

---

[329]The damage estimates from Table 2.A-1 were also adjusted for inflation--to a constant 1992 dollar basis--using the implicit price deflator for the Gross Domestic Product. (The estimates in Table 2.B-1, which are expressed as they were reported by the sources detailed, are re-expressed in 1992 dollars as detailed in Tables 2.A-1, 2.A-2 and 2.A-3.)

Table 2.A-1

Estimates of Efficient Emission Tax Rates Expressed in Dollars (1992) per Mile

Emission rates of ozone precursors:

		ZEV	ULEV	LEV	TLEV	Conv	92avg	00avg	UnocalAvg	UnocalMax
ROG g/m		0.004	0.04	0.075	0.125	0.25	3.76	1.8	16.6	85.4
NOx g/m		0	0.2	0.2	0.4	0.4	1.26	0.69	2.4	9

Cost ($/ton) estimates:

	ROG $/ton	NOx $/ton	ZEV	ULEV	LEV	TLEV	Conv	92avg	00avg	UnocalAvg	UnocalMax
South Coast:											
Damage cost estimates:											
NERA	2940	5192	0.00	0.00	0.00	0.00	0.00	0.02	0.01	0.07	0.33
Small and Kazimi	2920	10670	0.00	0.00	0.00	0.01	0.01	0.03	0.01	0.08	0.38
CEC	7701	16138	0.00	0.00	0.00	0.01	0.01	0.05	0.03	0.18	0.88
Sierra--overall	4862	0	0.00	0.00	0.00	0.00	0.00	0.02	0.01	0.09	0.46
Sierra--marginal	13565	0	0.00	0.00	0.00	0.00	0.00	0.06	0.03	0.25	1.28
Control cost estimates:											
CAPUC	20374	28524	0.00	0.01	0.01	0.02	0.02	0.12	0.06	0.45	2.20
SCAQMD	9471	33429	0.00	0.01	0.01	0.02	0.02	0.09	0.04	0.26	1.22
CEC	21060	29417	0.00	0.01	0.01	0.02	0.02	0.13	0.06	0.46	2.27
Other air basins--CEC											
Damage cost estimates:											
Ventura	319	1835	0.00	0.00	0.00	0.00	0.00	0.00	0.00	0.01	0.05
Sacramento	4601	6785	0.00	0.00	0.00	0.00	0.00	0.03	0.01	0.10	0.50
Bay Area	100	8184	0.00	0.00	0.00	0.00	0.00	0.01	0.01	0.02	0.09
San Diego	109	6194	0.00	0.00	0.00	0.00	0.00	0.01	0.00	0.02	0.07
Control cost estimates:											
Ventura	23511	18386	0.00	0.01	0.01	0.01	0.01	0.12	0.06	0.48	2.39
Sacramento	10140	10140	0.00	0.00	0.00	0.01	0.01	0.06	0.03	0.21	1.05
Bay Area	11366	11589	0.00	0.00	0.00	0.01	0.01	0.06	0.03	0.24	1.18
San Diego	19500	20391	0.00	0.01	0.01	0.01	0.01	0.11	0.05	0.41	2.04

Table 2.A-2
Estimates of Efficient Emission Tax Rates Expressed in Dollars (1992) per Year
(Assumes 12,000 miles driven per year)

	Cost ($/ton) estimates:		Emission rates of ozone precursors:								
	ROG $/ton	NOx$/ton	ZEV	ULEV	LEV	TLEV	Conv	92avg	00avg	UnocalAvg	UnocalMax
ROG g/m			0.004	0.04	0.075	0.125	0.25	3.76	1.8	16.6	85.4
NOx g/m			0	0.2	0.2	0.4	0.4	1.26	0.69	2.4	9
South Coast:											
Damage cost estimates:											
NERA	2940	5192	0	15	17	32	37	233	117	810	3936
Small and Kazimi	2920	10670	0	30	31	61	66	323	167	979	4565
CEC	7701	16138	0	47	50	98	111	651	330	2201	10611
Sierra--overall	4862	0	0	3	5	8	16	242	116	1067	5487
Sierra--marginal	13565	0	1	7	13	22	45	674	323	2976	15310
Control cost estimates:											
CAPUC	20374	28524	1	86	96	184	218	1487	745	5374	26388
SCAQMD	9471	33429	1	93	98	192	208	1027	530	3138	14665
CEC	21060	29417	1	89	99	190	225	1536	769	5553	27268
Other air basins--CEC											
Damage cost estimates:											
Ventura	319	1835	0	5	5	10	11	46	24	128	578
Sacramento	4601	6785	0	20	22	43	51	342	171	1225	6000
Bay Area	100	8184	0	22	22	43	44	141	77	282	1086
San Diego	109	6194	0	16	16	33	33	109	59	220	860
Control cost estimates:											
Ventura	23511	18386	1	61	72	136	175	1474	727	5741	28722
Sacramento	10140	10140	1	32	37	70	87	673	334	2546	12650
Bay Area	11366	11589	1	37	42	80	99	758	376	2861	14206
San Diego	19500	20391	1	64	73	140	172	1309	650	4925	24434

Table 2.A-3
Estimates of Efficient Emission Tax Rates Expressed in Dollars (1992) per Gallon
(Assumes 23 mpg)

	Cost ($/ton) estimates:		Emission rates of ozone precursors:								
			ZEV	ULEV	LEV	TLEV	Conv	92avg	00avg	UnocalAvg	UnocalMax
		ROG g/m	0.004	0.04	0.075	0.125	0.25	3.76	1.8	16.6	85.4
		NOx g/m	0	0.2	0.2	0.4	0.4	1.26	0.69	2.4	9
	ROG $/ton	NOx $/ton									
South Coast:											
Damage cost estimates:											
NERA	2940	5192	0.00	0.03	0.03	0.06	0.07	0.45	0.22	1.55	7.54
Small and Kazimi	2920	10670	0.00	0.06	0.06	0.12	0.13	0.62	0.32	1.88	8.75
OEC	7701	16138	0.00	0.09	0.10	0.19	0.21	1.25	0.63	4.22	20.34
Sierra--overall	4862	0	0.00	0.00	0.01	0.02	0.03	0.46	0.22	2.04	10.52
Sierra--marginal	13565	0	0.00	0.01	0.03	0.04	0.09	1.29	0.62	5.70	29.34
Control cost estimates:											
CAPUC	20374	28524	0.00	0.17	0.18	0.35	0.42	2.85	1.43	10.30	50.58
SCAQMD	9471	33429	0.00	0.18	0.19	0.37	0.40	1.97	1.02	6.01	28.11
OEC	21060	29417	0.00	0.17	0.19	0.36	0.43	2.94	1.47	10.64	52.26
Other air basins--CEC											
Damage cost estimates:											
Ventura	319	1835	0.00	0.01	0.01	0.02	0.02	0.09	0.05	0.25	1.11
Sacramento	4601	6785	0.00	0.04	0.04	0.08	0.10	0.65	0.33	2.35	11.50
Bay Area	100	8184	0.00	0.04	0.04	0.08	0.08	0.27	0.15	0.54	2.08
San Diego	109	6194	0.00	0.03	0.03	0.06	0.06	0.21	0.11	0.42	1.65
Control cost estimates:											
Ventura	23511	18386	0.00	0.12	0.14	0.26	0.34	2.83	1.39	11.00	55.05
Sacramento	10140	10140	0.00	0.06	0.07	0.13	0.17	1.29	0.64	4.88	24.25
Bay Area	11366	11589	0.00	0.07	0.08	0.15	0.19	1.45	0.72	5.48	27.23
San Diego	19500	20391	0.00	0.12	0.14	0.27	0.33	2.51	1.25	9.44	46.83

2.B ESTIMATES OF SOCIAL BENEFITS OF REDUCING EMISSIONS

Table 2.B-1 summarizes several estimates of the social costs of
ozone-precursor emissions--or, equivalently, the social benefits of
reducing those emissions--in the South Coast and other non-attainment
areas in California. The estimates are expressed in terms of dollars
per ton of emissions of ozone precursors.[330]

The sources of the estimates in Table 2.B-1 are detailed at the
bottom of the table. The estimates are based on two general approaches
to estimating the dollar benefits of reducing air pollution:

- Damage-cost estimates are based on linking emissions to the
  damage they cause--for example, damage to human health (e.g.,
  coughing spells, asthma, eye irritation, etc., due to ozone,
  premature deaths due to PM) and vegetation (ornamental and
  agricultural), and putting a dollar figure on health and
  vegetation damage per unit of damage.

- Control-cost estimates are developed under the theory that we
  can infer the value of reducing pollution from the costs we
  incur to avoid pollution. This theory is quite problematic, as
  discussed by CEC (1993, pp. 52-3), under the name of "revealed
  preference" (of regulatory authorities).

Conceptually damage-cost estimation is much more promising. In
practice, however, it has several limitations, not the least of which is
inability to apply it to all of the potentially significant sources of

---

[330]Some important studies on the economic costs of air pollution in
California are not listed in the table because they don't report their
results in dollars per ton. Especially notable examples are extensive
studies summarized in Krupnick and Portney (1991) and Hall et al.
(1992a), which estimate the annual dollar damages of prevailing air
pollution levels relative to NAAQS. The estimates of Krupnick and
Portney (1991) and Hall et al. (1992a) are, however, implicitly
represented in Table 2.B-1, because this work is drawn upon in studies
listed in the table. For example, Small and Kazimi (1995) use results
from both Krupnick and Portney (1991) and Hall et al. (1992), and Sierra
(1995b) draws heavily on the work summarized in Hall et al. (1992).

damage. The damage estimates presented in Table 2.B-1 include only the
following damage components:

- NERA: damage from ozone due to morbidity, and damage to
  materials and crops; damage from particulate matter due to
  mortality and morbidity, damage to materials, reduced
  visibility (Hahn, 1995, p. 228)

- Small and Kazimi: morbidity from ozone, morbidity and mortality
  from particulate matter

- CEC: damage to human health (not including chronic health
  effects of long-term ozone exposure), materials, plants and
  animals (not including effects of acid)

- Sierra: acute health effects of ozone, health effects of
  photochemically generated PM and benzene[331]

Damage-Cost Estimates Compared with Control-Cost Estimates

Damage-cost estimates are generally substantially lower than
control-cost estimates for the same regions. This is hardly surprising
given the concepts and methods underlying the two types of estimates.
Damage-cost estimates will tend to underestimate actual pollution costs
because some types of damage are not included in the estimates (often
because of lack of sufficient information). Moreover, control costs--
even if well measured--may substantially overestimate the social
benefits of the pollution reduced by the controls. This is because the
pollution controls that are instituted result from regulatory goals and
procedures driven by the federal Clean Air Act, which emphasizes
reduction of pollution without consideration of cost. Thus, costs of
controls may rationally--from a legal, but not economic point of view--
exceed the social benefits of the controls.

---

[331]Sierra develops its estimates under the assumption that all of
damage it quantifies is attributable to ROG. It seems this assumption
is used to avoid underestimation of benefits of controls on refueling
and evaporative (i.e., ROG) emissions, the application for which the
Sierra benefit estimates were developed. This assumption tends to
overestimate the pollution costs of ROG and (implicitly) underestimate
damage due to NOx emissions. In using the Sierra results, we apply
their estimates of ROG damage and assume that NOx damage is zero.

Table 2.B-1

Estimates of Benefits of Reducing Emissions of Ozone Precursors

Air Basin Estimation Approach	Source of Estimate*	ROG cost estimate ($/ton)	NOx cost estimate ($/ton)	Current dollar basis
South Coast:				
Damage cost	NERA	2,860	5,050	$1991
Damage cost	Small and Kazimi	2,920	10,670	$1992
Damage cost	CEC	6,911	14,483	$1989
Damage cost	Sierra--overall	5,071	0	$1994(?)
Damage cost	Sierra--marginal	14,148	0	$1994(?)
Control cost	CAPUC	20,374	28,524	$1992
Control cost	SCAQMD	8,500	30,000	$1991
Control cost	CEC	18,900	26,400	$1989
Other Air Basins:				
Ventura-damage cost	CEC	286	1,647	$1989
Ventura-damage cost	Sierra--marginal	812	0	$1994(?)
Sacramento-damage cost	CEC	4,129	6,089	$1989
Sacramento-damage cost	Sierra--marginal	417	0	$1994(?)
Bay Area-damage cost	CEC	90	7,345	$1989
Bay Area-damage cost	Sierra--marginal	337	0	$1994(?)
San Diego-damage cost	CEC	98	5,559	$1989
San Diego-damage cost	Sierra--marginal	958	0	$1994(?)

Table 2.B-1 cont'd.

Air Basin Estimation Approach	Source of Estimate*	ROG cost estimate ($/ton)	NOx cost estimate ($/ton)	Current dollar basis
Ventura-control cost	CEC	21,100	16,500	$1989
Sacramento-control cost	CEC	9,100	9,100	$1989
Bay Area-control cost	CEC	10,200	10,400	$1989
San Diego-control cost	CEC	17,500	18,300	$1989

*Sources of estimates are:
- NERA (National Economic Research Associates, 1992)--reported in Hahn (1995, pp. 228-9)
- Small and Kazimi (1995)--baseline estimates from Table 5
- CEC (California Energy Commission) --CEC (1993, Table 4-1)
- CAPUC (California Public Utilities Commission)--reported in Fulmer and Bernow (1995, Table 8-5)
- Sierra Research (1995b)--marginal and overall benefit-effectiveness ratios from Tables 3-2 and 3-4; estimates based on zero ppm as threshold for ozone damage
- SCAQMD (South Coast Air Quality Management District, 1992)--as reported in Hahn (1995, p. 229)

Range of Assumed Emission Changes

The damage-cost estimates are not all based on variations in emissions in even the same general range. The latter distinction is discussed with the aid of Figure 2.B-1. In the figure, the daily level of emissions (tons of ROG+NOx, say) is measured on the horizontal axis. On the vertical axis we measure the total dollar value of damage per day due to the pollution created by those emissions. The bold curve is the "social costs of pollution" function; for each emission rate, we can read off this curve the daily pollution costs that would result from emissions generated at that rate. The curve is drawn using the standard assumption that each additional ton of emissions generated per day in an area adds more to pollution cost than did the previous ton.

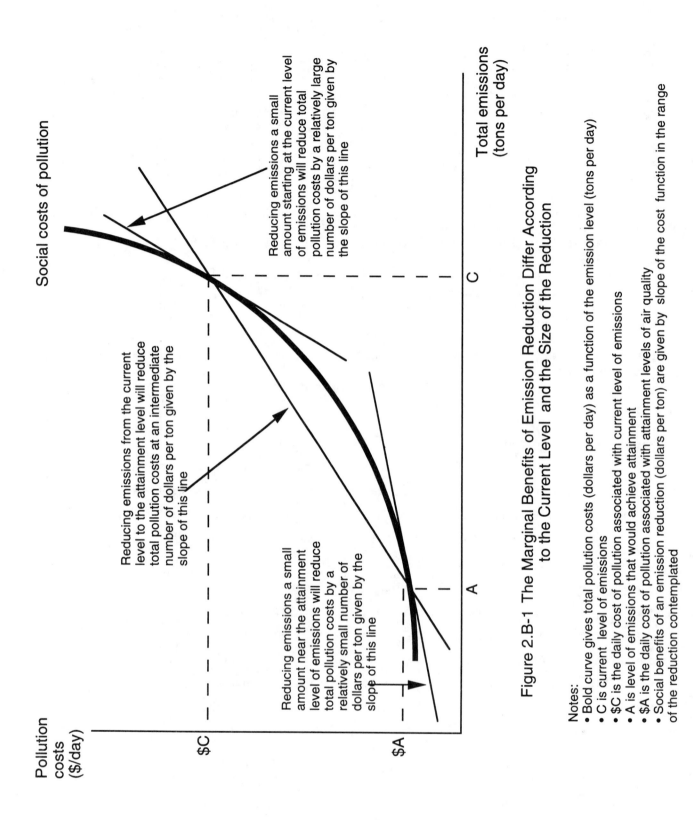

Social costs of pollution

Pollution costs ($/day)

Reducing emissions from the current level to the attainment level will reduce total pollution costs at an intermediate number of dollars per ton given by the slope of this line

Reducing emissions a small amount starting at the current level of emissions will reduce total pollution costs by a relatively large number of dollars per ton given by the slope of this line

Reducing emissions a small amount near the attainment level of emissions will reduce total pollution costs by a relatively small number of dollars per ton given by the slope of this line

$C

$A

C

A

Total emissions (tons per day)

Figure 2.B-1 The Marginal Benefits of Emission Reduction Differ According to the Current Level and the Size of the Reduction

Notes:
• Bold curve gives total pollution costs (dollars per day) as a function of the emission level (tons per day)
• C is current level of emissions
• $C is the daily cost of pollution associated with current level of emissions
• A is level of emissions that would achieve attainment
• $A is the daily cost of pollution associated with attainment levels of air quality
• Social benefits of an emission reduction (dollars per ton) are given by slope of the cost function in the range of the reduction contemplated

Two levels of emissions are delineated on the horizontal axis: C is the current emissions rate and A is the rate that would be necessary to achieve attainment with (federal, say) air quality standards. The corresponding levels of daily pollution damage are denoted by $C and $A. If we were to reduce emission rates from C to A, (we would achieve attainment, and) according to the figure pollution costs would fall by $C-$A per day. For this reduction in emissions, the dollar value per ton of emissions reduction would be ($C-$A)/(C tons - A tons) dollars of benefit (i.e., reduction in pollution cost) per ton. This rate can be read off the diagram as the slope of the line connecting the points on the curve corresponding to C and A. In contrast, suppose we were to reduce emissions by only a small amount starting at C. In that case dollar benefits per ton of emission reduction would be much higher (because of the assumption that pollution costs per ton get higher and higher as emission levels get higher). The benefits per ton for such a reduction would be measured by the slope of the line tangent to the social cost of pollution function above point C. Finally, for small reductions in emissions starting near A, dollar benefits per ton are relatively low, and can be measured from the figure as the slope of the line tangent to the curve above point A.

Thus, another source of difference between damage estimates in the table is the range of emission reduction assumed in forming the estimate. It is often not easy to tell what change in emissions is implicit in a damage estimation exercise. In fact, it often seems that information is combined from various (e.g., epidemiological) studies that reflect quite different levels of exposure to pollutants.[332] Small and Kazimi (1995, pp. 15-16) pay particular attention to this issue, and finesse it by assuming linearity of the relevant functions.[333] As reported in Table 2.B-1, Sierra (1995b) presents separate sets of estimates that involve different levels of emission reductions. In particular, their "marginal" and "overall" benefit-effectiveness ratios

---

[332]We have not reviewed the (very large) relevant literature in sufficient detail even to begin to sort this out.

[333] See, for example, the discussion in Small and Kazimi (1995, p. 21) of using estimates of Krupnick and Portney (1991) and Hall et al. (1992), which involve very large changes in pollution levels.

(BERs) are relevant to small and large changes in emissions from the status quo, respectively, as might result alternatively from a single regulation or an entire state implementation plan. (Sierra, 1995b, pp. 39-41.) As can be seen from Table 2.B-1, the marginal BER estimated for the South Coast by Sierra is almost three times as large as the estimated overall BER (i.e., $14,148/ton vs. $5,071/ton). In terms of the figure, the marginal BER might be interpreted as the slope of the tangent above C and the overall BER more like the slope of the line corresponding to emissions reduction from C to A.

South Coast Compared with Other Areas

Damage cost estimates per ton for the South Coast are much higher than those for other non-attainment areas in California. Since the South Coast has the worst air quality, these estimates provide some support for the view that the social cost of pollution function gets steeper (i.e., pollution causes increasing marginal damage) as the emissions rate gets higher.[334] Moreover, they suggest that some emission-reduction strategies that are economically worthwhile in the South Coast might not be economically worthwhile in other urban areas of California.

Similarity of Estimates

The variation in estimates in damage cost per ton for the South Coast is perhaps surprisingly small given the issues discussed above (i.e., differences in components of damage included and in the range of emission reduction implicit in the estimates). The largest damage-cost estimate is the Sierra marginal BER estimate, which should also be interpreted recalling that it is developed assuming that all costs are attributable to ROG (and implicitly that there is no damage due to NOx). Most important for our purposes is the fact that the ideas we develop in the text using estimates of the social costs of air pollution in California are broadly consistent with all of these estimates.

---

[334]They also reflect, however, the larger population exposed to pollution in the South Coast.

6.A SIERRA ESTIMATES OF INCREMENTAL COSTS OF TLEVS, LEVS, AND ULEVS

Sierra presents estimates of the total incremental costs of TLEVs, LEVs, and ULEVs over the cost of a Tier 0 vehicle and the incremental costs of a CA93 (same as Tier 1) vehicle over a Tier 0 vehicle (Sierra, 1994a, pp. 101). We subtract the incremental cost of a CA93 vehicle over a Tier 0 vehicle from the incremental costs of the low-emission vehicles over a Tier 0 vehicle to determine the incremental costs of the low-emission vehicles over a CA93 vehicle.

Sierra estimates incremental costs at production volumes equal to (1) California vehicle sales and (2) national vehicle sales. As shown in Table 6.A-1, incremental costs are between 10 and 35 percent lower at national volumes. Our analysis takes as given that twelve states in the northeast and the District of Columbia have adopted the California Low-Emission Vehicle Program (although only two have adopted the ZEV component of the program).[335] Judging by new-vehicle registrations by state in 1994, the combined sales of the twelve northeast states, the District of Columbia, and California, are 3.5 times the sales of California (*Automotive News*, May 24, 1995, p. 40). We thus use the Sierra estimates to estimate incremental costs at 3.5 California volume. We do this by linearly interpolating between the incremental cost at production volume equal to California sales (9.6 percent of national sales), and production volume equal to national sales. The resulting calculations are presented in Table 6.A-1.

Sierra does not directly report the breakdown of total incremental cost into fixed cost, variable cost, and dealer margin. Rather, it reports separate percentage breakdowns for TLEVs, LEVs, and ULEVs, but unfortunately, Sierra does not tie the percentage breakdowns to production volume. Applying these percentages to the incremental total costs is the only method available for decomposing total costs into fixed costs, variable costs, and dealer margin. The outcomes for 3.5

---

[335]The states are Connecticut, Delaware, Maine, Maryland, Massachusetts, New Hampshire, New Jersey, New York, Pennsylvania, Rhode Island, Vermont, and Virginia.

times California volume is reported in Table 6.1-2. These breakdowns should be used cautiously because the percentages should vary for different volume assumptions.

Table 6.A-1

Sierra Estimates of Total Incremental Costs of TLEVs, LEVs, and ULEVs Compared with 1993 California Vehicles (dollars per vehicle)

			ULEV	
	TLEV	LEV	4-cyl	6-cyl
Sierra manufacturer (discounted to 1993)				
California volume[a]	589	1,416	1,809	2,526
National volume[a]	393	1,018	1,395	1,956
3.5x CA volume[b]	538	1,312	1,701	2,377
Sierra best-case (discounted to 1993)				
California volume[a]	319	875	613	1,331
National volume[a]	200	631	466	1,203
3.5x CA volume[b]	288	812	575	1,298

[a]Sierra (1994a), p. 101

[b]Interpolated from estimates for California volume and national volume.

7.A COMPETITIVE, SHORT-RUN ANALYSIS OF MARKET EFFECTS OF THE NEW ICEV HARDWARE REGULATIONS

7.A.1 WHY FOCUS ON THE SHORT RUN?

We use a "short-run" competitive analysis to consider the effects of the new regulations on prices and quantities. What this means is that we consider effects during a time period shorter than it would take automobile manufacturers to adjust their production capacities, product offerings and dealer networks. We think of the short run as a period of at least several years.

In the short run, some costs are fixed or "sunk"--e.g., the costs of research, product development, plant, and equipment--and, hence, do not affect prices. A "long-run" analysis would be relevant to a time period long enough for every aspect of the business--production capacities, product offerings, dealer networks, and presence in the California market--to be adjusted.

Use of a long-run competitive model would predict that *all* cost increases due to the regulations would be passed on in prices (because companies would not be willing to invest further in serving the California market unless they expect to be able to cover their costs). We do not emphasize the long-run competitive interpretation for two reasons:

- The long run in the automobile industry would seem to involve many years, if not decades (and, as economists often remind each other: "in the long run we are all dead");
- The applicability of the long-run predictions of a competitive model to the California LDV market is equivocal because, for example, of the importance of (non-price) competition based on product styling, quality, innovation.

In sum, we think it very useful to apply a competitive model for a short-run analysis, but are much less sanguine about the applicability of a competitive model for a long-run analysis.

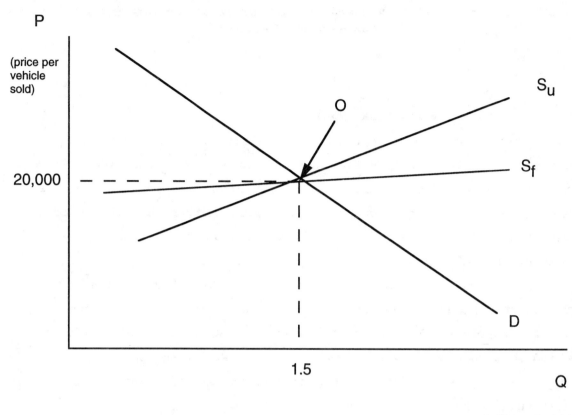

Figure 7.A-1

Short-Run Supply and Demand for New LDVs
Without the New ICEV Hardware Regulations

Note:
• Pertains to market for all LDVs (i.e., illustrates the "market interpretation")
• Q = quantity (in millions) of LDVs sold in California in a year
• P = (average) price ($/vehicle) of LDVs sold during the year
• D = demand curve without the new regulations
• S_f = relatively flat short-run supply function without the new regulations
• S_u = (distinctly) upward-sloping short-run supply function without the new regulations
• The two supply functions are alternative assumptions
• Point O is the competitive equilibrium point without the new regulations
• $20,000 = assumed average price of new LDVs in California without the new regulations
• 1.5 (million) = assumed quantity of new LDVs sold per year in California without the new regulations

7.A.2 SHORT-RUN PRICE AND QUANTITY DETERMINATION WITHOUT THE NEW REGULATIONS

Figure 7.A-1 depicts the short-run supply and demand conditions assumed to prevail in the entire California LDV market without the regulatory elements that require ICEV hardware improvements. These demand and supply conditions determine the total annual sales of LDVs in California and the (average) price of these vehicles in the absence of the new regulations.

We first discuss the supply and demand curves, then we consider how they are put together to determine the selling price that will prevail in the market and numbers of vehicles bought and sold (at that price). The discussion also provides segment-level interpretations. We then use this framework to characterize the market with the new regulations, thus allowing us to analyze how the new regulations affect market prices and quantities.

Demand. The demand curve (D) summarizes the market behavior of all potential buyers. This curve tells us for each potential price (measured on the vertical axis) the total number of vehicles (in the entire market or in a segment) that California buyers (individuals, households, fleets) will want to purchase if that price prevails in the market. As depicted in Figure 7.A-1, the demand curve slopes downward to reflect the standard assumption that the lower the price is--holding constant other factors that determine demand--the more vehicles buyers would be willing to purchase.

How much buyers respond to price. The steepness of the demand curve reflects the degree to which buyers in the California market are sensitive to price. In particular, the flatter this curve is, the more the quantity demanded falls in response to a particular price increase. Economists often find it useful to measure responsiveness of quantities to price in terms of *elasticities*. A demand elasticity, for example, measures the percentage decrease in quantity demanded that would result from a 1 percent increase in price.

To consider the effects of the new regulations quantitatively, we will have to put numbers on various parameters, including the elasticity of demand for new LDVs in the California market. Within the industry,

the elasticity of demand at the national market level is generally taken
to be very close to -1 (e.g., if the prices of all manufacturers were to
increase by 5 percent, all other factors held constant, industry
analysts would expect the number of vehicles sold nationwide to fall by
5 percent).

We take -1 as a lower bound (in absolute value) for the elasticity
of demand relevant for our purposes based on the following reasoning.
Many of the new regulations being analyzed apply only in California, so
they will tend to increase production costs for California vehicles more
than they will for vehicles produced for sale in other states.[336] Thus
we would expect the new regulations to have less effect on prices in
other states than in California. This means that as we consider the
responsiveness of California demanders to price increases in California,
we should be thinking in terms of prices in other states not rising
along with prices in California (or at least not as much). Since it is
possible for Californians to buy new vehicles outside the state,[337] we
would expect that buyers would be more responsive to price increases in

---

[336]Maximizing profits would lead manufacturers to incorporate
hardware modifications made in response to California regulations into
vehicles for sale outside of California, as well, when it is less costly
to do this than to produce different vehicles for sale inside and
outside of California. As long as vehicles sold in California under the
new regulations would have some hardware that is not incorporated in
vehicles for sale outside California, then production costs of vehicles
sold in California will increase more than for vehicles sold outside of
the state.

[337]There are some major disincentives to doing this, however. In
California, to register a vehicle with less than 7500 miles on it that
was purchased outside the state, the vehicle must meet California
certification standards and the buyer must pay California sales tax. In
addition, buying a vehicle outside the state involves time and
inconvenience (the more so the farther the buyer lives from the state
border). Many California residents may find it worthwhile to deal with
these impediments and buy a vehicle outside of California--for example,
buy a new vehicle and register it outside the state, bring it to
California, drive it for 7500 miles and then register it in California,
which requires passing I&M (but avoids the sales tax and the
certification requirement). Clearly, there is more incentive to do this
the larger the price premium is that one must pay to buy a vehicle in
California. It is unclear how much of this behavior we might reasonably
expect.

California than they would be if prices were rising in all states along with the prices in California.

We also consider an elasticity of -2. Elasticities of more than -2 would suggest that the possibility of buying new vehicles outside California would double the responsiveness of quantity demanded to price. An adjustment larger than this seems implausible.[338]

Supply. In a competitive model, the behavior of sellers (i.e., manufacturers and their dealers conceptualized as integrated entities) is represented by a market- (or segment-) level supply curve. This curve tells us for each potential price the total number of vehicles (in the market or a segment) that will be offered for sale by all manufacturers together if that price prevails in the market. The supply curve is the result of each company's choosing for each potential market price the production level that will maximize its own profits.

The position and slope of the supply curve is determined by the number of manufacturers and the costs to them of producing and selling additional LDVs in the California market--what economists call the *marginal* costs of LDVs. The basic idea is that when producers believe that their production or output levels will not affect the prevailing market price, they would be willing to produce and sell another LDV if and only if the selling price of that vehicle is at least as high as the extra cost of producing and selling the vehicle.

How much sellers respond to price. The slope of the supply curve plays an especially important role in the analysis because a fairly wide range of slopes is plausible. Figure 7.A-1 depicts two alternative supply curves: a distinctly upward sloping curve labeled S_u and a nearly flat one labeled S_f. Both supply curves incorporate the idea that more vehicles will be offered for sale if the selling price is higher. The two curves differ concerning how much the quantity offered for sale would increase in response to any particular increase in price: the flatter (more elastic) the supply curve, the more responsive is the industry-level quantity supplied to any particular increase in price.

---

[338]Because of the impediments to buying vehicles out of state and the fact that none of the major cities in California is nearby the border of another state.

In fact, the supply curve would be perfectly flat if the industry quantity supplied can be increased without increasing the marginal cost of producing and selling a vehicle in California. If production can be expanded for sales to the California market (generally in plants used to supply vehicles for many locations including California) without approaching planned or capacity production rates, then supply to California should be very elastic. In contrast, if expansion of production for the California market requires increases in marginal cost (for example, because assembly plants would need to operate overtime and pay premium wages), then the supply curve in the California market will be distinctly upward sloping. In short, if expanding production increases the cost of producing an additional vehicle, the market will have to offer manufacturers higher prices to induce them to increase the numbers of vehicles they will offer for sale.

How competitive markets determine short-run price and quantity.
Putting the supply and demand curves together (i.e., considering how buyer and seller behaviors interact in the market) allows us to determine the market price of each vehicle and the number of vehicles bought and sold. In a graphical representation of a competitive model like that in Figure 7.A-1, the market (or equilibrium) price and quantity can be found at the point where the supply and demand curve intersect--point O in Figure 7.A-1. (For convenience, Figure 7.A-1 is drawn so that this point is the same for either of the supply curves.) In the figure the equilibrium price and quantity are shown as $20,000 and 1.5 million vehicles, the values we use to represent the average price of LDVs and annual sales levels in California without the new regulations.

7.A.3 QUALITATIVE EFFECTS OF THE NEW REGULATIONS ON MARKET PRICES AND QUANTITIES

The ICEV hardware regulations affect the market price and quantity by affecting the costs of producing ICEVs. These cost increases imply (in terms of the model) that the supply curve with the regulations in place will shift upward by the amount that marginal production costs increase. Figure 7.A-2 analyzes the effects of such increases in marginal cost on market price and quantities.[339]

How cost increases affect supply. Figure 7.A-2 adds to the three curves in Figure 7.A-1 two supply curves that represent (cost and) supply conditions with the new regulations in place. The two new supply curves (labeled $S_{uw/}$ and $S_{fw/}$) are respectively the upward sloping and flat supply curves from Figure 7.A-1 each displaced upward by K dollars per vehicle.[340] The quantity K is generic notation for the increase-- which is assumed constant over vehicles--in the marginal cost of producing and selling a California ICEV associated with changes required to comply with the new regulations. Under the market interpretation of the model, K is the average, across all California LDVs, of the extra per-vehicle production cost incurred in the short run because of hardware modifications attributable to complying with the new regulations.[341]

Prices and quantities with the new regulations. In Figure 7.A-2, points U and F are the model's predicted equilibria with the new regulations in place, assuming alternatively that supply is relatively flat (point F) or supply is distinctly upward sloping (point U). The equilibrium prices and quantities with the new regulations in place under the alternative assumptions about the steepness of the supply curve are labeled ($P*_{fw/}$, $Q*_{fw/}$) and ($P*_{uw/}$, $Q*_{uw/}$). Comparing the equilibria with and without the regulations lets us predict how the new regulations will affect prices and quantities of new ICEV sales in California and how the sizes of the effects depend on the steepness of the supply curve, which reflects the value of the elasticity of supply.

---

[339]Again, because we focus on the short run, only variable costs of production are relevant to predicting price increases.

[340]I.e., the vertical distance between S_u and $S_{uw/}$ and between S_f and $S_{fw/}$ is exactly K for every value on the horizontal scale.

[341]In the figure, K appears to be large relative to the price of a vehicle; there is no quantitative significance to this, it is done merely to make it easy to see the qualitative implications of the analysis.

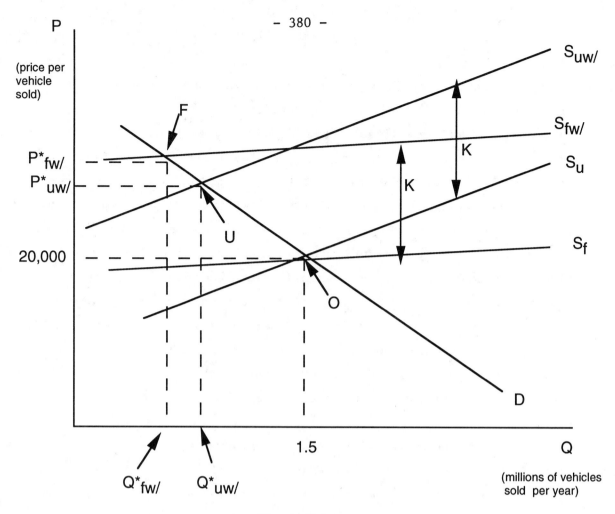

Figure 7.A-2

Effects of the New ICEV Hardware Regulations
on the Price and Sales of New LDVs in California

Notes:
• Situations with the new regulations are denoted by "w/"
• Q = quantity (in millions) of LDVs sold in California in a year
• P = (average) price ($/vehicle) of LDVs sold during the year
• D = demand curve both with and without the new regulations
• S_f = relatively flat short-run supply function without the new regulations
• S_u = (distinctly) upward-sloping short-run supply function without the new regulations
• K = increase in marginal cost due to the new regulations (assumed constant over units of production)
• $S_{fw/}$ = relatively flat supply function with the new regulations
• $S_{uw/}$ = (distinctly) upward-sloping supply function with the new regulations
• Point O is competitive equilibrium point without the new regulations
• Point F is competitive equilibrium point with the new regulations and relatively flat supply
• $P^*_{fw/}$ and Q^*_{fw} are predicted price and quantity with new regulations and relatively flat supply
• Point U is competitive equilibrium point with the new regulations and (distinctly) upward sloping supply
• $P^*_{uw/}$ and $Q^*_{uw/}$ are predicted price and quantity with new regulations and (distinctly) upward sloping supply

Qualitative effects on price and quantity. Some implications of the figure apply regardless of the size of K or the steepness of the supply or demand curve:

- The increase in marginal production cost will increase the price of new ICEVs in California
- The increase in marginal production cost will decrease the quantities of new ICEVs sold in California
- Profits of manufacturers and dealers will fall.

The first two predictions would result from the basic structure of the model as long as the demand curve is downward sloping and the supply curve is not exactly vertical.[342]

Profits--for both manufacturers and their California dealers--will tend to decrease for two reasons: increases in costs may not be completely passed on in prices and sales will fall because of the price increase.

How much of the increased cost of production should we expect the price increase to represent? How much should we expect sales of new LDVs to decrease in California? Given any assumed responsiveness of demand to price and the size of the cost increase, the sizes of these price and quantity effects depend on the steepness of the supply curve. Comparing points F and O provides predictions assuming that the supply curve is relatively flat (i.e., increases in production rates involve minor increases in marginal production costs), and comparing points U and O provides predictions assuming that the supply curve is relatively steep (i.e., increases in production rates to increase supply to California involve substantial increases in marginal production costs).

When the supply curve is relatively flat (point F), the increase in price is predicted to be larger than when the supply curve is relatively

---

[342]For example, the only ways--according to the model--that an increase in cost would not lead to an increase in price are: (i) if the demand curve were horizontal (i.e., demand were perfectly elastic), which would mean (totally implausibly) that an increase in price from the prevailing level would deter all potential California new LDV buyers from buying; or (ii) the supply curve were vertical (i.e., supply were perfectly inelastic), which would mean (also totally implausibly) that manufacturers would not be willing to expand production in response to a higher price in the market.

steep (point U); i.e., $P^*_{fw/} > P^*_{uw/}$). In the extreme, if the supply curve were completely flat (i.e., production can be expanded without any increase in marginal cost, which is not entirely implausible), the increase in cost of K dollars per LDV will result in an equal increase in price. (In common parlance, the entire cost increase will be passed on in price.)

Holding supply conditions constant, what would make effects of the new regulations on new LDV prices and quantities relatively large or small? For any given steepness of the supply curve:

- Holding demand conditions constant, the price increase and the quantity decrease will be larger the larger K is (i.e., the larger in the effect of the regulations on marginal production costs);

- Holding the cost increase constant, the price increase will be smaller and the quantity decrease larger, the more responsive demand is to price (i.e., the flatter is the demand curve).

The former prediction is a straightforward extension of the idea that it is the cost increase that is leading to the price and quantity effects of the new regulations. The later prediction reflects the common sense that a smaller portion of a cost increase will be "passed on" to buyers the more responsive they are to price increases (and the consequently larger effect on quantities).[343]

_____

[343]All of the price effects discussed here can be verified using the formula: $dP = (\kappa/(\kappa-\eta))K$, where dP represents the increase in price, K is the increase in marginal cost, κ is the elasticity of supply, and η is the elasticity of demand (which is defined to be negative). For example: i) if supply is perfectly elastic (i.e., κ is infinite), the increase in price equals the increase in cost as long as η is finite (i.e., demand is not infinitely elastic); ii) there will be a price increase unless supply is perfectly inelastic ($\kappa=0$) or demand is infinitely elastic (η is infinite); iii) otherwise the price increase will be between zero and the cost increase; iv) the price increase will be smaller, other things equal, the more elastic is demand; and v) the price increase will be larger, other things equal, the larger is the cost increase. (The formula can be derived, for example, along the lines of Garber and Klepper, 1980.)

7.B THE COURNOT MODEL AND SOME BASIC RESULTS[344]

The model. Suppose that there are only two firms competing in an LDV market segment--firms 1 and 2. Assume that they produce identical products and let the quantities each firm produces be denoted by q_1 and q_2, respectively. The price prevailing in the market--denoted by P-- depends on the total quantity offered for sale in the market: $Q = q_1 + q_2$. The demand curve is of the very simple linear form: $P(Q) = 1 - Q$. (note that if P > 1 the quantity demanded is zero.) Assume further that the firms each have constant marginal costs of production (both less than one) denoted by c_1 and c_2, respectively.   Under the Cournot assumption about strategic behavior, each firm maximizes its profits assuming that the other firm holds its output fixed at some conjectured level. An equilibrium (price and pair of quantities) has the property that the quantity conjectures of the two firms are consistent with profit-maximizing behavior by both firms.

Some basic results. In this very simple setup, the outputs of the two firms are given by

$$q^*_1 = (1/3) \ (1 - 2c_1 + c_2) \text{ and } q^*_2 = (1/3) \ (1 - 2c_2 + c_1).$$

Inspection of these equations shows that each firm will produce more output the lower is its cost and the higher is its rival's cost. The equilibrium market price (determined using the demand curve and the equilibrium market quantities q^*_1 and q^*_2) is given by:

$$P = (1/3)(1 + c_1 + c_2).$$

Thus, the market price is a compromise between the cost levels of the two firms.

Effects of increasing costs. Interpret the results above as giving price and firm quantities without a set of regulations. Now consider

---

[344]The development here borrows liberally from Tirole (1988, pp. 218-220).

regulations that increase the marginal production costs of the two firms. Assume that the firms incur compliance costs (increases in marginal costs due to the new regulations) of K_1 and K_2, respectively. Then, using the equations for q^*_1 and q^*_2 given above, it is easy to see that if neither firm's cost increase is at least twice as large as the other's, then the output of both firms fall. Using the price equation above, it follows that the increase in price is given by

$$DP = (1/3)(K_1 + K_2).$$

Finally, it can be shown that the profits of each firm decline because of the cost increases unless one firm's cost increase is two or more times as large as the cost increase of the other (in which case the profits of the low-cost complier increase).

7.C A MODEL OF PRODUCT DIFFERENTIATION AND SOME BASIC RESULTS[345]

The model. Suppose that there are only two firms competing in a market segment--firms 1 and 2. They offer products that are different from the point of view of buyers, whose tastes differ. Each firm charges the same price to all of its customers--firm 1 charges p_1 and firm 2 charges p_2--and attracts customers in competition with the other seller according to how each potential buyer evaluates the relative qualities of the two products (according to his or her personal tastes) and the prices set by the two sellers.

We need a way of representing the idea that the products offered by the firms are valued differently by different buyers. This is done by assuming that for each potential buyer there is a product variant that is ideal according to his or her tastes, and the quality of a product is judged by each buyer in terms of the distance between the actual quality and that buyer's ideal quality. To make these notions tangible, it is helpful to think explicitly in terms of geographic location of buyers and sellers. The model can be interpreted much more generally, but more abstractly.

Specifically, assume that buyers live at locations spread evenly over a street that is one mile long, and that the two sellers have stores located at two different places on the street. In order to buy from a seller, a buyer must visit a firm's store and doing so costs a buyer more the farther the buyer must travel from his or her residence to the store's location. (So, in the geographic-location interpretation of the model, what makes buyers differ in their valuations of the two products is that they live different distances from the places where they would have to go to buy the products.) Assume that if a buyer must travel distance X to buy from a seller, that the buyer experiences a cost of tX^2.

---

[345]The development here borrows liberally from Tirole (1988, pp. 279-281), but generalizes the results reported there to allow firms to have different levels of cost.

Assume that firm 1 is located a distance of $a < 1$ miles from the western end of the street and firm 2 is located $b < 1$ miles from the eastern end of the street. (E.g., if firm 1 is 1/4 mile from the eastern end of the street, $a = .25$.) Assume also that firm 1 is located to the east of firm 2.[346] Assume that the marginal cost of the product to firm 1 is c_1 and the marginal cost of the product to firm 2 is c_2.

To keep things simple, assume that each buyer will buy one unit of the good (one vehicle) from one of the two sellers. Each buyer will buy from the seller who offers the best package of location and price.

Here sellers compete by setting prices. The assumption about strategic behavior is that each firm chooses its price to maximize its profits assuming that the other firm holds its price fixed at some conjectured level. An equilibrium (pair of prices and quantities) has the property that the price conjectures of the two firms are consistent with profit-maximizing behavior by both firms.

Some basic results. In this model, the equilibrium prices of the two firms are given by

$$p^*_1 = (4/3)(a + .5 b)tk + tk^2 + (2/3)c_1 + (1/3)c_2 \quad \text{and}$$
$$p^*_2 = (4/3)(b + .5 a)tk + tk^2 + (2/3)c_2 + (1/3)c_1$$

where $k = 1-a-b$. The first two terms of these equations capture how pricing is affected by the locations of the two stores (a and b) and the travel costs of the customers (t)--which determine the relative attractiveness of their products given the distributions of customer locations or tastes. Our focus is on how costs (c_1 and c_2) affect pricing, and these effects are captured in the last two terms of each expression.

It can also be shown that the equilibrium quantities sold by the two firms are given by:

$$q_1^* = a + k/2 + (p_2-p_1)/2tk, \quad \text{and}$$
$$q_2^* = b + k/2 + (p_1-p_2)/2tk.$$

---

[346]This means that $a < 1 - b$.

Effects of increasing costs. Interpret the pricing equations above as applying in the absence of the new regulations (i.e., c_1 and c_2 are the firm's marginal costs without the regulations). Now consider regulations that increase the marginal production costs of the two firms by K_1 and K_2, respectively. Then, using the equations for p^*_1 and p^*_2 given above, it can be seen that:

- if both firms have the same cost of compliance (i.e., $K_1 = K_2$), then the two firms raise their prices by the same amount[347]
- if compliance costs are not identical, the firm with the higher compliance cost will raise price more than its rival

To see what happens to sales of each firm, use the equations for equilibrium quantities to conclude that:

- If both firms have the same cost of compliance, their quantities do not change;
- Otherwise, the firm with the larger cost of compliance will lose sales relative to its rival.

Thus this model suggests the conclusions summarized in the text.[348]

---

[347]The results also imply that the price increases are exactly equal to the cost increases, but this prediction is not emphasized because it is sensitive to the (convenient, but not at all substantively attractive) assumption that all buyers buy one unit of the product no matter what the prices are. In a model where buyers can react to higher prices by not buying at all (as in the previous two models), we would not expect cost increases to be fully transmitted into price increases.

[348]Because of the assumption that total market demand does not depend on prices, the model cannot address the effects of the regulations on sales of LDVs (but the conclusion that prices will increase is suggestive of decreases in sales) or on sellers' profits. The analysis in no way contradicts these conclusions.

9.A EFFECTS OF A LARGE, ONGOING AVR PROGRAM ON VEHICLE MARKETS

Most discussions or proposals for AVR programs assume that to be eligible for scrappage under the program, a vehicle must be at least a certain age (e.g., 12 or more years old); we refer to vehicles that are old enough to qualify for the program as "age-eligible" vehicles. AVR programs as implemented or proposed generally have other eligibility criteria such as having been registered in the region for the previous two years, being in running order, having recently failed an I&M inspection, having received an I&M waiver, or having relatively high actual or suspected emissions rates based on remote sensing.

An ongoing AVR program, like the one described in the state implementation plan, involves purchase and scrappage of vehicles for several successive years, and the operation of the program in a particular year affects the market environment in which the program operates in later years. In particular, taking older vehicles off the road in the present decreases--other things equal--the number of older vehicles on the road in the future and thereby affects the pool of older vehicles on which the AVR program operates in the future.

The age-eligible vehicle market. To begin to analyze the market effects of an AVR program, we consider first the relevant older-vehicle market in the South Coast in a particular year, which we refer to generically as "year T." The commodity whose market is studied in detail is age-*eligible* vehicles--that is, the market under consideration is the South Coast market for vehicles that meet the AVR program age criterion for scrappage in year T, regardless of whether they meet other eligibility criteria. We assume that, except for different emissions rates, these vehicles are identical in the eyes of buyers and sellers and hence all sell for the same price.

The measure of quantity in this analysis is *not* a number of vehicles bought and sold. It is, rather, the *absolute number or stock* of vehicles in the market during the period. This quantity concept is used because a primary interest is emissions from age-eligible vehicles, which depend on the number of age-eligible vehicles on the road and the number of age-eligible vehicles scrapped, regardless of whether these vehicles are bought and sold during the period.

Vehicles are considered to be in the market for age-eligible vehicles in year T if and only if:

- They are in use in the South Coast at the beginning of year T and remain in use in the South Coast during the year, or

- They are purchased from an owner in the South Coast and scrapped in the South Coast (either as part of the program or commercially), or

- They are purchased from an owner outside the South Coast and used during the year in the South Coast, or

- They are purchased from an owner outside the South Coast and scrapped in the South Coast during the year (presumably by commercial scrap yards because most AVR programs would not purchase a vehicle that was not in the region at the beginning of the year)

In sum, vehicles in the market under consideration in year T are age-eligible in that year and may have started the year either inside or outside the South Coast, but all end the year in the South Coast. Such vehicles can end the year in two situations: "in service" or "scrapped."

The quantity of vehicles in the market--i.e., the number in the South Coast (in service or scrapped) at the end of the year--is denoted as Q_e (the e denotes "(age)-eligible"), and the price of these vehicles is denoted P_e. The definitions of suppliers and demanders in this market are more subtle than in a new-vehicle market. In a new vehicle market, suppliers are potential or actual sellers and demanders are potential or actual buyers. This is not the case in a used-vehicle market (as treated here); the essential difference is that to understand a used-vehicle market we must deal with the fact that consumers start the period with stocks of the commodity (used vehicles). We address this complication as follows.

By definition, suppliers in this market either:

- Sell age-eligible vehicles to buyers in the South Coast, or
- Start the year with an age-eligible vehicle in the South Coast and keep it in the South Coast.

Suppliers in the second category are not sellers; they can be thought of as supplying vehicles to themselves during the year.

By definition, demanders in this market either:

- Buy a vehicle (that began the year inside or outside the South Coast), and either keep it in service in the South Coast or scrap it in the South Coast;
- Start the year with an age-eligible vehicle in the South Coast and keep it in the South Coast.

Demanders in the second category are one and the same as suppliers in the second category of suppliers; viewed as demanders, they can be thought of as demanding vehicles from themselves during the year.

Price and quantity effects of the AVR program. The market for age-eligible vehicles is depicted in Figure 9.A-1 with quantity measured horizontally and price measured vertically. The figure depicts the market both with and without the AVR program.

Demand conditions without the program are summarized by the line labeled $D_{Tw/o}$. As in the case of the competitive analysis of new ICEV markets in Section 7.2, the slope of the supply curve (elasticity of supply) plays a crucial role in the analysis. In the figure, we consider (as we did in Appendix 7.A) two alternative assumptions about supply conditions: S_{Tf} and S_{Tu} are respectively a relatively flat and a distinctly upward-sloping supply function for age-eligible vehicles. Using either supply function, point O is the equilibrium point in the market in the absence of the AVR program. (This assumption is made to simplify the diagram.)

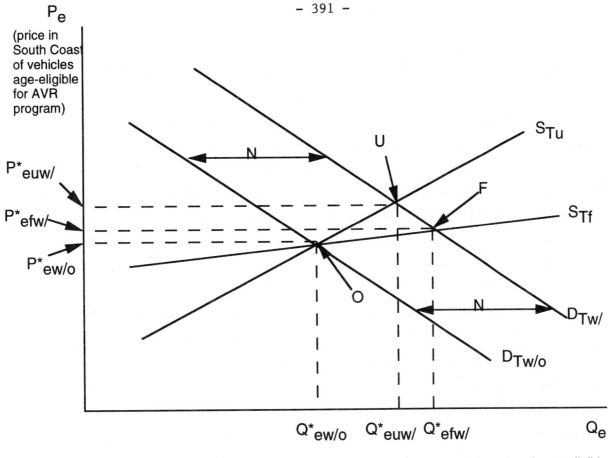

Figure 9.A-1

Year T Prices and Quantities in South Coast of Vehicles
That Are Age-Eligible for AVR Program With and Without Program

Notes:
• Situations with and without AVR program in South Coast denoted by "w/" and "w/o" respectively
• Q_e = quantity of age-eligible vehicles in South Coast in year T (number in service plus number scrapped)
• P_e = South Coast price ($/vehicle) of each age-eligible vehicle in year T
• $D_{Tw/o}$ = demand for age-eligible vehicles in year T without AVR program
• AVR program assumed to buy and scrap N vehicles in year T
• $D_{Tw/}$ = demand for age-eligible vehicles in year T with AVR program (quantity demanded is N vehicles more at every price than without the program)
• Supply of age-eligible vehicles is from vehicles in South Coast at beginning of year T and vehicles brought in during year
• S_{Tf} = relatively flat supply function with and without AVR program
• S_{Tu} = (distinctly) upward-sloping supply function with and without AVR program
• Point O is equilibrium point without AVR program
• $P^*_{ew/o}$ and $Q^*_{ew/o}$ are price and quantity of age-eligible vehicles without AVR program
• Point F is equilibrium point with AVR program and relatively flat supply
• $P^*_{efw/}$ and Q^*_{efw} are predicted price and quantity of age-eligible vehicles with AVR program and relatively flat supply
• Point U is equilibrium point with AVR program and (distinctly) upward sloping supply
• $P^*_{euw/}$ and Q^*_{euw} are predicted price and quantity of age-eligible vehicles with AVR program and upward sloping supply

How does an AVR program affect this market? The AVR program
introduces a new set of demanders in the market who buy vehicles with
the intention of scrapping or retiring them. Assume that the program
is designed to buy and scrap N age-eligible vehicles in year T.
Assume further that the program succeeds in doing this.[349] (For
example, in the program described in the state implementation plan, N
is 75,000 vehicles starting in 1999, and we are assuming that under
the program 75,000 vehicles will be purchased and scrapped in the
year under consideration.) In the figure the demand for age-eligible
vehicles with the program in place--denoted $D_{Tw}/$--then involves
quantities demanded at every price that are N vehicles higher than
without the program. (I.e., the demand curve with the program lies N
units to the right of the demand curve without the program.)

How does the program (i.e., this assumed shift in demand) affect
prices and quantities in this market? To see this we compare the
equilibrium without the program (point O) to the equilibrium with the
program. The equilibrium point with the program is U assuming that
the supply curve is distinctly upward sloping and is F assuming that
the supply function is relatively flat. In either case we conclude
that the program:[350]

- Increases the price of age-eligible vehicles;
- Increases the quantity of age-eligible vehicles in the
  region by less than N units.

The first conclusion has implications for projecting program
costs: estimation of the necessary bounty level to attract the target
number of vehicles should consider the price prevailing in the
presence of the program, not the price in the absence of attempts to

---

[349]We do not analyze how many of the vehicles scrapped in the AVR
program would have been scrapped even in the absence of the program.
This is a very important issue in designing and evaluating AVR programs,
but it is not crucial to the issues explored with our model: the
potential for price increases and drawing older vehicles into the South
Coast.

[350]Only if the supply curve is vertical (perfectly inelastic) or
horizontal (perfectly elastic) does the model predict a pure price or
pure quantity effect (respectively). We discuss the latter situation
below.

purchase a large number of vehicles. The second conclusion must be interpreted with special care. Recall that quantities in the market include vehicles in service and vehicles that are scrapped, and that these vehicles started the year in either the South Coast or outside the region. The number starting in the South Coast is fixed at the beginning of the year. The predicted increase in quantity, then, is the number of vehicles drawn into the region because of the AVR program and includes the N vehicles scrapped in the program. Since the increase in quantity is less than N (as can be seen by inspection of the figure, recalling that the horizontal distance between the two demand functions is exactly N vehicles), we conclude that the program draws less than N vehicles into the region and reduces the number of age-eligible vehicles in service (which is the market quantity with the program minus N).

Note further that:

- The increase in price is larger the steeper is the supply function;

- The increase in quantity is smaller the steeper is the supply function.

Because the increase in quantity due to the program includes a fixed number (N) of scrapped vehicles, the decrease in the number of age-eligible vehicles in service in the South Coast in year T will be larger the steeper is the supply function.

Consideration of an extreme (i.e., limiting) case is instructive. Suppose that the supply function were completely flat (horizontal), as is almost the case with S_{Tf}. In this case:

- There would be no increase in price;

- The increase in quantity would be exactly N vehicles;

- The program would have no effect whatever on the *number of age-eligible vehicles in service* in the South Coast in the year, even though the program is assumed to succeed in purchasing and scrapping N age-eligible vehicles. (This does not mean, however, that the program cannot have any effect on emissions, because (e.g.) the emissions levels of the vehicles scrapped need not be the same as those of the vehicles drawn into the region.)

This limiting case suggests that if the supply function were almost horizontal (very elastic), then the program would have almost no effect on the number of age-eligible vehicles in service in the South Coast in the year even though the program is assumed to succeed in purchasing and scrapping N age-eligible vehicles. This is because when supply is very elastic, no price increase is needed to draw vehicles into the region. Thus, as suggested above, the slope of the supply curve is indeed a crucial issue, and we should explore the conditions under which the supply function is relatively flat or relatively steep.

Are price or quantity effects likely to be more pronounced? The slope of the supply curve tells us how responsive the quantity of age-eligible vehicles supplied--to remain in service or be scrapped in the South Coast--is to the price in the South Coast. Age-eligible vehicles supplied in the South Coast must start the year either in the South Coast or outside the South Coast. The number that begin the year in the South Coast is a constant (when we are considering the effects of the operation of the program for a single year, as we are at the present). Thus the responsiveness of quantity (defined as we have defined it) supplied to price in a particular year is determined by the extent to which owners of age-eligible vehicles that begin the year *outside* the South Coast require higher prices to sell more of their vehicles in the South Coast.[351]

We would expect that if there were to be a significant inflow of vehicles into the South Coast, it would be accomplished largely by used-vehicle wholesalers responding to the realization that a profit can be made by buying older vehicles outside the South Coast,

---

[351]Nothing in the analysis denies or contradicts the fact that some AVR program participants will replace their vehicles with newer--or even new--vehicles. One factor that determines the extent to which older vehicles from outside the South Coast are drawn into the South Coast (presuming *some* price increase is necessary to attract them) is the preferences of owners for newer vs. older vehicles (i.e., the extent to which vehicles of different age groups are viewed as substitutes), which is reflected in the elasticity or slope of the demand curve.

transporting them to the South Coast, and selling them there.[352] For this activity to be profitable, the price of a vehicle must be higher in the South Coast than outside the area, and the price differential must be enough to cover the costs of buying vehicles outside the South Coast, transporting them to the South Coast, and selling them.

What does this all imply about whether the supply function is likely to be steep or flat? In any year of the program, supply would be very flat (elastic) if and only if there are 75,000 age-eligible vehicles available from outside the South Coast to be shipped into the South Coast in response to a quite minor increase in price. Is this plausible?

In the absence of the program, prices inside and outside the South Coast would be expected to be in balance (or equilibrium) with each other in the sense that there is no profit to be made by shipping vehicles in or out. In the first year of the program, it might be plausible for 75,000 vehicles to be available for shipping into the South Coast in response to a small price increase in the South Coast because there might be 75,000 such vehicles in counties bordering or otherwise quite nearby the South Coast--i.e., vehicles that could be brought into the South Coast at very low cost.

However, as years pass it seems likely that: a) shipping of vehicles into the South Coast from nearby areas in previous years will increase prices in those areas, thus requiring a larger price increase in the South Coast to attract more of them; and b) attracting vehicles into the South Coast from more distant locations will require higher prices in the South Coast because the transport cost will be higher the farther vehicles must be shipped.[353] Our

---

[352]The possibilities of owners bringing vehicles into the South Coast to sell them themselves or South Coast residents going outside the region to buy vehicles are also real. The basic economic considerations emphasized in the text apply equally to individuals bringing vehicles into the region. The text focuses on wholesalers for concreteness and simplicity in exposition.

[353]An additional factor supporting this conclusion pertains to vehicles that might be shipped into the South Coast from outside California: used vehicles brought into California must pay a $300 fee and pass an I&M test to be registered in the state.

conclusion, then, is that the supply function might be extremely elastic only during the early years of a large, ongoing AVR program in the South Coast--if at all--and in the later years of the program supply might be considerably less elastic than in the early years. Thus, even if the program does not have appreciable effects on prices of older vehicles in early years it may nonetheless have substantial price effects in later years. The good news is that the more price rises, the less in-migration tends to nullify the decrease in the stock of old vehicles caused by the AVR program.

There is another reason to predict that effects on the prices of older vehicles will grow over time. To the extent that the AVR program in any year scraps more vehicles than are attracted into the South Coast, the program reduces the stock of age-eligible vehicles with which the South Coast begins the next year. In terms of the supply and demand analysis, what this means is that the fact that the program has operated in the past decreases the supply (shifts the supply curve to the left) from where it would have been in the absence of the program, and decreases in supply tend to produce increases in price.

Effects on prices of newer vehicles. The AVR program may also be expected to increase the prices of vehicles that are too new to be age-eligible for the AVR program. We would expect a large, on-going AVR program to increase prices of newer used vehicles to some (unknown, perhaps small) extent, and have little if any effect on new vehicle prices.

If the AVR program increases prices for age-eligible vehicles-- and we have suggested reasons to expect this to happen--this will tend to increase the demand for newer used vehicles (which are substitutes for age-eligible vehicles). We would expect the supply of newer used vehicles to be more elastic than for age-eligible ones because the costs of bringing used vehicles of any age into the South Coast should be similar but any such cost represents a smaller percentage of the price of a newer vehicle. Thus we might expect some, perhaps minor, effects of the AVR on the prices of newer used vehicles. If price increases for newer used vehicles are relatively

minor, this suggests relatively small increases in demand for new
vehicles because newer used vehicles are closer substitutes for new
vehicles than are older used vehicles. With relatively small
increases in demand for new vehicles and--as discussed in Section
7.2--relatively elastic supply of new vehicles, we would not expect
prices of new vehicles to increase much, if at all.

10.A   SIMULATION OF EV INCREMENTAL LIFETIME OPERATING COSTS

In this appendix we first describe how we calculate incremental vehicle operating costs for a given set of parameter values. We then describe how we estimate the distribution of incremental operating costs given assumptions about the probability distributions about the values of the underlying parameters. For comparison with the distribution reported in Section 10.2 when the parameters are uniformly distributed, we conclude by reporting the distribution when the parameters follow normal and triangular distributions.

10.A.1 CALCULATION OF INCREMENTAL EV LIFETIME OPERATING COST

We calculate incremental electric vehicle lifetime operating costs using the following equations:

(1) $$\text{EV incremental operating cost} = \sum_{t=1}^{12} B^{t-1}(ev_t - gv_t)$$

(2) $ev_t = m_t(elec/eveff + gvrm*evrmfac) + battery_t$

(3) $gv_t = m_t(gas/gveff + gvrm)$

where

elec =	cost of electricity in \$/kwh,
eveff =	EV efficiency (wall to wheels) in mi/kwh,
evrmfac =	EV repair and maintenance costs as a fraction of ICEV repair and maintenance costs,
gas =	gasoline cost in \$/gallon,
gveff =	ICEV efficiency in miles per gallon
gvrm =	ICEV repair and maintenance costs (\$0.029 per mile)
m_t =	miles traveled in year t
B =	discount factor (1/(1+.04))
$battery_t$ =	battery purchase cost in year t.

The value for ICEV repair and maintenance costs (\$0.029 per mile) is taken from CARB (1994b), "Present Value Analysis" appendix. We select a

4 percent discount rate because it is the midpoint of the 3 to 5 percent range for discount rates found in the studies reviewed.

The vehicles are assumed to last 12 years and accumulate a total mileage of 129,000 as shown in Table 10.A-1 (the mileage time profile used in CARB (1994b), "Present Value Analysis" appendix).

We assume that two battery packs of equal cost are required during the vehicle lifetime: one when the car is purchased and the second at the beginning of year 6 when roughly half of the lifetimes vehicle miles have been accumulated. Battery costs in year 1 and year 6 are:

(4) $battery_1 = (129{,}000 \text{ miles/eveff})*chgeff*lifecost/2$

(5) $battery_6 = (129{,}000 \text{ miles/eveff})*chgeff*lifecost/2$

where

    chgeff =   efficiency of battery charging system (0.8),

    lifecost =   battery cost per kwh delivered ($/kwh delivered)

The total number of kwh required from the battery is determined by dividing lifetime vehicle miles (129,000) by the electric vehicle efficiency (wall to wheels) and then adjusting for charging losses (20 percent). This adjustment is required because the number of kwh needed from the battery is determined by battery-to-wheel efficiency, not wall-to-wheel efficiency. Multiplying the kwh required by each of the two batteries by the battery cost per kwh delivered produces the cost of each battery.

Table 10.A-1

**Mileage Accrued by EVs and ICEVs
by Year**

Year	Mileage
1	14,000
2	13,000
3	13,000
4	12,000
5	12,000
6	11,000
7	10,000
8	10,000
9	9,000
10	9,000
11	8,000
12	8,000
Total	129,000

Note that by specifying cost in terms of $/kwh we make no explicit assumptions about vehicle range. Vehicle range does affect the number and timing of battery-pack purchases during an EV's lifetime. It thus affects the sum of discounted battery costs (although it does not affect the total nominal battery costs given an assumption about battery cost in $/kwh delivered).

To give some idea of how different patterns of battery replacement during an EV's lifetime would affect discounted lifetime operating costs, we compared discounted battery costs for different assumed battery replacement patterns holding other factors constant. Assuming two battery packs are purchased causes discounted battery pack costs to be approximately 10 percent lower than they would be if only one pack were required using a 4 percent discount rate. Increasing the number of battery packs above two does not cause discounted costs to fall a great deal more: the discounted costs fall about another 5 percent when the number of packs required increases to 5. It is very unlikely that more than 5 packs would be required during 129,000 mile vehicle lifetime. Batteries account for 50 to 65 percent of EV operating costs, which attenuates the effect of battery pack replacement pattern on overall EV lifetime operating costs.

10.A.2 PROBABILITY DISTRIBUTION FOR INCREMENTAL EV OPERATING COSTS

In Section 10.2, we developed ranges for the values of five key parameters that enter into the calculation of incremental EV lifetime operating costs:

- EV efficiency,
- battery cost per kwh delivered,
- EV repair and maintenance cost relative to ICEVs,
- gasoline cost, and
- electricity cost.

We assume that these five parameters are statistically independent and alternatively follow three distributions over these intervals: uniform, triangular, and normal. In the uniform distribution each parameter has equal probability of being in any subinterval of the parameter range of fixed width. In the triangular case, the probability density for each parameter increases linearly from zero at the lower endpoint of its range until the midpoint of the range and the decreases linearly to zero at the upper endpoint. For the normal distribution, we center the distribution at the midpoint of the interval and assume that there is 5 percent probability that the parameter is below the lower endpoint and 5 percent probability that it is above the upper endpoint (we can calculate the variance of the distribution given these assumptions).

We use a modified numerical integration technique with a trapezoidal rule to approximate the distribution of incremental EV operating costs given the distributions of the five underlying parameters. To do this we divide each parameter interval into N subintervals of equal probability. Using available time and computing resources, we set N=6.[354] We then evaluate incremental operating costs for every combination (there are N^5) of the subintervals. Because the parameters are independently distributed, each of the combinations has equal probability. The technique is called trapezoidal because the function is evaluated at the 50th percentile of each parameter subinterval.

---

[354]Raising N to 10 affected the 5th and 95th percentiles of incremental operating costs by less than 2 percent when the parameters were uniformly distributed.

10.A.3 INCREMENTAL EV OPERATING COST WHEN PARAMETERS FOLLOW NORMAL AND TRIANGULAR DISTRIBUTIONS

Table 10.A-2 reports the distribution of incremental operating costs between 1998 and 2002 excluding gasoline taxes when the parameters follow normal or triangular distributions. These can be compared to the distribution in Table 10.2-7 when the uniform parameter distributions are used. We report results for the distribution only out to the 5th and 95th percentiles, because accuracy of the method decreases beyond these ranges.[355]

Table 10.A-2

Incremental EV Operating Costs Excluding Gasoline Taxes Between 1998 and 2002 for Normal and Triangular Distributions of Parameter Values
(dollars per vehicle)

	Passenger Car		Pickup or Minivan	
Percentile	Normal	Triangular	Normal	Triangular
5	2,997	4,251	3,540	5,071
10	3,806	4,828	4,557	5,856
15	4,419	5,263	5,328	6,441
20	4,933	5,627	6,003	6,917
25	5,386	5,950	6,615	7,372
30	5,804	6,247	7,188	7,793
50	7,342	7,341	9,324	9,323
70	9,003	8,491	11,796	11,028
75	9,504	8,827	12,537	11,528
80	10,071	9,206	13,430	12,115
85	10,748	9,650	14,484	12,786
90	11,622	10,208	15,901	13,672
95	12,959	11,040	17,934	14,926

---

[355]For uniform and triangular distributions, one can approximate percentile values farther out in the tails by linearly interpolating between the function values at the 5th (95th) percentile and the value of the function when all parameters are set at the lower end (upper end) of their ranges.

10.B. CALCULATION OF ELECTRIC VEHICLE NARROW COST EFFECTIVENESS

The narrow cost effectiveness ratio for electric vehicles sold between 1998 and year tau ($NCER_\tau$) is the ratio of the lifetime discounted costs and the discounted emission reductions of the vehicle sold:

$$(1) \qquad NCER_\tau = \frac{\displaystyle\sum_{t=1998}^{\tau} \beta^{t-1995} C_t}{\displaystyle\sum_{t=1998}^{\tau} \beta^{t-1995} E_t}, \qquad\qquad \tau = 2010, 2020, \infty$$

where

β = discount factor ($1/(1+$discount rate$)$),

C_t = lifetime incremental costs of EVs sold in year t discounted to year t (dollars),

E_t = lifetime ROG + NOx emission reductions of vehicles sold in year t discounted to year t (tons).

NCER is thus in units of \$/(ton ROG+NOx). We first describe the calculations that determine discounted incremental costs then turn to the calculations for discounted emission reductions.

10.B.1 INCREMENTAL ELECTRIC VEHICLE COSTS

The incremental costs of an electric vehicle sold in year t over a comparable ICEV sold in the same year are:

$(2) \quad C_t \qquad = \quad (incvar_t + incop_t)*evsales_t + fixed_t$

$(3) \quad evsales_t \quad = \quad mandate_t*sales$

where

$incvar_t$ = incremental variable production cost of EV over variable production cost of comparable ICEV in year t (\$ per vehicle),

$$incop_t \quad = \quad \text{incremental lifetime operating cost of an EV sold in year t over a comparable ICEV discounted to year t (\$ per vehicle).}$$

$$fixed_t \quad = \quad \text{fixed costs of EV program in year t (dollars)}$$

$$evsales_t \quad = \quad \text{EV sales in year t (vehicles),}$$

$$mandate_t \quad = \quad \text{EV mandate percentage in year t (percent of total light-duty vehicle sales),}$$

$$sales \quad = \quad \text{total annual light-duty vehicle sales (vehicles per year).}$$

Total annual light-duty vehicle sales are held constant at 2.48 million units throughout the analysis. This corresponds to 1994 LDV sales in California, Massachusetts, and New York. Incremental operating costs are incurred over the life of the vehicle, and then discounted back to the time of sale (year t) for inclusion in Equation (2). We discuss incremental variable production costs, fixed costs, and incremental operating costs in turn.

Incremental Variable Production Costs

During the first five years of the mandate, incremental EV variable production costs per vehicle are set to a fixed level. This value is specified in each simulation. After 2002, incremental EV variable production costs are determined by:

$$(4) \quad \ln(evar_t) \quad = \quad (\ln(rate)/\ln(2)) * \ln(N_t) + C_0$$

$$(5) \quad incrvar_t \quad = \quad evar_t - gvar \qquad \text{if } evar_t >= gvar$$
$$\qquad\qquad\qquad\quad = \quad 0 \qquad\qquad\qquad \text{if } evar_t < gvar$$

where

$$evar_t \quad = \quad \text{total EV variable costs predicted by experience curve,}$$

$$rate \quad = \quad \text{experience curve learning rate (between 0 and 1),}$$

$$N_t \quad = \quad \text{cumulative EV production from 1998 to year t,}$$

$$C_0 \quad = \quad \text{experience curve intercept for variable production costs,}$$

$$gvar \quad = \quad \text{variable production cost of ICEVs (\$10,000 per vehicle)}$$

Equation (4) implies that total EV variable production costs (as opposed
to incremental) decline by (1-*rate*)*100 percent each time cumulative EV
output doubles. C_0 is determined by solving Equation (4) given a total
EV variable cost and cumulative output. This sets the level of output
and cost at which long-term learning begins. As shown in Equation (5),
we assume that total EV variable production costs fall as predicted by
the experience curve until they equal ICEV variable production costs.

Fixed Production Costs[356]

Fixed EV production costs are calculated as:

(6) $\text{fixed}_t =$

fcest/7   t=1998, 1999, ... 2004,

fcest/(2*5)   t=2003, 2004, ... 2007,

fcest/(4*5)   t=2008, 2009, ... 2012,

.

.

.

where

fcest   =   estimate of fixed costs required during first
7-year product cycle.

Fixed costs are assumed to fall 50 percent in each consecutive 5-year
product cycle and are assumed to be spread out evenly during each
product cycle.

Incremental EV Operating Costs

Incremental EV operating costs per vehicle are set to a fixed level
during the first five years of the mandate in each simulation. These
levels are based on simulations described in Appendix 10.A. After 2002,
incremental EV variable production costs are projected by:

_____

[356]Note that fixed_t has two components in 2003 and 2004. This
reflects--following Booz·Allen--the idea that a second product cycle
begins in 2003 before the fixed costs of the first product cycle are
fully amortized.

(7) $\ln(evop_t)$ $= (\ln(rate)/\ln(2))*\ln(N_t) + C_1$

(8) $incop_t$ $= evop_t - gvop$ if $evar_t >= gvop + ultincop$

               $= ultincop$ if $evar_t < gvop + ultincop$

where

$evop_t$	=	total lifetime operating cost for an EV sold in year t, discounted to year t,
$gvop$	=	total lifetime operating costs of an ICEV sold in year t, discounted to year t ($6,500 per vehicle),
$ultincop$	=	eventual incremental EV discounted lifetime operating costs,
$rate$	=	experience curve learning rate (between 0 and 1),
N_t	=	cumulative EV production from 1998 to year t,
C_1	=	experience curve intercept for operating costs

The calculations for vehicles sold between 1998 and 2010 and vehicles sold between 1998 and 2020 (tau = 2010 and 2020) is straightforward. To calculate long-term NCER, we calculate costs through the year 2100 and then make an adjustment for costs in later years. We approximate costs in the later years by calculating the infinite discounted sum assuming that total incremental costs (variable production, fixed, and operating) remain at their 2100 level. This provides an upper bound for remaining costs. One half of this sum is then added to the discounted costs through 2100 to approximate the infinite sum of discounted costs. For the scenarios considered, this adjustment (and whether or not we divide by a factor of two) made very little difference.

10.B.2 ELECTRIC VEHICLE EMISSION REDUCTIONS

We first explain how emission reductions for EVs sold through 2010 and 2020 are determined and then how emission reductions are calculated for long-term NCER.

Emission Reductions for EVs Sold Between 1998 and 2010 or 1998 and 2020

Emission reductions for vehicles sold in year t are

$$(9) \quad E_t = \text{evsales}_t * \sum_{s=1}^{10} B^{s-1}(\text{emreduct}/10)$$

where

emreduct	=	lifetime emissions reductions of EV (tons of ROG + NOx).

We assume for simplicity that an electric vehicle stays on the road for 10 years and that the emission reductions generated during each year of the vehicle's life are constant. Constant annual reductions are needed in the calculations of long-term NCERs described below. It seems likely that the overall discounted emission reductions would not change a great deal if emission reductions varied to some extent over the life of the vehicle, or if the vehicle life was somewhat longer (say 12 rather than 10 years).

Emission Reductions for Long-Term Narrow Cost Effectiveness Ratios

The calculations of emission reductions for the long-term NCERs are based on determining the emission reductions for a constant number of EVs that are sold starting in a given year and continue to sell at that level every year thereafter. We first demonstrate how the emission reductions for such as set of vehicles can be calculated and then show how we generalize to an increasing number of EVs that are sold over time.

Assume that Z electric vehicles are sold in 1998 and every year thereafter. Also assume that an electric vehicle stays on the road for 10 years and, for simplicity, that the emission reductions generated in each year of the vehicle's life are equal to X (equal to emreduct/10). Then the emission reductions discounted to 1995 are

$$(10) \quad Z*B^3 \left[\sum_{s=0}^{\infty} B^s X + \sum_{s=1}^{\infty} B^s X + \dots \sum_{s=9}^{\infty} B^s X \right].$$

Equation (10) can be derived by writing out the 10 terms for the discounted benefits of cars sold in 1998, the ten terms for the discounted benefits sold in 1999, and so on. The result is the 10 infinite sums in Equation (10). This equation simplifies to:

(11) $Z*B^3* [10/(1-B)$

$$- 9 - 8B - 7B^2 - 6B^3 - 5B^4 - 4B^5 - 3B^6 - 2B^7 - B^8].$$

Now generalizing to the case where the number of EVs sold can increase over time, the denominator in the long-term narrow cost-effectiveness ratio is

(12) $\sum_{\tau=1998}^{\infty} B^{t-1998}E_t =$

$$\sum_{\tau=1998}^{\infty} B^{t-1998}(evsales_t - evsales_{t-1})*$$

$$(emreduct/10)*mult$$

(13) $mult = [10/(1-B)] - 9 - 8B - 7B^2 - 6B^3 - 5B^4 - 4B^5 - 3B^6 - 2B^7 - B^8$

where

$$evsales_t > = evsales_{t-1},$$
$$evsales_{1997} = 0.$$

Equations (10) through (13) require that the emission reductions of a single EV in any year of its life are constant.

11.A. TWO GENERAL APPROACHES TO PREDICTING EV DEMAND AND THEIR LIMITATIONS FOR OUR PURPOSES

Various researchers have studied the demand for EVs. Several studies have taken one of two general approaches: a) quantifying *potential* demand for EVs by counting households with travel patterns and other characteristics that appear to make them plausible candidates for EVs; and b) econometric analyses of survey responses to questions concerning willingness to buy an EV.[357] We describe these approaches, review leading studies pursuing them, and explain why we think that they provide little information about our central question: the demand for the kinds of EVs that Big 7 companies will market during 1988 to 2002.

Travel behavior, household characteristics and potential demand. Several studies have examined the *potential* market for EVs by estimating a number or fraction of households for which the technical limitations of EVs seem not to be a major problem. There are several papers in this tradition, going back at least as far as the 1970s.[358]

For example, following other researchers who focused on range limitations of EVs, Greene (1985) develops and applies a method for estimating the distributions of daily usage of individual vehicles from longitudinal data on refueling dates and odometer readings at the times of refueling. This enables Greene (1985, p. 355) to make inferences such as "...with 95 percent probability, 25 percent of the vehicles will travel less than 98.1 miles in a day, at least 98 percent of the days."

Nesbitt, Kurani and Delucchi (1992) emphasize the importance of home recharging in addition to range limitations for the near-term household demand for EVs. They use data from 1985 to estimate the "largest possible initial market for battery-powered electric vehicles," viewing households as potential buyers if and only if they: own a primary residence with a carport or garage, would also have a vehicle

---

[357]See Turrentine and Kurani (1995, pp. 17-21) for a review of studies discussed here and other studies.

[358]Greene (1985) reviews several such studies referring to them as "market niche" or "economic tradeoff" studies. GAO (1994, pp. 30-31) refers to such studies as "technical constraints" studies.

capable of long-range trips and have a vehicle used for purposes other than commuting more than 80 miles round-trip (Nesbitt, Kurani and Delucchi, 1992, p. 11). They conclude that in 1985, 28 percent of households (28 million in all) met these criteria. They caution the reader: "However, our analysis says nothing about whether those who *could* use an EV, as per our criteria, *would* actually buy one" (Nesbitt, Kurani and Delucchi, 1992, p. 18).

Econometric analyses of stated preferences for EVs. Observation and analysis of actual market choices cannot provide much information about the demand for EVs. This applies generally because EVs are very different from conventional vehicles, and consumers have not been offered EVs in the market place to any substantial degree.[359] Moreover, households and fleet managers have not been presented with any opportunity to purchase the kinds of EVs that the Big 7 are likely to offer under the mandate. Thus, researchers have attempted to assess the demand for EVs by presenting people with descriptions of different (hypothetical) vehicles and their prices and asking them to make choices. In some studies such information is analyzed using (rather advanced) econometric methods designed to analyze such discrete choices. We discuss three studies of households and one of fleet managers.

In Beggs, Cardell, and Hausman (1981), hypothetical choices of 193 respondents from nine different cities--selected because they were expected to be unusually receptive to the possibility of an EV purchase-- were obtained and analyzed. More specifically, each respondent was presented with descriptions of sixteen vehicles characterized by various combinations of nine attributes (e.g., price, fuel cost, range between refueling, time required to refuel, top speed, number of seats, length of

---

[359]Henderson and Rusin (1994. pp. 37-38) discuss the extent to which results of "hedonic studies" of consumers' willingness to pay for abstract vehicle attributes (e.g., acceleration, operating costs, reliability, safety) based on observed market behavior are likely to be useful in assessing demand for EVs. They conclude--and we concur--that the prospects are poor. For example, they write: "Because the current vehicle population does not have the limited range associated with EVs, there is no way to confidently use hedonic studies to value this attribute." (Henderson and Rusin, 1994, p. 37.) See also Gordon and Richardson (1995, pp. 5-6).

warranty) designed to reflect characteristics of gasoline and electric vehicles. Respondents were then asked to rank the choices with which they were presented from highest to lowest. Their estimates led Beggs, Cardell, and Hausman (1981, p. 19) to conclude that "Individuals do not seem receptive to electric vehicles that have limited range and long refueling periods."

In a study that is similar in some ways, Calfee (1985) analyzes 47 responses to a take-home survey form (administered in 1980). Each respondent was asked to make 30 separate vehicle choices from 30 sets of three hypothetical vehicles where each vehicle is described by five numbers representing the vehicle's purchase price, operating cost per mile, seating capacity, and (for EVs) range and top speed. Emphasizing that the most-viable market for EVs may be located in "odd market niches representing somewhat unusual tastes" (Calfee, 1985, p. 287), Calfee estimates separate preferences for each respondent and uses these to predict market shares for EVs (characterized in various ways) in competition with gas-powered vehicles. Attempting to estimate how many people would buy EVs under what conditions is an important aspect of Calfee's study,[360] but there are technical reasons to be concerned about the reliability of his estimates.[361] Calfee (1985, p. 298) concludes:

---

[360]In contrast, econometric demand studies often estimate demand functions characterizing an average or typical consumer; such demand functions are often of considerable interest. Average tastes are of limited interest in our context because the key question is the price at which a minority of buyers large enough to satisfy the mandate would buy an EV.

[361]Beggs, Cardell, and Hausman (1981) estimate their model alternatively assuming homogenous and heterogeneous tastes among their respondents and find considerable evidence of heterogeneity. But in analyzing the results for the model allowing for heterogeneity they focus nonetheless on the average tradeoffs among respondents who are estimated to have different tastes. (Beggs, Cardell, and Hausman, 1981, Table 4.) The authors apparently chose not to present and analyze separate estimates of individuals' tastes--e.g., to examine what fraction of respondents are somewhat receptive to EVs--because there is too little information to estimate reliably the tastes of each individual separately. In particular, there are only five degrees of freedom for estimating each individual's tastes (Beggs, Cardell, and Hausman, 1981, p. 14) and thus the "required asymptotic approximations are suspect." (Beggs, Cardell, and Hausman, 1981, fn. 10, p. 15.) Calfee's study design suffers from a similar difficulty--25 degrees of

"Electric vehicles of modest performance, such as could be produced very soon, are likely to have no significant market."

More recently, Bunch et al. (1993) studied responses to a 1991 mail questionnaire from 692 residents of the South Coast. Each respondent was presented with five choice sets of three vehicles each--with vehicles described in terms of fuel type, fuel availability, range, fuel cost per mile, level of pollution, performance--and asked to choose the most preferred vehicle in each of the five sets.[362] Preferences are assumed to be homogeneous, thus the results are interpreted as characterizing the preferences of an average or typical respondent.[363] The estimates suggest that, other things equal, the average respondent would require very large price discounts to compensate for limited vehicle range (e.g., $16,000 and $10,000 to compensate for a ranges of 75 and 125 miles, respectively) and limited availability of fuel ($8,000 and $2,000 to compensate for recharging capability at 10 percent and 50 percent as many locations as gasoline, respectively), but also a substantial willingness to pay for lower emissions (e.g., an extra $10,000 per vehicle to reduce emissions from that of gasoline vehicles to 10 percent of that level).

Hill (1987) analyzed data from 474 respondents in a phone survey during mid-1983 of managers of commercial vehicle fleets. Each respondent was presented with a scenario consisting of a pair of ranges (per charge) and life-cycle costs (purchase price plus lifetime operating costs) relative to conventional vehicles and was asked whether such a vehicle would be useful to the operations of the respondent's fleet and, if so, how many the respondent would buy. The three ranges considered were 30, 60 and 90 miles, and the three life-cycle costs were 10 percent less, 15 percent more and equal to the life-cycle costs of a conventional vehicle. Econometric analysis of the data led Hill (1987,

---

freedom even under the doubtful assumption of independence across observations for each individual respondent--but Calfee proceeds to estimate and analyze results estimated separately for individuals.

[362]Only half of the respondents were presented with choice sets including EVs. (The study examined demand for clean-fuel vehicles including non-electric vehicles.)

[363]Recruitment letters were sent to "a random sample of households in the California South Coast Air Basin." (Bunch et al., 1993, p. 240.)

p. 284) to conclude: "Our analysis provides strong evidence that firms would be willing to cope with the limited range of electric vehicles *if* these vehicles were able to provide a less costly means of doing business."

Synthesis. None of these studies, taken at face value, provides a basis for optimism about the demand for EVs.[364] The conclusions of the household demand studies speak for themselves. As far as fleet demand is concerned, Hill's fundamental conclusion is discouraging in light of our review of the evidence in Section 10.2, which indicates that during the time period under consideration, lifetime operating costs of EVs-- including *all* batteries--are likely to be $1,000 to $11,000 more than for comparable ICEVs. For life-cycle costs of EVs to be below those of ICEVs, then, purchase prices of EVs would have to be $1,000 to $11,000 below those of comparable ICEVs.

Usefulness for our purposes. The basic conclusion of Hill (1987)-- that fleet managers would trade off range and cost--seems unassailable. However, we have fundamental concerns about the relevance of the studies of household demand for the questions at hand. For example, Beggs, Cardell, and Hausman (1981) and Calfee (1985) analyze survey responses collected more than fifteen years ago; Beggs, Cardell, and Hausman (1981) and Bunch et al. (1993) characterize the preferences of average or typical respondents; and, perhaps most important, the respondents in all three studies have much less information about EVs than consumers would have if EVs were actually marketed under the mandate. Thus we conclude that the household studies provide quite limited information about the real-world demand for the kinds of EVs that the Big 7 are likely to market to households during 1998 to 2002, but that taken at face value the results of these studies are likely to understate substantially that demand.[365]

---

[364]See also, Henderson and Rusin (1994, pp. 41-42), who review results from "vehicle demand and hedonic studies," and calculate "a minimum estimated net penalty for passenger EVs of $6,700 to $7,700 per vehicle."

[365]GAO (1994, p. 32) in commenting on the pessimistic conclusions of two polls of consumer preferences for EVs reads: "Consumer preference studies about such an unfamiliar technology as EVs probably measure little more than consumers' underlying uncertainties about the

reliability and stability of EV technology itself and the relative importance of certain attributes of current ICEV technology that have previously received little consideration..." We are inclined to agree. See Gordon and Richardson (1995, pp. 6-7) for a contrary view.

11.B LONG-TERM CONSIDERATIONS IN BIG 7 EV MARKETING DECISIONS DURING 1998 TO 2002

The analysis of Big 7 company behavior in the text considers only the short-term costs and rewards of selling EVs. Some potential longer-term rewards warrant consideration. Is it likely that these potential longer-term rewards during 1998 to 2002 are large enough to outweigh the potential short-term losses and that Big 7 companies would market substantial numbers of EVs during 1998 to 2002 even without the mandate?

As is likely the case with many new products, and entirely consistent with basic economic principles, companies might be willing to market EVs at a loss (i.e., at prices that don't cover production and marketing costs) for a period of years, but only if and when doing so seems attractive to them in terms of long-term profitability. Long-term benefits to a company of marketing EVs could include the value to the company of:

- the knowledge gained about EV technology, effective EV marketing strategy, and EV owner behavior;
- getting ahead of the competition as an early successful innovator in electric-drive transportation;
- enhancing the company reputation for technical capability.

The information we have, however, is consistent with the idea that few, if any, of the Big 7 believe that--even once such longer-term advantages to the company are considered--the time to market EVs has come.

Companies are likely to value the knowledge they would gain by marketing EVs during 1998 to 2002. However, it may be that only one of the Big 7 has developed a product that could be expected to provide the company with major reputation benefits if marketed during the first five years of the mandate period. Specifically, the General Motors Impact appears to have the potential to please its owners, generate a lot of attention among car enthusiasts and car owners generally, and contribute to GM's reputation for technological capability.[366] With that single

---

[366]See the discussion in the text.

potential exception, it seems likely that companies believe that the
vehicles they could market in the near term would have negative long-
term effects on their companies because they would detract from their
reputations for technological capability and are not up to the standards
of drivability and convenience that companies believe characterize their
ICEVs and are essential to consumer perception of their products
generally.

11.C. AN ANALYSIS OF THE MARKET FOR EV CREDITS DURING 1998 TO 2002

As discussed in the text, according to the rules of the ZEV mandate during 1998 to 2002, every time that a non-Big 7 company sells an EV in California, it can sell an EV credit to a Big 7 company, which in turn can use the credit to offset one unit of its mandated quantity. Our analysis in the text emphasizes the production costs of vehicles marketed by Big 7 companies and the market for those EVs. In this appendix we consider how sensitive our conclusions might be to allowing explicitly for the possibility that the Big 7 companies will purchase credits from other EV producers. We do so using a model of the market for EV credits--i.e., the market in which these credits are bought and sold--during 1998 to 2002 and developing some simple, intuitively plausible implications.

While it would be useful to extend the present analysis in various ways, the model seems very helpful in sorting out some fundamental forces underlying the operation of the credit market. The analysis described here provides:

- Basic insights into the determinants of the prices and quantities of credits and the most likely sources of these credits;
- A foundation on which to develop more refined models and analyses of the EV credit market;
- A basis for explaining systematically our claims that if credits contribute substantially to the Big 7 companies' meeting of their mandated quantities, the major source of credits is likely to be ICEV companies that are subject to the mandate starting in 2003.

The Demand for EV Credits

Because only the Big 7 companies have any intrinsic use for EV credits, we assume that only Big 7 companies would buy (or demand) EV credits.[367]   We further assume that in determining their demand (or willingness to pay) for credits, the Big 7 companies pursue the goal of minimizing their costs in meeting their mandated quantities (a goal which is conducive to short-term profit maximization). An implication-- and the key to understanding the demand for EV credits--is that a Big 7 company would always be willing to buy an EV credit if the price of a credit is less than the cost to the company of any alternative means of satisfying one unit of its mandated quantity. The alternative means are:

a) producing and selling one of its own EVs, which involves a cost equal to the marginal loss to the company, if any, of doing so (i.e., the marginal revenue of its own EVs minus their marginal production cost);

b) paying the fine (non-compliance penalty) of $5,000, which involves a cost to the company of that $5,000 payment plus any additional cost that the company ascribes to paying a penalty.[368]

For simplicity we assume that all of the Big 7 companies impute a cost of $f (which may equal zero) for every unit of their mandated quantities covered by paying the fine. Then each company perceives a cost of $(5,000 + f) for each $5,000 fine it pays.

Figure 11.C-1 depicts the demand side of the credit market. The quantity of credits is denoted by C and the price of credits by P_C. This demand curve--labeled D_C--represents the combined demand for credits by all of the Big 7 companies. The height of the demand curve at any particular quantity of credits represents the willingness to pay of some Big 7 company for one additional credit.

---

[367]Thus we ignore the possibility that other companies (e.g., EV credit brokers) would buy credits to resell them.

[368]As discussed in the text, any additional cost would result from factors such as adverse publicity or reputation loss from paying the fine or additional risk of stockholders' suits.

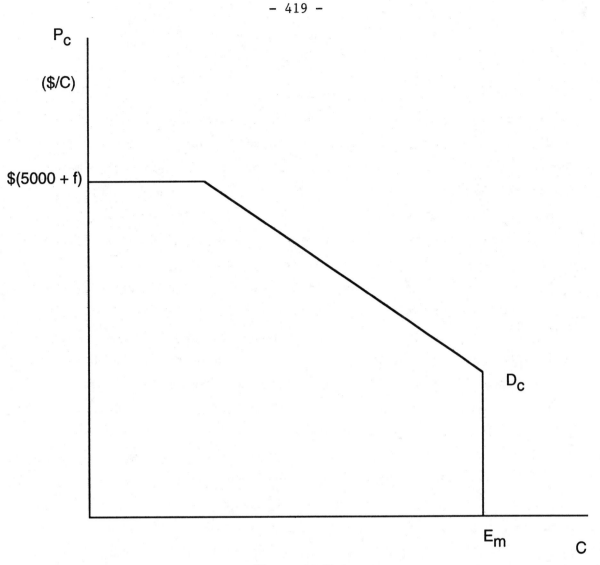

Figure 11.C-1

Market Demand Curve for EV Credits--1998 to 2002

Notes:
• C = quantity of EV credits
• P_c = price of credits ($/credit)
• D_c = demand curve for EV credits from all Big 7 companies together
• $f = cost Big 7 companies attribute to paying the fine in addition to the $5000 payment
• E_m = total number of EVs the Big 7 are mandated to sell

The horizontal segment at the level \$(5,000+f) reflects the implication of cost minimization that no company will pay more for a credit than the cost attributed to the alternative of paying the fine. The downward sloping segment of the demand curve represents the marginal loss levels of those companies (which may be all of them) that can produce and sell EVs at marginal losses less than $(5,000 + f)$.[369] The vertical segment represents the fact that the Big 7 companies would never buy more credits than E_m, the total mandated quantity of all Big 7 companies together, because additional credits are of no value if the Big 7 companies are meeting the mandate.

The figure incorporates the assumptions that Big 7 companies are willing to pay the fine, and sales of EVs are not profitable at the margin for at least some Big 7 EVs companies for some quantities below their mandated quantities. Some alternative possibilities deserve mention, but have such straightforward implications that they need not be analyzed in detail. First, suppose companies are not willing to pay the fine but selling EVs does involve marginal losses for Big 7 companies. In this case, there is no horizontal segment to the demand curve and each point on the demand curve represents a marginal loss associated with a Big 7 EV displaced by buying a credit. Second, if Big 7 companies can produce and sell EVs without incurring losses at the margin, then they would not be willing to pay anything for credits. If there is no demand for credits, there will be no credit market (i.e., no credits will be sold and no EV producer could get a positive price for a credit).

---

[369]When a Big 7 company can produce and sell an EV while incurring a loss of less than $(5,000+f)$, doing so is its best alternative to buying a credit and the cost of this alternative is the marginal loss from producing and selling another one of its EVs. In that situation the value of buying an additional credit is avoiding the marginal loss.

The Supply of EV Credits

We assume that the only companies that would sell credits are non-Big 7 companies.[370] These might include companies that convert ICEVs to EVs, producers of niche vehicles, and ICEV companies other than the Big 7. We assume that there are enough such companies selling EVs for there to be competition on the selling side of the credit market and enough companies potentially purchasing credits for there to be competition on the buying side of the market.[371]

The prices at which the non-Big 7 companies would be willing to sell (or supply) credits to the Big 7 depend on the costs to the non-Big 7 companies of producing *credits*. To produce an additional credit, a non-Big 7 company must produce and sell an additional EV. The (net) cost to the company of doing this is the marginal cost of producing the EV minus the price at which the EV is sold. Thus to analyze the supply of EV credits, we must examine the market for the EVs that produce the credits--i.e., the EVs produced and sold by companies not subject to the mandate. After doing so, we analyze the market for credits.

The Market for EVs of Non-Big 7 Companies

Figure 11.C-2 depicts the market for EVs produced by non-Big 7 companies. The quantity of EVs sold by all of these companies together is denoted by Z and the price at which these vehicles are sold is denoted by P_Z. We initially assume that the EVs sold by each non-Big 7 company are identical. We relax this assumption in applying the basic lessons derived from the simple model.

---

[370]This rules out the possibility, for example, that some Big 7 companies would sell more than their mandated quantities of EVs and sell credits to other Big 7 companies.

[371]Allowing for lack of strong competition among EV producers would be a worthwhile extension of the analysis. The most obvious implication (based on standard economic models of market power by sellers) is that companies that generate credits would be expected to take advantage of their power in the credit market, thus increasing the price and decreasing the quantity of credits relative to the competitive case. (This--see below--suggests that *fewer* non-Big 7 EVs would be produced than the analysis here predicts.)

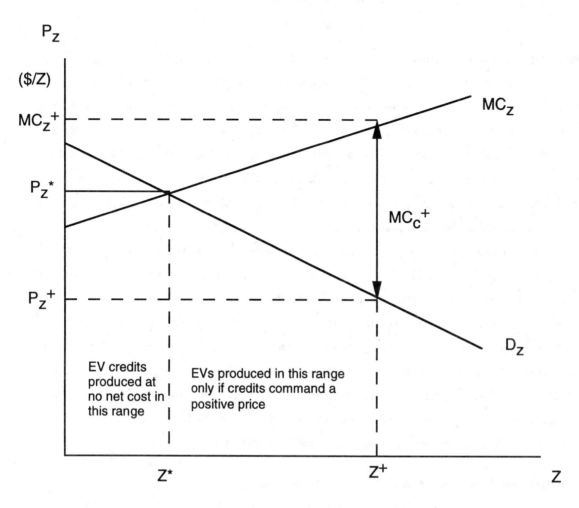

Figure 11.C-2

Market for EVs Offered by Non-Big 7 Companies

Notes:
- Z = quantity of EVs produced by non-Big 7 companies
- P_Z = price of EVs produced by non-Big 7 companies
- D_Z = demand for EVs produced by non-Big 7 companies given offerings by Big 7
- MC_Z = marginal cost of producing EVs
- Z^*, P_Z^* = equilibrium quantity and price of non-Big 7 EVs if Big 7 are not allowed to use credits
- Z^+ = arbitrary quantity of Z greater than Z^*
- P_Z^+ = price at which Z^+ non-Big 7 EVs could be sold
- MC_Z^+ = marginal production cost at of Z^+
- $MC_C^+ = MC_Z^+ - P_Z^+$ = marginal cost of producing *credits* if non-Big 7 produce and sell Z^+ EVs

The demand curve--labeled D_Z--represents the willingness of households and fleet managers to pay for the vehicles offered by the non-Big 7 companies. In thinking about the position of this demand curve, we must not only consider the physical attributes of these vehicles but also the fact that these vehicles will be competing with the vehicles being offered by the Big 7 at prices allowing them to satisfy their mandated quantities (in combination with any credits purchased and fines paid).[372]

The curve labeled MC_Z in the figure is the marginal production cost curves for EVs aggregated over all of the EV companies. Recall that we concluded that the marginal cost of an EV *credit* is the marginal production cost of an EV minus the price at which the EV is sold. Whether the marginal cost of a credit differs from the marginal cost of producing an EV, then, depends on whether credits command a positive price. This depends on the conditions in the market for non-Big 7 EVs and the quantity of these EVs sold.

First consider quantity levels below Z^*, which is the equilibrium quantity of non-Big 7 EVs sold in the absence of any *right* to sell credits (i.e., if the Big 7 were not *allowed* to use credits to cover part of their mandated quantities). For these quantities of EVs, the price of Z is greater than marginal production cost, and thus the marginal "cost" of producing a credit in this range is negative--EV companies would be willing to produce these units of EVs even if they cannot sell credits for a positive price. For quantity levels in this range, companies are willing to produce and sell EVs even without the extra incentive provided by the ability to sell credits, and because this is true credits will not command a positive price. (In a supply

_____

[372]Our analysis of the operating costs of EVs relative to ICEVs has led to the conclusion that Big 7 companies might have to price their EVs well below the price of comparable ICEVs. (The possibility that EV technology, especially battery technology, will not progress as rapidly as is hoped reinforces this prediction.) Since we do not expect EV companies to offer vehicles that are superior in performance to the EVs offered by the Big 7, EV companies may not be able to sell any significant numbers of their EVs (thousands per year, say) unless their prices are substantially below those of ICEVs comparable to the EVs offered by Big 7 companies.

and demand model, equilibrium prices equal marginal costs; if the cost of producing credits is zero, the price of credits will be zero.)

Next consider quantity levels greater than Z^*. In this range, the price at which an additional EV can be sold is less than the marginal cost of producing it. For example, consider Z^+, an arbitrary quantity greater than Z^*. If the non-Big 7 companies were to produce Z^+ units of Z, the price at which they could be sold would be P_Z^+, the marginal production cost would be MC_Z^+, and companies would suffer a loss of $MC_Z^+ - P_Z^+$ at the margin; this difference is the marginal cost of producing a credit at Z^+ units of EV production and sale. Non-Big 7 companies would be willing to produce that unit of Z, then, only if the price of credits is at least as high as $MC_Z^+ - P_Z^+$.

This example illustrates the following lessons:

- credits would be supplied up to a quantity of Z^* even at a zero price of credits;
- quantities of Z above Z^* will be produced only if the price of credits is positive;[373]
- for quantities above Z^*, the price necessary to get a marginal credit supplied is the distance between the MC_Z and D_Z curves.

With these results about the supply of credits, we can analyze the credit market and complete the discussion.

The Market for EV Credits

We start with two simple, but powerful, premises:

- For the price of credits to be positive, output of EVs by non-Big 7 companies must be above Z^*, the level that would be produced even if credits couldn't be sold.
- If the price of credits is positive in equilibrium, the number of *credits* sold must be equal to the number of *EVs* sold by the non-Big 7 companies.

The discussion just above establishes the former premise. Let Z^{**} denote the quantity of EVs produced by non-Big 7 companies in the presence of a credit market and C^* be the equilibrium number of credits

---

[373]If credits do command a positive price, the ability to sell credits can be thought of as a production subsidy mechanism.

sold. In technical terms, then, the latter premise is: if $P^*_C > 0$, then $Z^{**} = C^*$.[374] This allows us[375] to analyze both C and Z in Figure 11.C-3, which depicts the credit market. The demand curve is the same as Figure 11.C-1.

Figure 11.C-3 considers three alternative supply curves for credits, corresponding to three alternative sets of hypothetical conditions in the market for EVs offered by non-Big 7 companies (i.e., alternative views of what the MC_z and D_z curves in Figure 11.C-2 look like.)

The highest of the supply curves, S_1, represents a situation in which the cost of producing credits is very high (relative to what any Big 7 company would pay for a credit). In fact, as drawn, S_1, reflects a situation where the price of credits must be at least $(MC_{z10} - P_{z10}) > \$(5000 + f)$ to get even a single credit supplied. Based on the discussion of Figure 11.C-2, the term $(MC_{z10} - P_{z10})$ represents the marginal cost of the least-cost EV producer minus the price at which it could sell even its *first* EV.[376] Under these conditions, the cost of producing even a single credit (i.e., EVs offered by non-Big 7 companies are so unprofitable) is so high that no credits can be produced at a cost as low as any Big 7 company will pay for even a single credit. In this case no credits will be sold, and, in fact, other EV companies will sell no EVs.[377]

---

[374]This follows because: a) the other non-Big 7 companies cannot sell more credits than they produce and they can produce credits only by selling EVs (i.e., C is less than or equal to Z), and b) if there were a positive price for credits and not all of the (Z in number) available credits are being sold (i.e., Z > C), then EV companies with unsold credits would offer to lower the price of credits to sell their excess credits because they have no value any other way (this contradicts Z > C). Thus we have concluded that in equilibrium if $P_C > 0$ then we must have $C^* = Z^{**}$.

[375]Assuming that $P_C > 0$. This will be the case unless: production of EVs would be high enough even without credits to meet the mandate quantities of all of the Big 7; Big 7 companies are not willing to pay for credits; or both. (In either case the price of credits is zero).

[376]Visually, this means that the MC_z curve is higher than the D_z curve even at Z=0.

[377]As argued above, if an EV company sells an EV, this generates a credit, and the EV company would be willing to sell the credit for *any* positive price rather than not sell it at all. Thus, if no credits are

The lowest of the supply curves, S_3, represents a situation in which the cost of producing (at least some) credits is relatively low. As pictured, EV companies can produce Z_3* EVs profitably even without selling credits. To induce them to produce more EVs than this, credits must command a positive price, so (as drawn) the curve S_3 rise from that point. It takes higher and higher prices of credits (i.e., the supply curve is upward sloping) because to sell more and more EVs requires a lower price (i.e., D_Z is downward sloping as in Figure 11.C-2) and (perhaps less important) the marginal costs of producing EVs rises. The equilibrium price of credits is P_3* and C_3* credits are sold. Big 7 companies buy credits, produce some EVs themselves (since $C_3* < E_m$), but don't pay any fines. EV companies produce and sell a total of $Z** = C_3*$ EVs.

The supply curve S_2 represents a case where the costs of producing credits are in an intermediate range. Here EV companies would produce relatively few (i.e., Z_2*) EVs even without an ability to sell credits, but will not produce more EVs (and thereby produce more credits) unless the price of credits is positive. Big 7 companies buy C_2* credits at the price of $P_2* = \$(5000 + f)$. In this case, the Big 7 companies produce some EVs themselves, buy some credits and pay some fines. EV companies produce and sell a total of $Z** = C_2*$ EVs.

---

being sold we can infer that EV companies are not producing any credits (i.e., they aren't selling any EVs). (This is an example of the power of the result that if $P*_C > 0$, then $Z** = C*$.)

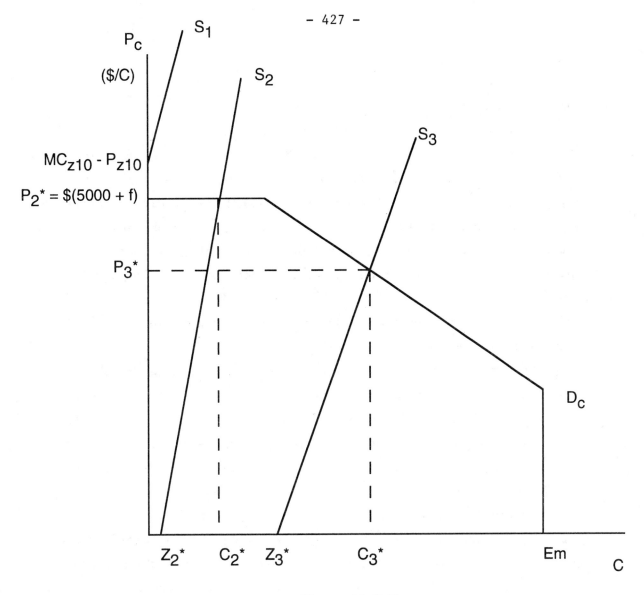

Figure 11.C-3

Market for EV Credits--1998 to 2002

Notes:
- C = quantity of EV credits
- P_c = price of credits ($/credit)
- D_c = demand for EV credits from all Big 7 companies together
- S_1, S_2, S_3 = alternative supply curves for EV credits (reflecting different hypothetical conditions in the market for EVs from non-Big 7 companies)
- MC_{z10} - P_{z10} = marginal loss on first unit of sales of Z under first set of hypothetical conditions in the market for EVs from non-Big 7 companies
- Z_2^*, Z_3^* = equilibrium quantities of EVs that EV companies would sell if Big 7 companies were not allowed to use credits
- $f = cost Big 7 companies attribute to paying additional fine in addition to the $5000 per-unit payment
- E_m = total number of EVs Big 7 companies are mandated to sell
- P_2^*, P_3^* = equilibrium prices of credits corresponding to supply curves S_2 and S_3
- C_2^*, C_3^* = equilibrium quantities of credits corresponding to supply curves S_2 and S_3

General Implications

We draw several lessons from this discussion.

If the Big 7 companies can meet the mandate on their own without selling any EVs at a marginal loss, then they would not be willing to pay anything for credits (i.e., there is no demand for credits) and the price of credits will be zero. EV companies will produce and sell EVs under these conditions only if they can do so profitably without any subsidy from the credit market and despite the competition from Big 7 EVs.

If Big 7 companies cannot meet their mandated quantities while avoiding marginal losses:

- The less profitably the Big 7 companies can produce and sell EVs, other things equal, the more credits they will tend to buy and the higher will be the price of credits.[378]

- The more profitably non-Big 7 companies can sell EVs (given the offerings of the Big 7), other things equal, the lower will the price of credits tend to be and the more EVs will be sold by non-Big 7 companies.[379]

- If EV sales by non-Big 7 companies are more unprofitable at the margin than are EV sales by Big 7 companies, then the price at which non-Big 7 companies are willing to supply credits is higher than the price at which Big 7 companies are willing to buy them. In this case non-Big 7 companies will not find it profitable to produce EVs even if they can sell the credits because they cannot sell the credits for enough to compensate for their marginal losses on EVs.

---

[378]This conclusion follows from the fact that the demand for credits increases with decreases in the profitability of Big 7 EVs.

[379]This follows from the fact that the supply of credits increases with increases in the profitability of non-Big 7 EVs. In the extreme, if EV companies can profitably (at the margin) sell enough EVs to meet the mandated quantities for the Big 7, credits will not be scarce, the Big 7 will meet the mandate entirely by buying credits (for next to nothing) and all of the mandate will be met by EV companies.

Will Many Credits Be Sold, and, If So, By What Companies?

Finally, the analysis here provides a systematic basis for explaining why we are doubtful that during the period 1998 to 2002 credits (i.e., production of EVs by non-Big 7 companies) will account for a substantial proportion of EVs produced because of the ZEV mandate, with the possible exception of credits generated by ICEV companies that become subject to the mandate in 2003.

The basic lessons from the analysis are:

- Non-Big 7 companies will find it profitable to sell EVs only if their marginal losses are smaller than those of the Big 7 and smaller than the cost Big 7 companies ascribe to paying fines.
- The marginal cost of producing credits will increase with more EV sales because prices will have to be lowered to sell more EVs.

Because of the ZEV mandate, the Big 7 companies will be tough competitors in the EV market. All indications are that they are gearing up to produce and sell at least large fractions of their mandated quantities.[380] We have concluded that they can be expected to produce and market EVs that are as similar as possible to their ICEVs of comparable size and body style, and to sell anything close to their mandated quantities, the Big 7 are likely to price their EVs below, and perhaps far below, the prices of comparable ICEVs. Under these conditions, demand for non-Big 7 EVs is likely to be quite low, and much lower than it would be if the Big 7 did not have the mandate pushing them to sell thousands of EVs.

For other companies to sell more than a small fraction of the total mandated quantities--say, more than 2,500 per year during 1998 to 2,000 and 6,000 during 2001 and 2002, which are not insubstantial numbers of vehicles in such an immature market--in competition with the Big 7 would seem to require quite low prices. Different types of EV producers are in different situations:

---

[380]Relatively little reliance on the EV credit market may be a self-fulfilling prophecy on the part of the Big 7. By gearing up to produce most--if not virtually all--of their mandated quantities themselves, they make it harder for other EV producers to compete and reduce the availability of EV credits.

- EV converters are competing directly with ICEVs and EVs
  produced by the Big 7. To sell more than a handful of vehicles
  per year would seem to require prices well below those of Big 7
  EVs, which themselves may be far below the prices of comparable
  ICEVs. Unless the production costs of converters are well
  below those of the Big 7, their marginal losses may not be much
  below those of the Big 7. To sell lots of vehicles, their
  prices might need to be very low and, if so, their marginal
  losses will approach the marginal costs of producing vehicles.

- Producers of niche vehicles that don't compete directly with
  ICEVs are likely to find some--and perhaps many--buyers who
  want an EV for uses other than those of an ICEV. But for them
  to be selling thousands vehicles per year at substantial prices
  (more than $10,000 per vehicle, say) during the introductory
  years in face of such stiff competition from other EVs does not
  seem plausible.

The most plausible scenario under which converters or producers of
niche vehicles would sell thousands of EVs per year before 2003 would be
if the Big 7 companies have very high willingness to pay for credits and
most of the revenues of EV companies are from credits.

We think it more likely that the predominant source of credits will
be the ICEV companies that are first subject to the mandate in 2003.
They must meet the 10 percent mandate level starting in 2003. These
companies--faced with selling substantial numbers of EVs in 2003--may
perceive substantial benefits (e.g., related to marketing, manufacturing
experience, public relations) to selling some EVs in California before
2002.[381] If so, such benefits would be viewed as (at least partial)

---

[381]This discussion assumes that the companies that become subject to
the mandate in 2003 will plan to produce EVs. We are doubtful that
these companies would plan to rely on paying fines after 2003 for the
same reasons we are doubtful that the Big 7 will rely heavily on fines
during 1998 to 2003. It also seems doubtful that they will plan to rely
heavily on buying credits, for example, from the Big 7. This is because
ICEV companies do seem to believe that the worldwide market for
electric-drive vehicles will be quite large eventually, and they are
unlikely to plan to fall far behind in the long-term competition to be
successful in those markets.

compensation for their marginal losses from selling EVs. This, in turn, suggests that the non-Big 7 ICEV companies may be more willing to sell EVs--and produce EV credits--than the short-term analysis here implies.[382]

---

[382]EV converters and producers of niche vehicles may also perceive substantial long-term benefits of selling EVs during 1998 to 2002, but they don't have the considerable incentive of having to gear up for very substantial mandated sales levels in 2003.

11.D ESTIMATING CONSUMERS' SURPLUS IN THE EV MARKET DUE TO THE ZEV MANDATE 1998 TO 2002

The two demand curves used to calculate consumers' surplus in the EV market (in Table 11.5-2) are depicted in Figure 11.D-1.[383] These are interpreted as market demand curves for the average Big 7 EV (on which the entire analysis is based).[384] Willingness to pay is expressed in terms of P^-, the price paid by buyers net of the 10 percent federal tax credit.

To calculate values for consumers' surplus in the EV market, we must specify the entire demand curve for EVs above the price expected to prevail in the market. As discussed in Section 11.3.2, there is very little empirical evidence available to guide us. We rely heavily on the range of views about the maximum prices that (all but very small fractions of) EV buyers would be willing to pay when comparing EVs to comparable ICEVs and the prevalence of buyers willing to pay substantial premiums. As above, we assume that buyers consider full life-cycle costs (i.e., purchase prices plus the present value of all future operating costs) when they compare EVs and ICEVs.

The demand functions are specified by choosing a value for the maximum premium a substantial fraction of EV buyers are willing to pay for an EV in terms of its full life-cycle costs relative to a comparable ICEV. It seems widely agreed that some substantial fraction of EV buyers are willing to pay a premium. The information we have leads us to conclude that a $5,000 premium would be considered optimistic by most

---

[383]Neither demand curve in Figure 11.D-1 looks like the one in Figure 11.3-1, which is more realistic. We use the simpler curves in Figure 11.D-1 to estimate upper and lower bounds for consumers' surplus (taking other assumptions as given) because--unlike the demand curve in Figure 11.3-1--the forms of these functions allow one to construct a demand curve by specifying values for a few parameters about which available information provides some guidance.

[384]In Appendix 11.H, we provide a more refined interpretation of these demand curves relying on our analysis of how the ZEV mandate may change the prices of ICEVs. (If the mandate does change ICEV prices, this shifts the demand for EVs--because they are substitutes for ICEVs-- and the more refined interpretation takes this into account.)

people and a premium of $1,000 would be widely considered pessimistic.[385] We use these values to construct bounds for consumers' surplus in the EV market. In both cases we assume that enough buyers are willing to pay the maximum premium to satisfy 25 percent of the mandate quantity.[386]

The bold demand curve--labeled D_{E1}--is constructed using relatively optimistic assumptions about the maximum premium and the alternative demand curve--labeled D_{E2}--is constructed using relatively pessimistic assumptions about it. Both demand curves are assumed to go through the point (E_m, P^-_m). (Table 11.5-2 presents two values for consumers' surplus for each assumed pair (E_m, P^-_m).) The two curves differ in their heights at quantities less than E_m, to represent different levels of willingness to pay of EV buyers for the EVs they purchase.[387]

Upper bounds on consumers' surplus. The bold demand curve incorporates the assumptions that:

a) the maximum premium over the full life-cycle costs of a comparable ICEV that any EV buyer would be willing to pay--net of the federal tax credit of 10 percent of purchase price--is $5,000,

b) enough consumers are willing to pay this $5,000 premium to satisfy 25 percent of the mandated quantity, and

c) from that point (.25E_m, P^-_m + 5000), demand falls off smoothly (linearly) to point (E_m, P^-_m).

---

[385]Recall that the analysis is being done in terms of the average Big 7 ICEV. For example, these bounding values are likely to strike readers as too small if they think in terms of a vehicle like the General Motors Impact, an expensive sports car, and too large if they think in terms of a small electric pickup truck or small electric sedan with a comparable ICEV selling for less than $15,000.

[386]Consider in this regard: "Our previous research, though informal, seems to confirm the opinion that not many consumers will pay extra for electric vehicles." (Turrentine and Kurani, 1995, p. 9.) "Our analysis provides strong evidence that firms would be willing to cope with the limited range of electric vehicles *if* these vehicles were able to provide a less costly means of doing business." (Hill, 1987, p. 284.)

[387]As seen presently, the heights of the demand functions for quantities greater than E_m are irrelevant to the calculations of consumers' surplus.

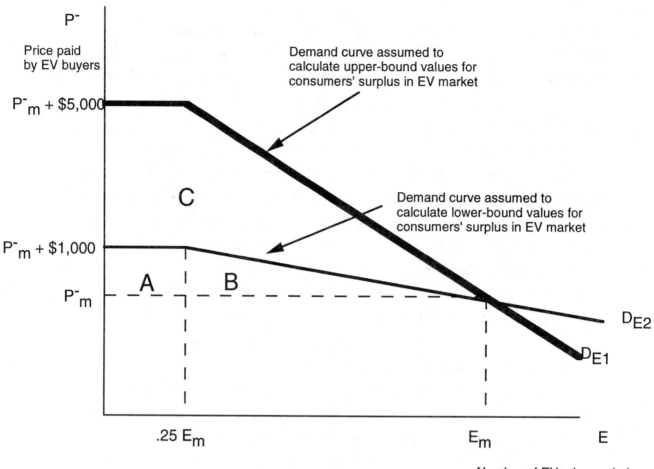

Figure 11.D-1

Alternative Demand Assumptions for Big 7 Companies' EVs During
1998 to 2002 Used to Estimate Consumers' Surplus in EV Market

Notes:
• D_{E1} and D_{E2} are alternative EV market demand curves for EVs offered by Big 7 companies
• D_{E1} is more optimistic about willingness of buyers to pay for Big 7 EVs

• P^- = price paid by EV buyers; i.e., price charged by companies minus federal tax credit (the purchase subsidy)

• P^-_m = price to buyers at which companies can sell mandated number of EVs (either $9,000 or $19,000 in simulations, see Tables 11.5-1 and 11.5-2)
• E = number of EVs demanded at market level
• E_m = mandated quantity for all Big 7 companies together

• A + B = lower bound on consumers' surplus in EV market (equals ($1,000) (5/8) E_m)

• A + B + C = upper bound on consumers' surplus in EV market (equals ($5,000) (5/8) E_m)

This demand curve implies for example, that if the price to buyers is $19,000, the higher of the assumed values in Table 11.5-2, half of the buyers of EVs would be willing to pay $22,333 or more despite the availability of comparable ICEVs for $20,000 and an operating cost disadvantage of EVs relative to ICEVs of $1,000.[388] If the price to buyers is $9,000 (the lower of our assumed values for P^-_m), half of the buyers of EVs would be willing to pay $12,333 or more despite the availability of comparable ICEVs for $20,000 and an operating cost disadvantage relative to ICEVs of $11,000.

Lower bounds for consumers' surplus. The demand curve labeled D_{E2} incorporates the assumptions that:

a) the maximum premium over the full life-cycle cost of a comparable ICEV that any EV buyer would be willing to pay--net of the federal tax credit of 10 percent of purchase price--is $1,000,

b) enough consumers are willing to pay this $1,000 premium to satisfy 25 percent of the mandated quantity, and

c) from that point $(.25E_m, P^-_m + \$1000)$, demand falls off smoothly (linearly) to point (E_m, P^-_m).

This second demand curve implies, for example, that if the price to buyers is $19,000, half of the buyers of EVs would have been willing to pay at least $19,667, $333 less than the price of a comparable ICEV despite an operating cost disadvantage of EVs relative to ICEVs of $1,000. If the price to buyers is $9,000, half of the buyers of EVs would have been willing to pay at least $9,667, despite the availability of comparable ICEVs for $20,000 and an operating cost disadvantage of EVs relative to ICEVs of $11,000.

Calculating consumers' surplus. Consumers surplus for each case considered in Table 11.5-2 is calculated as the area between the relevant demand curve and the horizontal line representing the (net of subsidy) price actually paid by EV buyers (P^-m). For D_{E2} this is the total--in Figure 11.D-1--area of the rectangle labeled A plus the triangle labeled B. For D_{E1} consumers' surplus can be calculated by

---

[388]Recall that the net price of $19,000 is derived assuming a price of $20,000 for a comparable ICEV and the lower-bound value of the operating cost disadvantage of an EV of $1,000,

adding to A+B the area between the two demand curves, which is labeled C in Figure 11.D-1. Given the shapes of these areas, consumers' surplus can be calculated as 5/8 of the product of the maximum premium and the mandated quantity.

11.E. PUTTING DOLLAR VALUES ON THE MARGINAL LOSSES TO A BIG 7 COMPANY FROM SELLING AN EV

How much might we expect a Big 7 company to lose from selling each additional EV during 1998 to 2002? Here we explain why this can be approximated by the difference between the average variable cost of producing EVs and the selling price of the EV.

Since losses are costs minus revenues, the additional losses due to selling an additional EV--which we call the "marginal loss on an EV"--is the additional cost of producing an EV (the "marginal cost" of an EV) minus the additional revenue from selling an additional EV (the "marginal revenue" of an EV).

Marginal costs relative to variable costs per EV. As discussed in Section 10.2, we expect average variable costs to be falling in the ranges of EV production relevant during 1998 to 2002 because larger levels of production will involve taking advantage of economies of scale experienced internally or by parts suppliers.[389] It is a logical necessity that if average variable cost is falling then marginal cost must be less than average variable cost. As reflected in Figures 10.2-1 and 11.4-2, we expect marginal costs to be less than average variable costs, but not dramatically so.

Marginal revenue relative to the price of an EV. What happens to revenues when an additional EV is sold? The company collects the price of this EV, but this is not the only factor changing EV revenues as a whole. This is because the company faces a downward sloping demand curve for its EV: in order to sell one more EV, the company must price all EVs a little lower than it could if it were to sell one fewer. To calculate marginal revenue, then, we must deduct from the selling price the amount of revenue the company gives up by lowering the price on all

---

[389]In the case of parts made by the vehicle manufacturer and vehicle assembly, economies of scale would directly lower average variable costs as production increases. In the case of parts purchased by the vehicle manufacturer, economies of scale in parts production would presumably allow the vehicle manufacturer to negotiate lower prices for parts if more parts are purchased.

of its EVs to sell the additional EV. For example, suppose that a company is selling 2000 EVs at $15,000 and that to sell an additional EV, it must lower the price of (all) EVs by one dollar per EV. Then marginal revenue is $12,999.[390] Thus, marginal revenue must be less than price (whenever a company has to lower price to sell more units), and how much less depends on how sensitive quantities demanded are to price. We have argued that once price is low enough to sell the mandated quantities, then demand should be quite responsive to price. Thus, we expect that marginal revenue for EVs would not be dramatically less than price at the level of EV sales relevant to determining the implicit costs of selling more ICEVs.

Putting the two pieces together, if marginal cost is below but near average variable cost and marginal revenue is below but near price, then the marginal loss--marginal cost minus marginal revenue--should be close to average variable cost minus price.

---

[390]I.e., the $14,999 selling price of the additional EV minus the $2000 forgone on the 2000 EVs that could have been sold at a price one dollar higher.

11.F CHOICES OF DEMAND ELASTICITIES FOR HYPOTHESES 1 AND 2 ABOUT PRICING BEHAVIOR OF NON-BIG 7 COMPANIES

Here we explain the choices of assumed demand elasticities facing the Big 7 companies under the two hypotheses about the pricing behavior of the non-Big 7 companies. The basic idea is that for any given price increase by the Big 7 companies, they will lose a smaller proportion of their sales if the non-Big 7 match the price increases than if they do not match.

Under Hypothesis 1, the non-Big 7 companies are assumed to match price increases by the Big 7, and hence both sets of companies are expected to experience comparable proportionate decreases in sales. This proportion will depend on how much prices increase and the elasticity of demand for new ICEVs in California in total. We use a value of -2 to represent this elasticity. As discussed in Section 7.2, this choice is based on the consideration that prices in neighboring states will not be increasing because of regulation-induced costs of selling vehicles in California and that some buyers are likely to respond to price increases in California by buying a new vehicle outside the state.

Under Hypothesis 2, the non-Big 7 companies are assumed not to increase their prices while the Big 7 companies do. In this case the responsiveness of demand for Big 7 vehicles to the Big 7 price increases will be larger than in the case where the non-Big 7 also raise their prices. This is because the increase in Big 7 prices relative to those of other companies will induce some buyers to shift their purchases from the Big 7 companies to the non-Big 7 companies. Under Hypothesis 2, then, the relevant elasticity of demand for Big 7 vehicles is larger than under Hypothesis 1. There is no precise basis for specifying a numerical value; we use a value of -4, twice the elasticity assumed under Hypothesis 1. This value means, for example, that if the Big 7 companies were to increase their prices by 2 percent then they would lose 8 percent of their sales. This choice reflects our view that demand should be considerably more responsive if the non-Big 7 hold their prices constant, but that many buyers would not shift their purchases to the non-Big 7 even if the Big 7 were to raise prices.

11.G DETAILED RESULTS FOR EFFECTS ON ICEV MARKETS ASSUMING NO DISPLACEMENT AND FULL DISPLACEMENT

The two tables in this appendix differ from Table 11.6-1 only in the degree to which EV sales are assumed to displace ICEV sales. (Table 11.6-1 assumes 50 percent displacement; i.e., that for every two EV sales one ICEV sale is displaced.) The tables in this appendix redo the calculations in Table 11.6-1, assuming alternatively that EV sales do not displace ICEV sales at all ("no displacement"--Table 11.G-1) and that EV sales displace ICEV sales one for one ("full displacement"-- Table 11.G-2). Results from Tables 11.6-1, 11.G-1, and 11.G-2 are collected and compared in Table 11.6-2.

Table 11.G-1

Projected Gains and Losses in California ICEV Market from ZEV Mandate
Assuming No Displacement of ICEV Sales by EV Sales (Ignores Benefits of Emission Reductions)

	Hypothesis 1 (prices matched):						Hypothesis 2 (prices not matched):					
Case assumptions:												
Cost to company of unit increase in mandate quantity	500	5000	14700	500	5000	14700	500	5000	14700	500	5000	14700
Mandate percentage	0.02	0.02	0.02	0.05	0.05	0.05	0.02	0.02	0.02	0.05	0.05	0.05
Implicit marginal cost of Big 7 ICEVs sold in CA ($/ICEV)	10	102	300	26	263	774	10	102	300	26	263	774
Average ICEV price without ZEV mandate ($ thousands)	20	20	20	20	20	20	20	20	20	20	20	20
Big 7 ICEV Sales without ZEV mandate (M vehicles/yr)	1.240	1.240	1.240	1.240	1.240	1.240	1.240	1.240	1.240	1.240	1.240	1.240
Other ICEV Sales without ZEV mandate (M vehicles/yr)	0.260	0.260	0.260	0.260	0.260	0.260	0.260	0.260	0.260	0.260	0.260	0.260
Elasticity of demand for Big 7 ICEVs	-2.0	-2.0	-2.0	-2.0	-2.0	-2.0	-4.0	-4.0	-4.0	-4.0	-4.0	-4.0
Elasticity of supply of ICEVs	5	5	5	5	5	5	5	5	5	5	5	5
Degree of ICEV demand displacement	0.00	0.00	0.00	0.00	0.00	0.00	0.00	0.00	0.00	0.00	0.00	0.00
Prices and quantities of Big 7 ICEVs:												
Big 7 price increase (dollars per ICEV)	7	73	214	19	188	553	6	57	167	15	146	430
Proportionate Big 7 price increase	0.000	0.004	0.011	0.001	0.009	0.028	0.000	0.003	0.008	0.001	0.007	0.021
Big 7 sales change (thousands of vehicles)	-0.9	-9.0	-26.6	-2.3	-23.3	-68.5	-1.4	-14.1	-41.3	-3.6	-36.3	-106.6
Proportionate Big 7 sales decrease	0.001	0.007	0.021	0.002	0.019	0.055	0.001	0.011	0.033	0.003	0.029	0.086
Big 7 sales with mandate (million vehicles/year)	1.2391	1.2310	1.2134	1.2377	1.2167	1.1715	1.2386	1.2259	1.1987	1.2364	1.2037	1.1334
Prices and quantities of other ICEV companies:												
Other ICEV companies price increase (dollars per ICEV)	7	73	214	19	188	553	0	0	0	0	0	0
Other ICEV companies sales change (thousands of vehicles)	-0.2	-1.9	-5.6	-0.5	-4.9	-14.4	0.7	7.0	20.7	1.8	18.1	53.3
Dollar gains and losses in ICEV market ($M/yr):												
Cost to California new ICEV buyers	11	109	318	28	279	806	7	70	203	18	179	510
Change in Big 7 revenues on ICEVs	-9	-91	-271	-23	-237	-723	-21	-212	-627	-54	-549	-1645
Change in Big 7 variable cost ($10K/ICEV)	-9	-90	-266	-23	-233	-685	-14	-141	-413	-36	-363	-1066
Change in Big 7 manufacturer and dealer profit in ICEVs	0	-1	-6	0	-4	-38	-7	-71	-214	-18	-187	-579
Change in other ICEV companies revenues	-2	-19	-57	-5	-50	-152	14	141	413	36	363	1066
Change in other ICEV companies variable cost ($10K/ICEV)	-2	-19	-56	-5	-49	-144	7	70	207	18	181	533
Change in other ICEV companies and dealer profit	0	0	-1	0	-1	-8	7	70	207	18	181	533
ICEV Cost to CA (Consumer loss-15% of profit change)	11	109	319	28	280	813	7	70	204	18	179	517

Table 11.G-2

Projected Gains and Losses in California ICEV Market from ZEV Mandate
Assuming Full Displacement of ICEV Sales by EV Sales (Ignores Benefits of Emission Reductions)

	Hypothesis 1 (prices matched):						Hypothesis 2 (prices not matched):					
Case assumptions:												
Cost to company of unit increase in mandate quantity	500	5000	14700	500	5000	14700	500	5000	14700	500	5000	14700
Mandate percentage	0.02	0.02	0.02	0.05	0.05	0.05	0.02	0.02	0.02	0.05	0.05	0.05
Implicit marginal cost of Big 7 ICEVs sold in CA ($/ICEV)	10	102	300	26	263	774	10	102	300	26	263	774
Average ICEV price without ZEV mandate ($ thousands)	20	20	20	20	20	20	20	20	20	20	20	20
Big 7 ICEV Sales without ZEV mandate (M vehicles/yr)	1.240	1.240	1.240	1.240	1.240	1.240	1.240	1.240	1.240	1.240	1.240	1.240
Other ICEV Sales without ZEV mandate (M vehicles/yr)	0.260	0.260	0.260	0.260	0.260	0.260	0.260	0.260	0.260	0.260	0.260	0.260
Elasticity of demand for Big 7 ICEVs	-2.0	-2.0	-2.0	-2.0	-2.0	-2.0	-4.0	-4.0	-4.0	-4.0	-4.0	-4.0
Elasticity of supply of ICEVs	5	5	5	5	5	5	5	5	5	5	5	5
Degree of ICEV demand displacement	1.00	1.00	1.00	1.00	1.00	1.00	1.00	1.00	1.00	1.00	1.00	1.00
Prices and quantities of Big 7 ICEVs:												
Big 7 price increase (dollars per ICEV)	7	73	214	19	188	553	6	57	167	15	146	430
Proportionate Big 7 price increase	0.000	0.004	0.011	0.001	0.009	0.028	0.000	0.003	0.008	0.001	0.007	0.021
Big 7 sales change (thousands of vehicles)	-21.4	-29.4	-46.6	-53.5	-73.6	-116.9	-21.9	-34.3	-61.2	-54.7	-86.0	-153.4
Proportionate Big 7 sales decrease	0.017	0.024	0.038	0.043	0.059	0.094	0.018	0.028	0.049	0.044	0.069	0.124
Big 7 sales with mandate (million vehicles/year)	1.2186	1.2106	1.1934	1.1865	1.1664	1.1231	1.2181	1.2057	1.1788	1.1853	1.1540	1.0866
Prices and quantities of other ICEV companies:												
Other ICEV companies price increase (dollars per ICEV)	7	73	214	19	188	553	0	0	0	0	0	0
Other ICEV companies sales change (thousands of vehicles)	-4.5	-6.2	-9.8	-11.2	-15.4	-24.5	-3.6	2.6	16.0	-9.0	6.6	40.3
Dollar gains and losses in ICEV market ($M/yr):												
Cost to California new ICEV buyers	11	108	315	28	274	790	7	69	202	18	175	500
Change in Big 7 revenues on ICEVs	-419	-500	-677	-1047	-1253	-1718	-431	-618	-1027	-1077	-1552	-2602
Change in Big 7 variable cost ($10K/ICEV)	-214	-294	-466	-535	-736	-1169	-219	-343	-612	-547	-860	-1534
Change in Big 7 manufacturer and dealer profit in ICEVs	-205	-206	-211	-513	-517	-549	-212	-275	-415	-530	-691	-1067
Change in other ICEV companies revenues	-88	-105	-142	-220	-263	-360	-72	52	321	-180	133	807
Change in other ICEV companies variable cost ($10K/ICEV)	-45	-62	-98	-112	-154	-245	-36	26	160	-90	66	403
Change in other ICEV companies and dealer profit	-43	-43	-44	-107	-108	-115	-36	26	160	-90	66	403
ICEV Cost to CA (Consumer loss-15% of profit change)	48	145	354	121	367	889	44	107	240	111	269	600

11.H CALCULATING CHANGES IN CONSUMERS' SURPLUS IN THE ICEV MARKET DUE TO THE ZEV MANDATE, 1998 TO 2002

In this appendix we explain how we calculate the consumers' surplus lost in the ICEV market (what we have called costs to consumers) if the ZEV mandate results in an increase in the price of ICEVs. (If not, there is no cost to consumers in the ICEV market due to the mandate.) The discussion also allows precise statement of how we decompose the sales effects of the ZEV mandate on the ICEV market into (demand) displacement effects and price effects, and explains a refinement of the interpretation of the demand curves used to calculate consumers' surplus gains in the EV market.

Conceptual Foundations

The policy being analyzed is the ZEV mandate during 1998 to 2002. It is analyzed in terms of annual effects--i.e., differences in equilibrium market conditions without and with the mandate--during each of those years. For simplicity, it is assumed that in the absence of the mandate, no EVs would be produced and sold in California.

We start with a simple description of how the effects of the policy are conceptualized. We then provide a (more detailed) graphical interpretation. The effects of the EV mandate on the ICEV and EV markets may be thought of as having the following components:

- The mandate leads the Big 7 (and perhaps other companies because of the ability to sell EV credits) to produce EVs (roughly 25,000 in each of the first three years and 60,000 in each of the next two years).

- Because EVs become available, the demand for ICEVs falls somewhat; this is what we have called the displacement effect. For example, the sale of 60,000 EVs might reduce demand for ICEVs by 30,000 vehicles, in which case we say there is a 50 percent displacement effect.

- The ZEV mandate increases the marginal cost of selling ICEVs in California and, as suggested by basic economic reasoning, these cost increases lead to increases in the prices of ICEVs in California.[391]

- The price increases for ICEVs tend to increase the demand for EVs.

All of these factors are represented in the two panels of Figure 11.H-1. The left panel (panel a) represents the ICEV market (with quantity denoted by Q and price by P_q). The right panel (panel b) represents the EV market (with quantity denoted by Z and price by P_z). Each panel contains two demand curves for vehicles. (D_q denotes demand for ICEVs and D_z denotes demand for EVs.) Another notational convention is that situations (demand levels, prices, quantities) without and with the mandate are denoted by "w/o" and "w/" respectively. The symbols used in each diagram are detailed in the notes below that diagram. The discussion here provides an overview.

The lower demand curve for ICEVs pertains to the situation with the mandate. The decrease (downward shift) in demand due to the mandate represents what we have termed the displacement effect. It is defined precisely as the horizontal distance between points A (the equilibrium without the mandate) and D. This distance is the decrease in demand due to the mandate, measured at the equilibrium price without the mandate. In the diagram, this distance is denoted by d. For example, if the ZEV mandate leads to the production of 62,000 EVs per year and the displacement fraction is 50 percent, d is 31,000 ICEVs. The movement up the lower demand curve (from point D to point B) is what we refer to as the price effect of the ZEV mandate.

---

[391]As discussed in Section 11.6, we do not dismiss the possibility that the ZEV mandate will not increase the costs of selling ICEVs in California. We have also discussed in the text the controversial issue of the extent to which ICEV cost increase would be factored into pricing decisions for California ICEVs. If there is no cost increase, there will be no effect on prices of ICEVs and there will be no consumer losses in the ICEV market due to the mandate. This appendix focuses on how the consumers' surplus analysis is performed for cases in which price effects are projected.

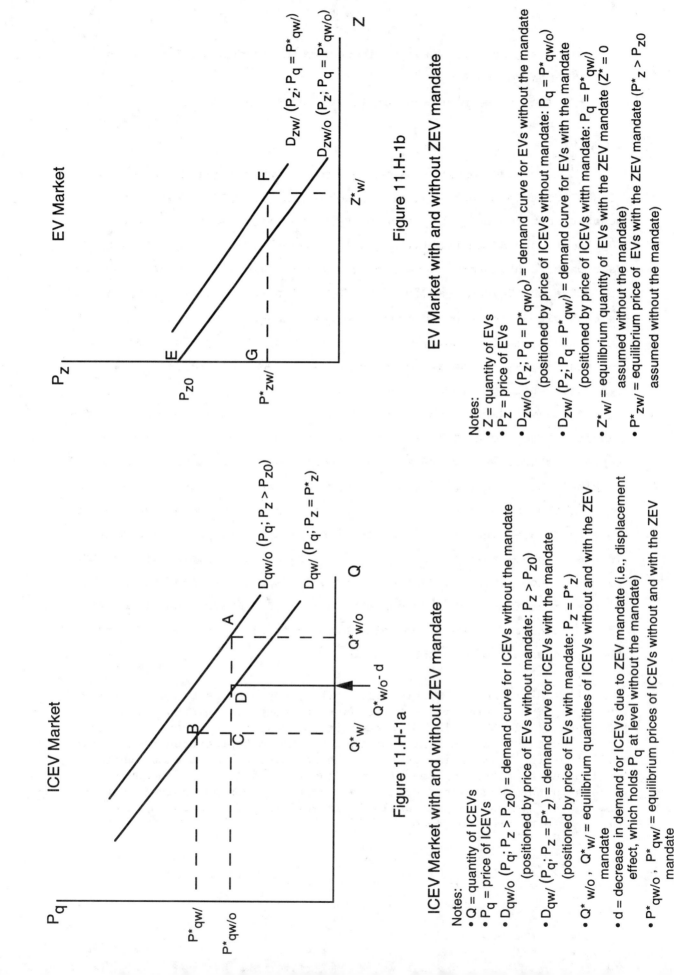

ICEV Market

Figure 11.H-1a

ICEV Market with and without ZEV mandate

Notes:
- Q = quantity of ICEVs
- P_q = price of ICEVs
- $D_{qw/o}$ $(P_q; P_z > P_{z0})$ = demand curve for ICEVs without the mandate
  (positioned by price of EVs without mandate: $P_z > P_{z0}$)
- $D_{qw/}$ $(P_q; P_z = P^*_z)$ = demand curve for ICEVs with the mandate
  (positioned by price of EVs with mandate: $P_z = P^*_z$)
- $Q^*_{w/o}$, $Q^*_{w/}$ = equilibrium quantities of ICEVs without and with the ZEV
  mandate
- d = decrease in demand for ICEVs due to ZEV mandate (i.e., displacement
  effect, which holds P_q at level without the mandate)
- $P^*_{qw/o}$, $P^*_{qw/}$ = equilibrium prices of ICEVs without and with the ZEV
  mandate

EV Market

Figure 11.H-1b

EV Market with and without ZEV mandate

Notes:
- Z = quantity of EVs
- P_z = price of EVs
- $D_{zw/o}$ $(P_z; P_q = P^*_{qw/o})$ = demand curve for EVs without the mandate
  (positioned by price of ICEVs without mandate: $P_q = P^*_{qw/o}$)
- $D_{zw/}$ $(P_z; P_q = P^*_{qw/})$ = demand curve for EVs with the mandate
  (positioned by price of ICEVs with mandate: $P_q = P^*_{qw/}$)
- $Z^*_{w/}$ = equilibrium quantity of EVs with the ZEV mandate ($Z^* = 0$
  assumed without the mandate)
- $P^*_{zw/}$ = equilibrium price of EVs with the ZEV mandate ($P^*_z > P_{z0}$
  assumed without the mandate)

To this point we have discussed the displacement effect in terms of the rate at which EVs sales displace (or reduce the demand for) ICEVs sales. In this appendix we follow standard economic reasoning--which allows us to apply standard tools of cost-benefit analysis--and interpret the decrease in demand for ICEVs as being due to a decrease in the price of EVs (a substitute for ICEVs). More specifically, and as detailed in panel b and its notes, we assume that without the mandate EV sales are zero because the price of EVs is higher than the price at which anyone would demand EVs (P_{z0} in the diagram, the vertical intercept of the demand curve for EVs without the mandate). An effect of the mandate is to induce companies to offer EVs for sale at a lower price, denoted $P^*_{zw/}$. Formally, this is what causes the demand for ICEVs to decrease.

Panel b of the figure indicates that the increase in the price of ICEVs tends to increase the demand for EVs. This is represented as an upward shift in the EV demand curve. (We refer back to this below.)

How Do We Measure Consumers' Surplus Lost in the ICEV Market?

As we have explained, the costs to buyers in the ICEV market are due to the increase in the price of ICEVs. These costs are the decreases in consumers' surplus in the ICEV market. In Figure 11.H-1(a), this is the sum of two areas:

- The rectangle with corners $P^*_{qw/}$, B, C, and $P^*_{qw/o}$, which represents the extra payments for ICEVs by consumers who buy ICEVs despite the price increase due the mandate.
- The triangle defined by the points A, B and C, which represents losses to consumers due to the decrease in the equilibrium quantity of ICEVs.

Thus, the lost consumers' surplus here is not--as is often taken to be the case--an area under a *single* demand curve. This is because the price change being analyzed (that of ICEVs) is itself the result of a price change in another market (the EV market), which causes the demand for ICEVs to shift.[392]

In our application, however, the area of the triangle DBA (which we do include in our measure of consumers' surplus lost in the ICEV market) is a small fraction of the total measure. The base of triangle DBA is of length d--the quantity displaced. Even for full displacement and the 5 percent mandate level, this is only 1/19 of the base of the area of the rectangle included in the measure of lost consumers' surplus. Noting that the heights of the rectangle and triangle are the same, we conclude that the area of the rectangle is at least 38 times as large as the area of the triangle.

Refining the Interpretation of Consumers' Surplus in the EV Market

In Appendix 11.D, we introduced two demand curves used to estimate upper and lower bounds on the gains to consumers in the EV market due to the mandate. For the same reasons that we cannot strictly conceptualize the lost consumers' surplus in the ICEV market as involving a single demand curve, we cannot strictly conceptualize the consumers' surplus gained in the EV market as involving a single demand curve when ICEV prices change because of the mandate: prices are changing in a related market and this shifts the demand for EVs. The proper interpretation of consumers' surplus in the EV market (when ICEV prices increase) is the

---

[392]The reasoning involved--which is intricate--is detailed in a different context in Sugden and Williams (1978, pp. 137-144). (Only especially dedicated readers will want to read on in this footnote. We are about to show in the text that the distinction is of little practical significance in the present application.) Adapting the arguments of Sugden and Williams to our application, the key to seeing why the area of the triangle DBA is part of the proper calculation (even though the movement from point A to point D is due to the shift in demand, not the ICEV price increase) is thinking of the price decrease of EVs and the price increase of ICEVs as taking place one infinitesimal unit at a time. As the price of EVs falls and the price of ICEVs rises, some buyers will shift from ICEV purchases to EV purchases. The tipping point for each buyer who does shift reveals the amount that buyer is just willing to pay for ICEVs, which is the key to measuring each consumer's surplus. Each of these valuations is revealed by a different pair of prices and hence the proper measures are taken from (slightly) different demand curves. (In many applications, where demand curves aren't shifting while prices change, there is only one demand curve to deal with.)

area of a triangle formed by the points E, F and G in panel b. While
this refinement is of conceptual relevance, we do not think it is of
practical significance in the current circumstances. For example, we
think the refinement is of very small quantitative significance relative
to the imprecision with which we are able to specify points like E and F
(which leads us to calculate bounds, ranges of effects, etc.).

REFERENCES

Abacus Technology Corporation, "Encouraging the Purchase and Use of Electric Motor Vehicles," draft report, prepared for Office of Transportation Technologies, U.S. Department of Energy, September 1, 1994.

Abernathy, William, J., and Kenneth Wayne, "Limits of the Learning Curve," *Harvard Business Review,* September-October 1974, pp. 109-119.

Adams, John W., overhead slides for presentation at CARB ZEV workshop, October 11, 1995, GM Ovonic, Indianapolis, IN, October 1995.

Alberini, Anna, David Edelstein, Winston Harrington, and Virginia McConnell, "Reducing Emissions from Old Cars: The Economics of the Delaware Vehicle Retirement Program," Washington, D.C.: Resources for the Future, Discussion Paper 94-27, April 1994.

Alberini, Anna, David Edelstein, and Virginia McConnell, "Will Speeding the Retirement of Old Cars Improve Air Quality?" *Resources,* Washington, D.C.: Resources for the Future, Spring 1994.

Alberini, Anna, Winston Harrington, and Virginia McConnell, "Estimating an Emissions Supply Function from Accelerated Vehicle Retirement Programs," Washington, D.C.: Resources for the Future, Discussion Paper 94-09, January 1994.

Alberini, Anna, Winston Harrington, and Virginia McConnell, "Determinants of Participation in Accelerated Vehicle Retirement Programs," Washington, D.C.: Resources for the Future, Discussion Paper QE93-18, June 1993.

Alberini, Anna, Winston Harrington, and Virginia McConnell, "Determinants of Participation in Accelerated Vehicle Retirement Programs," *RAND Journal of Economics*, Vol. 26, No. 1, Spring 1995.

Albu, Steve, Liwen Kao, and Tom Cackette, "The Effectiveness of the California Low-Emission Vehicle Program," paper presented to the Air & Waste Management Association, June 1992.

American Automobile Manufacturers Association, Comments Presented at the CARB Public Hearing on the State Implementation Plan, November 1994.

American Automobile Manufacturers Association, *Motor Vehicle Facts and Figures*, 1994.

Aroesty, Jerry, Lionel Galway, Louise Parker, Milt Kamins, Pamela Wyn Wicinas, Gwen Farnsworth, and David Rubenson, *Restructuring Smog Check: A Policy Synthesis*, Santa Monica, Calif.: RAND, DRU-885-CSTC, October 1994.

Automotive News, "Market Data Book," May 24, 1995.

Automotive News, "Ford Shows Part of Its Hand for Electric Ranger Pickup," June 19, 1995.

Automotive News, "EV Plant to Be Built in Kansas," September 18, 1995.

Automotive News, "GM to Sell EVs in Arizona, California in Fall," January 8, 1996.

Automotive News, "EV1 Serves as GM Halo Car With an Attitude," February 12, 1996.

Battelle Memorial Institute, *Vehicle Emissions: Statistical Analysis Report No. 6,* Second Draft, Columbus, OH: May 1995.

Beggs, S., S. Cardell, and J. Hausman, "Assessing the Potential Demand for Electric Cars," *Journal of Econometrics*, Vol. 17, 1981, pp. 1-19.

Berkovic, J., *Automobile Market Equilibrium*, Ph.D. Dissertation, MIT, 1983.

Booz, Allen & Hamilton, Inc., *Zero-Emission Vehicle Technology Assessment: Final Report*, prepared for the New York State Energy Research and Development Authority, NYSEROA Report 95-11, August 1995.

Bresnahan, Timothy F., and Dennis A. Yao, "The Nonpecuniary Costs of Automobile Emissions Standards," *RAND Journal of Economics*, Winter 1985, pp. 437-455.

Bunch, David, Mark Bradley, Thomas F. Golub, Ryuichi Kitamura, and Gareth P. Occhiuzzo, "Demand for Clean-Fuel Vehicles in California: A Discrete-Choice Stated Preference Pilot Project," *Transportation Research A*, Vol. 27A, No. 3, 1993, pp. 237-253.

Bureau of Automotive Repair, California Department of Consumer Affairs, *Revised State Implementation Plan for California's Motor Vehicle Inspection and Maintenance Program*, Sacramento, Calif.: June 1995.

Bureau of Labor Statistics, "Report on Quality Changes for 1996 Model Vehicles," U. S. Department of Labor press release, November 9, 1995.

Bureau of National Affairs, "California Air Resources Board Mobile Source Emission Standards Summary; Revised July 1, 1991," *Environment Reporter,* the Bureau of National Affairs, March 13, 1992.

Burns, Vaughn, R., Albert M. Hochhauser, Robert M. Reuter, Larry A. Rapp, Jay C. Knepper, Brian Rippon, William J. Koehl, William R. Leppard, James A. Rutherford, Jack D. Benson, and Louis J. Painter, "Gasoline Reformulation and Vehicle Technology Effects on Emissions-- Auto/Oil Air Quality Improvement Research Program," SAE Technical

Paper Series #952509, SAE International, Warrendale, PA: October 1995.

Calfee, John E., "Estimating the Demand for Electric Automobiles Using Fully Disaggregated Probabilistic Choice Analysis," *Transportation Research B*, Vol. 19B, No. 4, 1985, pp. 287-301.

California Air Resources Board, "Staff Report: Initial Statement of Reasons for Proposed Rulemaking. Public Hearing to Consider New Regulations Regarding Malfunction and Diagnostic System Requirements Applicable to 1994 and Later New California Passenger Cars, Light-Duty Trucks, and Medium-Duty Vehicles with Feedback Fuel Control Systems (OBD II)," Sacramento, Calif.: July 28, 1989a.

California Air Resources Board, "Technical Support Document: Revisions to Malfunction and Diagnostic System Requirements Applicable to 1994 and Later New California Passenger Cars, Light-Duty Trucks, and Medium-Duty Vehicles with Feedback Control Systems (OBD II)," Sacramento, Calif.: July 1989b.

California Air Resources Board, "Technical Support Document for a Proposal to Amend Regulations Regarding Evaporative Emissions Standards, Test Procedures, and Durability Requirements Applicable to Passenger Cars, Light-Duty Trucks, Medium-Duty Vehicles, and Heavy-Duty Vehicles, Mobile Source Division," Sacramento, Calif.: August 9, 1990a.

California Air Resources Board, "Reformulated Gasoline: Proposed Phase 1 Specifications, Technical Support Document," Sacramento, Calif.: August 13, 1990b.

California Air Resources Board, "Proposed Regulations for Low-Emission Vehicles and Clean Fuels: Technical Support Document," Sacramento, Calif: August 13, 1990c.

California Air Resources Board, "Proposed Regulations for California Phase 2 Reformulated Gasoline: Technical Support Document," Sacramento, Calif.: October 4, 1991.

California Air Resources Board, "Staff Report: 1994 Low-Emission Vehicle and Zero Emission Vehicle Program Review," Mobile Source Division, Sacramento, Calif.: April 1994a.

California Air Resources Board, "Technical Support Document: Zero Emission Vehicle Update," Mobile Source Division, Sacramento, Calif.: April 1994b.

California Air Resources Board, "Test Report of the Light-Duty Vehicle Surveillance Program, Series 12 (LDVSP 12)," Mobile Source Division, El Monte, Calif: July 1994c.

- 453 -

California Air Resources Board, "The California State Implementation Plan for Ozone," Sacramento, Calif.: November, 15, 1994d.

California Air Resources Board, "Summary of In-Use Vehicle Emission Compliance Testing and Recalls Implemented in 1994," Mobile Source Division, El Monte, Calif.: February 1995a.

California Air Resources Board, "Staff Report: Initial Statement of Reasons for Proposed Rulemaking for Adoption of On-Board Refueling Vapor Recovery Standards," Sacramento, Calif.: May 11, 1995b.

California Air Resources Board, "Proposed Amendments to the Low-Emission Vehicle Regulations to Add an Equivalent Zero-Emission Vehicle (EZEV) Standard and Allow Zero-Emission Vehicle Credit for Hybrid-Electric Vehicles," Preliminary Draft Staff Report, Sacramento, Calif.: July 14, 1995c.

California Air Resources Board, "California RFG, Fact Sheet 3," Sacramento, Calif.: August 1995d.

California Air Resources Board, "Methodology for Estimating Emissions from On-Road Motor Vehicles, Volume I," Draft Report, Mobile Source Emission Inventory Branch, Sacramento, Calif.: December 1995e.

California Air Resources Board, "Impacts of Individual Changes," presentation of John Ellis to CARB Workshop on Draft MVEI7G, December 15, 1995f.

California Energy Commission, *1992 Electricity Report*, Sacramento, Calif., January 1993.

California Motor Car Dealers Association, Government Affairs Office, "Re: The Zero Emission Vehicle Regulation," Letter to Assemblyman Katz and Senator Kopp, March 23, 1995.

California Public Utilities Commission, *Decision 91-06-022*, Sacramento, Calif., June 5, 1991.

CALSTART, Letter to Lloyd Dixon and Steven Garber from Bill Van Amburg and Paul Helliker, in authors' files, October 31, 1995.

Calvert, J.G., J.B. Heywood, R.F. Sawyer, and J.H. Seinfeld, "Achieving Acceptable Air Quality: Some Reflections on Controlling Vehicle Emissions", *Science*, Vol. 261, July 2, 1993.

Crandall, Robert W., Howard K. Gruenspecht, Theodore E. Keeler and Lester B. Lave, *Regulating the Automobile*, Washington, D.C.: The Brookings Institution, 1986.

Cropper, Maureen L., Sema K. Ayedede, and Paul R. Portney, "Discounting Human Lives," *American Journal of Agricultural Economics*, December 1991, pp. 141-145.

Cropper, Maureen L., and A. Myrick Freeman, III, "Valuing Environmental Health Effects," Washington, D.C.: Resources for the Future, Discussion Paper QE 90-14, 1990.

Cropper, Maureen L., and Paul R. Portney, "Discounting and the Evaluation of Life-Saving Programs," Washington, D.C.: Resources for the Future, Discussion Paper CRM 90-02, January 1990.

Dahl, Carol, and Thomas Sterner, "Analysing Gasoline Demand Elasticities: A Survey," *Energy Economics*, July 1991, pp. 203-210.

Delucchi, Mark, *Hydrogen Fuel-Cell Vehicles*, Institute of Transportation Studies, University of California, Davis, UCD-ITS-RR-92-14, September 1992.

Dino, Richard N., "Forecasting the Price Evolution of New Electronic Products, *Journal of Forecasting,* Vol. 4, pp. 39-60, 1984.

Doddapaneni, N., G. Nagasubramanian, and D. Ingersoll, *Solid-State Rechargeable Lithium Batteries for Electric Vehicle Applications*, Sandia National Laboratories and Jet Propulsion Laboratory, 1994.

Dohring Company, "Automotive News: California Electric Vehicle Consumer Study," Executive Summary, Glendale, Calif., December 1994.

DRI/McGraw-Hill and Charles River Associates, "Economic Consequences of Adopting California Programs for Alternative Fuel Vehicles," February 22, 1994.

Engineering-Science, Inc., *Vehicle Emission Reduction Studies (VERS), Part 2: Purchasing and Scrapping High Emitters*, Pasadena, CA, December 1994.

Environmental Defense Fund and General Motors, "Mobile Emissions Reduction Crediting," no date.

Fetcenko, M.A., S. K Dhar, S. Venkatesan, A. Holland, P.R. Gifford, D.A. Corrigan, and S.R. Ovshinsky, "Ovonic HiMH Battery Technology for Portable and Electric Vehicle Application," Ovonic Battery Company, Troy, MI, paper presented at 12th International Seminar on Primary and Secondary Battery Technology and Application, Deerfield Beach, FL, March 1995.

Freeman, A. Myrick, III, "Methods for Assessing the Benefits of Environmental Programs," in Allen V. Kneese and James L. Sweeney, eds., *Handbook of Natural Resource and Energy Economics*, Vol. I, Amsterdam: Elsevier, 1985.

Fulmer, Mark, and Stephen Bernow, "A Social Cost Analysis of Alternative Fuels for Light Vehicles," in Daniel Sperling and Susan A. Shaheen, eds., *Transportation and Energy: Strategies for a Sustainable*

Transportation System, Washington, D.C. and Berkeley, Calif.: American Council for an Energy-Efficient Economy, 1995.

GAO, see General Accounting Office.

Garber, Steven, and Steven Klepper, "'Administered Pricing' or Competition Coupled with Errors of Measurement?" *International Economic Review*, Vol. 21, 1980, pp. 413-435.

General Accounting Office (U.S. Congress), *Electric Vehicles: Likely Consequences of U.S. and Other Nation's Programs and Policies*, Washington D.C.: U.S. Government Printing Office, GAO/PEMD-95-7, December 1994.

German, John M., "Off-Cycle Emission and Fuel Efficiency Considerations," presentation to Sustainable Transportation-Energy Strategies Conference, Asilomar, CA, August 1, 1995.

Glazer, Amihai, Daniel B. Klein, and Charles Lave, "Clean on Paper, Dirty on the Road: Troubles with California's Smog Check," *Journal of Transport Economics and Policy*, January 1995, pp. 85-92.

Gordon, Peter, and Harry W. Richardson, "The Case Against Electric Vehicle Mandates in California," Los Angeles, Calif.: Reason Foundation, Policy Study No. 189, May 1995.

Greene, David L., "Estimating Daily Vehicle Usage Distributions and the Implications for Limited-Range Vehicles," *Transportation Research-B*, Vol. 19B, No. 4, 1985, pp. 347-358.

Gruenspecht, Howard K., "Differentiated Regulation: The Case of Auto Emissions Standards," *American Economic Review*, Vol. 72, May 1982a, pp. 328-331.

Gruenspecht, Howard K., *Differentiated Regulation: A Theory with Applications to Automobile Emissions Controls*, Ph.D. Dissertation, Yale University, December 1982b.

Hahn, Robert, "An Economic Analysis of Scrappage," *RAND Journal of Economics*, Vol. 26, Summer 1995.

Haines, Jonathan, *Comments of The Toyota Technical Center, ZEV Technological Progress Public Forum, October 11, 1995*, Toyota Technical Center, Los Angeles, CA, October 1995.

Hall, Jane V., Arthur M. Winer, Michael T. Kleinman, Frederick W. Lurmann, Victor Brajer, and Steven D. Colome, "Valuing the Health Benefits of Clean Air," *Science*, Vol. 255, February 14, 1992, pp. 812-817.

Harrington, Winston, and Michael A. Toman, "Methods for Estimating the Economic Value of Human Health Benefits from Environmental

Improvement," Washington, D.C.: Resources for the Future, Discussion Paper 94-41, August 1994.

Harrington, Winston, Margaret A. Walls, and Virginia McConnell, "Shifting Gears: New Directions for Cars and Clean Air," Washington, D.C.: Resources for the Future, Discussion Paper 94-09-REV, February 1995.

Henderson, Timothy P., and Michael Rusin, "Electric Vehicles: Their Technical and Economic Status," American Petroleum Institute, Research Study #073, January 1994.

Hill, Daniel H., "Derived Demand Estimation with Survey Experiments: Commercial Electric Vehicles," *Review of Economics and Statistics*, May 1987, pp. 277-285.

Honda, "1996 Honda Civic Models First to Receive LEV Certification", press release, Torrance, CA, August 29, 1995.

Hsu, Shi-Ling, and Daniel Sperling, "Uncertain Air Quality Impacts of Retirement Programs," Transportation Research Record 1444, 1994.

Hwang, Roland, Marshall Miller, Ann B. Thorpe, and Debbie Lew, *Driving Out Pollution: The Benefits of Electric Vehicles,* Union of Concerned Scientists, Berkeley, Calif.: November 1994.

Illinois Environmental Protection Agency, *Pilot Project for Vehicle Scrapping in Illinois*, May 1993.

Just, Richard E., Darrell L. Hueth, and Andrew Schmitz, *Applied Welfare Economics and Public Policy*, Englewood Cliffs, NJ: Prentice-Hall, 1982.

Kalhammer, F. R., A. Kozawa, C. B. Moyer, B. B. Owens, *Performance and Availability of Batteries for Electric Vehicles: A Report of the Battery Technical Advisory Panel*, California Air Resources Board, December 11, 1995.

Khazzoom, J. Daniel, "The Impact of a Gasoline Tax on Auto Exhaust Emissions," *Journal of Policy Analysis and Management*, Vol. 10, 1991.

Klausmeier, Rob, Sandep Kishan, Rick Baker, Andrew Burnette, and Joel McFarland, *Evaluation of the California Pilot Inspection/Maintenance (I/M) Program*, draft final report, de la Torre Klausmeier Consulting, Inc., and Radian Corporation, Austin, Texas, 31 March 1995.

Kliet, Andrew, "The Effect of Annual Changes in Automobile Economy Standards," *Journal of Regulatory Economics*, Vol. 2, 1990.

Kopp, Raymond J., "Discounting for Damage Assessment," Washington, D.C.: Resources for the Future, Discussion Paper 94-31, May 1994.

Krupnick, Alan J., and Paul R. Portney, "Controlling Urban Air Pollution: A Benefit-Cost Assessment," *Science*, April 26, 1991, pp. 522-528.

Krupnick, Alan J., and Margaret A. Walls, "The Cost-Effectiveness of Methanol for Reducing Motor Vehicle Emissions and Urban Ozone," *Journal of Policy Analysis and Management*, Vol. 11, 1992, pp. 373-396.

Kurani, Kenneth S., Tom Turrentine, and Daniel Sperling, "Demand for Electric Vehicles in Hybrid Households: An Exploratory Analysis," *Transport Policy*, Vol. 1, No. 4, 1994, pp. 244-256.

Lareau, Thomas J., "Improving Cost-Effectiveness Estimation: A Reassessment of Control Options to Reduce Ozone Precursor Emissions," American Petroleum Institute, Research Study #075, August 1994.

Lave, Lester, Chris T. Hendrickson, and Francis Clay McMichael, "Environmental Implications of Electric Cars," *Science*, Vol. 268, May 19, 1995, pp. 993-995.

Lippincott, Alan L., Jack S. Segal, and Shih-Chen Wang, "Emissions of California Phase 2 Gasoline in Advanced Technology Vehicles," SAE Technical Paper 932677, Warrendale PA, October 1993,

Mader and Associates, "Assessment of the U.S. Electric Vehicle Market," Los Altos, Calif.: October 1993.

McConnell, Virginia, and Winston Harrington, "Cost-Effectiveness of Enhanced Motor Vehicle Inspection and Maintenance Programs," Washington, D.C.: Resources for the Future, Discussion Paper QE92-18-REV, August 1992.

Moomaw, William R., Christopher L. Shaw, Wayne C. White, and Janet L. Sawin, *Near-Term Electric Vehicle Costs,* The Fletcher School of Law and Diplomacy and the Global Development and Environment Institute, Tufts University, October, 1994.

Moore, Taylor, "Producing the Near-Term Battery," *EPRI Journal*, pp. 7-13, April/May 1994.

Moss, Steven J., Richard J. McCann, et al., "Economic Analysis of the Proposed State Implementation Plan (SIP)--Conducted Prior to Its Consideration by the California Air Resources Board (CARB)," M.Cubed, San Franciso, CA, December 1995.

National Economic Research Associates, Inc., "Valuation of Air Pollution Damages," Cambridge, MA: 1992.

National Research Council, *Rethinking the Ozone Problem in Urban and Regional Air Pollution*, Washington, D.C.: National Academy Press, 1991.

Nesbitt, Kevin A., Kenneth S. Kurani, and Mark A. Delucchi, "Home Recharging and Household Electric Vehicle Market: A Near-Term Constraints Analysis," *Transportation Research Record*, 1992, pp. 11-19.

New York Times, "Chrysler-Electrosource Deal Seen on Battery for Electric Mini-Van", Matthew L. Wald, April 6, 1995.

Office of Technology Assessment (U.S. Congress), *Retiring Old Cars: Programs to Save Gasoline and Reduce Emissions*, Washington D.C.: U.S. Government Printing Office, July 1992.

PSA Peugeot Citron, "Peugeot 106 Electric," press information, Southfield, MI, June 1995.

Ross, Marc, Rob Goodwin, Michael Q. Wang, Rick Watkins, and Tom Wenzel, *Real-World Emissions from Model Year 1993, 2000 and 2010 Passenger Cars,* Washington D.C.: American Council for an Energy Efficient Economy, November 1995.

Scherrer, Huel C., and David B. Kittelson, "I/M Effectiveness as Directly Measured by Ambient CO Data," Warrendale, Penn.: Society of Automotive Engineers Technical Paper Series, No. 940302, 1994.

Sierra Research, Inc., "The Cost-Effectiveness of Further Regulating Mobile Source Emissions," Sacramento, Calif.: February 28, 1994a.

Sierra Research, Inc., "Evaluating the Benefits of Air Pollution Control: Method Development and Application to Refueling and Evaporative Emissions Control," Sacramento, Calif.: March 31, 1994b.

Sierra Research, Inc., Supplement to: "The Cost Effectiveness of Further Regulating Mobile Source Emissions--The Effects of Using EMFAC7F Instead of Mobile5a," Sacramento, Calif.: August 9, 1994c.

Sierra Research, Inc., "Evaluation of CARB SIP Mobile Source Measures," Sacramento, Calif.: November 9, 1994d.

Sierra Research, Inc., "Vehicle Scrappage: An Alternative to More Stringent New Vehicle Standards in California," Sacramento, Calif.: March 15, 1995a.

Sierra Research, Inc., "Achieving CARB's Mobile Emission Reduction Goals Without ZEVs," Sacramento, Calif.: May 30, 1995b.

Sierra Research, Inc., Letter from James Lyons to Lloyd Dixon, in authors' files, Sacramento, Calif.: July 18, 1995c.

Small, Kenneth A, and Camilla Kazimi, "On the Costs of Air Pollution from Motor Vehicles," *Journal of Transport Economics and Policy*, Vol. XXIX, No. 1, January 1995, pp. 7-32.

Sommerville, R.J., *Evaluation of the California Smog Check Program and Recommendation for Program Improvements: Fourth Report to the Legislature*, Sacramento, Calif.: California I/M Review Committee, February 16, 1993.

Sony Corporation, Sony Announces the Technological Development of Lithium Ion, Rechargeable Batteries for Electric Vehicle Applications, press release, September 28, 1995.

South Coast Air Quality Management District, *Amendment to the 1991 Air Quality Management Plan*, Los Angeles, Calif.: July 1992.

Sperling, Daniel, *Future Drive: Electric Vehicles and Sustainable Transportation*, Island Press, Washington, D.C., 1995.

Sperling, Daniel, and Susan A. Shaheen, (eds.), *Transportation and Energy: Strategies for a Sustainable Transportation System*, Washington, D.C. and Berkeley, Calif.: American Council for an Energy-Efficient Economy, 1995.

Sugden, Robert, and Alan Williams, *The Principles of Practical Cost-Benefit Analysis*, Oxford, UK: Oxford University Press, 1978.

Tirole, Jean, *The Theory of Industrial Organization*, Cambridge, MA: MIT Press, 1988.

Turrentine, Thomas, and Kenneth Kurani, "The Household Market for Electric Vehicles: Testing the Hybrid Household Hypothesis--A Reflexively Designed Survey of New-Car-Buying, Multi-Vehicle California Households," Davis, Calif.: Institute of Transportation Studies, UC Davis, UCD-ITS-RR-95-5, May 12, 1995.

Unocal, Inc., "SCRAP, A Clean-Air Initiative from UNOCAL," 1991.

USA Today, "Flap Over 'Clean' Engine," January 13, 1995.

U.S. Department of Energy, *Encouraging the Purchase and Use of Electric Motor Vehicles*, Washington, D.C.: September 1994.

U.S. Department of Energy, *Encouraging the Purchase and Use of Electric Motor Vehicles*, Washington, D.C.: Office of Transportation Technologies, May 1995.

Woodruff, David, "Shocker at GM: People Like the Impact," *Business Week*, January 23, 1995, p. 47.

ICJ PUBLICATIONS

Outcomes

General

Carroll, S. J., with N. M. Pace, *Assessing the Effects of Tort Reforms*, R-3554-ICJ, 1987. $7.50.

Galanter, M., B. Garth, D. Hensler, and F. K. Zemans, *How to Improve Civil Justice Policy*, RP-282. (Reprinted from *Judicature*, Vol. 77, No. 4, January/February 1994.) Free.

Hensler, D. R., *Trends in California Tort Liability Litigation*, P-7287-ICJ, 1987. (Testimony before the Select Committee on Insurance, California State Assembly, October 1987.) $4.00.

_____ , *Researching Civil Justice: Problems and Pitfalls*, P-7604-ICJ, 1988. (Reprinted from *Law and Contemporary Problems*, Vol. 51, No. 3, Summer 1988.) $4.00.

_____ , *Reading the Tort Litigation Tea Leaves: What's Going on in the Civil Liability System?* RP-226. (Reprinted from *The Justice System Journal*, Vol. 16, No. 2, 1993.) Free.

_____ , *Why We Don't Know More About the Civil Justice System—and What We Could Do About It*, RP-363, 1995. (Reprinted from *USC Law*, Fall 1994.) Free.

Hensler, D. R., and E. Moller, *Trends in Punitive Damages: Preliminary Data from Cook County, Illinois, and San Francisco, California*, DRU-1014-ICJ, 1995. Free.

Hensler, D. R., M. E. Vaiana, J. S. Kakalik, and M. A. Peterson, *Trends in Tort Litigation: The Story Behind the Statistics*, R-3583-ICJ, 1987. $4.00.

Hill, P. T., and D. L. Madey, *Educational Policymaking Through the Civil Justice System*, R-2904-ICJ, 1982. $4.00.

Lipson, A. J., *California Enacts Prejudgment Interest: A Case Study of Legislative Action*, N-2096-ICJ, 1984. $4.00.

Moller, E. *Trends in Punitive Damages: Preliminary Data from California*, DRU-1059-ICJ, 1995. Free

Shubert, G. H., *Some Observations on the Need for Tort Reform*, P-7189-ICJ, 1986. (Testimony before the National Conference of State Legislatures, January 1986.) $4.00.

_____ , *Changes in the Tort System: Helping Inform the Policy Debate*, P-7241-ICJ, 1986. $4.00.

Jury Verdicts

Carroll, S. J., *Jury Awards and Prejudgment Interest in Tort Cases*, N-1994-ICJ, 1983. $4.00.

Chin, A., and M. A. Peterson, *Deep Pockets, Empty Pockets: Who Wins in Cook County Jury Trials*, R-3249-ICJ, 1985. $10.00.

Dertouzos, J. N., E. Holland, and P. A. Ebener, *The Legal and Economic Consequences of Wrongful Termination*, R-3602-ICJ, 1988. $7.50.

Hensler, D. R., *Summary of Research Results on the Tort Liability System*, P-7210-ICJ, 1986. (Testimony before the Committee on Commerce, Science, and Transportation, United States Senate, February 1986.) $4.00.

Hensler, D. R., and E. Moller, *Trends in Punitive Damages: Preliminary Data from Cook County, Illinois, and San Francisco, California*, DRU-1014-ICJ, 1995. Free.

MacCoun, R. J., *Getting Inside the Black Box: Toward a Better Understanding of Civil Jury Behavior*, N-2671-ICJ, 1987. $4.00.

_____ , *Experimental Research on Jury Decisionmaking*, R-3832-ICJ, 1989. (Reprinted from *Science*, Vol. 244, June 1989.) $4.00.

_____ , *Inside the Black Box: What Empirical Research Tells Us About Decisionmaking by Civil Juries*, RP-238, 1993. (Reprinted from Robert E. Litan, ed., *Verdict: Assessing the Civil Jury System*, The Brookings Institution, 1993.) Free.

_____ , *Is There a "Deep-Pocket" Bias in the Tort System?* IP-130, October 1993. Free.

_____ , *Blaming Others to a Fault?* RP-286. (Reprinted from *Chance*, Vol. 6, No. 4, Fall 1993.) Free.

_____ , *Improving Jury Comprehension in Criminal and Civil Trials*, CT-136, July 1995. Free.

Moller, E. *Trends in Punitive Damages: Preliminary Data from California*, DRU-1059-ICJ, 1995. Free.

_____ , *Trends in Civil Jury Verdicts Since 1985*, MR-694-ICJ, 1996. $15.00.

Peterson, M. A., *Compensation of Injuries: Civil Jury Verdicts in Cook County*, R-3011-ICJ, 1984. $7.50.

_____ , *Punitive Damages: Preliminary Empirical Findings*, N-2342-ICJ, 1985. $4.00.

_____ , *Summary of Research Results: Trends and Patterns in Civil Jury Verdicts*, P-7222-ICJ, 1986. (Testimony before the Subcommittee on Oversight, Committee on Ways and Means, United States House of Representatives, March 1986.) $4.00.

_____ , *Civil Juries in the 1980s: Trends in Jury Trials and Verdicts in California and Cook County, Illinois*, R-3466-ICJ, 1987. $7.50.

Peterson, M. A., and G. L. Priest, *The Civil Jury: Trends in Trials and Verdicts, Cook County, Illinois, 1960-1979*, R-2881-ICJ, 1982. $7.50.

Peterson, M. A., S. Sarma, and M. G. *Shanley, Punitive Damages: Empirical Findings*, R-3311-ICJ, 1987. $7.50.

Selvin, M., and L. Picus, *The Debate over Jury Performance: Observations from a Recent Asbestos Case*, R-3479-ICJ, 1987. $10.00.

Shanley, M. G., and M. A. Peterson, *Comparative Justice: Civil Jury Verdicts in San Francisco and Cook Counties, 1959-1980*, R-3006-ICJ, 1983. $7.50.

_____ , *Posttrial Adjustments to Jury Awards*, R-3511-ICJ, 1987. $7.50.

Costs of Dispute Resolution

Dunworth, T., and J. S. Kakalik, *Preliminary Observations on Implementation of the Pilot Program of the Civil Justice Reform Act of 1990*, RP-361, 1995. (Reprinted from *Stanford Law Review*, Vol. 46, No. 6, July 1994.) Free.

Hensler, D. R., *Does ADR Really Save Money? The Jury's Still Out*, RP-327, 1994. (Reprinted from *The National Law Journal*, April 11, 1994.) Free.

Hensler, D. R., M. E. Vaiana, J. S. Kakalik, and M. A. Peterson, *Trends in Tort Litigation: The Story Behind the Statistics*, R-3583-ICJ, 1987. $4.00.

Kakalik, J. S., and A. E. Robyn, *Costs of the Civil Justice System: Court Expenditures for Processing Tort Cases*, R-2888-ICJ, 1982. $7.50.

Kakalik, J. S., and R. L. Ross, *Costs of the Civil Justice System: Court Expenditures for Various Types of Civil Cases*, R-2985-ICJ, 1983. $10.00.

Kakalik, J. S., P. A. Ebener, W. L. F. Felstiner, and M. G. Shanley, *Costs of Asbestos Litigation*, R-3042-ICJ, 1983. $4.00.

Kakalik, J. S., P. A. Ebener, W. L. F. Felstiner, G. W. Haggstrom, and M. G. Shanley, *Variation in Asbestos Litigation Compensation and Expenses*, R-3132-ICJ, 1984. $7.50.

Kakalik, J. S., and N. M. Pace, *Costs and Compensation Paid in Tort Litigation*, R-3391-ICJ, 1986. $15.00.

_____ , *Costs and Compensation Paid in Tort Litigation*, P-7243-ICJ, 1986. (Testimony before the Subcommittee on Trade, Productivity, and Economic Growth, Joint Economic Committee of the Congress, July 1986.) $4.00.

Kakalik, J. S., E. M. King, M. Traynor, P. A. Ebener, and L. Picus, *Costs and Compensation Paid in Aviation Accident Litigation*, R-3421-ICJ, 1988. $10.00.

Kakalik, J. S., M. Selvin, and N. M. Pace, *Averting Gridlock: Strategies for Reducing Civil Delay in the Los Angeles Superior Court*, R-3762-ICJ, 1990. $10.00.

Lind, E. A., *Arbitrating High-Stakes Cases: An Evaluation of Court-Annexed Arbitration in a United States District Court*, R-3809-ICJ, 1990. $10.00.

MacCoun, R. J., E. A. Lind, D. R. Hensler, D. L. Bryant, and P. A. Ebener, *Alternative Adjudication: An Evaluation of the New Jersey Automobile Arbitration Program*, R-3676-ICJ, 1988. $10.00.

Peterson, M. A., *New Tools for Reducing Civil Litigation Expenses*, R-3013-ICJ, 1983. $4.00.

Priest, G. L., *Regulating the Content and Volume of Litigation: An Economic Analysis*, R-3084-ICJ, 1983. $4.00.

Dispute Resolution

Court Delay

Adler, J. W., W. L. F. Felstiner, D. R. Hensler, and M. A. Peterson, *The Pace of Litigation: Conference Proceedings*, R-2922-ICJ, 1982. $10.00.

Dunworth, T., and J. S. Kakalik, *Preliminary Observations on Implementation of the Pilot Program of the Civil Justice Reform Act of 1990*, RP-361, 1995. (Reprinted from *Stanford Law Review*, Vol. 46, No. 6, July 1994.) Free.

Dunworth, T., and N. M. Pace, *Statistical Overview of Civil Litigation in the Federal Courts*, R-3885-ICJ, 1990. $7.50.

Ebener, P. A., *Court Efforts to Reduce Pretrial Delay: A National Inventory*, R-2732-ICJ, 1981. $10.00.

Kakalik, J. S., M. Selvin, and N. M. Pace, *Averting Gridlock: Strategies for Reducing Civil Delay in the Los Angeles Superior Court*, R-3762-ICJ, 1990. $10.00.

_____ , *Strategies for Reducing Civil Delay in the Los Angeles Superior Court: Technical Appendixes*, N-2988-ICJ, 1990. $10.00.

Lind, E. A., *Arbitrating High-Stakes Cases: An Evaluation of Court-Annexed Arbitration in a United States District Court*, R-3809-ICJ, 1990. $10.00.

MacCoun, R. J., E. A. Lind, D. R. Hensler, D. L. Bryant, and P. A. Ebener, *Alternative Adjudication: An Evaluation of the New Jersey Automobile Arbitration Program*, R-3676-ICJ, 1988. $10.00.

Resnik, J., *Managerial Judges*, R-3002-ICJ, 1982. (Reprinted from the *Harvard Law Review*, Vol. 96:374, December 1982.) $7.50.

Selvin, M., and P. A. Ebener, *Managing the Unmanageable: A History of Civil Delay in the Los Angeles Superior Court*, R-3165-ICJ, 1984. $15.00.

Alternative Dispute Resolution

Adler, J. W., D. R. Hensler, and C. E. Nelson, with the assistance of G. J. Rest, *Simple Justice: How Litigants Fare in the Pittsburgh Court Arbitration Program*, R-3071-ICJ, 1983. $15.00.

Bryant, D. L., *Judicial Arbitration in California: An Update*, N-2909-ICJ, 1989. $4.00.

Ebener, P. A., and D. R. Betancourt, *Court-Annexed Arbitration: The National Picture*, N-2257-ICJ, 1985. $25.00.

Hensler, D. R., *Court-Annexed Arbitration in the State Trial Court System*, P-6963-ICJ, 1984. (Testimony before the Judiciary Committee Subcommittee on Courts, United States Senate, February 1984.) $4.00.

_____ , *Reforming the Civil Litigation Process: How Court Arbitration Can Help*, P-7027-ICJ, 1984. (Reprinted from the *New Jersey Bell Journal*, August 1984.) $4.00.

_____ , *What We Know and Don't Know About Court-Administered Arbitration*, N-2444-ICJ, 1986. $4.00.

_____ , *Court-Ordered Arbitration: An Alternative View*, RP-103, 1992. (Reprinted from *The University of Chicago Legal Forum*, Vol. 1990.) Free.

_____ , *Science in the Court: Is There a Role for Alternative Dispute Resolution?* RP-109, 1992. (Reprinted from *Law and Contemporary Problems*, Vol. 54, No. 3, Summer 1991.) Free.

_____ , *Does ADR Really Save Money? The Jury's Still Out*, RP-327, 1994. (Reprinted from *The National Law Journal*, April 11, 1994.) Free.

_____ , *A Glass Half Full, a Glass Half Empty: The Use of Alternative Dispute Resolution in Mass Personal Injury Litigation*, RP-446, 1995. (Reprinted from *Texas Law Review*, Vol. 73, No. 7, June 1995.) Free.

Hensler, D. R., A. J. Lipson, and E. S. Rolph, *Judicial Arbitration in California: The First Year*, R-2733-ICJ, 1981. $10.00.

_____ , *Judicial Arbitration in California: The First Year: Executive Summary*, R-2733/1-ICJ, 1981. $4.00.

Hensler, D. R., and J. W. Adler, with the assistance of G. J. Rest, *Court-Administered Arbitration: An Alternative for Consumer Dispute Resolution*, N-1965-ICJ, 1983. $4.00.

Lind, E. A., *Arbitrating High-Stakes Cases: An Evaluation of Court-Annexed Arbitration in a United States District Court*, R-3809-ICJ, 1990. $10.00.

Lind, E. A., R. J. MacCoun, P. A. Ebener, W. L. F. Felstiner, D. R. Hensler, J. Resnik, and T. R. Tyler, *The Perception of Justice: Tort Litigants' Views of Trial, Court-Annexed Arbitration, and Judicial Settlement Conferences*, R-3708-ICJ, 1989. $7.50.

MacCoun, R. J., *Unintended Consequences of Court Arbitration: A Cautionary Tale from New Jersey*, RP-134, 1992. (Reprinted from *The Justice System Journal*, Vol. 14, No. 2, 1991.) Free.

MacCoun, R. J., E. A. Lind, D. R. Hensler, D. L. Bryant, and P. A. Ebener, *Alternative Adjudication: An Evaluation of the New Jersey Automobile Arbitration Program*, R-3676-ICJ, 1988. $10.00.

MacCoun, R. J., E. A. Lind, and T. R. Tyler, *Alternative Dispute Resolution in Trial and Appellate Courts*, RP-117, 1992. (Reprinted from *Handbook of Psychology and Law*, 1992.) Free.

Moller, E., E. S. Rolph, P. Ebener, *Private Dispute Resolution in the Banking Industry*, MR-259-ICJ, 1993. $13.00.

Resnik, J. *Many Doors? Closing Doors? Alternative Dispute Resolution and Adjudication*, RP-439, 1995. (Reprinted from *The Ohio State Journal on Dispute Resolution*, Vol. 10, No. 2, 1995.) Free.

Rolph, E. S., *Introducing Court-Annexed Arbitration: A Policymaker's Guide*, R-3167-ICJ, 1984. $10.00.

Rolph, E. S., and D. R. Hensler, *Court-Ordered Arbitration: The California Experience*, N-2186-ICJ, 1984. $4.00.

Rolph, E. S., and E. Moller, *Evaluating Agency Alternative Dispute Resolution Programs: A Users' Guide to Data Collection and Use*, MR-534-ACUS/ICJ, 1995. $13.00.

Rolph, E. S., E. Moller, and L. Petersen, *Escaping the Courthouse: Private Alternative Dispute Resolution in Los Angeles*, MR-472-JRHD/ICJ, 1994. $15.00.

Special Issues

Kritzer, H. M., W. L. F. Felstiner, A. Sarat, and D. M. Trubek, *The Impact of Fee Arrangement on Lawyer Effort*, P-7180-ICJ, 1986. $4.00.

Priest, G. L., *Regulating the Content and Volume of Litigation: An Economic Analysis*, R-3084-ICJ, 1983. $4.00.

Priest, G. L., and B. Klein, *The Selection of Disputes for Litigation*, R-3032-ICJ, 1984. $7.50.

Resnik, J., *Managerial Judges*, R-3002-ICJ, 1982. (Reprinted from the *Harvard Law Review*, Vol. 96:374, December 1982.) $7.50.

_____ , *Failing Faith: Adjudicatory Procedure in Decline*, P-7272-ICJ, 1987. (Reprinted from the *University of Chicago Law Review*, Vol. 53, No. 2, 1986.) $7.50.

_____ , *Due Process: A Public Dimension*, P-7418-ICJ, 1988. (Reprinted from the *University of Florida Law Review*, Vol. 39, No. 2, 1987.) $4.00.

_____ , *Judging Consent*, P-7419-ICJ, 1988. (Reprinted from the *University of Chicago Legal Forum*, Vol. 1987.) $7.50.

_____ , *From "Cases" to "Litigation,"* RP-110, 1992. (Reprinted from *Law and Contemporary Problems*, Vol. 54, No. 3, Summer 1991.) Free.

_____ , *Whose Judgment? Vacating Judgments, Preferences for Settlement, and the Role of Adjudication at the Close of the Twentieth*

Century, RP-364, 1995. (Reprinted from *UCLA Law Review*, Vol. 41, No. 6, August 1994.) Free.

Areas of Liability

Auto-Accident Litigation

Abrahamse, A., and S. J. Carroll, *The Effects of a Choice Auto Insurance Plan on Insurance Costs*, MR-540-ICJ, 1995. $13.00.

Carroll, S. J., and A. Abrahamse, *The Effects of a Proposed No-Fault Plan on the Costs of Auto Insurance in California*, IP-146, March 1995. Free.

Carroll, S. J., and J. S. Kakalik, *No-Fault Approaches to Compensating Auto Accident Victims*, RP-229, 1993. (Reprinted from *The Journal of Risk and Insurance*, Vol. 60, No. 2, 1993.) Free.

Carroll, S. J., A. Abrahamse, and M. E. Vaiana, *The Costs of Excess Medical Claims for Automobile Personal Injuries*, DB-139-ICJ, 1995. $6.00.

Carroll, S. J., J. S. Kakalik, N. M. Pace, and J. L. Adams, *No-Fault Approaches to Compensating People Injured in Automobile Accidents*, R-4019-ICJ, 1991. $20.00.

Carroll, S. J., J. S. Kakalik, with D. Adamson, *No-Fault Automobile Insurance: A Policy Perspective*, R-4019/1-ICJ, 1991. $4.00.

Hammitt, J. K., *Automobile Accident Compensation, Volume II, Payments by Auto Insurers*, R-3051-ICJ, 1985. $10.00.

Hammitt, J. K., and J. E. Rolph, *Limiting Liability for Automobile Accidents: Are No-Fault Tort Thresholds Effective?* N-2418-ICJ, 1985. $4.00.

Hammitt, J. K., R. L. Houchens, S. S. Polin, and J. E. Rolph, *Automobile Accident Compensation: Volume IV, State Rules*, R-3053-ICJ, 1985. $7.50.

Houchens, R. L., *Automobile Accident Compensation: Volume III, Payments from All Sources*, R-3052-ICJ, 1985. $7.50.

MacCoun, R. J., E. A. Lind, D. R. Hensler, D. L. Bryant, and P. A. Ebener, *Alternative Adjudication: An Evaluation of the New Jersey Automobile Arbitration Program*, R-3676-ICJ, 1988. $10.00.

O'Connell, J., S. J. Carroll, M. Horowitz, and A. Abrahamse, *Consumer Choice in the Auto Insurance Market*, RP-254, 1994. (Reprinted from the *Maryland Law Review*, Vol. 52, 1993.) Free.

O'Connell, J., S. J. Carroll, M. Horowitz, A. Abrahamse, and D. Kaiser, *The Costs of Consumer Choice for Auto Insurance in States Without No-Fault Insurance*, RP-442, 1995. (Reprinted from *Maryland Law Review*, Vol. 54, No. 2, 1995.) Free.

Rolph, J. E., with J. K. Hammitt, R. L. Houchens, and S. S. Polin, *Automobile Accident Compensation: Volume I, Who Pays How Much How Soon?* R-3050-ICJ, 1985. $4.00.

Asbestos

Hensler, D. R., *Resolving Mass Toxic Torts: Myths and Realities*, P-7631-ICJ, 1990. (Reprinted from the *University of Illinois Law Review*, Vol. 1989, No. 1.) $4.00.

_____ , *Asbestos Litigation in the United States: A Brief Overview*, P-7776-ICJ, 1992. (Testimony before the Courts and Judicial Administration Subcommittee, United States House Judiciary Committee, October 1991.) $4.00.

_____ , *Assessing Claims Resolution Facilities: What We Need to Know*, RP-107, 1992. (Reprinted from *Law and Contemporary Problems*, Vol. 53, No. 4, Autumn 1990.) Free.

_____ , *Fashioning a National Resolution of Asbestos Personal Injury Litigation: A Reply to Professor Brickman*, RP-114, 1992. (Reprinted from *Cardozo Law Review*, Vol. 13, No. 6, April 1992.) Free.

Hensler, D. R., W. L. F. Felstiner, M. Selvin, and P. A. Ebener, *Asbestos in the Courts: The Challenge of Mass Toxic Torts*, R-3324-ICJ, 1985. $10.00.

Kakalik, J. S., P. A. Ebener, W. L. F. Felstiner, and M. G. Shanley, *Costs of Asbestos Litigation*, R-3042-ICJ, 1983. $4.00.

Kakalik, J. S., P. A. Ebener, W. L. F. Felstiner, G. W. Haggstrom, and M. G. Shanley, *Variation in Asbestos Litigation Compensation and Expenses*, R-3132-ICJ, 1984. $7.50.

Peterson, M. A., *Giving Away Money: Comparative Comments on Claims Resolution Facilities*, RP-108, 1992. (Reprinted from *Law and Contemporary Problems*, Vol. 53, No. 4, Autumn 1990.) Free.

Peterson, M. A., and M. Selvin, *Resolution of Mass Torts: Toward a Framework for Evaluation of Aggregative Procedures*, N-2805-ICJ, 1988. $7.50.

_____ , *Mass Justice: The Limited and Unlimited Power of Courts*, RP-116, 1992. (Reprinted from *Law and Contemporary Problems*, No. 3, Summer 1991.) Free.

Selvin, M., and L. Picus, *The Debate over Jury Performance: Observations from a Recent Asbestos Case*, R-3479-ICJ, 1987. $10.00.

Aviation Accidents

Kakalik, J. S., E. M. King, M. Traynor, P. A. Ebener, and L. Picus, *Costs and Compensation Paid in Aviation Accident Litigation*, R-3421-ICJ, 1988. $10.00.

_____ , *Aviation Accident Litigation Survey: Data Collection Forms*, N-2773-ICJ, 1988. $7.50.

King, E. M., and J. P. Smith, *Computing Economic Loss in Cases of Wrongful Death*, R-3549-ICJ, 1988. $10.00.

_____ , *Economic Loss and Compensation in Aviation Accidents*, R-3551-ICJ, 1988. $10.00.

_____ , *Dispute Resolution Following Airplane Crashes*, R-3585-ICJ, 1988. $7.50.

Executive Summaries of the Aviation Accident Study, R-3684, 1988. $7.50.

Employment

Dertouzos, J. N., E. Holland, and P. A. Ebener, *The Legal and Economic Consequences of Wrongful Termination*, R-3602-ICJ, 1988. $7.50.

Dertouzos, J. N., and L. A. Karoly, *Labor-Market Responses to Employer Liability*, R-3989-ICJ, 1992. $7.50.

Environmental Litigation: Superfund

Acton, J. P., *Understanding Superfund: A Progress Report*, R-3838-ICJ, 1989. $7.50.

Acton, J. P., and L. S. Dixon with D. Drezner, L. Hill, and S. McKenney, *Superfund and Transaction Costs: The Experiences of Insurers and Very Large Industrial Firms*, R-4132-ICJ, 1992. $7.50.

Dixon, L. S., *RAND Research on Superfund Transaction Costs: A Summary of Findings to Date*, CT-111, November 1993. $5.00.

_____ , *Fixing Superfund: The Effect of the Proposed Superfund Reform Act of 1994 on Transaction Costs*, MR-455-ICJ, 1994. $15.00.

_____ , *Superfund Liability Reform: Implications for Transaction Costs and Site Cleanup*, CT-125, 1995. $5.00.

Dixon, L. S., D. S. Drezner, and J. K. Hammitt, *Private-Sector Cleanup Expenditures and Transaction Costs at 18 Superfund Sites*, MR-204-EPA/RC, 1993. $13.00.

Medical Malpractice

Danzon, P. M., *Contingent Fees for Personal Injury Litigation*, R-2458-HCFA, 1980. $4.00.

_____ , *The Disposition of Medical Malpractice Claims*, R-2622-HCFA, 1980. $7.50.

_____ , *Why Are Malpractice Premiums So High—Or So Low?* R-2623-HCFA, 1980. $4.00.

_____ , *The Frequency and Severity of Medical Malpractice Claims*, R-2870-ICJ/HCFA, 1982. $7.50.

_____ , *New Evidence on the Frequency and Severity of Medical Malpractice Claims*, R-3410-ICJ, 1986. $4.00.

_____ , *The Effects of Tort Reform on the Frequency and Severity of Medical Malpractice Claims: A Summary of Research Results*, P-7211, 1986. (Testimony before the Committee on the Judiciary, United States Senate, March 1986.) $4.00.

Danzon, P. M., and L. A. Lillard, *The Resolution of Medical Malpractice Claims: Modeling the Bargaining Process*, R-2792-ICJ, 1982. $7.50.

_____ , *Settlement Out of Court: The Disposition of Medical Malpractice Claims*, P-6800, 1982. $4.00.

_____ , *The Resolution of Medical Malpractice Claims: Research Results and Policy Implications*, R-2793-ICJ, 1982. $4.00.

Kravitz, R. L. , J. E. Rolph, K. A. McGuigan, *Malpractice Claims Data as a Quality Improvement Tool: I. Epidemiology of Error in Four Specialties*, N-3448/1-RWJ, 1991. $4.00.

Lewis, E., and J. E. Rolph, *The Bad Apples? Malpractice Claims Experience of Physicians with a Surplus Lines Insurer*, P-7812, 1993. $4.00.

Rolph, E. S., *Health Care Delivery and Tort: Systems on a Collision Course?* Conference Proceedings, Dallas, June 1991, N-3524-ICJ, 1992. $10.00.

Rolph, J. E., *Some Statistical Evidence on Merit Rating in Medical Malpractice Insurance*, N-1725-HHS, 1981. $4.00.

_____ , *Merit Rating for Physicians' Malpractice Premiums: Only a Modest Deterrent*, N-3426-MT/RWJ/RC, 1991. $4.00.

Rolph, J. E., R. L. Kravitz, K. A. McGuigan, *Malpractice Claims Data as a Quality Improvement Tool: II. Is Targeting Effective?* N-3448/2-RWJ, 1991. $4.00.

Williams, A. P., *Malpractice, Outcomes, and Appropriateness of Care*, P-7445, May 1988. $4.00.

Product Liability

Dunworth, T., *Product Liability and the Business Sector: Litigation Trends in Federal Courts*, R-3668-ICJ, 1988. $7.50.

Eads, G., and P. Reuter, *Designing Safer Products: Corporate Responses to Product Liability Law and Regulation*, R-3022-ICJ, 1983. $15.00.

_____ , *Designing Safer Products: Corporate Responses to Product Liability Law and Regulation*, P-7089-ICJ, 1985. (Reprinted from the *Journal of Product Liability*, Vol. 7, 1985.) $4.00.

Garber, S., *Product Liability and the Economics of Pharmaceuticals and Medical Devices*, R-4285-ICJ, 1993. $15.00.

Hensler, D. R., *Summary of Research Results on Product Liability*, P-7271-ICJ, 1986. (Statement submitted to the Committee on the Judiciary, United States Senate, October 1986.) $4.00.

_____ , *What We Know and Don't Know About Product Liability*, P-7775-ICJ, 1993. (Statement submitted to the Commerce Committee, United States Senate, September 1991.) $4.00.

Moller, E., *Trends in Civil Jury Verdicts Since 1985,* MR-694-ICJ, 1996. $15.00.

Peterson, M. A., *Civil Juries in the 1980s: Trends in Jury Trials and Verdicts in California and Cook County, Illinois*, R-3466-ICJ, 1987. $7.50.

Reuter, P., *The Economic Consequences of Expanded Corporate Liability: An Exploratory Study*, N-2807-ICJ, 1988. $7.50.

Workers' Compensation

Darling-Hammond, L., and T. J. Kniesner, *The Law and Economics of Workers' Compensation*, R-2716-ICJ, 1980. $7.50.

Victor, R. B., *Workers' Compensation and Workplace Safety: The Nature of Employer Financial Incentives*, R-2979-ICJ, 1982. $7.50.

Victor, R. B., L. R. Cohen, and C. E. Phelps, *Workers' Compensation and Workplace Safety: Some Lessons from Economic Theory*, R-2918-ICJ, 1982. $7.50.

Trends in the Tort Litigation System

Galanter, M., B. Garth, D. Hensler, and F. K. Zemans, *How to Improve Civil Justice Policy*, RP-282. (Reprinted from *Judicature*, Vol. 77, No. 4, January/February 1994. Free.

Hensler, D. R., *Trends in California Tort Liability Litigation*, P-7287-ICJ, 1987. (Testimony before the Select Committee on Insurance, California State Assembly, October 1987.) $4.00.

_____ , *Reading the Tort Litigation Tea Leaves: What's Going on in the Civil Liability System?* RP-226. (Reprinted from *The Justice System Journal*, Vol. 16, No. 2, 1993.) Free.

Hensler, D. R., M. E. Vaiana, J. S. Kakalik, and M. A. Peterson, *Trends in Tort Litigation: The Story Behind the Statistics*, R-3583-ICJ, 1987. $4.00.

Mass Torts and Class Actions

Hensler, D. R., *Resolving Mass Toxic Torts: Myths and Realities*, P-7631-ICJ, 1990. (Reprinted from the *University of Illinois Law Review*, Vol. 1989, No. 1.) $4.00.

_____ , *Asbestos Litigation in the United States: A Brief Overview*, P-7776-ICJ, 1992. (Testimony before the Courts and Judicial

Administration Subcommittee, United States House Judiciary Committee, October 1991.) $4.00.

_____ , *Assessing Claims Resolution Facilities: What We Need to Know*, RP-107, 1992. (Reprinted from *Law and Contemporary Problems*, Vol. 53, No. 4, Autumn 1990.) Free.

_____ , *Fashioning a National Resolution of Asbestos Personal Injury Litigation: A Reply to Professor Brickman*, RP-114, 1992. (Reprinted from *Cardozo Law Review*, Vol. 13, No. 6, April 1992.) Free.

Hensler, D. R., W. L. F. Felstiner, M. Selvin, and P. A. Ebener, *Asbestos in the Courts: The Challenge of Mass Toxic Torts*, R-3324-ICJ, 1985. $10.00.

Hensler, D. R., M. A. Peterson, *Understanding Mass Personal Injury Litigation: A Socio-Legal Analysis*, RP-311, 1994. (Reprinted from *Brooklyn Law Review*, Vol. 59, No. 3, Fall 1993.) Free.

Kakalik, J. S., P. A. Ebener, W. L. F. Felstiner, G. W. Haggstrom, and M. G. Shanley, *Variation in Asbestos Litigation Compensation and Expenses*, R-3132-ICJ, 1984. $7.50.

Kakalik, J. S., P. A. Ebener, W. L. F. Felstiner, and M. G. Shanley, *Costs of Asbestos Litigation*, R-3042-ICJ, 1983. $4.00.

Peterson, M. A., *Giving Away Money: Comparative Comments on Claims Resolution Facilities*, RP-108, 1992. (Reprinted from *Law and Contemporary Problems*, Vol. 53, No. 4, Autumn 1990.) Free.

Peterson, M. A., and M. Selvin, *Resolution of Mass Torts: Toward a Framework for Evaluation of Aggregative Procedures*, N-2805-ICJ, 1988. $7.50.

_____ , *Mass Justice: The Limited and Unlimited Power of Courts*, RP-116, 1992. (Reprinted from *Law and Contemporary Problems*, Vol. 54, No. 3, Summer 1991.) Free.

Selvin, M., and L. Picus, *The Debate over Jury Performance: Observations from a Recent Asbestos Case*, R-3479-ICJ, 1987. $10.00.

Environmental Issues

Califonria's Clean-Air Strategy

Dixon, L. S., S. Garber, and M. E. Vaiana, *Making ZEV Policy Despite Uncertainty: An Annotated Briefing for the California Air Resources Board*, DRU-1266-1-ICJ, 1995. Free.

Superfund

Acton, J. P., *Understanding Superfund: A Progress Report*, R-3838-ICJ, 1989. $7.50.

Acton, J. P., and L. S. Dixon with D. Drezner, L. Hill, and S. McKenney, *Superfund and Transaction Costs: The Experiences of Insurers and Very Large Industrial Firms*, R-4132-ICJ, 1992. $7.50.

Dixon, L. S., *RAND Research on Superfund Transaction Costs: A Summary of Findings to Date*, CT-111, November 1993. $5.00.

_____ , *Fixing Superfund: The Effect of the Proposed Superfund Reform Act of 1994 on Transaction Costs*, MR-455-ICJ, 1994. $15.00.

_____ , *Superfund Liability Reform: Implications for Transaction Costs and Site Cleanup*, CT-125, 1995. $5.00.

Dixon, L. S., D. S. Drezner, J. K. Hammitt, *Private-Sector Cleanup Expenditures and Transaction Costs at 18 Superfund Sites*, MR-204-EPA/RC, 1993. $13.00.

Reuter, P., *The Economic Consequences of Expanded Corporate Liability: An Exploratory Study*, N-2807-ICJ, 1988. $7.50.

Economic Effects of the Liability System

General

Carroll, S. J., A. Abrahamse, M. S. Marquis, and M. E. Vaiana, *Liability System Incentives to Consume Excess Medical Care*, DRU-1264-ICJ, 1995. Free.Carroll, S. J., A. Abrahamse, M. S. Marquis, and M. E. Vaiana, *Liability System Incentives to Consume Excess Medical Care*, DRU-1264-ICJ, 1995.

Johnson, L. L., *Cost-Benefit Analysis and Voluntary Safety Standards for Consumer Products*, R-2882-ICJ, 1982. $7.50.

Reuter, P., *The Economic Consequences of Expanded Corporate Liability: An Exploratory Study*, N-2807-ICJ, 1988. $7.50.

Product Liability

Dunworth, T., *Product Liability and the Business Sector: Litigation Trends in Federal Courts*, R-3668-ICJ, 1988. $7.50.

Eads, G., and P. Reuter, *Designing Safer Products: Corporate Responses to Product Liability Law and Regulation*, R-3022-ICJ, 1983. $15.00.

_____ , *Designing Safer Products: Corporate Responses to Product Liability Law and Regulation*, P-7089-ICJ, 1985. (Reprinted from the *Journal of Product Liability*, Vol. 7, 1985.) $4.00.

Garber, S., *Product Liability and the Economics of Pharmaceuticals and Medical Devices*, R-4285-ICJ, 1993. $15.00.

Hensler, D. R., *Summary of Research Results on Product Liability*, P-7271-ICJ, 1986. (Statement submitted to the Committee on the Judiciary, United States Senate, October 1986.) $4.00.

_____ , *What We Know and Don't Know About Product Liability*, P-7775-ICJ, 1993. (Statement submitted to the Commerce Committee, United States Senate, September 1991.) $4.00.

Peterson, M. A., *Civil Juries in the 1980s: Trends in Jury Trials and Verdicts in California and Cook County, Illinois*, R-3466-ICJ, 1987. $7.50.

Wrongful Termination

Dertouzos, J. N., E. Holland, and P. A. Ebener, *The Legal and Economic Consequences of Wrongful Termination*, R-3602-ICJ, 1988. $7.50.

Dertouzos, J. N., and L. A. Karoly, *Labor-Market Responses to Employer Liability*, R-3989-ICJ, 1992. $7.50.

Compensation Systems

System Design

Darling-Hammond, L., and T. J. Kniesner, *The Law and Economics of Workers' Compensation*, R-2716-ICJ, 1980. $7.50.

Hammitt, J. K., R. L. Houchens, S. S. Polin, and J. E. Rolph, *Automobile Accident Compensation: Volume IV, State Rules*, R-3053-ICJ, 1985. $7.50.

Hammitt, J. K., and J. E. Rolph, *Limiting Liability for Automobile Accidents: Are No-Fault Tort Thresholds Effective?* N-2418-ICJ, 1985. $4.00.

Hensler, D. R., *Resolving Mass Toxic Torts: Myths and Realities*, P-7631-ICJ, 1990. (Reprinted from the *University of Illinois Law Review*, Vol. 1989, No. 1.) $4.00.

_____ , *Assessing Claims Resolution Facilities: What We Need to Know*, RP-107, 1992. (Reprinted from *Law and Contemporary Problems*, Vol. 53, No. 4, Autumn 1990.) Free.

King, E. M., and J. P. Smith, *Computing Economic Loss in Cases of Wrongful Death*, R-3549-ICJ, 1988. $10.00.

Peterson, M. A., and M. Selvin, *Resolution of Mass Torts: Toward a Framework for Evaluation of Aggregative Procedures*, N-2805-ICJ, 1988. $7.50.

Rolph, E. S., *Framing the Compensation Inquiry*, RP-115, 1992. (Reprinted from the *Cardozo Law Review*, Vol. 13, No. 6, April 1992.) Free.

Victor, R. B., *Workers' Compensation and Workplace Safety: The Nature of Employer Financial Incentives*, R-2979-ICJ, 1982. $7.50.

Victor, R. B., L. R. Cohen, and C. E. Phelps, *Workers' Compensation and Workplace Safety: Some Lessons from Economic Theory*, R-2918-ICJ, 1982. $7.50.

Performance

Abrahamse, A., and S. J. Carroll, *The Effects of a Choice Auto Insurance Plan on Insurance Costs*, MR-540-ICJ, 1995. $13.00.

Carroll, S. J., and A. Abrahamse, *The Effects of a Proposed No-Fault Plan on the Costs of Auto Insurance in California*, IP-146, March 1995. Free.

Carroll, S. J., and J. S. Kakalik, *No-Fault Approaches to Compensating Auto Accident Victims,* RP-229, 1993. (Reprinted from *The Journal of Risk and Insurance*, Vol. 60, No. 2, 1993.) Free.

Carroll, S. J., A. Abrahamse, and M. E. Vaiana, *The Costs of Excess Medical Claims for Automobile Personal Injuries*, DB-139-ICJ, 1995. $6.00.

Carroll, S. J., A. Abrahamse, M. S. Marquis, and M. E. Vaiana, *Liability System Incentives to Consume Excess Medical Care*, DRU-1264-ICJ, 1995. Free.Carroll, S. J., A. Abrahamse, M. S. Marquis, and M. E. Vaiana, *Liability System Incentives to Consume Excess Medical Care*, DRU-1264-ICJ, 1995.

Carroll, S. J., J. S. Kakalik, N. M. Pace, and J. L. Adams, *No-Fault Approaches to Compensating People Injured in Automobile Accidents*, R-4019-ICJ, 1991. $20.00.

Carroll, S. J., J. S. Kakalik, with D. Adamson, *No-Fault Automobile Insurance: A Policy Perspective*, R-4019/1-ICJ, 1991. $4.00.

Hensler, D. R., M. S. Marquis, A. Abrahamse, S. H. Berry, P. A. Ebener, E. G. Lewis, E. A. Lind, R. J. MacCoun, W. G. Manning, J. A. Rogowski, and M. E. Vaiana, *Compensation for Accidental Injuries in the United States*, R-3999-HHS/ICJ, 1991. $20.00.

_____ , *Compensation for Accidental Injuries in the United States: Executive Summary*, R-3999/1-HHS/ICJ, 1991. $4.00.

_____ , *Compensation for Accidental Injuries: Research Design and Methods*, N-3230-HHS/ICJ, 1991. $15.00.

King, E. M., and J. P. Smith, *Economic Loss and Compensation in Aviation Accidents*, R-3551-ICJ, 1988. $10.00.

O'Connell, J., S. J. Carroll, M. Horowitz, and A. Abrahamse, *Consumer Choice in the Auto Insurance Market*, RP-254, 1994. (Reprinted from the *Maryland Law Review*, Vol. 52, 1993.) Free.

O'Connell, J., S. J. Carroll, M. Horowitz, A. Abrahamse, and D. Kaiser, *The Costs of Consumer Choice for Auto Insurance in States Without No-Fault Insurance*, RP-442, 1995. (Reprinted from *Maryland Law Review*, Vol. 54, No. 2, 1995.) Free.

Peterson, M. A., *Giving Away Money: Comparative Comments on Claims Resolution Facilities*, RP-108, 1992. (Reprinted from *Law and Contemporary Problems*, Vol. 53, No. 4, Autumn 1990.) Free.

Peterson, M. A., and M. Selvin, *Mass Justice: The Limited and Unlimited Power of Courts*, RP-116, 1992. (Reprinted from *Law and Contemporary Problems*, Vol. 54, No. 3, Summer 1991.) Free.

Rolph, J. E., with J. K. Hammitt, R. L. Houchens, and S. S. Polin, *Automobile Accident Compensation: Volume I, Who Pays How Much How Soon?* R-3050-ICJ, 1985. $4.00.

Special Studies

Hensler, D. R., and M. E. Reddy, *California Lawyers View the Future: A Report to the Commission on the Future of the Legal Profession and the State Bar*, MR-528-ICJ, 1994. $13.00.

Merz, J. F. and N. M. Pace, *Trends in Patent Litigation: The Apparent Influence of Strengthened Patents Attributable to the Court of Appeals for the Federal Circuit*, RP-426, 1995. (Reprinted from *Journal of the Patent and Trademark Office Society*, Vol. 76, No. 8, August 1994.) Free.

An annotated bibliography, CP-253 (12/95), provides a list of RAND publications in the civil justice area through 1995. To request the bibliography or to obtain more information about the Institute for Civil Justice, please write the Institute at this address: The Institute for Civil Justice, RAND, 1700 Main Street, P.O. Box 2138, Santa Monica, California 90407-2138, or call (310) 393-0411, x6916.